In the Beginning Was the Pun

Comedy and Humour in Samuel Beckett's Theatre

By Tatiana Chemi

AALBORG UNIVERSITY PRESS

In the Beginning Was the Pun. Comedy and Humor in Samuel Beckett's Theatre
By Tatiana Chemi

1. Edition

© Aalborg University Press, 2013

Layout: Hofdamerne ApS Grafisk Design v/ Lea Rathnov
Printed by Toptryk Grafisk ApS, 2013
ISBN: 978-87-7112-110-0

Translated by Julia Campbell Hamilton and Tatiana Chemi
Cover illustration by Tatiana Chemi

Published by:
Aalborg University Press
Skjernvej 4A, 2nd floor
9220 Aalborg
Denmark
Phone: (+45) 99407140
aauf@forlag.aau.dk
forlag.aau.dk

> This book is financially supported by Lillian og Dan Finks Fond and by Department of Learning and Philosophy, Aalborg University, Denmark.

All rights reserved. No part of this book may be reprinted or reproduced or utilized in any form or by any electronic, mechanical, or other means, now known or hereafter invented, including photocopying and recording, or in any information storage or retrieval system, without permission in writing from the publishers, except for reviews and short excerpts in scholarly publications.

* INDEX *

Preface by Gabriele Frasca	7
Acknowledgments	11
Introduction	13
1. "Crritic!" Beckett, humour and scholars	19
1.1. State of the art	19
1.2. Irony	23
1.3. Tragicomic	27
1.4. Carnival	31
1.5. Which tradition?	37
2. "The labour of nesting in a strange place". Upbringing	47
2.1. Beckett and the theatre	47
2.2. Music-hall	62
2.3. Le Cirque Beckett	69
2.4. Beckett and cinema	83
3. "Dans un espace pantin". Body. Gesture. Movement	101
3.1. Bowler hats and other toys	101
3.2. "J'ai naturellement pensé au pseudo-couple"	113
3.3. Banana skin	126
3.4. Body in-action: the gag	140
3.5. Portrait of Beckett as a director	155
4. "Tray bong". Noise. Rhythm. Music	173
4.1. Only a manner of speaking	173
4.2. Words and music	179
4.3. Noise and silence	191

5. "Words fail us". Words. Speech. Text	201
5.1. The betrayed tradition	201
5.2. "…a moi de jouer"	210
5.3. The speaking clown	225
5.4. "I was merely cursing"	239
5.5. "It had never been a good joke"	250
6. All that *laugh* according to Beckett	267
6.1. Comic Beckett?	267
6.2. "Rien n'est plus drôle que le malheur"	269
6.3. "Pourquoi en ris-tu toujours?"	288
6.4. Angelic smiles and satanic guffawing	305
6.5. The suffocated reaction	317
References	335
Texts by Beckett	335
Beckett bibliography	343
General bibliography	418

This book is dedicated to my masters and mentors in the theatre,
Eugenio Barba and Franco C. Greco.

I am grateful for the honour of their guidance and advice.

* PREFACE *

by Gabriele Frasca

I couldn't say what came first – the desire to speak Beckett in Italian or to rewrite him in a study. First and foremost, of course, there is the passion of the reader, which impels you to go over and over the work of the writer you have unaccountably chanced upon, rushing around after it, just as it comes. At a certain point, it ends up being a part of what you are becoming, which to some extent also depends on how that same work has got you going again. This happens to all enthusiastic readers, by their very nature always ready to make something of what they are gradually experiencing, something in the nature of a therapy, and a looking after. And it happens, fortunately, more than once in a lifetime. In this way you create your line-up of favourite authors, with an array of works that is practically endless. There are some works that swiftly become the musical score of our life and the first time we play them we know we will play them again, because we sense that they have not entirely given up all their elements, and perhaps for the very fact that they contain more, that *more than us* which seems elusive, but then invites us to try again. To finish again. *For to end yet again...* There is a subtle pleasure in this feeling of inadequacy (Beckett, expert in foolishness, knew all about this), because it is precisely this that gets us going again, and this is how, at the same time, a writer's work takes flight.

For me, with Beckett's work, this is what happened – and the book you now have in your hands is the fruit of a similar passion.

If you love a writer's work (not the author, of whom you swiftly become either a fierce, jealous custodian or humble priest, no matter which) – and you only love it if you feel it is revolutionary (able to *revolutionise you*, get you going etc.) – then it explodes inside you, you don't want to keep it to yourself, you want to spread the word.

In translating Beckett, I was also spurred on by the possibility of direct contact with him – I had actually already been in touch with him on a matter of literary criticism. The study I had decided to write on *Watt* (my best-loved book of all) led me to contact Beckett with a series of timid requests (sent, in fact, to Minuit and Beckett replied to me personally, for he was an incredibly courteous man). I wasn't asking for explanations (I already knew that Beckett did not enjoy giving them) but for help in finding the text, for example, because all my attempts at finding the Calder edition had been unsuccessful (I only had the subsequent French translation, on which Beckett had worked). To cut a long story short, he answered, he wished my work well and he sent me the book, with his best regards – utterly amazing! It was 1983. After that we had a short correspondence (a couple of letters each year - I was naturally delighted to correspond with him but I also knew how precious was his time). And his "best regards" became increasingly spirited (those I put at the beginning of *Dante in Beckett* were, of course, given the circumstances, the ones I held dearest). So, after the first letter I sent him (again via Minuit once, to return my discretion, he replied to me at Corpo 10, my publishers at the time), written in my timid, awestruck, very formal English, I began writing to him directly in Italian (a language Beckett knew very well, better, he said, than German in fact he would have collaborated in translating his works into Italian, as he did with the Tophoven German translations, if our Italian editors had not discouraged him). He replied to me in English or in French (I think it depended on the language he was using at the time). I sent him *Rame* (my first collection of poems) as soon as it came out (then my first novel, *Il fermo volere*, and, of course, *Cascando*). He was a man of great generosity, and in that period he ended up being of great help to me (I don't think he ever stinted on encouragement for the various young writers who contacted him).

Translating Beckett arises from the circumstance whereby all readers of Beckett acquire a sort of affection for the author. Strangely, because he is apparently very cold and depicts levels of extreme decrepitude that ought to put the reader off. Translating him was like paying off a debt. In the only "moving" letter I wrote to Samuel Beckett (his description), I told him I remembered every instant and every second of my first reading of *Watt*, I remembered what Watt was doing and what I was doing. My anxiety to translate I think came from this affection for the author. And, given that for about thirty years we were contemporaries, I was fortunate enough for about fifteen of them to be awaiting his new works with the same anxiety, and emotion, with which I waited, let's say, for the records of my favourite bands. When I came to hear that he was bringing out a new book, I couldn't wait to get my hands on it – to where would it lead me this time, where would I be off to in his company? And he never disappointed me. I don't know how much he influenced my writing - others may be the judge of that.

Many think Beckett struck the imaginary of a vast public with the newness of his theme, the cyclical, the absurd and things like that. But I am convinced that what fascinated the crowds ("in transports… of joy", as Clov jokingly described them in *Fin de partie*) was his technical experimentation into sound, rhythm and light. Beckett was a genius with lighting – perhaps not only on stage. Spectators were fascinated by Beckett's stage wonders, where he demolished the fourth wall, only to draw them into the trap. You call this bourgeois drama? It's baroque theatre!

The present volume addresses Beckett in a similarly passionate way. Through the fascination of Beckett's theatrical score, it aims to uncover what has not yet been fully addressed: humour, comedy, tragicomedy or comitragedy.

This book is the result of an ardent need to disseminate the experience of a reader and spectator in Beckett's literary and theatrical universe.

Gabriele Frasca teaches Comparative Literature and Comparative Media at the University of Salerno, Italy, and is author of poetry, prose, plays and essays. He has been a Beckett expert for many years, editing and translating from French and English into Italian several texts, such as Murphy, Watt, Company, Mal vu mal dit, Worstward Ho. Beckett is also the favourite theme of many of his essaistic contributions, among the others: Cascando, Dante in Beckett, In nessuna lingua ancora and the forthcoming Lo spopolatoio: Beckett con Dante e Cantor. He has been directing, writing and radio-hosting for radio-programmes at the Italian national broadcast, RAI.

* ACKNOWLEDGMENTS *

This book is the product of many years of hard work and passion and it would not have come to an end without the qualified help and creative support of several colleagues and friends. First of all my gratitude goes to the amazing staff at the Samuel Beckett Archive, which during my field-work in 1996-1998 was housed at the Reading University Library, UK. Thanks go to Julian Garforth for having endured all my curiosity and helped me in finding books, articles, manuscripts and connections; for having assisted me in deciphering Beckett's handwriting and for having discussed texts, theatre productions and biographical events; for having shared the same passion for Beckett's universe. At the University of Reading in the same period, I enjoyed the incredibly competent help of James Knowlson and John Pilling: thanks to them for having specified some biographical data that had direct influence on the topic of the present work. Thanks to Walter Redfern for providing me with a preview of his article "A Funny-bone to Pick with Beckett", later to be published in the Journal of Beckett Studies. I am grateful to Giancarlo Alfano for having endorsed my work and to Antonella Valoroso, who helped me with the English versions of Pirandello's theory on humour. Inspiring conversations with Gabriele Frasca, Christian Ludvigsen, Bent Holm and Sigvard Bennetzen have greatly enriched my discoveries in the world of Beckett's humour, not only with textual exegesis but also with unique information on Beckett's life, personal opinions and broadcasts. Frasca has also contributed to this work in a more intangible manner: as a scholar he has aided me as described above, and as an author he has shown me the Beckett legacy in the flesh. Similarly, I have found a great deal of inspiration in the works of Paul Auster whose Trilogy wonderfully reinterprets several of Beckett's elements. To both authors I owe the deep understanding and appreciation of rhythm and musicality in Beckett and Joyce.

Lorenzo Mango must be acknowledged for his supervision and kindness with which he guided my work in the direction of scientific and rhetoric coherence. Even though he greatly contributed to the development of this work, any inaccuracies are entirely mine. A due acknowledgment goes to my parents, who supported me emotionally and economically in this complex digging into Beckett's materials throughout Italy, UK, Ireland and Denmark.

This study would not have been published in book form without the trusting support of Annette Lorentsen at the Department of Learning and Philosophy at Aalborg University, Denmark, and the competent translation of Julia Campbell Hamilton.

Last but not least, I need to address a special heartfelt acknowledgment to my husband for his unconditional love, trust and encouragement since the very first day we met, when we were ironically brought together by a Scandinavian Godot. Godot came to us, embodied in our two beautiful boys, to whom all my love and gratitude goes for keeping me sane and real.

* INTRODUCTION *

This book is a matter of love. Science informs its method, approach and coherence, but this book is no science matter. Rather, it is a matter of love, passion and perseverance. The Beckett universe has been following me throughout almost a couple of decades. Its images, philosophy, poetry and musicality have formed both my aesthetical understanding and artistic preferences. The Promethean loss of certainties and endless resurrections have never ceased to move me deeply, as well as the seemingly pathetic comedy of Beckett's characters, which still provokes in me bursts of hilarity and genuine enjoyment. This book is the product of a life-long passion, to which I am still bound and of which I do not intend to be cured. The core of the book is the systematic monographic study that I engaged in during the period 1994-1999, followed by further sub-theme reflections and communications, up to the present date. The former consists of the research I carried out during my PhD studies, which bears almost the same title as this book. The latter consists of academic courses, conferences, workshops, publications, events and a single theatre directing experience (*Come and Go*, Aarhus 2nd-4th November 2006, director Tatiana Chemi, artistic producer Laurence Kaye, with Anni Bjørn, Eva Brow Simonsen and Helle Brokjær). My intention is to address this passion by channelling it into scientific frames and methods and by means of analytical tools. The intended result is an original and worthwhile contribution to Beckett studies.

The novelty of the present volume lies in its approach drawn from theatre studies rather than literary criticism and in the orderly in-depth investigation of texts, performances and biographical data in order to clarify the relationship between Beckett and comedy. Humour and comedy have been almost overlooked by Beckett scholars worldwide. Few have ventured into this topic and even fewer have triangulated texts and performance analysis with biography, as is done in the present volume. My readers, who I imagine are comprised of Beckett experts either in the academic or theatrical fields, will find exhaustive examples of comedy and humour in Beckett's works, together with biographical corroboration of cultural knowledge and appreciation of several forms of comedy. An additional element of novelty is that this research is based on the thorough analysis of all of Beckett's works, including those less known. My intention was to avoid the frequent popular identification of Beckett's drama with the most famous *En attendant Godot* and *Fin de partie*. With rare but brilliant exceptions such as Gontarski, Brater, Knowlson, Esslin and Zilliacus, the most studied Beckett plays are the big ones, while the less studied ones are the very short pieces, which are full of oneiric suggestions. While taking into account a clear evolution of Beckett's dramas from tragicomic forms towards the progressive rarefaction of form and content, I have attempted to give voice also to the unknown or little known Beckett productions.

Samuel Beckett is one of the preferential topics of contemporary criticism. Critical contributions on his work and staging or broadcasting of his plays or scripts are numerous. His popularity among contemporary critics and audiences is both taken for granted and astonishing. What is the obvious or incomprehensive appeal of this author in our Western, postmodern culture? Why has such an obscure and seemingly gloomy author become beloved by critics and widely known within popular awareness? My hypothesis is that Beckett built a fine network of reciprocally contradicting meanings by means of semantic and stylistic clashes. This complex system enacts rather than expresses chaos, leaving to the reader or audience the responsibility of actively contributing to the semantic exchange. Author and receiver, holding hands, dance a grotesque dance on the debris of culture, philosophy and artistic genres. They dance and they laugh, knowing that it is no laughing matter. How to critically address this postmodern complexity? How to take a scholarly approach to such an organic matter? As far as possible, the present contribution intends to address such an effort towards dispelling the stereotype of a Beckett essentially writer and fundamentally devoted to the expression of pessimism and anxiety. The present research and textual analysis discover a Beckett who does not only know an endless variety of comedy tools, but is also aware of specific theatre-making as a director and then as a radio, film and television-maker. With this technical knowledge of comedy and theatre, Beckett treated both the comic and the pathetic with a rare balance, making them interact and blend on stage.

I begin this discussion with a review of the critics' views on comedy and humour in Beckett. This question is organised by looking at to what extent Beckett's texts are understood as containing elements of comedy or humour and by describing how comedy and humour in Beckett are conceptualised or defined. In order to classify the analytical material, I make use of a necessarily discontinuous and heterogeneous conceptualisation, clustering in the same overview categories of comedy, such as "irony", "tragicomedy" and "carnival". These are somewhat unsuitable to be applied to Beckett in absolute and uncritical ways, but they are amply warranted by means of critical references, textual evidence and biographical data. The first chapter reviews specific contributions on Beckett and comedy and examines their theatrical traditions in context. The second chapter gives a thorough account of Beckett's cultural background regarding comedy and comic genres. His knowledge of and passion for the comic, both in its literary and performed forms, are evidenced by biographical data and some unpublished documents. The attention here is, once again, given to the less known areas in Beckett's biography: his attendance at theatre performances, circuses, vaudeville and cinema comedies. At the same time, textual analysis has searched for the signs of these performances attended, looking for what belongs to the language and what to the body on stage. Examples of experiences within comedy or quotes from comedy genres are numerous in Beckett's texts and this chapter emphasises them. The following chapters are defined thematically as comedy in the body, in the word and in the sound. The third chapter investigates embodied comedy. Evidence of comedy in gesture is found in its simplest forms (the body itself, in its outward appearance) and as well in more complex forms (the body in movement, gesture and proxemics). The fifth chapter is devoted to the comic in speech, taking into account the function of the word itself and also its organised articulation in speech and dramatic texts. Both chapters are the core of the present study, with their exposition of textual evidence of a wide scope of comedy, ranging from basic pratfall to sophisticated forms of pun and verbal humour. An eclectic dimension is introduced in the fourth chapter, where sound, music and noise are considered to be the intermediate steps between body and words. From silence to indistinct sound, this rhythmic organisation of sound finally reaches codified meaning of music and words. The emphasis is here given to the instrumental use of sound, silence, noises and music in order to generate or enhance comedy effects. The last chapter, the sixth, is devoted to a Beckett theory of comedy and humour. As well known, not only Beckett did never nurture any theatrical or literary theory, but he always stubbornly and steadfastly refused to provide explanations of his artistic products. Yet Beckett scattered throughout his writings detailed and accurate information that can be helpful in understanding his approach to and philosophy of comedy. Peeking between the lines of prose, poetry and theatre, Beckett's conceptualisations on comedy and humour, even though they are not conceived as theoretical contributions, shed light on Beckett's awareness on the hermeneutics of comedy. I also paid attention to the moments in which the characters laugh and to the type of laughter that Beckett's texts enhance in audiences and readers.

With regard to critical tools, I have endeavoured to give the reader as broad an overview as possible. This includes a large bibliography divided as following: 1) Beckett's published texts and manuscripts, which show the original edition of the first versions and any later translations to and from French and English, 2) critical bibliography on Beckett, 3) a general bibliography on humour, silent movies, circus, theatre theories and semiotics. This critical apparatus is meant to be an active tool for the Beckett reader and scholar.

The main target group of the present book, framed as a research monograph, is postgraduate-level students and academic scholars. However, performance artists or theatre professionals and professionals at cultural institutions at large can also benefit from it. In terms of teaching application the book could be well suited for theatre, drama and performance studies; English, French and Italian literature; philosophy, aesthetics, philosophy of art and cultural studies.

A last piece of important information concerns the method of reporting quotes. Quotes from Beckett's texts are chosen in the original language of the first edition, even though it was Beckett who took care of his own translations from and to French and English. Beckett revised his texts any time he had to translate one of his works, or even when he had to translate the plays into the performing language of the stage, often giving critics reason to wonder which version best voices Beckett's spirit - the very first version or the latest revision. My choice of taking the original version and its language is dictated by the need of going back to the very roots of Beckett's ideas about and expressions of humour and comedy. However, when necessary, the two versions are quoted together and compared to each other.

let's get as many laughs as we can out of this horrible mess

the key word in my plays is 'perhaps'

Samuel Beckett

* CHAPTER ONE *

"CRRITIC!"
BECKETT, HUMOUR AND SCHOLARS

1.1. State of the art

The existence of comic elements in Beckett's texts, so well recognised by critics, might seem a topic closed long ago. In reality, the constant return by scholars to this interpretative key and the extremely fragmentary nature of many of these studies call for a different, more complete approach. The only monographs hitherto dedicated to the comic in Beckett are *Samuel Beckett: the comic gamut* by Ruby Cohn (1962); *The Humour of Samuel Beckett* by Valerie Topsfield (1988) and *Beckett's Critical Complicity. Carnival, contestation and tradition* by Sylvie Debevec Henning (1988).

Of these, the book by American scholar Ruby Cohn remains an essential point of reference, despite its date of 1962. It is the only specific study to use detailed textual analysis to identify the comic techniques used by Beckett. In the wake of a widespread movement which took place in the United States in the Fifties of critical re-evaluation of Henri Bergson's work, Cohn makes prevalent use, as her interpretative tool, of the comic categories proposed by the French philosopher in his study of laughter.[1] Her choice would appear quite unchallengeable, given the evidence showing that Beckett undoubtedly knew Bergson's theories. Some sources[2] note that the young Beckett, while teaching at Trinity College, Dublin, in the Thirties, gave his students a monographic lesson on the French philosopher, while others[3] limit his still considerable interest to numerous quotes during lessons dedicated to other authors. Very valuable student notes show that Beckett often used Bergson as an element of comparison to further clarify Proust and Gide, using Bergson's concept of time to discuss that of Proust and his theories on language to differentiate them from those of Gide. Also, in a letter to Tom MacGreevy from the same period, Beckett defines *Le Kid* as something halfway between Corneille and Bergson.[4] A clear nod to the French philosopher is found in *More Pricks Than Kicks*, when Chas attempts to explain the world to his pupils: "the difference [...] between Bergson and Einstein, the essential difference, is as between philosopher and sociologist" (p. 63), and a few lines later he bewails the fact that "it is the smart thing now to speak of Bergson as a cod" (p. 64). Beckett studies Bergson, uses him as a comparative aesthetic type and is probably also influenced by him. Moreover, as Bergson is one of our greatest 20th century theorists of the comic, he is an essential interpretative key to the study of those mechanisms that he identified. Consequently if, on the one hand, one cannot fault Cohn's choice, on the other, her exegetical orientation is too partial for material such as Beckett's humour, which contains several interpretative levels. Cohn's analysis explores those phenomena of the comic in words, situations and characters covered by Bergson's philosophical categories, while other degrees of comicality – though present in the texts – are not taken into consideration. Cohn was well aware of this limit when she wrote the book, for she states that from *Watt* onwards "we find Bergson's analysis is less descriptive of Beckett's comic"[5] and that, while she found Bergson's analysis useful in examining comic elements before *Watt*, from this novel on, Beckett's comicality changes radically, so that "corrective and consolidating theories of comedy are irrelevant to *Watt*"[6] and all the works that follow. Yet, though she evidently sees the limitation of Bergson's categories, Cohn keeps to her analysis of the comic in words, situations and characters, because her attention is not specifically focussed on the theatre, nor does she make a clear distinction between the writing of a literary text and of one for the stage. The theatre as dramatic literature and comicality as the comic word exclude physicality on stage and the corporeality of the comic from the pages of this work, extremely useful though it may be, while it is evident to other scholars that "Beckett's fool elicits laughter that is almost outside the Bergsonian categories".[7]

Rather than being the exception in criticism of Beckett, this approach is the model most commonly found. Critics' attention to the Beckett/comic relationship dates from after the Second World War, when critical interest in comicality was growing in direct proportion to interest in Beckett's works. Many scholars of the time made a connection between the two questions, finding in Beckett evident comic elements: in France Nadeau, in Germany Anders, in Great Britain and in the United States Cohn, Esslin, Kenner and later Hoffman, Jacobsen, Mueller, Scott, Fletcher and Robinson (Italian criticism would merit separate consideration, given the as yet undiscovered reasons for its scarce attention to issues of the comic in Beckett).[8] Some, however, have perceived in this temporal proximity the seeds of a clamorous error: Richard Simon holds that Samuel Beckett is *not* comic, instead "Beckett's texts are clearly anticomic [...]; Beckett's literature is [...] a perversion of the comic".[9] According to Simon, the fact that Beckett's texts have been interpreted as comic – wrongly in his view – lies precisely in this interpretative "fashion", common in the late Fifties and in the Sixties in France, Germany and Great Britain, but above all in the United States where, now free from wartime censorship, Jewish humour was widespread. In actual fact, studies do exist into the comic in Beckett outside of this interpretative "vogue" and their conclusions seem to us to be indisputably legitimate, despite the very obvious limits of their analyses. The weightier studies on the subject take a theoretical, philosophical or literary approach, which ignores the specificity of the theatrical stage and comic practice upon it. So despite that fact that clowns, carnivalesque obscenity and vaudeville routines are often mentioned, they seem to have lost any "technical" connotation, being transfigured into general categories of the comic. Other shorter critical contributions analyse a specific comic technique without relating it to the general context of the text or texts, or again to a recurring, significant construction. The result is an overall, unchallenged agreement as to the comic nature – to a greater or lesser degree - of all Beckett's work; a generic reference to the traditions of the circus, the music-hall and of Hollywood comic films that is stereotyped and in the long run sterile, being frozen into a cliché; the possibility of associating Beckett's comic with materials that are very different and sometimes contradict each other, the eclectic nature of Beckett's texts is such that one risks being able to state anything and its contrary; and philosophical theorising to the detriment of pragmatic analysis. The last point, in particular, applies to the majority of critical studies of Beckett and the comic, including the above-mentioned volumes by Topsfield and Henning. From the latter, one can derive useful thoughts on "philosophical laughter" in Beckett. The former, on the other hand, demonstrates how all Beckett's work is nothing less than progressive evolution and continuous tension towards the "risus purus" in Beckett's *Watt*.[10] In Beckett's early works Topsfield notes a prevalence of the ethical and intellectual laugh, while in his last works he seems to tend towards a philosophical acceptance of existence. Humour, as defined by the English author, takes on a "balancing" function, since it helps the audience/reader find a sense of proportion when the tears/laughter conflict is no longer felt: in a situation of interpretative confusion, comic and tragic are perceived as one and the same thing.[11] The purgatorial situation of mankind, constantly shifting between tears and laughter, is experienced in Beckett's universe by the author: Beckett himself sees "a positive side to the purgatory of being a writer, because it is a pensum, or task, not a punishment, so that if the task is completed, there is a positive result".[12] But it is also experienced both by his characters (the "quest" to which they are condemned makes these "ineffective heroes"[13] resemble those of Dante) and by his public, which is obliged to maintain an equilibrium between the tragic and the comic.

Topsfield's study also investigates the literary, philosophical, theatrical and cinematic antecedents of the idea and practice of the comic in Beckett. From Dante to Joyce, from Heraclitus to Bergson, by way of Jarry, Artaud, Synge and O'Casey, each of these authors seems to have left his mark on Beckett's texts, as shown by Topsfield in numerous examples. These analytical essays can be grouped around three different themes: 1) irony; 2) tragicomedy; 3) the carnivalesque.

1.2. Irony

"Irony is usually seen as something that undermines clarities, opens up vistas of chaos, and either liberates by destroying all dogma or destroys by revealing the inescapable canker of negation at the heart of every affirmation".[14] Irony is created through ambiguity in the communication process, which the receiver must "decode" and reconstruct with "another" meaning, different from the one explicitly stated and hidden between the lines of the actual message transmitted. Saying one thing and meaning another implies a space where the meaning is broken up as it is spoken, but also a space for its logical reconstruction while being decoded. Once the original meaning has been reconstructed, it becomes defined and stable. Stable irony is based on a shared system of rules between a receiver and an implicit author and enables the play between what is spoken and the hidden meaning. This is what is undermined by Beckett, who rather uses what Lloyd Bishop defines as "romantic irony".[15]

Beckett's universe is not so much open to visions of chaos as at the complete mercy of it. Entropy conveys an effect of "miniaturisation" and ironic, or rather auto-ironic collapse, which results in the implosion of the writing. The very narrative structures are threatened by systematic aggression from within. The writing seems to no longer have fixed points of reference, it seems reduced to silence, yet it continues to persist, continues to speak the unspeakable. In Lloyd Bishop's analysis of the *Thrilogy*[16] and its internal deflation, to the detriment of hero, narrator and narrative, he considers this process as the result of exasperation of the romantic irony. The hero in his classic function as narrator has disappeared, has shrunk, says Bishop, to the dimension of a litotes: an attenuation who implies more than he says, an anti-hero incapable of carrying out any function, not even that of the former hero. A figure that completely reverts to a larval state in the trilogy, but which inhabits all of Beckett's pages with his passivity, "he is a passive questor, waiting for something to happen rather than making things happen".[17] The anti-hero is condemned to suspend his judgement of the world, for he lives bound by a total compresence of contraries, which prevent him from having a clear view of events around him. The simultaneous presence (*cum-praesentia*) of black/white, alive/

dead, sad/happy clouds his Cartesian clarity, or the possibility of certain, scientific knowledge of the world around him. His hopeless waiting is that of perpetual gnoseological paralysis. Although Bishop only considers the *Thrilogy*, these judgements can be extended to the entire bestiary of Beckett's work: Didi and Gogo do nothing but wait *ad infinitum*, just like Krapp, Hamm, Clov, just as the couples Mr/Mrs Rooney and Winnie/Willie constantly repeat the same routines. All these characters are "philosophically paralysed by aporia"[18] and can no longer enjoy the certainty of being creatures born of the fantasy of a traditionally omniscient narrator, since the latter proves completely unreliable, not to say dishonest: he admits to lying and, even when he tries to convince us that his story is true, he fills it with so many verbs indicating uncertainty, so many adverbs and conjunctions of probability, that a huge doubt remains as to its reliability. The narrator, who often admits to being an ungovernable narrator, as well as an ungovernable liar, gratifies us with his self-parody. But even in this comic effect there is no consolation, since it serves to deflate the narrator and his narrative. Beckett's narrator is aware of the self-deconstruction he is pursuing in his narrative and invites readers to participate in it, involving them in a strong feeling of bewilderment, by means of many meta-narrative comments and frequent mingling of different stylistic registers. Beckett appears in his own fiction as a clearly recognisable puppet-master and as an incompetent ventriloquist.[19] This definition of Bishop's may be illustrated by *Dream of Fair to Middling Women*, where the narrator several times calls on the author, Mr Beckett, revealing the narrative convention: he first says "thanks Mr Beckett" (p. 69, repeated then in the less colloquial "thank you Mr Beckett" in *More Pricks than Kicks*, p. 197), then "oh but the bay, Mr Beckett, didn't you know, about your brow" (p. 141), ending with a sort of verbal attack on Mr Beckett, "behold, Mr Beckett [...] a dud mystic" to which the author retorts "he meant mystique raté, but shrank always from the mot juste" (p. 186). In his drama, too, "mister" Beckett makes the author's function and the theatrical fiction clear. What Bishop sees in the fiction and in the *Thrilogy* in particular can be applied to the theatre. Beckett quotes himself ironically in *Eleutheria*, where the Spectator complains to the author: "[...] qui a fait ce navet? (*programme*) Beckett (*il dit:«Béquet»*), Samuel,

Béquet, Béquet, ça doit être un juif groenlandais mâtiné d'Auvergnat" (p. 136). There are also numerous nods to the audience and meta-theatrical references, which destroy the naturalistic fiction of the scene and make it possible for the author to be replaced by the characters: they take over from him as explicit masters of the stage play and they, too, turn out to be unreliable *maîtres du jeu*. Reason is totally defeated: the identity of the characters on stage is larval, diminished, completely unsuited to human life. The spectator shares their bewilderment for a reality he thought was "measurable", or at least knowable, which turns out to be elusive. The narrator struggles against an enunciative system that escapes him and seems to have a life of its own. The inadequacy of languages is stated but also contradicted by continuing to write, to communicate albeit in an imperfect, defective, partial, exhausting way. Continuing to speak despite the impossibility of saying, persisting in affirming silence, making silence speak, constructing a building and deriving the only possible meaning from its ruins. "Only romantic ironists create, then deliberately break, the fictional illusion".[20] Compresence of affirmation and negation - we are deep in paradox. If we look more carefully at the structure and the function of paradox, we realise that this figure of speech is a fundamental part of irony and that the two are often inextricably linked.

Rolf Breuer's study of paradox in Beckett[21] clarifies, albeit using a purely philosophical and logical approach, some of the concepts already expressed by Bishop: endurance (persistence against odds), oxymoron (figure of speech combining opposites), meta-irony (boomerang irony) and allegories (ironic tools used on allegory itself) can all be defined as immovable paradoxes. A paradox (from the Greek παρα'-δο'ξαν= contrary to wisdom) is a statement that seems absurd but which has not (yet) been refuted. Within this generic definition, Breuer recognises various logical types such as sophism (an innocuous paradox) and antinomy (contradictory affirmations deduced from syllogisms founded on premises that are apparently true and generally accepted). Or again, one can find paradoxes acting on logic or on reality. Beckett uses both and Breuer's study analyses them, together with their linguistic and textual forms. The logical paradoxes are developed on a literary plane, where the antinomies are created by confusing the literary level with the meta-literary one - the literature, with its recursive, circular, repetitive nature, seems to re-create itself. Structures seem to reproduce themselves, stimulated simply by endless repetition of the same elements. A typical example might be the final *tableau*, which repeats the opening one, in *Fin de Partie*, formal reiteration also found in *Happy Days, Play, Not I, En attendant Godot*.[22] Paradoxes of reality consist of the simultaneous existence of opposing elements, both justified and justifiable, both accepted or acceptable as true. They are the perfect *coincidentia oppositorum* in the unresolved complementarity of opposites: beginning/end, to be/not to be, tears/laughter, words/silence. This latter pair, especially, defines the intimate nature of the oxymoron. The negation that affirms (or the affirmation that negates) stimulates a new, different reality, alive with the pulsating trauma of artistic paradox: expressing the inexpressible through an imperfect medium. "To be an artist is to fail, as no other dare fail".[23] So art can be only the manifestation "of his insight into the relativity of all attempts at categorization, into the impossibility of differentiation".[24] However, for the paradox to become a source of philosophical laughter it must attain the more elevated viewpoint of romantic irony.[25] Only then can it be considered, in a certain sense, an instrument of self-knowledge - that elusive knowledge that remains ever open and unresolved, like the paradox itself.[26] By philosophical laughter I intend that defined by Sylvie Debevec Henning as the fruit of Menippean satire:[27] a problematic reflection on the search for truth, which takes us on a journey towards an idea of the world, in a philosophical system.

Beckett explodes western thinking from within and from its epistemic foundations, giving us a character obsessed with "wholeness" and monism. Murphy lives in a perpetual separation of mind and body, resolving in inactivity his inept ascetic tendencies. Murphy is ridiculed constantly as the story unfolds, in a progression that sees him gamble his own ontology in a profane game of chess against his ideal adversary, Mr. Endon (from the Greek=that which is, as opposed to Murphy, who attempts to flee life's course by imprisoning himself naked on a rocking chair). We laugh at Murphy, up to the final apotheosis of his death (which occurs following a very trivial, paradoxical accident) and his "funeral" celebrated involuntarily in a squalid bar, on whose floor his ashes are carelessly scattered. Our laughter is joined by that of the laughing philosopher, Democritus[28] – the laughter of the materialist who mocks the ascetic's attempt to stop life's eternal rhythm (the rocking with its perpetual oscillations) by retreating to a lunatic asylum, perfect example of a place of non-being. Democritus, whose atomic theory envisages a compresence of atoms/void and man as a microcosm containing all the elements of the macrocosm, laughs at Murphy's quest, for he knows that the soul is made of atoms – that is, of matter – and that there is no real dualism of body and soul, given that the body is essential to the integrity of the soul. The Menippean satire brings Murphy's philosophical "quest" down to earth, radicalises opposites into being problematic and, in the attempt to find a form that accommodates the chaos, offers a possible solution – that of laughter, of comic aggression, of carnivalisation, which creates a breaking of the binary oppositions. *Murphy* does not embody a particular philosophical position but is a satire against all of western thought and its certainties. The totality opposing it has itself a problematic and dialectical nature and provides for the possible reversal of any given into their opposites.[29] The instrument used by Beckett is the sharp weapon of comedy, or rather tragicomedy, since it disorientates the audience or reader with a cognitive shock. It is in the highly theatrical nature of the irony that the attention of the audience (reader) is re-oriented through the traumatic alternation of comic and tragic.

1.3. Tragicomic

The comic in Beckett is most frequently defined as "tragicomic", a mixture of comedy and pathos. Here, however, we find differences in critical opinions: does the tragic balance out the comic and vice versa, or do comic and tragic occur simultaneously in the texts? Richard Dutton saw a connection between modern tragicomedy, identified in examples from Beckett, Pinter, Stoppard, Albee and Storey, and the historical tradition of this theatrical genre that goes by the name of "tragicomedy".[30] To this end, Dutton explored the roots of the genre and followed the evolution over the centuries of a tradition that dates from Italian, French and English Renaissance drama. In the classical world the two genres were never mingled, indeed Aristotle, Horace and Cicero considered them as incompatible opposites. Dutton did note that Latin satire had experimented with something similar to tragicomedy in the satire of Plautus. In his *Amphytryon*, Plautus has Mercury say that he has the powers to derive comedy from tragedy and vice versa, or to mix the two (*tragicomœdia*). The Middle Ages made a scarce contribution to this evolution, with a few examples from popular plays of situations overturned, serious king/comic clown, in a carnival-like atmosphere. This paved the way for the true age of tragicomedy - the Renaissance. It was during this cultural period that the genre was cultivated on stage and studied analytically (among early theories one might mention *Pastor Fido* by Giovanbattista Guarini and *Discorso sulle comedie e sulle tragedie* by Giraldi Cinthio). Renaissance practice and theory teaches us that the tragic/comic mixture was never by chance "[...] but a deliberate blending of traditionally tragic and comic dramatic elements for specific purposes and effects".[31] Certain distinctive characteristics of the genre can be identified: forms that are unrealistic, though everyday; an intricate plot founded on an unlikely hypothesis; characters that are not supernatural but certainly "Protean"; touches of passion and emotion (pathos).[32] It might perhaps seem risky to make a connection between two types of drama so different and so far apart in time as the Theatre of the Absurd[33] (which Dutton, in the light of the analyses mentioned here, proposes re-christening Modern Tragicomedy) and European Renaissance Theatre. But for Dutton, both forms have the same rituality at their base. Moreover, "tragicomedy" is the only definition used explicitly by Beckett himself, in the first edition of the text of *En attendant Godot* – attracted, perhaps, by the very ambiguity of the term. I believe that Beckett used the term consciously, as he knew the historical tradition to which it referred. From biographical sources, we know that at Trinity College Dublin he was able to study and analyse texts from the Italian, French and English Renaissance while taking a course on Foreign Literature and that in subsequent years he continued to read the drama of that period.[34] Traces of this interest and knowledge are disseminated in Beckett's drama and, in particular, we find various veiled allusions to Shakespeare: Lucky in his famous speech names Miranda, a character from *The Tempest*; again in *En attendant Godot* various themes record *topoi* from classical culture taken from the Renaissance (wounds to legs and feet like Oedipus; Estragon as a Protean model similar to Christian redemption); Hamm in *Fin de Partie* recalls Prospero from *The Tempest* and the storytelling of many Shakespearian characters.[35] But above all, over these heterogeneous allusions prevails the perception of drama as a single, unitary body "where ideas are raised and either not pursued at all, or pursued with a perversity which leads nowhere, to nonsense or to music-hall routines".[36] In reality, the Beckett spectator is not led "nowhere", but towards the paradoxical system of nonsense of certain comic traditions (comic cinema, circus, music-hall), a universe whose principal creed is aggressive deconstruction of fixed, unshakeable forms. The comic exists to give form to that which has none, to generate order from chaos. In the universe dominated by this positive, stimulating disorder, tragedy is no longer possible unless derived from comedy and vice versa. Forms can no longer be pure and the "contaminated" genre of tragicomedy expresses the deeper tensions of contemporary life - "it mirrors the passionate anarchy our artists oppose to an absurd world, a meaningless society, devitalized speech. It embodies our puzzlement with the world, and suggests the groping for a question rather than an answer".[37]

The Theatre of the Absurd was to explore the absurdity of human life and speech and try to express it. In a biological and psychological system dominated by chaos, we see the illogicality of space/time and cause/effect relationships. The Theatre of the Absurd puts this chaos on stage, playing with atmospheres that are part folly, dream and reality. It shows an existence that is irreverent towards all traditional logic and is apparently without motive. To J. L. Styan this seems the materialisation of Artaud's theatre of cruelty.[38] The critic indicates this mixture of tragic and comic as "dark comedy", explaining the frustrating effect it has on the public: "dark comedy" is a drama "which impels the spectator forward by stimulus to mind or heart, then distracts him, muddles him, so that time and time again he must review his own activity in watching the play".[39]

In fact, there are many terminological definitions for the same concept: instead of tragicomedy one might speak of comic drama, tragic farce, pseudo-drama, comi-tragedy, black humour, schizo-comedy.[40] The most complete list of the various "labels" attributed to the Theatre of the Absurd is found in *Le théâtre de dérision* by Emmanuel Jacquart, where, in addition to those already mentioned, we find: anti-theatre, avant-garde theatre, experimental, critical or protesting theatre, meta-theatre, obscure comedy, modern tragicomedy, metaphysical farce, theatre of the human condition, apocalyptic theatre, atheatre, theatre of shock, theatre of misfits or – as Jacquart prefers – theatre of derision.[41] Equally numerous are the ways of expressing the same notion with equivalent judgements: Peter Brook speaks of the contemporary existence of the awful and the funny;[42] Alan Schneider considers *Godot* as a text that is terrible and comic at the same time, *Fin de partie* as constantly turning the sublime to the ridiculous and the ridiculous to the sublime, *Krapp* as comic and moving;[43] James Knowlson notes that the mixture of humour and pathos is fruit of a tragicomic vision of the world;[44] Ruby Cohn suggests using the term "comitragedy" as, if tragicomedy is a tragedy with a happy ending, in Beckett we have the exact opposite, a comedy with a sad ending.[45]

Some have seen in Beckett's tragicomedy more profoundly Shakespearian references. Verna Foster[46] notes that the narration of tragic events is overlaid, in both authors, by a comic, light-hearted tone that produces a tragicomic effect. Thus seen, however, tragic and comic have two different, distinct functions that occur simultaneously: the former deals with the content and the latter with the form of the discourse. Both can be manifested thanks to the structure of the storytelling. In Beckett and in Shakespeare's last works (from *Pericles* to *The Tempest*[47]) there are frequent situations where a character interrupts the dramatic flow to tell a story. Vladimir and Estragon do it to pass the time, Pozzo out of egoism, Winnie because it is in his nature, Krapp plays with the duplication of his own voice (recorded and live) and converses with himself, Hamm tyrannically insists that people listen to the same old, oft-repeated story. But Nagg, too, tells his own funny tale, Mr Rooney tries to distinguish the story from his own, the protagonists of *Play* are obliged to do so. Beckett's world is crowded with characters that tell of their unhappiness, thus the storytelling is transformed, paradoxically, from narrative into dramatic technique. The drama is not negated by the story, but modified, re-oriented by it, for the story itself has a "dramatic" structure, in accordance with the dialectic contrast between content (tragic) and form (comic). The function of this dialectic, according to Foster, "consists in consolation and recuperation, in giving to suffering some kind of meaning or framework",[48] since the storytellers "narrate tragic events but in the telling modulate them towards comedy and by their presence reassure the audience of some more consoling resolution than the story itself at first seems to offer".[49] If this is possible in Shakespeare, I nurture strong doubts about Beckett - the laughter provoked is certainly not the free and liberating laughter of "pure" comedy, but is always a reluctant laugh that long ago shed any cathartic and/or consolatory connotation. In Beckett, comic and tragic appear simultaneously rather than alternately[50] and appear to be interchangeable. This creates bewilderment in the spectator who is not used to the superimposition of opposing dramatic conventions: "the members of the audience are confused by this mixing of conventions, and they find themselves being amused by the kind of events that normally evoke compassion and sympathy".[51] Bewilderment, but also complete involvement of the spectator, who takes on an active role in trying to find the right referentiality and whose imagination is stimulated, together with his ability to act within the spell of artistic pretence. The impossibility of clearly distinguishing comic from tragic in Beckett has not, however, restricted critical attention to the category of tragicomedy. In fact a great deal of attention has been devoted to seeking comic techniques in Beckett's texts.

1.4. Carnival

Several studies have made the connection between Beckett and carnivalesque fantasy with its collection of stage and dramatic techniques and its mythological fascination. The most authoritative of these is the already-mentioned *Beckett's Critical Complicity. Carnival, contestation and tradition* by Sylvie D. Henning. As the title indicates, Carnival is placed between contestation and tradition, but this is a "categorical" Carnival, not the lay-religious festival of historical delimitations and connotations. Henning finds that, though Beckett has been interpreted as the clearest symptom of the 20th century's crisis of values, as expression of the Absurdist and/or Existentialist movement, in actual fact his works contain a greater complexity, which escapes these definitions. Beckett challenges western cultural tradition with its desire for integral totality, even in dissent. His is a radical opposition, with no half measures. It shakes even the most unshakeable foundations of tradition, ranging from morality to the alienated mechanisms of society, from dogmatic certainties to aesthetics. Closed systems, all-inclusive logic that sees all and knows all, are rendered useless by the compresence of opposing tensions that never cancel each other out. Beckett stages the ongoing confusion through concomitance of impulses and counter-impulses. His might be defined as "criticism of repressive thought" and has an illustrious antecedent in the carnivalised universe of Bakhtin.[52] Henning takes the mediaeval Carnival with its literary production as a comic phenomenology and theoretical criterion of laughter, outside of any historicist periodisation, and uses it as a philosophical category of joyful and playful destabilisation. Western thought can no longer deal with the chaos. It is completely lost within a world of problems that defies all ratification. Beckett reveals the limits of "serious" thought without totally discrediting it, for his aggression still needs a target and the rules of the anarchic game require both poles of opposition. Beckett's work becomes a "carnivalised" place of confrontation between the culture of order (or of the ordered disorder of alternative thinking) and that of chaos, without ever solving the dilemma. The carnivalesque is the instrument of this aggression, the place where values are overturned, the time of the prank without payback. Using Bakhtin's categories, Henning notes that the stylistic nature of the carnivalesque is dialogic heteroglossia, where heteroglossia means language having a plurality of contrasting perspectives, values and ideologies, while dialogism indicates the symbolic exchange between speakers. The tensions set up by this situation are uncontrollable, especially when we are in the presence of dialogisation, that is to say, an even more creative form of heteroglossia. In this case, the possibility of dominating the contrasting forces is even less likely: "when carnivalization is absent, or when its playfully ironic contestation of official structures has broken down, the opposed forces within heteroglossia can more easily approach simple domination".[53]

Dialogisation, in the sense of an interpretative category opposed to monologism, pursues a strategy of deconstruction, which sets preferential elements of the argument against latent or repressed ones, insinuates its subversive voice into the dominant argument and leaves both sides to coexist without repression. The "dialogic" quality of the writing is obtained in Beckett by the coexistence of various different interpretations at the same time. This provokes, in the audience, a certain vertigo regarding the sense, as well as confusion - often traumatic. As he or she is no longer given any stable reference for interpretation, "a reader/spectator can never really be certain of the 'vantage point' from which he or she is viewing the play. The very idea of stable reference is subjected to critical scrutiny".[54] Yet this is also the reason for Beckett's fascination - "an intellectually challenging writer because he works through complex problems".[55]

This is the vital spirit of his art, this balancing between opposing pulsations - the need and the desire for order along with denial of this possibility; the awareness of the elusive nature of chaos and the will to insist in expressing it. Disorder brings creative stimulation to thought and gives it the illusion of dealing with chaos and conflict is its formal manifestation, the dramatic tension of/in the text that reacts to paralysing despair. But in this evident multi-dimensionality of Beckett also lies the hermeneutical danger, since it is possible to affirm everything and its opposite, should one not manage to decipher the obscure clarity of his argument. The obscene, grotesque physicality of carnivalesque laughter inverts official values and shatters the unitary vision of the world. Contemporary rationalism, which had tried to eliminate all traces of the non-conceptual, maintaining pure logic alone, is attacked by the most vulgar physicality and the same fate awaits empiricism, the scientific faith in knowing and classifying chaos. Consider the logical-mathematical vertigo of Watt, completely futile and ridiculous, or Clov's "Galilean" clumsiness, when he points a telescope (supremely "Galilean" instrument) at the audience and says he sees a crowd of madmen: "a public that accepts uncritically the propositions of a conventional science [...] is delirious, if not mad".[56] Nor does anthropocentrism bring any consolation. Man, like Hamm, has lost his centre and, hard as he tries to find it, his eyes are immersed in eternal darkness and his body is at the mercy of an untrustworthy servant.

Carnivalesque comedy attacks all totality with a physicality that is childlike and, therefore, playful, containing infinite bodily humours that move through the body inside and out. Physiology not only of the human organism itself but also of its verbal expression. Language becomes the bearer of triviality, expressing itself through metaphors of the bodily functions, by means of imprecations, parodies, that is, by "doubling" of the identity which can be verified through its opposite sign. Dialogism, in fact, allows the double to exist freely in a single context and undermines our notion of logic founded on the hegemony of monologism. Dialogism was to destroy the unity of context, with the presence of speaking voices of mixed or ambivalent truths in the same space of text. The monologism of institutional literary tradition, on the other hand, reduced all voices to the intonations of one single speaking voice.[57] The literary strategy (narrative or dramatic) that envisages the interaction of two criteria of different truths is the dialogic couple or, better, pair of parodic look-alikes. The tradition of the comic duo is a classic of literature and comic theatre. One might recall the *zanni* of the Commedia dell'Arte, but also the clowns (*clown blanc/auguste*) and American movie couples (Laurel and Hardy, Abbot and Costello). Here are two different elements, with opposing signs, which interact schizophrenically within the text, as they repeat each other's speeches with reverse trends[58] and reciprocally re-orientate their declarations and the different criteria of truth that underlie them. Beckett's characters have been defined variously as clowns, 'masks' from the Commedia dell'Arte, *clochards* and gagmen, since they very clearly embody the quality of the parodic couple. Critic Frederik Busi has used the stock characters of the Commedia dell'Arte as archetypes to which both Beckett and Cervantes refer. The characters of *En attendant Godot* appear to owe a debt to the tradition of the Spanish author, with their interdependent buffoonery that seems to personify the carnivalesque compresence of opposites. Vladimir and Estragon are buffoons who complete each other, opposites who receive sense from their reciprocal difference and from the impossibility of separating, as do the stock couples of servants in scenes from the *Improvvisa*, or Don Quixote and Sancho Panza. Unfortunately, however, Busi's brilliant intuition was not corroborated by any objective evidence from Beckett's biography, nor by more detailed investigation. In fact, Busi based his study on the hypothesis that "it would be unthinkable that one of this century's major novelists was unfamiliar with the masterpiece created by that genre's principal developer"[59] and does not go beyond analysis of *Godot* and its onomastics in comparison with that of *Don Quixote*. Today, thanks to the work of academics from the University of Reading,[60] we know that Beckett did read *Don Quixote*. John Pilling, in discussing what later was called the "*Murphy* notebook" – notes made by Beckett when writing his novel *Murphy* – found among the quotations listed several from *Don Quixote*, both translated into French and in the original Spanish.[61] From Knowlson's biography of Beckett we learn that Beckett not only read Cervantes' work but also studied in depth the whole tradition of the picaresque novel.[62] So he was well aware of the techniques of these authors who used the rhetorical figures of the comic. This, however, should not be a reason for simply comparing the styles of Beckett and Cervantes, authors separated by time and space, or of Beckett and picaresque writers. Rather, it should help us understand how Beckett used a given tradition. In this way we should read critical intervention linking Beckett and the Commedia dell'Arte. Some elements of the *Commedia all'improvviso* are found in Beckett as comic categories: anti-realism, the grotesque, comic routines. The relationship of the Commedia actors with their audience breaks the "magic one-ness"[63] and tends to surprise spectators in a mixture of distance and attraction. This, according to Edith Kern, is the basis of the meta-theatricality that links Beckett to the spirit of the Commedia dell'Arte. Hamm, Pozzo and their colleagues constantly reveal theatrical convention, at the same time provoking surprise and horror from the audience, as well as an overturning of viewpoint that recalls the upside-down world of carnival. The dramatic technique inherited by Beckett from this stage practice is the *lazzi*, stock characters who will be examined below.

    Another element in common with the imaginary of the Commedia dell'Arte is that of playfulness, also shared with entire Theatre of the Absurd and the carnival universe. The rules of play are mandatory but subversive, too - they regulate the progress of the *ludus*, but result in a mechanism of make-believe, so that all illusions (from in-ludo=in the play) can be accepted. Between Beckett's characters "joking relationships" prevail, that is to say, "a peculiar combination of friendliness and antagonism",[64] which may be symmetrical (both characters make fun of each other) or asymmetrical, with one victim and one executioner. Beckett's characters use both dynamics and are nearly always involved in a physical and verbal game,[65] or use games and toys to pass the time (chess, bicycles). They also use common, everyday objects, transfigured for use in play (Winnie with her bag, the hats of Vladimir and Estragon, Krapp's tapes). But in Beckett there is an extra complication: if the system of play must express itself using everyday language, that of an elementary psychological world, the language of the affections, he adds to this another level, that of awareness of code. Vladimir and Estragon do not merely play (at insulting each other, hanging each other, at Pozzo and Lucky etc.) - they also discuss the problem of instructions, of "how" to play.[66] This in effect gives the game connotations of an autonomous meta-system, a carnival universe and an upside-down world. This is a "child's" universe that attacks adult thought with the logic of the body, the shameless, obscene body, fascinated by physiological and bodily functions as only children can be. Although one notes a certain restraint on the part of Beckett when translating the trivial expressions from texts originally written in French into his mother tongue (a little Irish Puritanism, perhaps?),[67] obscenity is a recurring motif in his work. Scatological references, so beloved of children, are especially frequent. "La merde universelle"[68] in Beckett becomes a conscious symbolic universe, in opposition to that of rationalist seriousness, another chance to attack logical thought. The reader/spectator finds it hard to extricate himself among a mass of expressions marked by ambiguous interpretation and the coprolalia makes him even more confused. Especially when excrement becomes a metaphor for artistic production and the act of defecation, the work of the artist. For Celati, the function of Beckett's scatology is to highlight the "vice" underlying reading: for the writer it is an act of exhibitionism, for the reader it is a sin of indiscretion. But even this revelation takes place with the complicity of the writer and provokes an appalling promiscuity of the I/you relationship.[69] Besides, it is in juxtaposing heterogeneous systems like bodily and intellectual functions that Beckett's tragicomedy lies. A striking example of this is *Krapp's Last Tape*. Krapp is a failed writer, unable to write even one more line, as he is unable to defecate. He is physically and intellectually constipated and none of his most intimate production, whether organic or cerebral, is moving freely or easily - "with Krapp, neither crap nor thought moves freely, though mere words do; in both cases, only gas flows".[70] The obscene metaphor is then amplified in *Krapp* by the play on bananas, which aggravate his constipation and which introduce another bodily level – sex. The bananas encourage his "masturbatory" narcissism and are used for the banana skin routine. But, in Beckett, the *"tendance scatologique, quelle régression infantile au stade anal"*[71] takes on a very particular connotation, in line with the whole ideological and formal structure: excrement, like mud, is an indistinct and shapeless mass, potentiality in its purest form that will never be transformed into action and will always remain in its eternal potentiality. The permanent catastrophe in which man lives is put on stage in the cosmic/comic epic of mud, by the apotheosis of shapeless obscenity. Faeces become an attribute of the world. And thus the words for expressing this mess are mixed up with the mud itself and the faeces become similar to words, as it was for Joyce, Freud and even more so for Swift.[72]

1.5. Which tradition?

Among the comic categories that we have hitherto used in an equally arbitrary and instrumental manner, one is clearly missing - that of humour. Yet humour is an essential analytical tool for any comic form of our times. This apparent hiatus in the catalogue reflects critical attitudes towards Beckett that consider humour almost as a super-category of the comic, for which different analysis is required. For our purposes, we think it important to discuss Beckett's humour in relation to the influence that Pirandello had upon it. The profound links between the comic aesthetic of Beckett and of Pirandello have been inexplicably ignored by critics, despite the numerous points of contact between both authors. The only study specifically dedicated to the subject was the disappointing *Pirandellism and Samuel Beckett's Plays*.[73] The reference to Pirandello and previous ones to Freud, Joyce and Swift – as also earlier references to Shakespeare, Cervantes and Renaissance literature – raise for us the question of which comic tradition Beckett knew, used, rejected, and in what way - by removal, quotation or allusion etc.? This question becomes particularly relevant when linked with investigation of the comic types used by Beckett. Too often they have been made to derive automatically from a precise, defined tradition, thereby losing the overall vision necessary to analysis. The heterogeneity of Beckett's cultural stimuli, aptly defined by Tagliaferri as a "hyper-determined"[74] cultural background, is such that these stimuli ought not to be arbitrarily limited. Yet, critics have attributed the comic types of Beckett's texts to one or another different literary and/or dramatic tradition known to him. And this tradition has been viewed in the light of limited analysis of types, ignoring the complexity and totality of Beckett's erudition. This imbalance in the criticism had occurred because the lack of information about Beckett's life and his unwillingness to discuss his work had not hitherto allowed proper investigation of the author's actual cultural background. Analyses published up till now were founded on hypotheses and intuitions derived from reading the texts, but had no documentary corroboration. Now the educated reader can glean very precise, unmistakeable signs from the texts, so these hypotheses are often reliable, though they reveal the danger of being able to relate Beckett to all of human knowledge. Beckett was one of the most learned intellectuals of our century, with a lively and curious erudition that moved in several directions contemporaneously - European literature and drama, ancient and modern philosophy, psychoanalysis, the exact sciences, Christian theology, the figurative arts, music, new means of mass communication. It is understandable, then, that critics should have a variety of opinions as to the relationship between Beckett and tradition. But which tradition?

The first to discover links between Beckett and a precise cultural background was Martin Esslin who associated Beckett with what he calls the Theatre of the Absurd. This tradition has very ancient origins, identifiable in classical mime, which left traces in the pantomime of the Commedia dell'Arte (thence to Molière and Marivaux), whence, in turn, it became the basis of the clown's art (Esslin cites the Grimaldis as most obvious examples). Then, from the circus, this tradition moved to English and Irish music-hall, to American vaudeville and, from there, to early comic cinema. The list of literary antecedents, on the other hand, goes from the comic Baroque novel to twentieth-century avant-garde theatre: Lewis Carroll, Edward Lear, Flaubert, Calderon, Swift, Walpole, Joyce, Kafka, Jarry, the Symbolists, the Surrealists, Brecht, Aragon, Artaud, Cocteau, Salacrou, Garcia Lorca (with *El Paseo de Buster Keaton*) and S. J. Perelman who wrote most of the Marx Brothers movie scripts. This line of evolution missed, however, Beckett's attention towards Irish literature, a doubt that occurred to Esslin himself later. He sought confirmation of this in an interview with Cohn Leventhal at the 1971 Beckett symposium in Reading, when he discussed with him whether Beckett's humour could be considered as typically Irish. Leventhal replied that an answer might be found in the first Irish performance of *Godot* with Irish actors,[75] where the text worked wonderfully with 'Irishness' of the production. Vivian Mercier maintains that Beckett, like many English-speaking Irish, had absorbed many traditional elements from oral culture and, even more, from reading widely across the Gaelic literary tradition.[76] Moreover, Beckett read the plays and saw the theatre productions (at the Abbey Theatre, Dublin) of the Irish tragicomic (O'Casey, Synge) and tragic-symbolist (W.B. Yeats) literary traditions. This relationship, undoubtedly of knowledge, but also of love/hate, produced a certain influence, but also a hidden refusal - John Orr believes Beckett suffered from amnesia as far as Irish tradition was concerned, since he repudiates more or less consciously his own cultural identity by voluntary exile in Paris and, even more, by not writing in his mother tongue.[77] This repudiation was often underscored by sarcasm towards the traditional Irish bigot. The more recent position taken by John Pilling[78] tends to mitigate over-drastic affirmations of Beckett as a son of his homeland or outcast and exile. We agree with Pilling that Ireland was at the same time the place of Beckett's roots and the place from which he fled, of conflicting sentiments that became clear to the young writer only when he moved to London and was far enough away from the place of his birth and upbringing to be able to feel clearly both attraction and repulsion for it. To this Irish substrate Mercier adds the classic French author Racine, whom Beckett studied at Trinity College, and the stage conventions of the circus, the music-hall and the Commedia dell'Arte, from all of which he gained "technical" knowledge of performance genres. The traditions of the circus and music-hall, together with that of Hollywood comedies, are those most frequently mentioned when searching for a precise background in Beckett: "l'univers du spectacle où ils [the characters] évoluent, n'est pas vraiment celui du théâtre, mais plutôt celui du cirque, du music-hall, des lieux où l'acteur joue d'abord de son corps contre la pesanteur, l'opacité, la roideur des choses, en virtuose pour l'acrobate, en pantin maladroit pour le clown".[79] Circus, pantomime, music-hall, as well as the tradition of English and Irish comic realism (Synge, Wilde, Shaw, Behan) are noted by Michael Worton as reference elements for the meta-theatrical essence of Beckett's theatre and for its perpetual swinging between modernism and post-modernism.[80] The critical studies, in their turn, might be grouped according to the performing tradition indicated as of greater influence on Beckett: some discuss exclusively the circus and clowns (Pringent, Restivo, Serreau, Simon, Dort), others vaudeville (Miller), some speak of American comic movies (Clausius, Celati, Gontarski, Kalb), while others again group the various stimuli into a single, heterogenous melting pot (Fletcher, Mayoux, Smith, Styan, Cohn, Kern, Knowlson, Pilling, Bair).

The latter hypothesis is that of this present study, not only owing to a conviction that all cultural events are the fruit of a series of complex, concomitant causes, but also because documentary research and – above all – analysis of Beckett's texts confirm this supposition.

Notes

1. Bergson 2002.
2. Topsfield 1988, p. 21; Cronin 1997, p. 127; Pilling 1976, p. 7.
3. Pilling 1997, p. 28.
4. Letter of 24th February 1931, cited by Knowlson 1996, p. 727, no. 15. *Le Kid* was a review parody written in Goliardic university spirit. In the Thirties, the Department of Modern Languages of Trinity College, Dublin used to put on a show organised by students, lecturers and professors, members of the Modern Languages Society. In February 1931, while Beckett was a lecturer there, they staged a burlesque, *Le Kid*, inspired by Corneille's *Le Cid* and alluding to *The Kid* by Charlie Chaplin. In the past, this parody was unconditionally attributed to Beckett (in collaboration with Georges Perolson). James Knowlson, however, has revised this and maintains that the myth of a very early sortie by Beckett into theatre should be severely redimensioned: "according to Georges Perolson, the idea of the play was his alone and the cutting up of Corneille's text which produced the one-act burlesque was also done almost entirely by himself, with very little help and advice from Beckett" (Knowlson 1996, p. 123). The myth was, and still is, sustained by the fact that until now no copy of the work has been traced and any information about it chiefly derives from articles published in the TCD journal - the review of the performance and Beckett's satirical reply to the review, entitled "The Possessed".
5. Cohn 1962, p. 66.
6. Ibid. p. 94.
7. Takahashi (1975, p. 36) also notes that the pun, fundamental to Beckett's comedy, is dismissed by Bergson as the least recommendable form of humour.
8. The "tragic" interpretation is well summarised by Strehler: "En lisant et en relisant ce texte [*Oh les beaux jours*], qui m'apparaît de plus en plus comme une tragédie, je suis surtout frappé par cette affirmation de vie qu'il contient" (Strehler 1990, p. 213). Exceptions to this view in Italy are Celati 1986; Tagliaferri 1967; Restivo 1991; Locatelli 1990a; Frasca 1988.

9   Simon R. K. 1987, p. 90. For further information on Beckett's relationship with the comic and for critical contributions on comic theories from the Twenties to the Sixties, see the useful bibliographical indications attached to the present study.
10   See here para. "Rien n'est plus drôle que le malheur".
11   Topsfield 1988, p. 2.
12   Ibid. pp. 2-3. The author later explores the concept of writing as consolation for Beckett, likening his detachment from suffering to that of Dante, who was, however, comforted by the divine presence.
13   Ibid. p. 9.
14   Booth 1975, p. IX.
15   Bishop L. 1989, passim.
16   Beckett wrote the novels *Molloy*, *Malone meurt* and *L'Innommable* in a single creative rush. He conceived and wanted them published, as soon as possible, in one volume. For this reason they are normally referred to as the Trilogy.
17   Bishop L. 1989, p. 187.
18   Ibid. p. 194.
19   Ibid. p. 190.
20   Bishop L. 1989, p. 189.
21   Breuer R. 1993, pp. 559-580.
22   The examples are all from Breuer, who however specifies in a note that these identities or repetitions are never perfect copies, in fact often an involution of the situation can be seen: Pozzo and Luck come back but one is blind and the other is dumb; Winnie sinks very noticeably downwards; Auditor's gestures are increasingly less visible, and so on.
23   "Three Dialogues", in *Disjecta*, p. 145.
24   Breuer R. 1993, p. 580.
25   Gianni Celati sees the difference between paradox (mere coincidence of opposites, self-referentiality) from romantic, black humour is a higher point-of-view. Both systems are then different from the comic of comedies, which plays on the empirical ego that must be isolated within the social group. See Celati 1975, pp. 92-95.

26 See "The paradoxes remain unresolved, but tellingly explore identity and relationships through notions of sound and silence", Little R. 1994, p. 193.

27 Henning 1985, pp. 5-20. Menippean satire is a literary genre named after Menippus, a cynical philosopher who lived in Palestine in the 3rd century B.C. His satires contained fierce, moralistic criticism of society, in which Menippus saw the corruption of the natural course of life. He therefore preached the total abandonment of civilisation, which corrupted the purity of nature, and a return to the original natural state. The parodic demistification was associated with colourfully realistic forms. Henning uses this term, not so much as a historically defined literary genre, as a comic category applicable to a treatise that is theoretical rather than historical.

28 Henning maintains that "the sound of the Abderite's guffaw [...] disturbs Murphy's experience of the supposed primordial void" (1985, pp. 74-75), but the definition of Democritus as the "laughing philosopher" is Beckett's own, *More Pricks than Kicks*: "Now among our wise men, I doubt not but many would be found, who would laugh at Heraclitus weeping, none which would weep at Democritus laughing" (p. 175).

29 Tagliaferri 1996, p. XXVII.

30 I refer particularly to Dutton 1986.

31 Ibid. p. 15.

32 All characteristics are listed by Dutton, based on an article by Waith 1952, pp. 36-42.

33 The definition is Martin Esslin's (in his famous study *The Theatre of the Absurd*). Because it groups together authors who are very different, it has been repeatedly rejected by other critics and by the authors themselves. Adamov said, "le mot *théâtre absurde* déjà m'irritait. La vie n'est pas absurde, difficile, très difficile seulement" (in Adamov 1968, p. 111) and for Ionesco the definition "c'est un mot à la mode qui ne le sera plus. [...] il est dès maintenant assez vague" (Ionesco 1962, p. 194). Beckett himself in *Molloy* is ironical about the Camus' myth of Sisyphus whence Esslin derives his definition:

"mais même à Sisyphe je ne pense pas qu'il soit imposé de se gratter, ou de gémir, ou d'exulter, à en croire une doctrine en vogue, toujours aux mêmes endroits exactement" (p. 206). The "doctrine en vogue" to which Beckett refers is precisely that of Camus, as he himself confirmed to Tagliaferri in a message dated 21st December 1985 (see note 11 in *Trilogia*, 1996, p. 145). Moreover, the Theatre of the Absurd was never a school, but a convenient label for some post-war authors who shared the same concerns, but resolved them in many different forms. The term will be used, bearing in mind these necessary clarifications.

34 See Knowlson 1996, Cronin 1997 and Bair 1990.
35 These and other examples are from Dutton again.
36 Dutton 1986, p. 65.
37 Lamont 1965, p. 385.
38 Styan 1968, p. 219.
39 Ibid. p. 262. It should be noted that this definition recalls Brecht's theories on theatre. The Beckett/Brecht relationship is still fairly unexplored, as is the political nature – hitherto denied by most – of Beckett's theatre. See Brecht's theories in *Schriften zum Theater* and in his "work diary" *Theaterarbeit* (Brecht 1964; id 1969).
40 All definitions are from Lamont 1965, p. 385, apart from the last two, which are, respectively, Mayoux 1966, pp. 33-41, and Thiher 1983, p. 87.
41 Jacquart 1974, p. 38. Also on p. 96 the concept of derision is placed beside that of the tragic and the ulterior definition is "absurdité tragi-dérisoire". In the text in question there is an excursus among the critical analysis of Beckett and the comic, though he is discussed together with another two authors, Ionesco and Adamov.
42 Brook 1976.
43 Schneider 1958.
44 Knowlson, "Beckett and John Millington Synge", in Knowlson-Pilling 1979.
45 Cohn 1962, p. 8.
46 The article "'A sad tale's best for winter'. Storytelling and Tragicomedy in the Late Plays of Shakespeare and Beckett" can be found in the interesting volume analysing the links on various lev-

els between Shakespeare and Beckett, edited by Anne Marie Drew (see Foster, V. A. 1993).
47 Foster V. A. 1993, p. 15.
48 Ibid. p. 16.
49 Ibid. p. 15.
50 Beckett "usually mingles the tragic and the comic simultaneously rather than alternately" for Dukore too, 1973, p. 353.
51 Lowe 1995, p. 17.
52 Bakhtin 1968.
53 Henning 1988, p. 200, n. 1.
54 Ibid. p. 120.
55 Ibid. p. 6.
56 Ibid. p. 105.
57 Celati 1986, p. 109.
58 Ibid. p. 108.
59 Busi 1980, p. 12.
60 One of the most active and up-to-date centres for research into Beckett, also home of the "Beckett International Foundation" and the Samuel Beckett Archive in the university library. This is currently one of the largest Beckett collections, together with that of Trinity College, Dublin and the Harry Ransom Humanities Research Center of the University of Texas, Austin. For Beckett archives worldwide see Jacquart-Chabert 1990, p. 427.
61 Pilling 1992, pp. 1-20. The document referred to is conserved at the Beckett archive in Reading, MS 3000/1.
62 Knowlson 1996, p. 216.
63 Kern 1966, p. 260.
64 Booth 1974, p. 30.
65 In nearly all European languages, the word for 'to play' also means 'to act': in French jouer, in German spielen, in Danish at spille, in Russian igrat (to have fun, to act a role).
66 Betty Rojtman defines these levels of the discourse as "direct expression" and "secondary expression", adding a third, "surrespression" typical of meta-theatrical situations: see Rojtman 1976, p. 18.
67 Raymond Federman, in Beckett 1971, p. 11: "Beckett's French is based on innumerable idiomatic phrases which disappear in Eng-

lish [...], when Beckett translates himself into English he removes a number of idiomatic or almost obscene expressions".
68 From *Nouvelles et textes pour rien*, "La fin", p. 119.
69 Celati 1986, p. 182.
70 Dukore 1973, p. 352. It should be noted that the character's name recalls excrement, see Campbell 1997.
71 Simon A. 1983, p. 96.
72 Tagliaferri 1996, p. LIII.
73 Uwah Okebaram 1989. Otherwise see: Chemi 2006.
74 Id. 1967, where on p. 11 there is an explanation of the term "hyperdetermination": "the event is determined not once but several times, not by one cause but by many causes".
75 Conversation between Esslin and Leventhal in Beckett 1971, p. 10. Leventhal's precise reply was: "to have a proof that Beckett's humour was Irish, one should have seen the first Irish performance of *Waiting for Godot* in a very, very tiny theatre in Dublin in which the actors were Irish".
76 Mercier 1977.
77 Orr 1991.
78 Pilling 1997, pp. 120-121.
79 Simon A. 1990b, p. 75.
80 Worton 1994, pp. 67-87.

* CHAPTER TWO *

"THE LABOUR OF NESTING IN A STRANGE PLACE". UPBRINGING

2.1. Beckett and the theatre

It is commonly held that Beckett became a dramatist by chance. He himself encouraged the story of a man of letters who began and who saw himself as a poet, who did not disdain "lyrical" prose and who, as repose from his purely literary efforts, enjoyed writing plays. It is true that his creative impulse was without doubt initially towards academic writing (his study of Proust was intended to have been followed by one on Gide),[1] then to literature, while his first finished plays would only see the light after twenty years of experimentation.

Beckett started moving towards theatre at the same time as he was writing the largest part of his prose in French - the short stories and the *Thrilogy* – during a period packed with creativity and fertile imagination that ran from 1946 to 1950. At that time Beckett was overcome with a frenetic impulse to write. He completed *Mercier et Camier* and composed "L'expulsé", "Premier amour" and "Le calmant". His very first attempt at drama dates from January 1947 – *Eleutheria*, a play that remained unpublished until 1995 and was never staged at the author's wish until 2005, when it was performed by Naqshineh Theatre at the City Theatre of Tehran. It was a pleasant distraction before plunging into the long and difficult writing of the *Thrilogy*, from May 1947 to January 1950. His second foray into drama was *En attendant Godot*, written right in the middle of the *Thrilogy*, from October 1948 to January 1949.

When *Godot* was put on for the first time it was 1953 and Beckett was 47 years old. After a while, he was acclaimed by critics as one of the most brilliant examples of contemporary theatre, then they discovered that *Godot* was the one and only play he had written (*Eleutheria* continued to remain unknown to the public, as Beckett already saw it as a failure and had begun to "remove" it). As his fame grew, Beckett increasingly attracted the attention of journalists, critics and young academics who became ever more intrusive. They were particularly curious about his tardy, sudden conversion from prose to drama and they began to question him directly about the reason. For his part, Beckett, always torn between attraction and repulsion towards critics, always teetering between shyness and generosity, put them all off the scent by repeating that he had chosen the dramatic genre as a chance *divertissement*, to serve as mental repose from the more serious, more difficult writing of prose in French.[2]

According to this explanation, Beckett came to the theatre by chance, without specific instruments and with a deep-seated prejudice against the genre - writing prose was difficult work while writing for the theatre was a pleasant relaxation. The success he later earned as a dramatist and director could be explained by his tardy (self) education in the genre.

In reality the biographical data[3] show that Beckett had been going to the theatre since a child and that, during his university career as student and lecturer he had studied the classics of dramatic literature and moved in Irish theatrical circles both as a keen spectator and as an occasional amateur actor. We can discern a technical knowledge of the stage and of dramatic writing, as well as a precocious awareness of the problems of staging a play, that go far beyond a supposedly casual encounter with the dramatic genre. Or more correctly, beyond the performing arts and broadcasting, for his dramatic experiments would pave the way for another suppressed youthful passion, cinema, and thence to new means of mass communication, television and radio. This is in no way to maintain that Beckett was already thinking as a dramatist – simply that, despite the common view, he had a cultural background sufficient to explain his astounding skill in writing *Godot* and subsequent plays. It should, however, be noted that in the failed, then abandoned dramatic attempt

Human Wishes in 1936, "Beckett had not obviously been thinking hard about dramaturgy, or indeed thinking like a dramatist at all" and that in his notebooks dedicated to the project we can find no "evidence of an embryonic dramatist".[4]

His awareness of the theatrical medium does not necessarily indicate an early consciousness of being a dramatist, but is a certain sign of his personal, undetected consideration of problems of the stage and of drama and his long-standing encounters with a variety of performing genres.

Though born into a family with very strict Protestant principles, from a child Beckett was encouraged towards the arts, thanks to some of his lively and rebellious relations. Music, in particular, enlivened his days as a child, when his aunt Cissie (his father's sister) played the piano and sang and when he himself tinkled away on the same instrument, with, it seems, some success.

As a boy his first encounter with the theatre was the Christmas pantomime to which his mother May regularly took her two sons, Sam and his elder brother Frank.[5] Every year the Gaiety Theatre in Dublin put on pantomimes, which had become part of the Irish Christmas tradition, as they already were for the English. The English pantomime was an entertainment derived from the mime tradition of the Commedia dell'Arte. It became established in England in the 18th century, with its varied contents of stock characters, music, dance, acrobatics and elaborate scenic effects. The Pantomime, whose name recalled its origins as a mime show, elaborated the techniques of classic pantomime and included short scenes of "fairy tales and nursery stories".[6]

In these years of 1913-15 Beckett enjoyed another type of theatre – the Gilbert and Sullivan productions put on by the English touring company, the "D'Oyly Carte Opera Company".[7] The company was named after its manager, Rupert D'Oyly Carte (born in Hampstead on 3rd November 1876), son of theatrical impresario Richard D'Oyly Carte. Born into the profession, Rupert studied at Winchester College and began his career as assistant to his father at the Savoy Theatre in London until 1913, when he became chairman of the Savoy Theatre Ltd and sole proprietor and manager of the "Opera Company". The company performed at the Savoy and in the larger British towns and became famous for its performances of Gilbert and Sullivan musicals.[8]

Sir William Schwenk Gilbert (London, 1836-1911), like many respectable middle class Europeans in the 19th century with artistic leanings, was educated as a lawyer and called to the bar, but in his leisure hours enjoyed writing farces and burlesques. He dedicated himself to the law, while cultivating his writing as a socially acceptable hobby until its extraordinary success enabled him to choose the theatre as a full-time profession. His close association with the composer Sir Arthur Sullivan began in 1871, but only in 1875 was success assured, with a production by Richard D'Oyly Carte. No less than 14 productions by the trio were to follow. The Savoy operas[9] were essentially based on the musical brilliance of the composer and of the author: catchy tunes and rhyming text came to the rescue of a somewhat unoriginal and obvious story based on surprise encounters, babies exchanged at birth, confusion with twins and convoluted switches.[10] All this was presented in charming good taste and with the satire, irony and taste for the fantastic of "fairy comedies", where the comic mingled with the pathetic-sentimental, all homogenised in an atmosphere of sparkles and sequins. Gilbert's sharp wit permeated the topsy-turvy mechanisms of an overturned, upside-down world, but his paradoxical spirit was never lacking in verbal elegance. The "Gilbert and Sullivan" brand long outlived the authors themselves and the D'Oyly Carte Company continued to produce their musical comedies until 1941, going on tour as far afield as Canada and New York.

The case of this English company taking its productions to Ireland was no exception for Irish theatrical production at the turn of the century. Rather, it was a key example of the authentic colonisation that had marked Irish theatrical life since the end of the 19th century. And it was common for English touring companies, part of the central London touring system, to call in at the larger Irish towns without a resident company of their own, although the theatre managers were still Irish. The repertories of these companies were the Gilbert and Sullivan musicals, the "*pieces bien faites*" from light French dramas and Sardou, sometimes staged as an Irish version. The cultural colonisation included, therefore, both the production system and the dramatic content.

A real uprising against this cultural oppression took place in the shape of the foundation of the Irish Literary Theatre in Dublin in 1899, with a manifesto signed by W.B. Yeats, Lady Gregory and Edward Martyn. This operation, conceived by a small group of intellectuals, sometimes provoked violent criticism and dissent, but it did bring to the Irish theatrical panorama renewed focus on national (occasionally nationalist) questions and provided an always-open space for young Irish writers and actors. This space was metaphorical, but physical too - the Abbey Theatre and its experimental spin-off, the Peacock. These two adjoining theatres attracted the new, enlightened intelligentsia both onstage and off. Their public consisted of young university students or ordinary people who were starting to become aware of the problem of Irish independence. The Abbey Theatre's productions were not always acclaimed. Though their programmes were presented as typically Irish, they were often criticised by the most radical among the nationalists themselves, who saw in the strong colours of the Abbey's often cruel naturalism an unacceptable insult towards Irish culture. It was the paradox of a theatre conceived and run by intellectuals, who wanted to describe the most cruel and aberrant aspects of daily life, often full of degradation and conflicts.

The Twenties of the new century were, for the Abbey, its most active and fertile period. At this very sensitive time in Irish history,[11] the Abbey acted as a sounding board for the social and political tensions of the entire nation. And it was during this period that Beckett was going to the theatre in Dublin. At that time he was a university student, studying languages at Trinity College, Dublin. From 1923 to 1927 he frequently went to the Abbey with his friend Geoffrey Thompson and they always tried to occupy the same seats.[12] The repertory of those years mainly favoured the realism and pathos of Irish nationalistic theatre, though without disdaining occasional sorties into the comic genre, or the grotesque and tragicomic. When asked by John McCormick about his memories of Abbey productions he had seen at that time, Beckett replied by underlining productions from a list sent him by McCormick. This list, offered by McCormick to James Knowlson in the Seventies,[13] is a mine of information for those investigating Beckett's relations with the theatre and stage tradition of his youth. The plays Beckett remembered were: *Never the Time and the Place* ("comedy") and *The White Blackbird* ("play") by Lennox Robinson; *Look at the Heffernans!* ("comedy") by Brinsley Mac-Namara; *Oedipus the King*; *Oedipus at Colonus* (by Sophocles, "prose version" by Yeats) by W. B. Yeats; *Fanny's First Play* ("play") by G. B. Shaw; *Professor Tim* ("comedy") by George Shiels; *The Emperor Jones* ("play") by Eugene O'Neill; *Autumn Fire* ("play") by Thomas Cornelius Murray.[14] Apart from O'Neill, these are all Irish authors, mostly interested in describing Irish country life, apparently having started a specific genre of "peasant plays".[15] Clear examples of this were Murray, Lennox Robinson and Brinsley MacNamara who told of "new aspects of life in provincial towns".[16] The first of these wrote *Autumn Fire*, a small, personal tragedy in a setting that was provincial both geographically and culturally speaking. In the same genre, but with decidedly comic overtones, was *Professor Tim*, by the only playwright from Ulster on the list, a work that has been defined a "well-wrought kitchen-comedy".[17] Very different, by contrast, were the plays of Yeats and O'Neill, inspired by theatrical and dramatic symbolism, very far from the others' realist pathos.

Beckett's favourite authors who influenced and enthused him most were Sean O'Casey and John Millington Synge, as well as some works by Yeats. The latter occupied an entire shelf of his private library (a sizeable presence, next to Joyce's two shelves),[18] having been the subject of study as well as of enjoyment. Some went so far as to say that Yeats was responsible for introducing Beckett to the influence of Nô[19] theatre, however Beckett denied this, saying that he had never been acquainted with the forms of that Japanese theatre, having never seen a performance.[20]

In 1956, for the centenary of the birth of G.B. Shaw, the Gaiety Theatre in Dublin invited Beckett to compose a tribute to the author. Beckett's answer was an unequivocal refusal:

> you ask me for a tribute to G. B. S., in French, for your souvenir programme. This is too tall an order for me. I wouldn't write in French for King Street. I wouldn't suggest that G. B. S. is not a great play-wright, whatever that is when it's at home. What I would do is give the whole unupsettable apple-cart for a sup of the Hawk's Well [*At the Hawk's Well* by W. B. Yeats], or The

Saints [*The Well of the Saints* by Synge], or a whiff of Juno [*Juno and the Paycock* by O'Casey], to go no further. Sorry.[21]

In the Twenties, by O'Casey, Beckett saw *The Shadow of a Gunman* (12th April 1923), *Juno and the Paycock* (3rd March 1924) and *The Plough and the Stars* (8th and 11th February 1926).[22] He also seems to have seen lighter works by the author, which the Abbey called "curtain raisers", short one-act plays like *Nannie's Night Out* and *Cathleen Listen In*, much closer to music-hall tradition and than to the "serious" theatre of the Abbey.[23] The version of *The Plough and the Stars* seen by Beckett and Thompson was the one that would become famous, giving rise to fierce debate. According to Cronin, the two friends, having seen the opening night of the play on Monday 8th February in front of a very agitated audience, returned to see it a few days later. The performances had seen a crescendo of discontent until hostilities broke out on Thursday 11th when the audience (including Beckett and his friend) physically attacked the actors, who gave as good as they got, in the face of insults and an attempt by protesters to invade the stage.[24] *The Plough and the Stars* was inspired by an explicit, fervent socialism, albeit perfectly humanitarian and nationalist. The story was set during the "Easter Week Insurrection" that had caused so many deaths and growing resentment towards British troops. The characters, all from the Dublin working class, thronged the debris of the slums, in the city's poorest area. These characters were poor, but generous and good to each other, ignorant but with high ideals, indolent but ready to fight for their homeland. O'Casey fully supported the Irish Labour Party's ideals of independence and nation, but his good intentions were misunderstood and extremists in the fight for independence rose up against what they considered an unacceptable insult. They were particularly scandalised by the presence on stage of the glorious banner of the Irish Republican Labour Party (The Plough and the Stars being the name of this flag) and by the irreverence shown in presenting the 1916 martyrs -the Easter Rising was still an open wound. The characters spoke the local "brogue", often swearing, and there was even a prostitute among them. This representation of the martyrs of the revolution as such wretched folk led the "angry" factions to rise up. O'Casey was accused of anti-Catholic sentiments (an easy charge against an Irish Protestant) and foul language and the actors were criticised for having taken part in such impudence. The clashes that followed were the result of a huge misunderstanding caused by the electric state of social life in Dublin during those years.

Beckett does not appear to have any memories of the clashes, nor do they seem to have particularly affected his career as a young student. But O'Casey's production left a distinct mark on him, though it was sometimes recalled in an obscure or simply allusive manner.

Beckett's interest in this author was not limited to theatregoing – it also extended to reading and it would have involved him personally if Jack MacGowran's project to present both authors – something Beckett would have enjoyed - had been successful.[25] He certainly read *Windfalls*, a collection of poetry, prose and plays by O'Casey, which he reviewed for *The Bookman* in '34 (now part of *Disjecta*).[26] Although brief, the piece is full of interest for the comprehension of both Irish authors. Through his examination of what is "essential" and what is "incidental" in O'Casey (the title of the article being "The Essential and the Incidental"), Beckett throws great light on his own aesthetic. In order to define the compresence of what is good and what is secondary in all authors, he takes as example an author, an actor and director: Molière, Chaplin and Ejzenštejn.[27] In the first, he approves his dialogic prose writing, but much less his trite Alexandrine verse. In the second, he praises the comic strength that balances out unnecessary sentimentality and in the third, the screenwriting "*via* his Moscow copybook" (p. 82). The best part of O'Casey, for Beckett, is the knockabout. O'Casey is a master of knockabout in the highest possible sense of the term. His works are founded on the explosion of sense and its vehicles, "the principle of disintegration in even the most complacent solidities" (p. 82). His theatre is an expression of chaos, or rather of "chassis", as Beckett defines it, quoting from Juno and the Paycock, which he considers to be O'Casey's best work.[28] Knockabout is its vehicle: "this is the energy of his theatre, the triumph of the principle of knockabout in situation, in all its elements and on all its planes" (ibid.). An explosive energy which also pervades the poetry, despite poems being the "*ne plus ultra* of inertia" (p. 83), an inertia that fixes in frozen moments attitudes that continue to be comical, producing the paradoxical effect of looking at Walt Disney frames one by one.[29]

O'Casey influenced Beckett through his dramatic writing, since the stage presence was obviously expressed through the Abbey's actors and their "school" of interpretation. O'Casey's texts are full of notes that were taken up by Beckett, after he had purged them of all the pathos and sentimentality with which they were imbued - the macabre from the crime news that finds its way into everyday conversation, until it becomes commonplace; the proverbs and popular saws that become senseless repetitions; the almost blasphemous irony; the mixture of tragedy and comedy; the characters' backchat and their quaint way of talking, getting "difficult" words wrong. All these elements can be recognised in Beckett. Some of his characters recall those of O'Casey: Mr and Mrs Rooney are the mirror image of Mr and Mrs Grigson in *The Shadow of a Gunman*. In the same work, the stereotype figure of the landlord demanding his rent recalls the landlady in *Eleutheria*. Joxer and Mr Boyle in *Juno and the Paycock* converse comically by quoting proverbs.

Synge, even more than O'Casey, has left a clear mark on Beckett's dramatic work, with his tramp characters, his cross-talk and his macabre, unreal atmosphere. Apart from the strongly dialectal and typical choral elements of Synge's theatre, it contains numerous images that must have made an indelible mark on the young Beckett's imagination. In an interview in 1972 James Knowlson asked Beckett who he thought had been the greatest influence on his theatre and the only name mentioned was that of Synge.[30] He himself has said that he saw *The Playboy of the Western World*, *The Well of the Saints* and *The Tinker's Wedding*, at a time when Synge was already considered an Irish classic. About ten years older than O'Casey,[31] Synge's artistic career led him to have a more profound influence on Irish theatre. After studying at Trinity College, Dublin, he moved for a while to Paris, where he freed himself of the dour Irish provincialism of the time, but where he was inspired to return to Ireland and to observe it with fresh eyes. The meeting between Synge and Yeats in Paris has become one of the myths of modern Irish culture. The older man advised the younger, trying to free himself from the influence of

Irish cultural limitations, to direct his restlessness precisely towards his native land. There was a place, in Ireland, where one could be a native and a foreigner at the same time, where the physical nature of the place and the psychological nature of the people were a model of harmony and simplicity - the Aran Islands. Fascinated by the description, but somewhat sceptical, Synge went there in 1898 and had an authentic illumination - from then on, he would write stories of ordinary people, without shame for what Ireland might be - a naïve country, but astute and lively. The tragicomic atmosphere held stories that were often macabre, where the characters delivered their frequently blasphemous obscenities in a poetic, rhythmical rural idiom with strong Gaelic overtones. The humour that pervades even the most – apparently – anguished tales makes it difficult to classify these works. Is *The Playboy of the Western World* a tragedy or a comedy? It is the story of a boy who kills his father, but told in a light tone and with a macabre irony that caused right-thinking people to rise up and cry scandal. Synge and O'Casey were both accused of amorality, blasphemy and anti-clericalism and are both impossible to categorise. Though Synge's works are defined as tragedies, they contain "some of the most boisterous comedy in the modern theatre".[32]

Synge's influence on Beckett's imaginary can be clearly deciphered in the mix of tragic and comic, making it possible to laugh about something sad[33] - about a man who feigns death to discover his wife's unfaithfulness (*The Shadow of the Glen*), about the search for the identity of a drowned body washed up by the sea (*Riders to the Sea*), about the wedding of two penniless tinkers (*The Tinker's Wedding*) or about two blind beggars cheated by destiny (*The Well of the Saints*). The story of this latter play is the one with the strongest connections to Beckett. Two beggars, husband and wife, hear of a miraculous well with power to restore their sight. Drawn by this promise, they undergo the test and the experiment is successful but tricked by fate, they discover that the delightful spouse they thought to have at their side is nothing less than an old cripple. Their happiness for their recovered sight, so often longed for, turns out to be a demon of disappointment. This hope for a better future only in dreams and this love-hate relationship foreshadow the interaction of Beckett's couples.[34]

Beckett's passion for Synge lasted throughout his life and was accompanied by a passion for James Joyce.[35] He studied Synge, for his private library contained the work by David and Stephens Greene, with M. Edward, *J. M. Synge, 1871-1909*, New York, Macmillan, 1959.[36] He continued to attend Synge's performances even in the Fifties. From a letter to Pamela Mitchell in '54 we know that, on one of his occasional trips back to Ireland from his permanent home in Paris, he saw *The Playboy of the Western World* at the Gaiety in Dublin, directed by Cyril Cusack,[37] an artist specialised in productions of O'Casey and who was to become a memorable Krapp.[38]

As far as the actors interpreting his favourite authors in the Thirties were concerned, we know that Beckett had the chance to see, among others, F. J. MacCormick, W. O'Gorman and M. J. Dolan. Of the latter he was struck by his powerful gestures, especially playing Job in *Autumn Fire*, where the mere posture of his hands was enough to express all the tragic tiredness of the character.[39] At the time Beckett was very young, but was already fascinated by the expressive power of gesture, so much so that he developed the subject in his lessons on Molière, while lecturing at Trinity College. Notes of these lessons taken by some of his students are kept in Trinity College. These are reasonably reliable records of Beckett's unrehearsed speech, his slow delivery interspersed with frequent, very long silences. The subjects of the lessons are Racine, Balzac, Celine and Molière and they show a surprising technical awareness of the stage. For example, Beckett gives a visual description of the stage in Phèdre (Beckett had given a monographic course dedicated to Racine in 1931, entitled "Racine and the Modern Novel").[40] He describes the centre with a light from above splitting the darkened stage and shows that he had, long before becoming a playwright, precise pictorial and sculptural canons for the stage. He remarks on the gestural quality that pervades the writings of Racine and Molière and appreciates Shakespeare's theatrical skill, even more than his literary ability. These lecture notes have been hitherto little used as material, apart from by W.H. Lyons, then one of Beckett's students, who in a short article entitled "Backtracking Beckett" made some passing, though significant comments: "those who heard Mr Beckett lecture on Molière in the early Thirties will recall his insistence on this element [movement and gesture] in the comic theatre, his reference to 'muscular dialogue generated by gesture'[...]."[41]

Of the actors Beckett knew, McCormick[42] was the one who became most famous and liked by critics. This most versatile of Irish actors was able to go from tragedy to kitchen comedy, showing that he was "the most gifted of the lot".[43] He acted for most of his life at the Abbey, where he always took on very varied parts. He was Oedipus in *Oedipus Rex*, based by Yeats on Sophocles, and adapted to the symbolist text, which required a "singsong" delivery. He was long remembered as Joxer in *Juno and the Paycock*. The part of Seamus Shields (*The Shadow of a Gunman*) was practically created by him, as "the lazy, unwashed, self-respecting coward of a war-torn Dublin".[44] His preference was for character parts, where he used the acting techniques of the early Abbey Theatre, noted for "simplicity of movement and clarity of diction".[45] Not by chance, out of this same school came a young Irish actor destined to become one of Beckett's favourites - Jack McGowran, who debuted at the Abbey on 12th March 1947. MacGowran's acting career was influenced by the myth of McCormick and he had to measure himself against his idol when he was offered the older actor's past roles. This emulation was often noted by Kenneth Tynan, a critic who linked the two actors and thought that the latter had overtaken his master in the part of Joxer.[46] Beckett often made use of this fantastic, genial actor in his productions. For him he wrote *J. M. Mime* and he would have liked him for *Film*. He allowed him – exceptionally – to adapt parts of his novels for the stage. Their friendship was not sufficient to explain the extremely close bond felt by Beckett, a feeling strengthened even more by mutual esteem and by the special consonance between MacGowran's acting and the universe of Beckett. And this consonance had its roots in a tradition absorbed, in different ways and forms, by both men - that of the Abbey Theatre, Dublin.

The Abbey continued to be part of Beckett's life even after his time at university. In August 1934 he saw Yeats last works, *Resurrection* and *The King of the Great Clock Tower*, which did not impress him particularly.[47] In August 1938 he went with his mother to the Abbey.[48] In 1954 he was still in touch with the Abbey authors when he went to the Gaiety for

Cusack's⁴⁹ *The Playboy of the Western World*. Again in 1961 he followed the Abbey productions on tour in Paris.⁵⁰

Theatre became a constant interest of Beckett's in the Thirties - there was no genre that did not whet his curiosity and his horizons grew to include European writers, musical theatre and amateur productions. In Paris, between 1928 and 1930, he came into contact with productions by Baty, Dullin, Jouvet, Pitoeff and the surrealists, although his preference was towards productions of the classics. He certainly saw performances of works by Racine (perhaps *Bérénice* at the Odéon)⁵¹ and *La Mandragola* by Machiavelli produced by Madame Valsamaki, which he enjoyed very much and still spoke of excitedly in '37.⁵² The Parisian programme could boast great variety, ranging from the classics of European literature to new foreign writers. But even Dublin under the enlightened aegis of the Abbey and Gate theatres began to put on Ibsen together with other European classics and there Beckett, in about 1932, saw at the Abbey Ibsen's *Et Dukkehjem* (*A Doll's House*), *En Folkefiende* (*An Enemy of the People*), *Peer Gynt*⁵³ and *Vildanden* (*The Wild Duck*), as well as *Romeo and Juliet* by Shakespeare produced by MacLiammóir-Edwards at the Gate.⁵⁴ In Dresden, in 1937, he had his first encounter with opera. Mozart's *The Marriage of Figaro* made such an impression on him that he wrote out in his notebook entire passages of text.⁵⁵ Strangely, Beckett began to desert the theatre when his fame had made him sought after and recognised as a playwright. He began to find the stalls cramped and suffered unbearable feelings of frustration (he could not bear to see his own mistakes) and anguish (he felt trapped by the public).⁵⁶ Apart from the understandable dislike of a shy man for crowds and the clamour of unwelcome publicity, the reason for his desertion probably lies elsewhere. He confessed to Mel Gussow in '78 that he lost his appetite after having gulped down all sorts of theatre productions at the Abbey. Despite this, sometimes Beckett did go to other people's productions, mostly those of playwright friends, perhaps driven more by sense of friendly duty than by real desire. Whatever the truth may be, we know that he saw Alan Schneider's *Who's Afraid of Virginia Woolf?* written by Edward Albee at the Piccadilly Theatre, London, in 1964, that he followed the plays of Pinget and of "some other writers",⁵⁷ and that he went with Jack MacGowran to a performance of

Chekhov's *Djadja Vanja* (*Uncle Vanja*), interpreted by Laurence Olivier.[58] For Beckett, the Abbey and the Gate became mythical, poetical places in his imaginary and their seriousness was ridiculed in *Murphy*. The Gate Theatre is mentioned when Murphy meets Ticklepenny and asks him if he hadn't had the "misfortune" of meeting him in Dublin – "can it have been at the Gate?" (p. 61). The Abbey becomes the actual setting for Murphy's grotesque funeral, when he expressly asks to be "buried" in its toilet. His last wishes were:

> with regard to the disposal of these my body, mind and soul, I desire that they be burnt and placed in a paper bag and brought to the Abbey Theatre, Lr. Abbey Street, Dublin, and without pause into what the great and good Lord Chesterfield calls the necessary house, where their happiest hours have been spent, on the right as one goes down into the pit, and I desire that the chain be there pulled upon them, if possible during the performance of a piece, the whole to be executed without ceremony or show of grief. (p. 183)

Murphy spends his happiest moments in that necessary place, unmentionable in polite society, which is the toilet. The young Beckett, presumably, spent them in the audience, where his interest soon moved from simply being a spectator to being a "doer". In the Thirties, in fact, he actually began playing an active part in the amateur or semi-professional circuit that gravitated around intellectuals looking beyond the city's provincialism and linked in different ways to Trinity College.

In February 1931 he was involved in the performance of *Le Kid* as actor and writer's assistant. The production, intended as an academic *divertissement*, was based on a text by Perolson to which Beckett had made a very small contribution. The assembled public must have thought that the pair had collaborated much more closely than was in fact the truth, because criticisms of the show's superficiality were directed to both young writers in equal measure.[59] Yet Beckett had taken a very limited part in it - He certainly came up with the title, explicitly parodying *Le Cid* and linking to Chaplin's film, *The Kid*. His, too, was the suggestion of interpreting Don

Diègue with an alarm clock. As far as we know this was Beckett's only appearance as an actor. He also made a scarce contribution to preparations for the performance. He hardly ever took part in rehearsals, preferring to practice on his own. During the three nights of performance (19th-21st February 1931 at the Peacock Theatre) he grew increasingly embarrassed and Professor Rudmose-Brown's outburst did not help. "Beckett found the first night acutely embarrassing" and "dreaded having to face an audience again".[60] Despite this, the play seems to have contained some true comic elements that, perhaps due to the players' immaturity, did not come sufficiently to the fore. To the textual parody were added numerous visual comic effects, acting as parodic counterpoint to entire parts taken from *Le Cid*. One of the more comic figures was the character of Don Diègue, interpreted by Beckett wearing a long white beard, an umbrella instead of a sword and an alarm clock. When this rang, it awoke a silent character who sat on a ladder, smoked a pipe and amused himself by turning anti-clockwise the hands of a large clock hanging on the wall. The ringing of the alarm clock had been suggested by Beckett for his monologue in the first act and it was to go off right in the middle of a lyrical moment, interrupting the tragic atmosphere and speeding up the rhythm of gestures and words in a crescendo that recalls Lucky's monologue in *En attendant Godot*. The occasion and scenic effects of this university skit recall very strongly *Ubu Roi* by Jarry, in the same period echoed by the "merde and remerde" (similar to the "merdre" in *Ubu*) of the *Dream of Fair to Middling Women* (p. 146). Beckett was not insensible to student pranks. After the manner of Borges, he wrote a brief profanation (now collected in *Disjecta*) on Concentrism, an imaginary literary movement founded by an imaginary author, Jean du Chas. In analysing the work of du Chas and the movement invented by him, Beckett used all the academic instruments he had acquired. The same student travesties are found in the parody on contraception bans in Ireland, "*Che Sciagura*" (signed D.E.S.C. – which stands for "*d'esser senza coglioni*" – the continuation of the sentence in Italian taken from *Candide* by Voltaire),[61] and in "*The Possessed*", a reply to the negative criticism of *Le Kid*.

Le Kid was Beckett's first and last experience of amateur dramatics at university, but not his only active involvement in amateur productions.

It seems that in 1936 he helped his cousin Mary Manning Howe revise her play *Youth's the Season* for its performance in Dublin at the Gate Theatre, directed by Hilton Edwards and Micheál MacLiammóir,[62] with a repeat performance in London. It appears that Beckett advised his cousin to insert a totally dumb character into the action and that she accepted the idea with pleasure.[63] During this period Beckett went to the rehearsals of the Dun Laoghaire Theatre Group and the productions of the Drama League of Mrs W. B. Yeats and Lennox Robinson. He discussed his ideas on theatre with playwright Denis Johnston.[64]

Far from being an occasional spectator, Beckett followed the theatre in several directions and acquired knowledge of it in a systematic manner by reading scripts, seeing performances and through personal experience in fleeting, brief – but significant – occasions.

2.2. Music-hall

In Dublin in the Twenties and Thirties, the theatrical circuit offered numerous and varied productions. Each theatre had its "speciality" and the public could choose their genre by going to a particular theatrical address. The Abbey put on Irish realist authors with occasional sallies into European classics (old and new). The Peacock, the small stage of the Abbey, preferred highly experimental theatre.[65] The Queen's put on melodrama, while the Theatre Royal, Gaiety and Olympia showed vaudeville. The Gate chose modern European authors or much-loved classics (Aeschylus, Shakespeare, Chekhov, Shaw, O'Neill, Goethe, Ibsen, Strindberg etc.), as well as a small number of Irish realists. The type of production changed over time from a predominance of "visiting dramatic and operatic companies from London" who fixed "long-term commitments",[66] particularly in the "light" theatres (Gaiety, Royal), to a slow autonomy not only regarding the text, but also the staging. Each theatre had its own history, interwoven with the story of the company or of artists in search of their cultural, professional identity.

Irish variety, sprung from the English tradition, was very similar to American vaudeville and may have been taken across to the United

States by migrant Irish or English actors, where it then developed independently. In Ireland there were fewer scantily clad girls, probably due to Catholic censorship and Protestant respectability, but the numbers were similar to all the European variety programmes: singers, comics, acrobats, various wonders, such as trained dogs or seals. The comic numbers were the main attraction. There were usually two comics - a straight man, who was the "puzzled and uncomprehending one",[67] accompanied by a funny man who had the comic lines. Their dialogue was made up of cross-talk and their actions were gags where they exchanged hats, boots and trousers, or got into a muddle with ladders and chairs, from which they fell. The scenes might turn into longer sketches, involving two or more actors and becoming absurd and chaotic.

Beckett was a frequent spectator of this genre, too, though evidence is lacking, for it was usually a solitary experience. Beckett did not go to the music-hall with the faithful friend who accompanied him to see "serious" theatre, perhaps imagining that he could not propose a similar genre to a cultured intellectual. Music-hall "was also a solitary matter, such shows being probably beneath the intellectual level of Geoffrey Thompson and his few other friends".[68] These were solitary and perhaps unplanned visits - Cronin, when tracing a map of Dublin vaudeville theatres, realised that they were all within a short distance of each other and on the route that Beckett would have taken daily, while studying or lecturing at university.[69] He suggests the performances might have been chosen by chance, aided by the fact that theatres offered morning and afternoon shows and that there was no need to book in advance.

Even if this were so, it would not seem to us to diminish Beckett's interest in the genre. His passion for music-hall also took other directions, following the texts – surely most significant.

Music-hall comedy, mainly based on stereotype elements from the comic genre, easily understood and enjoyed, found its space even in the "serious" Abbey theatre. The authors alternated writing tragedies with writing plays that could be best defined as comedies (Robinson, Murray, MacNamara) or mixed both dimensions for a tragic-comic effect. Beckett's favourite authors followed the latter route. O'Casey and Synge, though writing for an educated public and telling tragic stories, alongside the pathos also inserted humorous elements, often farcical. Beckett had a clear idea of this combination, in fact in the review of O'Casey's *Windfalls* mentioned earlier he praises the comic quality of his work as the most brilliant moment of his texts: "the music-hall side of O'Casey's work was something Beckett would have clearly recognized because he had also become a regular attender at the places where 'variety', as it was called in Dublin, was on offer; developing a taste for it which never left him".[70]

Beckett's approach to the genre started early, when as a child his Aunt Cissie played on the piano "popular music-hall numbers, songs like 'I feel so funny when the moon comes out'".[71] The short songs performed by the actors in English and Irish variety shows, known as "ditties", had catchy melodies and often humorous, suggestive words, inasmuch as Irish moralism allowed. The young Samuel quickly learned the parodic techniques of the ditties and began to gain first-hand experience of them from Gilbert and Sullivan musicals. On returning home after performances, he repeated the songs, which he knew from records, putting his own irreverent verses to Sullivan's music: "he sang irreverent, ribald Beckett *libretti* in substitution for Gilbert's words".[72]

During his university years, especially in 1925-26, Beckett saw "politically engaged" plays, as well as "light" performances such as reviews, music-hall and circus. The theatres he went to were the Gaiety, the Olympia and the Royal.[73] Again in August 1937, after his brother Frank's wedding on the 24th, he went with his mother and a cousin to the Gaiety to see a variety performance of "the great Dublin comedian Jimmy O'Dea".[74]

In Paris, towards the end of 1952, he took some visitors from Dublin to the Bobino, a variety theatre in the Rue de la Gaîté on the Left Bank. Together with the Olympia on the Right Bank, this was the last remaining music-hall in Paris. Initially a local café-concert, in the Twenties and Thirties the Bobino had become "un véritable music-hall sous la direction de Castille junior".[75] In the Fifties, as well as performances from *chansonniers* like Brassens and Juliette Greco, the Bobino "offered comedians and acrobats who appealed to less rehearsed tastes and were just as much an attraction as far as Beckett was concerned. He went there frequently, even in the afternoons, and nearly always by himself, though sometimes [...] with visitors whom he was showing around Paris".[76] Vaudeville, therefore, continued to fascinate him even in Paris and he thought it one the best forms of entertainment for tourists worth going to in the French capital. He also went there so frequently that he perfectly understood the special "argot" used by the artists. Again in autumn 1959 he was going to the Parisian music-halls and at an unspecified date, probably during the Fifties, he was taken to one of these performances in London by his cousin John Beckett and his friend Aidan Higgins, the Irish novelist: "[Beckett's] fondness for the music-hall was known about, so in the end they decided on the last of the London music-halls - Collins, in Islington. [...] The show they saw included a comedian who delivered a long and hilarious monologue about cod liver oil as a cure for all ills [...], when the comedian came through and the other stopped him to offer congratulations, Beckett, on being introduced, joined in the assent, saying politely, 'I loved your stuff'".[77]

Despite the clear influence on Beckett of the genre, he often minimised its importance in his work. When James Knowlson asked him if he had gone to the London music-hall, Beckett replied laconically "little acquaintance".[78] If Beckett as an author wants us to believe he had little knowledge of the genre, his texts speak very differently. As do his choices as a director. For the first performance of *Godot* in 1953, it was not by chance that Roger Blin got Beckett's approval of Lucien Raimbourg for the part of Vladimir. Raimbourg was a cabaret singer and music-hall actor who played the "Bouffes du Nord" in Paris and cleverly met "the circus and music-hall features of Beckett's play".[79] Beckett liked the choice of Raimbourg, as later he did that of Jack MacGowran, whose artistic career had begun in vaudeville, for Clov (London, 1958). He also approved of Leslie Sarony for the part of Nagg in *Endgame* in 1964 at London's Aldwych Theatre, directed by Donald McWhinnie. "[Beckett] especially liked the way Nagg's voice was done in this production. When he heard Leslie Sarony do the part of Nagg, he said, 'Oh, he's an old music hall actor is he? I've never heard the tailor's speech better given'".[80]

It was not for its comic techniques that music-hall first entered Beckett's work, but as a metaphor, an allusion and a distancing effect.

Already in Proust he refers to this genre, opining that opera is "less complete than vaudeville, which at least inaugurates the comedy of an exhaustive enumeration" (p. 92). Beckett uses Labiche's vaudeville as a negative paragon, too, in the pseudo-study "Le Concentrisme", written in about 1930: "[...] vous ne ferez que dégrader en vaudeville de Labiche cet art [...]".[81] With *Proust* and "Le Concentrisme", however, we are in the field of literary criticism and the quotations come from a context not specifically about vaudeville, rather about the musicality of Proust's prose in the first case and the aesthetic of Jean du Chas in the second.

But the allusions in Beckett's novels and drama are much more intriguing.

In *More Pricks Than Kicks* the word vaudeville is used to indicate an unexpected, amusing situation that might take place from one moment to the next. For Belacqua, wandering the streets, a "vaudeville situation" is something that might hit you when least expected: "it had not to shun the unforeseen nor turn aside from the agreeable odds and ends of vaudeville that are liable to crop up" (p. 41.). But then the adventure that happened to him was indeed "unforeseen", but not quite "vaudeville": "this was unforeseen with a vengeance, if not exactly vaudeville" (p. 47).

In *Murphy*, on the other hand, reference to vaudeville is more subtle and personified in the comic figure of Ticklepenny, a qualified "cabaret poet". The expression used by Beckett in the original English version is "Pot Poet" (p. 61), which derives its meaning from a fairly ancient semantic origin, associating "pot" with burlesque.[82] Just as his characteristics are typically those of the "pot poet's bulk and induration to abuse" (p. 65). Beckett here is clearly alluding to the lively atmosphere of the music-hall audience, habitually "brightened up" by taunting insults to the actors, especially to the comedians. Picking up on the public's provocation and improvising on these was one of the qualities of a good cabaret artist, directly inherited from his predecessors in vaudeville. In Beckett's satirical description, the technique of composition of these artists resembled the art of connecting up cables. This is why Ticklepenny was so strongly drawn towards the difficult task of joining two pipes: "this was a difficulty whose fascinations were familiar to him from the days when as a pot poet he had laboured so long and so lovingly to join the ends of his pentameters" (p. 119).

Beckett was clearly well acquainted with the techniques and the repertory of Anglo-Irish music-hall, since he mentioned some classic elements from it in his writing and in his private life.

In one of countless letters to MacGreevy, Beckett tells him the joke about the centipede: "do you know the story of the chaste centipede, who said to her suitor, crossing her thousand legs: 'no, a thousand times no'".[83] The joke, in itself a typical example of music-hall humour, refers to an old music-hall song, a ditty entitled "No, no, a thousand times no" that, as might be easily imagined, "is about a woman refusing a man's advances".[84] Beckett had grown up with these songs from an early age and there is no need to prove that he knew this particular ditty to assume that these stereotypes were familiar to him, turning up also in his prose (in *More Pricks Than Kicks* Chas quotes the first verse of the popular ditty "Love's Old Sweet Song",[85] p. 55).

He uses ditties again in *Godot*, in the English version, with a phrase that had been the title of a famous one. In the first act Pozzo has just finished his speech and asks his audience, Didi and Gogo, how they liked it:

VLADIMIR: [*First to understand.*] Oh very good, very very good.
POZZO: [*To ESTRAGON.*] And you, sir?
ESTRAGON: Oh tray bong, tray tray tray bong. (p. 38)

Quite unnoticed until now,[86] Estragon's reply uses the title of a song made popular by Charles Chaplin sr., father of the more famous Charlie Chaplin jr. between 1890 and 1896 on the stage of London music-halls. The song was entitled "Oui! Tray Bong!" and was subtitled "My Pal Jones". Lyrics and music were by Norton Atkins and the sheet music was published in 1893 by musical publishers Francis, Day & Hunter, one of the most prestigious in London. Like other successes by Chaplin sr. by the same publishers, the cover showed "his portrait prominent on the cover. This honour was accorded only to artists whose reputation the publishers were certain would sell copies".[87] The song's lyrics are unknown, but the title clearly makes fun of an Englishman trying to speak French - "tray bong" being an anglicised attempt at the French "très bon" – and it is in this sense that Estragon repeats it several times. The French version underlines the fact that this is not merely a remark to Pozzo, but also a comic turn by Estragon, since it is marked "accent anglais" (p. 53). Estragon is playing around, acting the part of the vain and silly Anglophone dandy, enamoured of French fashions, much employed in European vaudeville parodies and also found in the sister tradition of the circus. In the first half of the nineteenth century the English clown Boswell (James Clement 1826-1859) had found success with parodies of Shakespearian speeches in an Anglo-French accent and these had become fashionable.

Or perhaps Estragon is alluding to the habit of nomadic circuses, of gathering artists who had to have a smattering of all languages, speaking that particular circus "argot" that mispronounces words and is still today a characteristic.

And he insists on mentioning the circus as an alternative to Vladimir's vaudeville. The two players, Didi and Gogo, are greatly enjoying Pozzo's performances and, to show their pleasure, declare that the scene is like a show:

> VLADIMIR: - Charmante soirée.
> ESTRAGON: - Inoubliable.
> VLADIMIR. - Et ce n'est pas fini.
> ESTRAGON. - On dirait que non.
> VLADIMIR. - Ça ne fait que commencer.
> ESTRAGON. - C'est terrible.
> VLADIMIR. - On se croirait au spectacle.
>   [English: "Worse than pantomime", p. 34]
> ESTRAGON. - Au cirque.
> VLADIMIR. - Au music-hall.
> ESTRAGON. - Au cirque. (pp. 47-48)

2.3. Le Cirque Beckett

Circus performances are of very ancient origin and can be dated from the classical period, from the Greek hippodromes and the Latin circuses. This tradition that lasted through the centuries and is still alive in the form devised by Philip Astley (1742-1814) in Europe in the 18th century. Astley, considered the founder of the modern circus, set up London's first circus ring in his home country and then took the new formula to Paris, thence throughout Europe. The first modern circuses offered mainly equestrian acts, to which other acts were added gradually with acrobats and clowns on horseback. By the mid-19th century the circus programme had settled into the one which has come down to our present time – equestrian numbers, balancing acts, acrobatics, magic, trained animals and clowns. In the second half of the nineteenth century, the cultural colonisation of North America also included the spread of popular spectacles like the circus and in 1871 the biggest and most memorable circus of the United States was founded - the Barnum Circus.

At the turn of the century, popular entertainment enjoyed one of its liveliest periods with the music-hall. This genre, constructed in a similar way to the circus, appeared in 19th century England as a type of light, carefree entertainment offered to clients by the owners of bathing establishments, in line with the holidaymakers' desire for carefree, light-hearted enjoyment. The programme included songs, pantomime and brief comic interludes. Apparently in error the music-hall was also called "vaudeville", an older genre founded and widespread in France, which took its name from the witty songs that were inserted into theatre performances from the 16th century onwards. The error would appear to lie in the fact that true vaudeville consisted of light comedies with musical interludes of popular airs of the kind composed by Scribe and Labiche and evolved into actual comedies with Meilhac, Hennequin and Feydeau. This impression of error, however, becomes less grave if we consider French vaudeville as a mixed genre of different specialities – singing and plays – similar to that of music-hall and especially if we take into account its development in America. "American vaudeville" describes the type of music-hall that travelled from Europe to North America and adapted there to local tastes.

The new genres were not so much total novelties on the European entertainment scene as stereotypes, technical instruments and rhetoric mechanisms from popular tradition "recycled" into new production processes and new aesthetic forms. The result was that a single type changed its form in various ways, so that the common origin of the end products is often lost. Through the history of popular entertainment runs a common thread of logical and chronological development that links the Commedia dell'Arte and burlesque to the circus, the circus to music-hall, the music-hall to vaudeville and vaudeville to early comic cinema. Rooted in what Celati calls "nomadic theatre",[88] which maintains its "inner" nomadism even when permanent, we can trace the mutual influence and borrowing between circus and music-hall, not only aesthetically, but also materially. The programme constructed as a deliberate composition of different numbers and the importance of the visual code and physicality common to both genres exploited the same wealth of human participants and of rhetoric. The structures of the comic sketches obeyed the same clichés so the actors could easily adapt to the more popular show. And the artists are the real promoters of these contacts, because whenever a "new" kind of entertainment appears in theatrical history, the artists must adapt to it, bringing to this task their entire cultural heritage. On several occasions in the material history of entertainment we see artists moving from a traditional genre to a newer, more popular, better paid one. Such was the move from circus to music-hall. Two former British circus owners, Sir Garrard Tyrwhitt-Drake and John Smith Clarke, gave evidence of similar exchanges in their memoirs, recalling their experiences from the late nineteenth-early twentieth centuries. Clarke places the origins of clowning in mediaeval jesters, in pantomime and in the masks of the Commedia dell'Arte, but he also links it to music-hall and Chaplin, noting how in the first half of the 19th century a new character appeared in the circus - the "funny man", also called "music-hall comedian", with grotesque characteristics, performing in the arena and eventually taken up by Chaplin in films.[89] Tyrwhitt-Drake gives even more details of this mutual influence, studying circus owners such as Carmo, originally connected with music-hall[90] and why artists left the circuses for the halls at the end of the Twenties: "so bad was business that many of the old tenting shows packed up their big tops and obtained engagements on the halls at stage circuses".[91] Big circus stars were engaged by music-hall where they had to adapt their traditional knowledge to a different context. The famous clown Grock began his career as a circus artist, but then worked contemporaneously as a circus apprentice and music-hall player for over twenty years.

This common heritage of music-hall and circus would in itself be enough to explain the presence of circus elements in Beckett's writing. However, his biography also reveals a "direct" contact with the genre, not only in its original forms, but also in the more "modern" ones of music-hall and cabaret.

During the Twenties Beckett went to the circus and, less frequently than to other types of performance, he certainly went there in Paris in autumn '59[92] and in Berlin in 1971, when he saw clown Charlie Rivel's farewell tour.[93] He had recurring links with circus imaginary in the Fifties, and in 1956 wrote *Acte sans paroles I* for the mime artist-clown Deryk Mendel of Sadler's Wells, performing at the Parisian cabaret "Fontaine des Quatre Saisons".[94] In that period ('53-'54) in Paris he occasionally met up with Robert Pikelny, painter of "circus themes" and, also in Paris, he often went to the Bobino and the Cirque Medrano with his friends Roger Blin and Jean Martin.[95] In 1962 Beckett showed that he knew of "clown" Marcel Marceau, whose pantomime may be considered as a contemporary interpretation of clown gestuality, when in an interview with Charles Marowitz he spoke of his own "acts without words", citing the French mime-artist and comparing him with his own idea of pantomime.[96]

The most recent clown known to Beckett would appear to be Bill Irwin, introduced to him by American critic Mel Gussow, who was the first to mention him in their conversations and to speak of his ability as clown, actor and mime-artist. Irwin played Lucky in the Eighties in the highly controversial American production of *Godot* with Steve Martin and Robin Williams, but it seems that the "reports" on him pleased Beckett and he reminded him of the assortment of actors and clowns of silent cinema of his youth.[97] With Gussow's words of praise to him, Irwin won the esteem of Beckett and the latter suggested, through Gussow, that he try out his clown skills in *Acte sans paroles I*. Then, when the actor expressed a wish to meet him in person, Beckett consented and took Irwin's emotional reaction in his stride. Born in 1950, Irwin is one of the most famous artists (actor, author, "entertainer") of the so-called "New Vaudeville", a theatre form that mixes the tradition of circus and vaudeville with the techniques of experimental theatre. "Irwin attempts to make innovative use of his clown skills to create exciting visual metaphors for the broader actions and emotions of the play".[98] His style has been defined as "metaphysical slapstick"[99] and owes much to the tragicomic atmosphere of Beckett's theatre. In his case, rather than of Beckett antecedents, it would be more accurate to speak of influence by Beckett on western experimental theatre. We feel, however, that Beckett's wish to make contact with Irwin, his appreciation of the eccentric clown and his suggestion about *Acte sans paroles* are meaningful, the latter showing that Beckett had immediately associated Irwin's art and sweet-sour sensibility with his own idea of the character in *Acte*.

Of circus, Beckett particularly loved the clowns' performances, their gestural and comic qualities. When Beckett scholars consider his humour it is a commonplace to mention the clownery of his characters. Every reference to Vladimir and Estragon defines them as clowns and tramps. But Beckett's allusions to the world of circus go far beyond this limited and generic indication and show a detailed precision that only a connoisseur of circus could possess.

When he visited Berlin in 1971 he did not miss the chance to see the last show by a clown famous for his imitation of Chaplin, Charlie Rivel, stage name of José Andreu (Cubellas 1896-S. Pedro de Ribas 1983). Rivel began his career early with "the Andreu family", where he took the role of the clown Auguste, displaying considerable gifts of mimic and acrobatics. He went down in history, however, with his parody of Charlot, which Chaplin himself – normally very critical of those imitating his character[100] - is supposed to have liked. One of Rivel's most famous numbers was "Charlot on the trapeze", taken up by his son, Juanito Rivel, and used throughout his career. From the exaggerated comedy of Auguste with his square, purplish face, red nose and extravagant poses, Rivel had moved on to greater elegance with his Chaplin imitation, done with "[...] indescriptible ironie, faite de tendresse et de nostalgie".[101] His entrances were made slowly and majestically. He was awarded the "Clown d'or" in Montecarlo in 1975 and a few years later retired at the age of 75. This was when Beckett saw him in Berlin and was entranced, despite his heaviness that hinted at incredible agility as a young man. It was actually because of this strongly melancholy note that Beckett was transported back in time - he saw the artist's weariness and felt he was reliving moments of his own youth, when he went to the circus and music-hall in his home town and when, many years earlier, he had met the cabaret "clown" Karl Valentin.

The comic German actor Karl Valentin, stage name of Valentin Ludwig Fey (Munich 1882-1948), had trained in variety where he had begun his career as a musical clown. He conceived and built the *orchestrion*, a device incorporating the sounds of various musical instruments that together sounded like a small orchestra. His pieces in Bavarian dialect encountered a fair success and in 1908 he took his stage name, which he would maintain until his death. In 1911 he convinced a soubrette of Italian origin, Elisabeth Wellano, to become his stage partner under the stage name of Liesl Karlstadt. They formed a duo performing scripts written by him, inspired by details of everyday life among the poor of Munich. His greatest popularity with the public occurred between the wars, but then dwindled until he was totally forgotten, principally due to Nazi censorship that disapproved of how he showed the poverty of the suburbs, sometimes verging on authentic social and political protest.[102] In 1937, during one of Beckett's frequent visits to Germany, Valentin was playing the Benz Cabaret in Munich. Beckett went on his own to see the comic sketches of this skinny actor with Liesl Karlstadt, a comely brunette who could play all kinds of comic effects, even interpreting male roles. Beckett noted in his diary: "real quality comedian, exuding depression, perhaps past his best [...] Don't follow half of his dialect. Reduced here and there to knockabout".[103] Despite his inability to understand the heavy Bavarian dialect, Beckett appreciated the gestural quality of their comedy and loved it. It is curious that Beckett noted the high artistic quality together with the existential depression, perhaps due to the onset of artistic decline, or more probably to Valentin's actual stage character.

Brecht describes his dry, interior comic quality, revealing the *inadequacy of all things*. Through Brecht we can recognise Beckett's interest in Valentin, for that perfect marriage of tragedy and comedy, of exhilarating and pathetic, for that irresistible dianoetic laugh that miserably reveals the "inadequacy of the human capacity for knowledge".[104] A month after Beckett's visit to the Benz Cabaret, the cinema actor Eicheim, who had become friendly with Beckett, hoping to please his friend organised a meeting with Valentin. But after visiting the star in his home, Beckett confirmed to himself the impression of sadness and melancholy for the good old days that he had got when watching him on stage.[105] All in all, Valentin as a private individual was a simple man with few airs, lazy and sedentary. This perhaps disappointing encounter was to leave, in the years to come, a double trace - the sadness of the private approach and the exhilaration of the stage dimension.[106]

Valentin had the physique of a circus athlete, thin and agile, and his slight build was often emphasised in contrast to his powerful opposite parts. His character, a mixture of timid ingenuity and wily scoundrel, kept getting entangled in absurd situations without losing its impassive element of the eternal loser. His worn, unsuitable clothing, along with his unusual use of everyday objects, were a direct link with circus tradition, but his particularly alienated relationship with the world associated him with a surreal atmosphere. According to Fazio his sketches are a catalogue of failed experiments, broken actions and a whole reality that is breaking up: Valentin's madmen seem to embody a sort of analytical dementia, observing a correct but diagonal logic, always out of phase, useless and absurd.[107] His characters act for excess of logic, associating the un-associable and spiralling into a grotesque apotheosis of banality. His folly recalls that of the clowns, as do some of his chosen settings - see, for example, his performance as a barber in the 1923 film *Die Mysterien eines Frisiersalon* (directed by a young Bertolt Brecht), which is nothing other than the replica of a circus sketch. But his elegance kept him away from the ring, winning him, on the other hand, the favour of famous intellectuals like Bertolt Brecht who actually as a young man "in Munich was for a while part – as clarinettist – of his band",[108] as well as that of other intellectuals like Feuchtwanger, Bronnen, Hermann Hesse, Alfred

Polgar, the Mann family, Walter Mehring and Tucholsky.[109] With Liesl Karlstadt he formed an irresistible couple, especially in their mature years when he was skinny and she was chubby and, both in their aspect and in their exchanges, they repeated the clichés of the comic couple, in a verbal skirmish of crossed lines and cynical repartee.

Another "*clown triste*" whose show Beckett rushed to see was Buster Keaton. This childhood hero of Beckett performed at the Cirque Medrano in Paris in 1954, in the same period when Beckett was a frequent visitor there.[110] Weary, disappointed and forgotten by cinema, Keaton was trying to re-launch himself in Europe in the circus world, which perhaps suited him better than talking movies. The personal and artistic relationship between Beckett and Keaton, however, does not so much concern the circus ring as cinema, of which more later.

Beckett's knowledge of circus clowning, which is found in biographical data, can also be read in his writing. Both in his prose and his plays, Beckett makes reference to contemporary circus players whom he presumably knew, although there is no biographical confirmation of this.

The very famous Swiss clown, Grock, appears in Beckett's universe quite early, in a novel published posthumously but dating from the early Thirties, *Dream of Fair to Middling Women*, which contains a continuous, separate commentary that recurs at regular intervals throughout the story, almost functioning as meta-discursive abstraction from the "seriousness" of the narrative. On p. 9 of the novel we find, in enigmatic italics, "*Inquit Grock…*", an unfinished comment on the plot which we later discover refers to the clown's motto: "voice of Grock: *Nicht möööögliccchhh…!*" (p. 115). Continuing our journey of the *Dream of Fair to Middling Women* with its protagonist Belacqua, we learn that "he was inclined to agree with Grock, when that faithful philosopher blew from his French horn the first throaty cui bono of the meditation" (p. 136). Also that one of his girlfriends, Alba, was able to mock someone "in the style of Grock" ("'sans blahague!' [Alba] mocked grockly", p. 173). Towards the end we find "*Grock ad libitum inquit*" (p. 204). And in a "false" ending (false because, though it feels as if it is the end, it briefly takes up the narration again, only to break off abruptly) "*Voice of Grock…*" (p. 237). Grock's voice is almost an obsession for readers of *Dream of Fair to Middling Women*, an incomprehensible riddle that can only be solved by putting all the quotations together and accumulating the clues. The figure of Grock is outside the narrative, but follows it and comments on it ("inquit", "voice", "ad libitum inquit"). His wisdom (he is even called a philosopher) makes him a behavioural model for the play's characters (Belacqua agrees with him and Alba behaves "grockly") and he even has the last word following the speech that fades on suspension points. But what does Grock say? What is his voice declaring when it comments *ad libitum*? The key lies in the expression "*Nicht möööögliccchhh...!*" (p. 115), the catchphrase of the Swiss clown, which may be better understood by looking at the collection of short stories, *More Pricks Than Kicks*, derived by Beckett from *Dream of Fair to Middling Women* and with Belacqua as protagonist.

Grock is certainly quoted less frequently in *More Pricks Than Kicks* than in *Dream...*, but the symbolism of these mentions are clearer and more evident. The reduction of the mentions has concentrated their meaning more explicitly. In the short story "Yellow", Belacqua, torn between tears and laughter, finally decides to support a "clownish universal", which paradoxically associates a trio of clowns with Democritus, the philosopher of laugher: "it was this paramount consideration that made him decide in favour of Bim and Bom, Grock, Democritus, whatever you are pleased to call it, and postpone its dark converse to a less public occasion" (p. 176). Whatever it is called, the concept is the same, whether it takes the name of a clown or of a philosopher - the comic, laughter is for Beckett a free space where the frontier between serious and facetious dissolves in a single universal proposition. The disrespectful familiarity of the clowns with philosophical austerity creates in the reader an association of circus/philosophy and the mutual overflowing of one into the other. Are Bim, Bom and Grock philosophers, despite their "levity", or is Democritus a comedian despite being a thinker?

Grock, who seems to be referenced also in Croak of *Words and Music* (the name sounds too similar to be a mere chance) also appears with the mention of his famous catchphrase. The first (and only) person to note the "short circuit" was Ruby Cohn, who associated the expression with Beckett's entire comic vision comprising vaudeville, gags and *laz-*

zi.[111] In *More Pricks Than Kicks*, the short story "A Wet Night" contains a peculiar waking nightmare of Belacqua: Grock appears to him, his face substituting that of the curate and scolding him in his own way:

> the face on the curate faded away and Grock's appeared in its stead.
> 'Say that again' said the red gash in the white putty.
> Belacqua said it all and much more.
> '*Nisscht möööööghlich*' moaned Grock, and was gone. (my emphasis, p. 58)

"Nisscht möööööghlich" is spelled differently than in *Dream…* to better reproduce the sound of Grock's "drawling" speech, probably mocking the emphatic diction of German speakers, compared with the different accent of Switzerland. Occurring again on p. 86, it is one of Grock the clown's recurring catchphrases, considered even to be his motto and may be translated as "rien à faire", "nothing to be done", which is the opening line of *En attendant Godot*.

The clumsy clown would come out with these words when he gave up, unable to get a grip on the world around him over which, with his *naivetée*, he had no control. "Nisscht möööööghlich" was his cry of defeat, a *débâcle* of a simple soul, ready to make the same mistakes again – but a light-hearted one, as confirmed by the drawn-out pronunciation that makes fun of the serious meaning. "Rien à faire" is the very first cry of Beckett's theatre characters and declares the impossibility of starting any kind of action, right at the opening of the dramatic action. It declares defeat before the challenge even begins. It is the tragic sense of human impotence that the clowns Didi and Gogo will interpret in their own playful and paradoxical ways, falling down and rising endlessly without ever learning the trick of the game.

Grock was the stage name of Adrien Wettach, born in Recouvilliers, Switzerland on 10th January 1880. Born into the profession, he began his artistic career as circus and music-hall clown extremely young, specialising in various acts, as a contortionist, juggler, trapeze artist, acrobat and rider, as well as playing numerous musical instruments. He took the nickname of Grock for the first time in 1903, in a duo with Brick (Marius Galante), then continued with other partners or as a solo act in circus and music-hall. He performed with the Medrano for several years, before founding his own circus, retiring in '57 at the age of 74. This clown, who had also entertained Chaplin in '53 in Vevey, wore an Auguste costume, over-sized with large, colourful checks, or a too-small black jacket and trousers with white gloves. His make-up consisted of a completely white face and bald head, with a strikingly large red mouth to emphasise his satisfied smiles and winks. His numbers were constructed around the absurd logic of an effort disproportionate to the result – he has a huge suitcase containing a tiny violin; to get closer he pushes the piano to the piano-stool and not vice versa. Others concerned the uselessness of striving to obtain results, which only happen by chance – he tries in vain to throw his violin bow over his shoulder and catch it, but only succeeds by chance.

Beckett must have known Grock well for him to quote his motto, although we do not know whether he ever actually saw him perform. A similar doubt exists regarding the pair of clowns, Bim and Bom. Mentioned together with Grock in *More Pricks Than Kicks*, where they inspired "Belacqua's bravado in the face of death",[112] they recur several times in Beckett's imaginary:

In *Murphy* there are two nurses with their names – "Mr Thomas ('Bim') Clinch" and "Mr Timothy ('Bom') Clinch" (pp. 109 and 115). In *Comment c'est*, the narrator plays with the reader, deciding on the spot the name of his character, Pim, then changing it to Bom, or perhaps preferring Bim or Bem. Beckett's very last work of drama, *What Where*, sees Bim and Bom as protagonists together with their parodic-assonant amplifications, Bam and Bem. Originally also *Godot* and *Fin de partie* contained references to the comics, which were later removed from the final versions. The first version of *Godot* read:

> ESTRAGON. - On se croirait au spectacle.
> VLADIMIR. - Au music-hall.
> ESTRAGON. - Avec Bim.
> VLADIMIR. - Et Bom.
> ESTRAGON. - Les comiques staliniens.[113]

These "Stalinist comedians",[114] the Russian clown duo Bim and Bom, had an excellent reputation in Soviet Russia, at a difficult time for the Russian circus. Indeed a Soviet decree had decided to nationalise the Russian circus, which was accused of being unoriginal and of following European fashions too much, but Bim and Bom maintained the high reputation of the Russian show, accommodating differing tastes and requirements.[115] In "Avant *Fin de partie*", one of the preparatory manuscripts for *Fin de partie*, Beckett describes the action between X and his Factotum (F) as correlated to the number of Bom, giving the comic not only universal significance over and above the show in itself, but also a dramatic function: "[X and Factotum disguised as his mother] should concern themselves with 'the affair of Bom'. The allusion to the Russian clown Bom and her unanswered plea for water – suggesting an alternative to the kind of drama just parodied. That alternative would be at once more comic and more tragic and more universal".[116] Also in the preparatory study for *Fin de partie* is a vaudeville pun on 'end' ("X makes a joke about the eternal order of things. To F's 'everything has an end', X replies with the music-hall joke, 'Except the sausage… it has two' […]").[117] This, according to Ruby Cohn, may be taken from the *routines* of Bim and Bom.[118] The two comics had the ability to launch critical attacks on those in power while remaining unpunished and their cynical humour was even tolerated by the Soviet regime, because it was mild and in good taste: "emblems of human cruelty, disguised under a comic garb". Beckett also probably alludes irreverently to them when Molloy, speaking of his castration, refers to his genitals as "frères de cirque" (p. 52).

Although in *Mercier et Camier* the figure of authority cautions Mercier, Camier and Watt that "ceci est un trottoir […], pas une piste de cirque" (p. 196), the impression we have of their adventure is completely different. The three tramps are performing one of the most exhilarating pieces of their journey, a lively argument accompanied by shoves and skirmishes. The confusion attracts the attention of a policeman, who admonishes them, saying that they are in a street, not a circus. The immediate reaction of the reader ought to be that these characters are not so much clowns as *clochards*, belonging to the dust of the street, not of the circus ring. In reality, neither Mercier, nor Camier, nor Watt, nor any other of Beckett's characters give us solely the impression of being tragic tramps. Indeed their tragedy is always combined with clowning. They therefore give the observer the feeling of moving within "une piste de cirque".

This clownish air is common to all Beckett's characters: Belacqua, Watt, Murphy, Didi, Gogo, Clov, Nagg and Nell, and so on, in unbroken succession between prose and drama. The clownish attitudes and actions that were merely evoked in prose, imagined in the mind of the reader, on stage take on a three-dimensional aspect that emphasises their physicality, requiring special gestural ability on the part of the actor. Beckett's clowns mimic those of the circus, but they use their 'turns' in a deliberate manner – they shift between the serious and the facetious, creating portraits of universal clowns that prevent us from ever interpreting their activity in a banal or mono-tone fashion. They raid the circus clowns' wealth of invention and insert their booty into their own routines, stripping away the "facile" comic effects and giving them a different sense. Their grotesque appearance and stumbling gait, between a tightrope walker and a comic miming a fall, the clownish violence, the ludic dimension that prevails over all other activities, the objects whose function has been reinterpreted – these are all circus elements.

Clov, the servant in *Fin de partie*, is a synecdochic allusion to all the other clown characters in Beckett's universe, in his aspect, but first and foremost in his name itself. The sound of "clov" is too similar to "clown" (especially if considered with Anglo-Irish pronunciation) not to bring it to mind in attentive readers like Adorno (who insisted on this interpretation, even ignoring Beckett's flat denials).[119] But it is not only his name. Clov started out with a decidedly clownish appearance, eliminated by Beckett, particularly after the Berlin productions in the Seventies, in order to obtain a more balanced tragicomic effect. Yet Clov began as a clown, just like Hamm, Nagg and Nell and Krapp. To all of them Beckett attributed unashamedly clownish connotations, evolved by him through attenuating colours, but which were equally symbolic. When Beckett first directed *Endspiel* (Schiller Theater Werkstatt, Berlin 1967), he removed from the scene the too-comic elements, like the red faces of Hamm and Clov, but he kept the comic routine, which he made slicker and more animated, for example, by substituting Clov's trouser buttons with elastic, speeding up the gag about the flea. The same occurred when directing *Das letzte Band* (Schiller Theater Werkstatt, Berlin 1969), where Krapp had his red nose and too-short trousers taken away, and all the movements were stylised.[120]

Reduction was a recurring process in the construction of Beckett's texts. He re-worked his plays several times before releasing them for print, taking subsequent advantage of his translating and directing his own works to make new changes. "Beckett's creative process is marked not only by gestation, by accretion, but by deletion [...]. In much of his creative process he struggles to undo himself".[121] This can be noted in nearly all his artistic workings - Pilling clarified it for *Watt*[122] and Gontarski for *Krapp*, *Play* and *Happy Days*, a work he maintains was composed not as "an evolution toward fuller explanation of character and situation, but the opposite. The process of composition in *Happy Days* was essentially contraction, decomposition, diffusion".[123] This internal development of the texts, practically a physiological necessity, would sometimes last over twenty years (as in the case of *Fin de partie*) and always followed the same principle - "subtraction", as he himself theorised in *Proust*, for "the artistic tendency is not expansive, but a contraction" (p. 47). Beckett worked by subtraction, but it is fascinating to note how his reduction of impulses always maintained the original energy, concealing it in the form of hints, of hyper-allusive construction. This process resulted in forms Beckett called definitive, but which never ceased moving towards the same direction - restraining the energy of text and scene to obtain a more intense effect. Thus elements that were too obviously clownish and farcical were eliminated or attenuated, while maintaining a strong trace even in their absence.

Even subtracting the clownish insolence, the comic impulse remains in all the characters, enriched by an ever-improved balance of tragedy and comedy. Sometimes, for example, an object may suffice to allude to the circus, like Pozzo's ringmaster's whip, or the one that appears in a take from *Film*, which was then edited out of the final film. Or all the clown props – bags full of assorted objects, bicycles, ropes and hats. But at times, even a movement can transport us into the circus dimension – not only a gesture, a mime, a fall, a fake balancing act, but even a direction. In directing *En attendant Godot* and *Fin de partie*, Beckett insists on circular movements for the characters that attract our attention, being coherent with the space of the circus.

The circus ring is normally circular (only rarely oval) and this obliges artists who perform there to organise their numbers as a consequence. This means that most movements involving a fair number of artists and/or animals (the opening and closing parades, the performances of horses, elephants or trained zebras) take place around the edge where the ring meets the public, thereby delineating a circular path. When Beckett directed *Warten auf Godot* (Schiller Theater Werkstatt, Berlin 1975), he conceived and introduced circular and semicircular movements that established a real, recurrent model - these were small gestures of hand or foot and movements in space that invariably followed a clockwise or anticlockwise direction. That these simple spatial elements constituted a complex network of a subliminal, significant stage imaginary is demonstrated by their coincidence with verbal references to temporal, earthly existence - both in the micro- and the macro-movements "clockwise motion is associated with life in the temporal world and counter-clockwise motion with attempts to escape from it".[124] The same pattern occurs in the production of *Endspiel* mentioned above (Schiller Theater Werkstatt, Berlin 1967), where the clockwise movements are associated with activity and earthly matters and anticlockwise ones with escaping. Though for Clov and Hamm the former uses angular movements and the latter uninterrupted curved lines, "both move in patterns that suggest circles or semicircles".[125] These are rendered even more explicit by Hamm's obliging his servant to move him around in his wheelchair, along the imaginary edge of a ring, or by his obsession for the centre.

> HAMM. - Fais-moi faire un petit tour. (*Clov se met derrière le fauteuil et le fait avancer.*) Pas trop vite! (*Clov fait avancer le fauteuil.*) Fais-moi faire le tour du monde! (Clov fait avancer le fauteuil.) Rase les murs. Puis ramène-moi au centre. (Clov fait avancer le fauteuil.) J'étais bien au centre, n'est-ce pas? (p. 41)

His desire to be at the perfect centre of a hypothetical world that moves round him is a parody of outdated anthropocentrism, or rather symptom of a profound sense of disorientation. The jolly circus parade has lost its carefree and self-referential nature and has become, in Beckett, a sign of discomfort, of a space and time that are closed and can no longer be crossed or (re)discovered.

2.4. Beckett and cinema

The final component of Beckett's comedy consists of the comic cinema, its origins, the silent films and the first 'talkies'. In fact, careful observation reveals that all the comedy seen by Beckett in his youth was distilled in the capacious vessel of cinema. This new means of communication increasingly for the masses recycled all the resources of traditional theatre entertainment and gave rise to new aesthetic developments between the old and the new. The result was a change in artists' lives and in their habits, as well as in how entertainment was produced and consumed. This radical change could only occur by going through a process of metabolisation of the pre-existing tradition.

When Lumière's *cinématographe* was shown in public in 1895 it was quite successful, but the problem arose of what to do with this wonderful technical instrument. Right from the beginning, the aesthetic possibilities were explored, as were the places of projection. Music-halls were used for the first experiments with this invention, at first simply offering "motion pictures", literally, pictures that moved. By the final years of the 1890s in London, the success of "motion pictures" within venues for music-hall was assured, and so the first actual showings were taken from the repertory of "light" theatre: "condensations of vaudeville turns, circus acts, and minute excerpts from popular plays".[126] As an entertainment form, cinema preferred to borrow from the comic heritage of vaudeville, which could offer known, reassuring material to public and actors, in addition to a repertory that was always lively and packed with novelty. The main problem, that of the actors' adaptation to a different acting technique, was overcome by metabolising pre-existing abilities, already used in treading the boards. Early producers recruited their artists from those already available in the theatre and comic actors were easily transferred from vaudeville to cinema. American vaudeville, in particular, played a key role in the changeover from one medium to another, with its origins in the circus, minstrel shows and concerts and its adoption of a pre-established, rigid format: "as vaudeville developed [...] this ensemble format changed to a specialized, fragmented format with each performer or act working autonomously and not participating in the closing sketch".[127] This structuring of the programme according to an internal order that gave prominence to the better numbers and homogenised differing abilities was a principle already adopted by the modern circus. It would later be adopted by the talkies, associating comic scenes with song or dance as in the films of Fred Astaire and Ginger Rogers, or also in many Marx Bros. films, whose storyline was broken by sketches and musical performances.

Music-hall and circus repertories were ransacked by those who, having begun their career in the music-hall and in the circus, had moved on to work in the new entertainment industry. The migration of theatre actors to the cinema gained momentum when Hollywood organised production according to very modern criteria, effective and successful. The dream of Hollywood stardom began to spread to Europe and to attract young, unknown artists, who would quickly become the leading lights of the system. The majority of "Keystone cops", in a comic series produced by Keystone centring round American police forces, were "ex-circus clowns",[128] actors who had learned their trade in European or American vaudeville, as was their director, Mac Sennett. Sennett, who had begun his artistic career as a vaudeville actor, clown and silly policeman, became a director by chance when he took over from a sick colleague and went on to launch the famous Keystone series, gathering around him promising young artists such as Chaplin. The young Chaplin, along with Stan Laurel, was already an attraction in the theatre company of Fred Karno in London, when he arrived in the United States and settled there, starting out on his cinema career. The same thing would happen to Laurel before meeting Oliver Hardy who was meantime working in American cabaret, to Keaton who as a child had followed his parents on tour in American vaudeville, to Langdon who worked both in circus and music-hall, to

Ben Turpin, to Roscoe Arbuckle and right through to the Marx Brothers dynasty. All of them were the human material made use of by the Hollywood system and whose technical know-how cast light on the new road ahead. Cinema operators left it to the actors themselves to use their skills to enrich the experiments on celluloid. As Chaplin confirmed, at the beginning of the century the technical possibilities of cinema acting were quite limited and it was the theatre folk who supplied the necessary elements: "[at the Keystone] they knew little about technique, stagecraft, or movement, which I brought to them from the theatre. They also knew little about natural pantomime".[129] But this debt to the circus and to vaudeville would soon be paid in the form of open tributes: Chaplin's films *Caught in a Cabaret* (1914), *The Circus* (1927), in part *Limelight* (1952) and *At the Circus* (1939) by the Marx Bros. were set in the milieu where these artists had begun their professional growth and the references to this were explicit.[130] The influences became reciprocal.

Once the cinema experiment had begun, the material life of comic theatre had to adapt to new production habits and this consequently modified its aesthetic.

Beckett had experience of circus, of music-hall and of cinema, separately as independent genres, as well as of the thread of development that connected and ran through them. He was, in fact, a very keen cinema-lover, so much so that for a time he played with the idea of working and studying with Ejzenštejn[131] and of using him in his novels as a significant rhetorical figure. In *More Pricks Than Kicks*, cinema is a metaphor for a fantasy world where even the seizing of a sailing ship is child's play. Lucy gets round Belacqua so cleverly that "it was nearly as good as catching an ocean greyhound on the pictures" (p. 113). In *Comment c'est* the allusion is more cryptic and unfinished: "cette famille d'où me vient ce cinéma" (p. 50). But it is in *Murphy* that the author reveals his attention for the big silent screen, comparing Ticklepenny's behaviour to a scene by Griffith, "as though thrown on the silent screen by Griffith in midshot soft-focus sprawling on the bed" (p. 132).

Beckett was a particularly fervent fan of comic cinema, especially silent movies, which he considered far from extinct even at the end of the Thirties: "he thought that the possibilities for the silent film had been far from exhausted".[132] The bowler hats worn by Vladimir and Estragon have often been linked with images of Charlot in the Twenties, but rarely has detailed investigation been carried out into the genre's influence on Beckett's imaginary and writing, an influence deriving from his frequent visits as a spectator and which led to just one experience as actor-director.

Between 1906 and 1915 his uncle Howard (his father's brother) encouraged Samuel's budding interest for cinema, taking him and his brother to films in Dublin or in a small cinema in Dún Laoghaire, a suburban town then known as Kingstown.[133] As a university student in his home town, Samuel mostly went by himself and, it would seem, in an unplanned way to the cinema to see the masters of silent tragicomedy, Chaplin, Harold Lloyd and Keaton and then of the 'talkies', Laurel and Hardy and the Marx brothers.[134] When he went to Paris as the Thirties were approaching, his attention for mass culture led him to proudly cultivate his passions for the circus, the music-hall, jazz and silent movies. It was in 1928 that he saw Buñuel's film, *Un chien andalou*, which apparently gave him the idea for *Happy Days* with the image of a man sinking into the sand.[135] In London, where he spent some time in 1935, from July onwards he went to the cinema alone,[136] while in Berlin in 1937 he went sometimes with the film actor Eicheim.[137] In January 1938 in Paris he took Nora and James Joyce, who were going through a difficult time, to relax at the cinema, choosing Chaplin's film *Modern Times*, because he knew that he and Joyce both shared a passion for Charlot – "James and Beckett at least enjoyed themselves".[138] Throughout the Fifties he continued to go to the cinema, sometimes with his wife Suzanne – it seems to be a rare interest they had in common – or with his nephew Edward Beckett (his brother's son) who was visiting his aunt and uncle.[139] Edward recalls that they went to a cinema on the Champs Elysées and chose films like *The General* with Keaton and *The Hustler* with Paul Newman, which Beckett liked very much.[140]

The Hollywood comic repertory he saw included Charlie Chaplin, Buster Keaton, Laurel and Hardy, Harold Lloyd, Harry Langdon and the Marx brothers.[141] It is singularly difficult to read between the lines of Beckett's statements and discern his true opinion of the various artists. Indeed, when it became clear that the routines of Didi and Gogo were an integral part of the comic numbers from this cinema, the critics began to question Beckett about his relationship with these films and his replies became increasingly evasive. A letter from Beckett to James Knowlson on 10th January 1971 offers some information on the subject.[142] The scholar asked him if "it would be true for me to state that you admired some of the comic stars of the silent-screen and early talkies i.e. Laurel & Hardy, Buster Keaton and, of course, Charlie Chaplin. Any additional names here? (e.g. Roger Blin told me he admired greatly Harry Langdon?)". The reply he received, apparently laconic, but intrinsically eloquent was: "yes, but much less Langdon. Strong weakness for Bill Turpin". In that short "yes", Beckett seems to say little, but he was in reality confirming his preference for Chaplin, Keaton and Laurel and Hardy, going on to specify a lesser preference for Langdon, the sad hero, his lunar mime often in opposition to his alter-ego, Keaton, and a "strong weakness" for "Bill" Turpin. Beckett makes a mistake here, whether voluntary or not we do not know, in writing down the actor's Christian name, which is Ben.

Ben Turpin (New Orleans 1868 or 1874 - Hollywood 1940) was a very famous face among the Hollywood comics. This thin little man with a squint and impressive, pretentious moustache mostly played the parts of the jealous father, the useless husband or the eternal butt of jokes. Cinema stole him from vaudeville, where he had spent 11 years of his career at the Sam T. Jack's Burlesque Company as an impressionist, turning him into one of the most unusual figures of silent slapstick comedy. Hired by Sennett, he became known for playing opposite Chaplin. He was always a "sidekick", a minor character, but with his stage presence, constructed around his physical characteristics but also on his mime as acrobat and trapeze artist, he managed to remain unforgotten even in his last working years, when "[he] played support to comedy stars".[143]

In the same document Beckett replied in the negative on being asked whether he had ever seen *Duck Soup* by the Marx Bros. and if he had been thinking of Chaplin's *The Kid* when he chose the title of *Le Kid*. We find these latter replies, unlike the others, rather suspicious, since they deny textual evidence already revealed by Ruby Cohn, who maintained that the hat routine in *Godot* was taken from *Duck Soup*.[144] Considering that the American scholar often verified her opinions on texts directly with Beckett, having over the years built up a friendly relationship, we may imagine that she used not only textual evidence, but also some allusion by Beckett to the film, although she does not mention it. As far as Chaplin's masterpiece is concerned, over and above the too-evident syncretism parodying the titles *Le Cid/The Kid*, it was well known that Beckett of all Chaplin's works particularly liked *The Kid*.[145]

In any case, his favourite actors-writers remained for a long time Chaplin and Keaton and it was with them he had the most constant relationship. Regarding Chaplin, we know that he never missed a film, that he also enjoyed good quality imitations of Charlot (the clown Charlie Rivel) and that he often cited formal elements of his films. In the Thirties the Anglo-American comic became an authentic aesthetic model that Beckett used in his academic work, as an author and university professor. We have already seen how, in reviewing O'Casey's *Windfalls*, he expresses his opinion on the "best" of Chaplin, which he identifies in the comic effects free of sentimentality. Some years before, however, he had already mentioned him in his lessons at Trinity College. To illustrate comic gestuality in Molière, he dwells on the kinetic elements - movement and gesture – of comic theatre, making "repeated allusions to Charlie Chaplin".[146]

Beckett maintained this line in the Fifties, when he wrote to Adam Tarn, who was organising the translation, publication and diffusion of his texts in Poland, that he thought the production of *Godot* (Warsaw, 1957) well done because it was very "Chaplinesque".[147] Again, for the first production of *Godot* he suggested to Blin the association with Chaplin and Keaton, rather than with the circus, which the director had been working on.[148] I also like to think that the Charlot Chassepot mentioned by Winnie in *Oh les beaux jours* (p. 21, repeated on p. 62), a translation of Charlie Hunter from the original English in *Happy Days* (p. 142 and p. 161) is another allusion, this time a hidden one, to the star of silent comedy.

The comic films of Charlie Chaplin that critics and biographers are sure that Beckett saw are *The Kid* (1921), *The Pilgrim* (1923), *The Gold Rush* (1925) and *Modern Times* (1936). For Buster Keaton, in addition to the short films, *Sherlock Jr.* (1924), *The Navigator* (1924), *Go West* (1925), *Battling Butler* (1926) and *The General* (1927).[149]
Buster Keaton was the only actor of slapstick comedies with whom Beck-

ett had professional contact, though Roger Blin thought that the ideal cast of *Godot* would have been Chaplin as Vladimir, Keaton as Estragon and Charles Laughton as Pozzo.[150] In 1955 Beckett was disappointed to hear the news that the Broadway production of *Godot* would not take place due to the actors' other engagements. This production had been conceived by U.S. director Leo Kerz with Buster Keaton as Vladimir and Marlon Brando as Estragon. Far from being too daring, the strange couple seemed to have stirred Beckett's fantasy and expectations and he was truly delighted at the idea of the cast.[151] About ten years later, the abandonment of this project was made up for by Beckett's first and only attempt at cinema, for which he hired the famous Buster Keaton.

Film was intended as part of a trilogy of episodes in one single feature film including work by Pinter and Ionesco. Beckett's contribution was the only one actually made. The preparations for *Film* began in 1964 with a complex choice of protagonist. The first suggestion was (perhaps from Beckett) Chaplin. He sent an unceremonious reply to producer Barney Rosset, who had sent him the script to read: "there was at first no reply, but when Barney wrote again the reply was a letter stating, 'Mr Chaplin does not read scripts', to which Barney responded in rather juvenile fashion with another letter saying he was sorry that Mr Chaplin couldn't read".[152] Another candidate who was not available was Zero Mostel, a comic of Jewish origin (his real name was Samuel Joel Mostel, New York 1915-Philadelphia 1977) who had used his huge stature to win success with his comic characters. Jack MacGowran, too, was unavailable and already had engagements that clashed with the work schedule of director Alan Schneider. Finally, Beckett himself suggested Keaton "[...] for he had never forgotten his early passion for Keaton's films".[153] This decided, Alan Schneider insisted that Beckett meet Keaton before shooting started. Overcoming his proverbial terror of the United States, Beckett went – and his first encounter with the actor, according to Schneider, was nothing short of disastrous. Beckett's famous shyness, accentuated by the huge esteem he had for Keaton as an artist, was met with open hostility by the aging Keaton, half-forgotten by the cinema and beset by severe financial problems. In fact the actor's economic difficulties were the only reason he agreed to participate in this – to him, incomprehensible - avant-garde work and the enthusiastic American director had his work cut out trying to set up a relationship between him and the author. This real indifference initially shown by Keaton need not surprise us, for it reflected the general aversion of Hollywood comics for what were considered to be intellectualist experiments. This can be seen in Chaplin's unconditional refusal (the situation was different for MacGowran, already a "Beckett" actor, and for Mostel, who had also acted in "serious" theatre, both effectively unavailable because of previous engagements), and also in Groucho Marx's cool reaction to the passion expressed by some intellectuals, such as Joyce and Eliot, for his humour. Groucho expressed a violently sarcastic opinion of Beckett's work: commenting on one of Genet's plays, he wrote that he had never understood it, just as he had never understood *Krapp's Last Tape*. And he added that a change in the word order of the title would give an idea of his opinion on it.[154]

Nonetheless, during the making of *Film*, Keaton's aversion gave way to, at first, a collaborative attitude and then to open appreciation. Schneider tells how, when the atmosphere on the set was more relaxed, Keaton regaled the staff with anecdotes about the "good old days" of silent cinema, explaining the production mechanisms used at that time. Not only, Keaton began to make an active contribution to the work, suggesting some comic touches. It was he who suggested wearing the funny squashed hat that had become almost a trademark of his sad character, also the very special way of doing the cat and dog gag ('O' chases one off while the other comes back in, "this was straight slapstick, a running gag, the little man versus a mutely mocking animal world").[155]

Beckett, for his part, could only appreciate Keaton's professionalism and be enchanted by that impassive face, which managed to be funny despite its intrinsic melancholy. The Keaton of silent movies, with his small, very athletic physique, able to do any kind of acrobatics, had interpreted to perfection Beckett's juvenile fantasies – with his delirious expression, hardly ever smiling, he could be considered the true incarnation of Beckett's comic aesthetic. He was charmed by this "becoming reality" and when shooting was over he paid his own respects to the great artist. Before leaving the United States, in 1964, he read Keaton's autobiography *My Wonderful World of Slapstick* and in February 1965 in Berlin he went back to see *The General*, which he seems to have already seen more than a dozen times:[156] "in deference to his recent work with Buster Keaton, he went to see Keaton again in his 1927 film, *The General*, finding it, however, disappointing".[157] Chaplin, Keaton and their colleagues had by the Sixties been assimilated into the imaginary of Beckett, who had certainly found nourishment in their adventures, and they had found new paths of inspiration therein. Beckett had now constructed his own humour and his texts were moving towards the inexpressible and towards silence. His characters were starting to fade into troubling, elusive ghosts. The clumsy figurines of the early novels and plays spoke their lines in increasingly constricted, claustrophobic places. Although they do not cease to be self-deprecating, sarcastic, obscene and cynical, though they never stop laughing even in the most extreme psycho-physical dimensions – think of Mouth in *Not I* delivering her heartbreaking monologue of cruel laughs, or May in *Footfalls* who shifts in an ironic dimension though imprisoned on her illuminated strip. Their sense of humour has definitely changed, compared with the brazen, open pantomime of Vladimir and companions.

So *The General* could only disappoint Beckett when he went to see it again at the end of the Sixties, at a time when slapstick was undergoing a process of disintegration in his texts and one of the films and actors that had most stimulated his fantasy had now subsided into another context (his work) and had become something different from the original. Keaton's comedy, which the young Beckett had so enjoyed, had filtered into his literary work in the form of images, characters and actions, but had become something other than the original model, no longer recognisable even to the author making use of them. Comic material from cinema, but also from music-hall and the circus, having collided with Beckett's material lost its authenticity and was destined never to find it again. Beckett's universe put its own stamp on it, though a hint of the original provenance was always left.

Notes

1 See Pilling 1997 who quotes Beckett's letter to Charles Prentice (8th February 1932) and to Thomas MacGreevy (1932) conserved in RUL and TCD respectively (p. 235, no. 2).

2 See Cohn 1973, though she mentions this commonly held view without giving it too much weight. Gontarski 1985, on the other hand, attributes the move towards drama to a more likely "literary cul-de-sac" (p. 25).

3 Knowlson 1996; Cronin 1997.

4 Both quotations from Pilling 1997, p. 164.

5 From Knowlson 1996, pp. 27-28. The source was a friend of Beckett, now deceased, who used to go to performances with the Becketts (James Knowlson, letter to the author, Reading, 6th November 1997).

6 WBE 1977, vol. 15, p. 112.

7 Knowlson, p. 28.

8 See Who Was Who 1978, vol. II, p. 697.

9 In 1881 the structure and repertory of the Savoy Theatre had been renewed, in line with more modern, professional taste. The end results were remembered as "Savoy operas" and their supporters were known as "savoyards". See McGraw-Hill 1972, vol. II, pp. 145-160.

10 They contained every stereotype of light comedy from Aristophanes onwards.

11 In 1920 the British Parliament divided Ireland into two separate nations. In 1921, southern Ireland became a British dominion with the name of "Irish Free State". In 1922 civil war was officially declared and was to characterise the entire history of the young independent parliament, which only very slowly began to cut its ties with the United Kingdom (the most decisive steps were taken between 1932 and 1937 by De Valera).

12 Knowlson 1996, p. 56 (from an interview with Beckett on 13th September 1989). Other mentions of attending the Abbey Theatre are: Cohn 1973, p. 122; Cronin 1997, p. 55; Bair 1990, pp. 62-62; Pilling 1976, pp. 2, 69, 152.

13   Knowlson then gave it to the RUL, MS1227/1/2/16.

14   All definitions of genre are from Robinson 1951, pp. 135-141 (see this text for further information on the history and productions of the Abbey Theatre, Dublin). All the indications refer to the above-mentioned MS1227/1/2/16, apart from that of Murray's play, found in Knowlson 1996, p. 56.

15   Ó hAodha 1974, p. 117.

16   Ibidem.

17   Fitz-Simon 1983, p. 162.

18   Mel Gussow (1996) personally visited the collection in Boulevard St. Jacques.

19   See studies by Takahashi and Pilling 1976, p. 75.

20   See Gussow 1996. But Beckett had authorised a Nô version of *Rockaby* and *Ohio Impromptu* for the Edinburgh Festival (ibidem).

21   A. J. Leventhal in Knowlson 1971, p. 14.

22   MS1227/1/2/16.

23   This piece of information is given in Cronin 1997, p. 57, but as the author does not specify his source, we cite it with a margin of doubt.

24   Here, too, we cite from Cronin with the benefit of the doubt, as the information (p. 6) does not refer to any source. Other documents (MS1227/1/2/16) bear witness to Beckett having been present only at the "rowdy" performance: Knowlson 1996, p. 623.

25   The actor maintained that Beckett yearned to meet O'Casey personally (Gussow 1996). At the end of the Eighties, at the suggestion of O'Casey's widow, Beckett took steps to promote the works of his beloved author, proposing the Gate's staging of Juno and the Paycock at international theatre festivals (See Ibid. p. 54).

26   See pp. 82-83.

27   In the text, written by Beckett as "Eisenstein", according to the accepted British spelling.

28   See ibid. p. 112, note 1.

29   "Walt Disney inspected shot after shot on the celluloid", p. 83.

30   Knowlson 1996, pp. 56-57 and p. 716, no. 59 (interview of 11th April 1972).

31 Synge: 1871-1909; O'Casey: 1880-1964.
32 Fitz-Simon 1983, p. 168.
33 "Beckett and John Millington Synge" by James Knowlson, in Knowlson-Pilling 1979.
34 Another possible model for Beckett's couples might be the two beggars, one blind, the other lame, who go to the magic well of Saint Coleman and are miraculously cured – the protagonists of *The Cat and the Moon* by Yeats. Gontarski (1985, p. 56) says that this "may have been one of Beckett's sources for *Godot*", although no documentary evidence is given to show that Beckett knew the work.
35 Knowlson 1996, p. 98.
36 Ibid. p. 842. Knowlson was able to consult personally Beckett's library in his home at 38 Boulevard Saint-Jacques in Paris, being authorised to work there by Beckett himself (letter from James Knowlson to the author, 6th November 1997).
37 Ibid. p. 401. Beckett was not very pleased with the play, commenting "didn't much enjoy myself, in spite of alternate stout and whiskey" (letter from Beckett to Pamela Mitchell on 12th July 1954, cit. Ibid. p. 781, no. 68).
38 Fitz-Simon 1983, p. 190.
39 Knowlson 1996, p. 56 (source: Bill Cunningham, interview on Radio Telefís Éireann April 1976, See p. 716, no. 56).
40 Gontarski 1985, p. XVI, where the notes of the then student, Rachel Burrows, are cited.
41 Lyons 1980, p. 214.
42 Stage name of Peter Judge, born in Skerries, near Dublin, in 1891. He died in Dublin in 1947. He began his professional acting career at the Queen's Theatre in melodrama. His first appearance at the Abbey was in 1918. Here he played about 400 parts until his death at the early age of 56, at the height of his artistic career.
43 Young 1987, p. 29.
44 Ibid. p. 51.
45 Ibidem.
46 *The Irish Times*, August 3rd 1966, cit. in Young 1987, p. 51.

47 Cronin 1997, p. 206; Knowlson 1996, p. 189.
48 Cronin 1997, p. 303.
49 Knowlson 1996, p. 401.
50 Cronin 1997, p. 522.
51 Knowlson 1996, p. 107. See also p. 724, no. 82: probably the performance of 2nd December 1929, with its bare set and places referred to only by associative allusions. Beckett still remembered it when he wrote on 21st January 1937 in his German diary that he had seen "Racine at Odéon, when the set didn't matter" (GD, notebook 4).
52 Ibid. p. 107. Beckett had spoken enthusiastically of the text to Kay Boyle (see Cohn 1975, p. 16) and, several years later, to the German director Eggers-Kastner (GD, notebook 6, 19th March 1937).
53 Pilling 1976, pp. 152-153.
54 Cronin 1997, p. 183. He does not seem to have liked either of them.
55 Ibid. p. 246. Also see *Whoroscope/Murphy Notebook* (RUL MS3000/1, p. 36, 39 et seqq).
56 Both are opinions of Beckett in Gussow 1996.
57 See Ibid. The quotation is of the words of Edward Beckett, interviewed by the author on 15th December 1995.
58 Told by MacGowran himself to Mel Gussow (ibid.) in an interview on 9th January 1973.
59 Beckett loved and respected Professor Rudmose-Brown, "who had played no part in the choice of the plays, [and who] insulted both Perolson and Beckett and stormed away, apoplectic with rage and disgusted by what he regarded as a stupid, shameful charade that reflected badly on the entire Department". Knowlson 1996, p. 125.
60 Ibidem.
61 The lament of the eunuch Farinelli on seeing a very beautiful girl. Voltaire 1968, p. 139.
62 Pountney 1988, p. 2.
63 This and the information of the *reprise* in London are from Cronin 1997, p. 256.
64 Pountney 1988, p. 2.
65 Here Beckett saw the experimental plays of Yeats, where the lack of events was replaced by the circularity of what happened on stage. Cronin 1997, p. 142.

66   Fitz-Simon 1983, p. 135.
67   Cronin 1997, p. 57.
68   Ibidem. Deidre Bair (1990, p. 63) also emphasises his solitary visits to these performance, information confirmed by some friends and acquaintances (See p. 78, no. 43).
69   Cronin 1997, p. 57.
70   Ibidem.
71   Knowlson 1996, p. 8 (the source is an interview with Cissie's son, Morris Sinclair, dated 22nd May 1991; See p. 707, no. 40).
72   Ibid. p. 28. Geoffrey Perrin, childhood friend of Beckett, interviewed by Knowlson on 3rd February 1993 (Ibid. p. 710, no. 143).
73   Ibid. p. 57, but also Cronin 1997, p. 57; Cohn 1973, p. 122; Bair 1990, pp. 62-63.
74   Cronin 1997, p. 262.
75   Damase 1965, p. 1556.
76   Cronin 1997, p. 440. The visitors were Thomas and Vincent Hickey. See Bair 1990, p. 468 (from an interview with Caroline Beckett Murphy on 17th January 1974).
77   Cronin 1997, p. 566.
78   RUL MS1227/7/17/2.
79   Knowlson 1996, p. 386.
80   Interview with Donald McWhinnie in 1976, in McMillan-Fehsenfeld 1988, p. 177. For both productions (*Godot* in Paris in '53 and *Endgame* in London in '64) Beckett did not personally undertake the direction, but he followed it assiduously, orientating the official directors, Blin and McWhinnie, in their respective tasks.
81   In *Disjecta*, p. 42.
82   Apperson 1993, p. 508. "Pot", however, is also associated with suffering and begging ("to go to pot"=to beg), see also Freedman 1996, p. 201.
83   Redfern 1998, p. 4, mentions the original conserved in TCD (MS1042/72).
84   The ditty's name and the quotation were suggested by Walter Redfern, in a letter to the author, Reading, 11th May 1998.
85   See also Pilling 1976, p. 58.

86 If we exclude Miller 1991.
87 Robinson 1985, p. 9, for a reproduction of the cover.
88 Celati 1976, p. 23.
89 Clarke 1936, p. 14.
90 Tyrwhitt-Drake 1946, p. 42.
91 Ibid. p. 44.
92 Cronin 1997, p. 496.
93 Knowlson 1996, p. 585. Information on the event and on Beckett's impressions in a letter from him to Josette Hayden on 15th September 1971 (see p. 813, nos. 66-67).
94 Ibid. p. 418. From interviews with: Deryk Mendel (3rd March 1993 and 5th February 1994), John Beckett (8th July 1992). See p. 785, no. 2.
95 Ibid. p. 389.
96 Marowitz 1962, p. 44.
97 Gussow 1996.
98 Wilmeth-Miller 1993, p. 250
99 Ibidem.
100 AA.VV. 1984, p. 193. Chaplin had numerous imitators in the circus: as well as Rivel, there was Doug Ashton in the United States and Charlie Bale in the United Kingdom. See Hugill 1980.
101 Renevey 1977, vol. II, p. 114.
102 See his sketch "Father and Son Discuss the War" in Valentin 1980, pp. 97-102.
103 GD, notebook 6, 14th March 1937.
104 Hesse 1980, p. 207.
105 GD, notebook 6, 1st April 1937.
106 For the first, see Beckett's letter to Peter Gidal, 12th September 1972 ("Yes, I saw K. V. [sic] in a shabby cafe-theatre outside Munich. Evil days for him. I was very moved", in Gidal 1986, p. 212) and for the second, his letter to Josette Hayden, 15th September 1971 (cit. in Knowlson 1996, p. 813, nos. 66-67).
107 Fazio 1980, p. 15.
108 Jhering 1954-1968, p. 1392.
109 See Fazio 1980, p. 13.

110 Knowlson 1996, p. 779, no. 5. The source is a letter from Beckett to Pamela Mitchell on 12th January 1954. Keaton had toured more than once with the Cirque Medrano as he wanted, in the Fifties, to re-launch himself as an artist in Europe, where he was almost forgotten (in the USA he was still working in television).
111 Cohn 1980, p. 12.
112 Opinion of Cohn 1973, p. 35.
113 Cited in Cohn 1962, p. 204.
114 Cohn 1973, p. 231.
115 See Cervellati 1956, p. 211.
116 McMillan-Fehsenfeld 1988, p. 167, who quote from "Avant *Fin de partie*", the typewritten original of which is conserved in the RUL, MS1227/7/16/7.
117 Gontarski 1985, p. 40 (Gontarski's citations are from the manuscript "Avant *Fin de partie*").
118 Cohn 1980, p. 177. For more information on "Avant *Fin de partie*", see Restivo 1991 and Gontarski 1985.
119 See Knowlson 1996, p. 479.
120 For further information on textual modifications in Beckett's own productions see the above-mentioned McMillan-Fehsenfeld 1988.
121 Gontarski 1985, pp. XIII-XIV.
122 Pilling 1997, p. 179, maintains that *Watt* was created "by elimination".
123 Gontarski 1985, p. 75.
124 McMillan-Fehsenfeld 1988, p. 121.
125 Ibid. p. 196. Also see Fehsenfeld 1990b, p. 364.
126 Allen 1980, p. 102.
127 Ibid. p. 48.
128 Chaplin 1992, p. 143.
129 Ibid. p. 153.
130 Vice versa, the circus also owed a debt to cinema. The circus players, having been transformed into celluloid clowns, returned to the ring with cinematic connotations, where they imitated not only Charlot, but also Keaton and Laurel and Hardy, who were used as models by the clown Rhum.

131 I think Gontarski, in mentioning Beckett's letter of '36 to Pudovkin (1985, p. 103), is in error, perhaps because in the Thirties in Dublin Beckett was indeed reading the theories of Pudovkin and Arnheim and owned a vast collection of the cinema magazine *Close Up*. But it was to Ejzenštejn that he wrote, with the idea of studying at the Moscow State Cinema Institute. His approach, however, came to nothing when the Russian master predictably ignored the letter from the unknown young Irishman. See Knowlson 1996 (the source is a letter from Beckett to MacGreevy of 25th March 1936, see p. 748, no. 161), p. 226; Cronin 1997, p. 228 and Bair 1990, pp. 233-34. Gidal believed that the refusal was due to the critical state of all Ejzenštejn's activities in '36 because of his opposition to the Regime and quotes from a letter he received from Jay Leyda on 22nd February 1984: "Beckett's letter would certainly have attracted Eisenstein's [sic] attention (that closeness to Joyce was recommendation enough) –and action- if it had not arrived in the last half of 1936. That was a year that turned bad for Eisenstein. […] Beckett's application was lost in the shuffle" (Gidal 1986, p. 278).

132 Knowlson 1996, p. 226.

133 Ibid. p. 10 (from an interview with Beckett on 9th July 1989, see p. 707, no. 50).

134 Cronin 1997, p. 58 and Bair 1990.

135 Cronin 1997, p. 82. The hypothesis of a link between the image of Winnie sinking and that of Buñuel is also found in Brater 1989, p. 100.

136 Knowlson 1996, p. 203.

137 Ibid. p. 234 and 249.

138 Cronin 1997, p. 281, but also Knowlson 1996, p. 98 maintain their shared "fondness" for Chaplin and Synge.

139 Bair 1990, p. 468. But also Cronin 1997, p. 496 confirms that Beckett went to the cinema in Paris until autumn 1959.

140 Edward Beckett to Mel Gussow (1996).

141 Bair 1990, p. 63; Cronin 1997, p. 58.

142 This was from an interview Knowlson sent by letter to Beckett, which was returned by the author with the replies handwritten in the margin. RUL MS 1227/7/17/2. The quotations that follow are from this document.
143 Robinson 1985, p. 776.
144 Cohn 1973, p. 133.
145 Knowlson 1996, p. 57, who probably got this information from a conversation with Beckett (Knowlson, letter to the author, Reading, 6th November 1997).
146 Lyons 1980, p. 214.
147 Bair 1990, pp. 623-624.
148 Beckett and Blin met in Paris in summer 1950 to discuss the production. Tactfully, Beckett turned the conversation away from the circus (Blin was thinking of setting it in a circus and interpreting Didi and Gogo as clowns) and towards the silent cinema of these two actors. Bair 1990, p. 453.
149 Knowlson 1996, p. 57.
150 Melese 1966-1969, pp. 146-148.
151 Ibid. p. 413 (from a letter by Beckett to Pamela Mitchell on 17th February 1955, see p. 784, no. 139).
152 Cronin 1997, pp. 530-531.
153 Knowlson 1996, p. 522.
154 Given the similarity of Krapp/crap, Groucho would seem to be suggesting "the last crap tape". Marx 1992, p. 195. See also ibid. (p. 167 et seq.) for the correspondence and meeting between Groucho and T. S. Eliot, with the same childish awe of the intellectual for the comic (and the same cynical indifference of the comic for the intellectual) that had dominated the Keaton-Beckett meeting.
155 Schneider 1987, p. 361. For the full account of the preparation of *Film*, see this text and Bair 1990, pp. 638-642; Cronin 1997, pp. 530-536; Knowlson 1996, pp. 522-523.
156 Cronin 1997, p. 530: "[Beckett] had a profound admiration for Keaton and saw *The General* upwards of a dozen times".
157 Knowlson 1996, p. 528 (in a letter from Beckett to Judith Schmidt of 1st March 1965, see p. 803, no. 77).

* CHAPTER TREE *

"DANS UN ESPACE PANTIN". BODY. GESTURE. MOVEMENT

3.1. Bowler hats and other toys

When Beckett began to depict his fantasies on the space of a stage rather than on a blank page, his creative universe was enriched by the three-dimensionality of the theatre. With prose and poetry, physicality was alluded to, albeit strongly pushed back by the *logos*, but on the stage the body could become real and the comic could be expressed using the body.

By means of the inherent potential of theatre productions, Beckett's comic element could establish a dialogue with the performative traditions on which the young Beckett had been nurtured - circus, vaudeville and cinema.

In this chapter I shall examine the elements of comic gesture, starting from the character's physical appearance, human relations and behaviour in comedy and, finally, spatial dynamics.

Beckett's characters have been defined as clowns, tramps, *clochards*, ghosts and puppets, but let us see what is concealed behind these labels.

Starting with the names of the characters, the circus is frequently evoked. The names of Pozzo and Gogo, but also Godot (Beckett requested it be pronounced with the accent on the first syllable "Go'do") follow the vaudeville habit in the first years of the 20th century of giving actors shortened stage names ending in "o". If we think of the Marx Brothers, we have Groucho, Chico, Harpo (his musical speciality was the harp, hence harp + circus "o"), Zeppo and Gummo. Another clownish element is found in the play on similar-sounding names of many couples, "trios" and "quartets": Winnie/Willie, Nagg/Nell, Vi/Ru/Flo and Bam/Bem/Bim/Bom all exploit a basic assonance that immediately associates them as a comic couple, trio or quartet. This is not only because of the reference to the world of clowns, but also because of the sound of the nicknames, at the same time similar and different.

If the names first qualify the characters as clowns, this is then emphasised by their first impact on the audience, which is visual. But how do these characters present themselves to the public? What kind of first impression do they make?

Godot contains few indications in the stage directions regarding dress, since this information was mostly given by Beckett during rehearsal or – rarely – left to the sensibility of the players.[1] Nonetheless, some actions required by the stage directions help us to gain a clearer idea of the characters' appearance. When the curtain rises Estragon seems struggling with a pair of boots, which he is trying to take off, and his trousers are held up by a cord that eventually loosens, leaving him in his underwear (p. 87). Vladimir wears a coat with capacious pockets, where he keeps turnips, carrots and all kinds of disgusting things ("*il fouille dans ses poches, archibondées de saletés de toutes sortes*", p. 18). Lucky carries Pozzo's coat, later to be put on by the latter. They all wear bowler hats. Beckett's note for the published version was "tous ces personnages portent le chapeau melon" (p. 46). This characterisation was already found in his novels and short stories, where one sees an obsessive use of bowler hats (Cooper and the county coroner wear it in *Murphy*, as do Molloy and the tenant in *Molloy* and the protagonists of *Le calmant* and *La fin*), as well as of other comical hats.

The bowler hat was a symbol of bourgeois respectability in British society at the turn of the century, along with the black umbrella and the briefcase, status symbols of the man who works and produces, who follows the rules of society wherein he is a leader - "the bowler hat was of course *de rigueur* for male persons in many social contexts when Beckett was growing up in Foxrock".[2] But the bowler worn by Beckett's characters, rather than pertaining to social conformity, references the irreverent decontextualisation of the hat by the comic cinema of Laurel and Hardy,

Sennett's heroes and Chaplin. The character of Charlot, tramp and hero, had been constructed according to the principle of bringing together dissimilar elements, in a jumble of contradictions - the upper-class bowler, the too-small suit of the poor fellow, the too-large shoes of the clown,[3] and each element made the other look ridiculous.

In Beckett the bowler hat is derived from the tradition of comic cinema and of the circus and is an emblem by means of which he was imagining his characters, long before they were expressed through his art. While in his work for publication he consciously constructed a universe of funny little men doing comic actions, in his manuscripts there was space for his quite unconscious fantasies. When words escaped him or the form resisted his efforts, to help his concentration or to relax from the exertions of writing, Beckett distractedly drew strange little figures.

This gives his manuscripts a special space for freedom of thought that has not yet taken the form of words, consisting of the doodles Beckett used draw in the margins or amidst the written words. These eccentric documents allow us to visualise a sort of hidden level of his creative process, like a stream of consciousness that is solitary and quite involuntary.

The doodles are mostly funny figures wearing weird hats, often bowlers, like those in children's comics, which Beckett had indeed devoured as a child.[4] Their clothes resemble those of comedians from vaudeville and silent cinema: skimpy suits, striped trousers, bowler hat or boater. Their movements are grotesque, with shuffling bodies, contortions and grimaces. As an alternative to the bowler hat, we find the music-hall boater used on film by Harold Lloyd, or hats that are oversize or decked with floral decorations. The physical aspect of these little men always has a hint of clumsiness: the stooping walk, the scuttling like a spider, the ungainly run or the disjointed limbs, like a puppet or acrobat. The face always stands out as disproportionately large for the tiny body and certain abnormalities – big ears, a large nose or mouth or a surprised, staring expression – give it a grotesque appearance.[5]

Beckett's characters have been defined by some critics as "puppets", noting their fixed, puppet-like attributes. Beckett indeed knew some elements of puppet theatre and their use as textual metaphors. We know that Beckett had read Heinrich von Kleist's "Über das Marionettentheater" and had mentioned it during rehearsals for the TV drama *Ghost Trio* in 1976, saying that "puppets possess a mobility, symmetry, harmony and grace greater than any human dancer (or *a fortiori* any actor) can possibly achieve, because they lack the self-consciousness that puts human beings permanently off balance".[6] The Seventies were a time when Beckett was experimenting with the "ghostly aspect" of characters and actions and von Kleist's dimension provided him with a theoretical complicity specifically for the theatre. Von Kleist's marionette is a puppet animated by the spirit of the dance, inspired by metaphysics and matter, albeit light matter, who almost challenges the law of gravity following the same principle of dance, just as actors of Beckett are encouraged by their director to act using dance-like rhythm and balance. The popular tradition of puppet theatre, in Beckett as in most avant-garde thinking of the twentieth century, maintained very little of its original *naïveté*, but on it was based its symbolic content.[7]

In Beckett's texts the bowler hat is not merely part of costume, but enters the action on stage with all its power of evocation, becoming in *Godot* an authentic prop. There are no bowler hats in *Fin de partie*, but their function is interpreted by other types of headgear and props: Hamm wears a mortarboard, the rimless hat once worn by magistrates, lawyers and university professors; Nell, a lace cap; Nagg, a nightcap. In *Happy Days* Winnie's head is regally adorned with a "*small ornate brimless hat with crumpled feather*" (p. 142), Willie appears with a "boater, club ribbon" (ibid.); in *All That Fall* we learn that Mr Tyler has a beret and in *Film*, Keaton wears his signature felt hat. These various forms were part of the common lexicon referring to past grandeur, now lost and no longer missed. Beckett's characters seem quite unaware of the signs of the past they are wearing. They are made unknowingly ridiculous, for the bourgeois glory referenced externally is constantly contradicted by their irrational behaviour and worn garments.

Winnie is the clearest example of this decadence: "*about fifty, well-preserved, blonde for preference, plump, arms and shoulders bare, low bodice, big bosom, pearl necklace*". She wears the provoking sleeveless, low-cut dress and pearls of high society receptions and balls, then sinks into the sand and seems to pay no heed to her inevitable end and to the vanity of her speeches. Winnie has remained in the world she came from, the world of pearl necklaces, of good manners and small talk, unaware that the feather on her hat is as bedraggled as her life itself. So she continues to praise the wonderful day she is having, which the spectator finds hard to recognise as such. This contrast is comic and pathetic at the same time, a true "feeling of the contrary" in the manner of Pirandello. Winnie reminds us strongly of the elderly lady Pirandello uses as an example of his concept of humour, a faded beauty who ludicrously refuses to accept reality, a fossil that we refuse as ab-normal and that we stigmatise with a punishing laugh.[8]

Similarly, we imagine that Mrs Rooney wears her best frock to go to meet her husband at the station. We imagine it, because *All That Fall* is a radio drama and the physical aspect is evoked by the character's lines. Poor Mrs Rooney has put on her corset to support her "two hundred pounds of unhealthy fat" (p. 191), as Mr Rooney kindly calls it. She has put on a frock she is afraid of spoiling and which unfortunately does get torn in the car door ("my frock! You've nipped my frock! [...] My nice frock! Look what you've done to my nice frock!" p. 178). She is also wearing, perhaps on her hat, a feather, which she risks damaging on getting out of the car ("Mind your feather, Ma'am", p. 179). Mrs Rooney, like Winnie, is an image of gauche, provincial respectability, a female version of normally male clownishness. This attempt at dignified bearing that crumbles before our eyes is a quintessentially clownish attribute that, taken to extremes, leaves the actor in his underpants. Winnie and Mrs Rooney are sad, pathetic clowns who inspire contradictory feelings of commiseration and ridicule.

Of the male characters, Krapp is the one whose appearance is closest to that of a clown:

> *rusty black narrow trousers too short for him. Rusty black sleeveless waistcoat, four capacious pockets. Heavy silver watch and chain. Grimy white shirt open at neck, no collar. Surprising pair of dirty white boots, size ten at least, very narrow and pointed.*
> *White face. Purple nose. Disordered grey hair. Unshaven.*
> *Very near-sighted (but unspectacled). Hard of hearing.*
> *Cracked voice. Distinctive intonation.*
> *Laborious walk.* (p. 215)

Krapp's clothes are an authentic manual of the appearance and manner of a clown. The trousers are tight and too short like Charlot's, showing the ankles. The jacket has four big pockets, needed to hold the various objects magically produced by clowns in their comic routines, among which accessories are frequently found clocks and alarm clocks with impossibly huge dimensions, which may well be referred to by Krapp's heavy pocket watch. And the shoes are the real circus touch - enormous, narrow, pointed shoes that, were it not for their colour, might resemble those of Charlot. All these elements are tinged with Beckett's brush: the waistcoat and trousers are faded, the shirt and white shoes are grubby, all share the same uniform grey that is the colour of shabbiness, of a life that was once but is no more. This tonal limbo also affects the body, with its disordered hair, white face "dirtied" by stubble, as well as voice, hearing and sight, now "grey", opaque, not quite lost, but no longer as efficient as they were.

Although Beckett toned down the clownish content of Krapp in his German production, the character continued to be coloured by the comic atmosphere of the first stage directions. Gone was the red nose, hinting at drunkenness,[9] along with the clown's make-up, but the clown's movements remained in his halting walk and small, anxious steps.

Beckett's characters have faces that express their isolation from the surrounding world, with their crossed eyes, albeit not actually crossed like Ben Turpin's. Reality is thus distorted into a ludic, surreal atmosphere, able to contain both the "expression incrédule" (p. 31) of Vladimir and Estragon looking at Pozzo, and the vacant gazes of Lucky, of Clov, of Pozzo feigning indifference, of Nagg and Nell and of Krapp. The latter are using a classic technique from comic cinema – the deadpan look, the impassive face. In cinema aesthetics, techniques such as cuts and close-ups allowed more scope for expression and deadpan meant the character staring impassively into the camera. There are various examples of this in Hollywood comedy, as each actor interpreted the gaze according to his character's personality: Buster Keaton's deadpan was the absurd impassivity of the little man in the face of the havoc he has unwittingly caused, that of Oliver Hardy was asking for the spectator's agreement regarding Stan Laurel's idiocy. The deadpan of Beckett's characters affects the entire body with a physical and psychological immobility. It is an interior rather than exterior attribute, requiring suspended pauses during the stage action.

From the start, the physical bearing of Estragon and Vladimir is maladroit clumsiness - we find the one struggling to remove his shoes without success, while the other goes up and down with "*petits pas raides, les jambes écartées*" (p. 9). Both immediately appear as physically uncomfortable - they cannot free themselves of this, they fight against it but succumb. The day spent by the two friends unfolds into frenetic activity that to us appears senseless, but at certain times is frozen in moments of immobility when gesture, face, action and words are suspended in a void: "*ils demeurent immobiles, bras ballants, tête sur la poitrine, cassés aux genoux*" (p. 24). In *Godot*, Lucky impersonates extreme impassiveness, to a seemingly pathological extent - this silent servant, indifferent to the tyrant's dishonesty, is always there waiting for orders, gazing into space. His physical immobility is the same as the psychological immobility of the other servant, Clov, who in between his obsessive rocking, alternates his "*démarche raide et vacillante*" (p. 13) with moments when "*il reste un moment immobile*" (p. 16), interrupting the action. The sense of the scene is not suspended, but rather finds its true content in these same "frozen moments".

The same model underlies Hamm's flow of speech and Nell's facial expressions, which give us a clear example of deadpan, in the very situation where we would expect a different reaction. Nell's response to Nagg's joke about the tailor is a vacant gaze ("*il fixe Nell restée impassible, les yeux vagues*", p. 38). The comic effect is amplified by the fact that Nell realises she has not responded adequately and forces a shrill laugh, which prompts Hamm's fury.

As his awareness of theatre-making grows, Beckett adds to the stage directions descriptions of the impassive faces of his characters. From the mime deadpan in *Acte sans paroles I* suggested by "*il réfléchit*" (p. 95), a mere allusion to expression, he goes on to give clear indications of physical appearance. Krapp "plays" with the banana and suddenly remains "*motionless, staring vacuously before him*" (p. 216); in *Fragment de théâtre I*, character B pities A con with a gaze "*sans émotion*" (p. 21 and repeated on p. 24); all components of the love triangle in *Play* must have *"faces impassive throughout"* (p. 307); *Film* ends with a long close-up *"of the unblinking gaze"* (p. 329) of O, perfectly played by the king of impassive comedy, Buster Keaton; Joe in *Eh Joe* is caught by the TV camera standing completely still, his face must be "practically motionless throughout, eyes unblinking during paragraphs, impassive except in so far as it reflects mounting tension of *listening*" (p. 362); the anguished eyes of the woman in *Rockaby* are "now closed, now open in unblinking gaze" (p. 433); the castrating stare of Protagonist in *Catastrophe* who *"relève la tête, fixe la salle"* (p. 81), while the audience's applause fades before such courageous passivity.[10]

The effect of these stares is disconcerting, as the immediate reaction is neutered by the apparent lack of sense. Deadpan annuls expectations of reactions coherent to stimulus and blocks the cause/effect mechanism, revealing the "mechanical" essence of the body, as Bergson would say.[11] This contrast between non-functional immobility and its potential connection with the situation surprises us and makes us see the characters as pathetic clowns, unfit for life. But just when the gloomy atmosphere is dispelled by clownish levity, we are driven to doubt this too. We realise that the clown-characters are aware of their own clumsiness and their indifference towards "normal" logic. This discovery shakes the audience's conviction that they are watching a performance by clowns and sows doubts that the characters' actions-reactions might not be dictated by complete absence of logic, but by the presence of a different logic, an alternative to rational logic. The model that inspires Beckett's characters might well be that of clowns, but it is used with a self-awareness not found in the circus ring.

The logic underlying their actions is partly the ludic, maladroit logic of clowns, with their clumsy gestures, obscene allusions to the body, sexual and physiological aspects and their archetypal hunger. All these elements are clichés that can be found in any comedy show, from mediaeval carnival to the performances of the Commedia dell'Arte, from the circus to cinema.

The characters use their bodies in a way that is anything but rational, harmonious or "economical". They all struggle with their own clumsiness and with the material world that turns against them. The comic situations are multiplied when they interact with the world around them, in the material form of objects or other human beings. Their stage costumes have many accessories, needed for their games, for somehow passing the time, immobile and unchanging.

Beckett's stage, though bare, is cluttered with objects needed for stage business. Pozzo appears, boasting a circus tamer's whip, with Lucky on a lead of rope. Whip and ropes recur often in Beckett: there is a whip in the script of *Film* (p. 324) in the part that was filmed but then cut; also in *Pochade radiophonique* where Dick, a character who is dumb (note Beckett's derision, inserting a mute character into a play for radio, an entirely audio medium…) expresses himself only by cracking a "nerf de bœuf" (p. 65); and the unpublished MS2932 is all based on ropes. In the latter, probably dating from 1952, there are two characters, l'Englouti and l'Anonyme, tied to each other by a rope that winds round their necks and occasionally tightens, causing them to stagger and stumble. Made of rope, too, is the ladder from which they descend "envoyés". This unpublished typescript, presumably preparatory to *Godot*, groups together various elements of interest that relate it, on the one hand, to earlier prose (there is a Camier) and on the other, to future dramatic works: the gong at the start of action, equivalent to Winnie's alarm clock or the whistle in *Acte sans paroles I*; the speeches without a clear sense and without any real dialogue; the clumsy, ungainly movements of the arms; the violence which explodes unexpectedly without motive; the frozen gestures of the *tableaux* (Camier "s'immobilise dans une pose qu'il gardera jusqu'à la fin").[12] All these are elements shortly to be developed in an organic and complete fashion.

Returning to whips and ropes, it should be noted that these are basic circus accessories - animal tamers work with whips, acrobats with ropes. Pozzo's dominating behaviour and the act of wielding the whip justify the resemblance to an animal tamer or circus master, just as the whistle around Hamm's neck, used in the circus to call the chaotic spinning of the clowns to order, is a metaphor for controlling power that is never exercised or is ineffective.

Other clown's equipment consists of bags and suitcases and their "portable" alternative, jacket pockets, all full of junk that gets pulled out and used: such is Winnie's bag, her sole salvation on a day that is monotonous to the point of desperation. The bag gives its owner the illusion of not being alone, as well as a pretext for busying herself in everyday activities without interrupting her phantasmagorical self-deception. Winnie keeps toys in her bag for passing the time, it contains her entire world, her fantasies, nostalgia, everyday matters, it is her last desperate link with reality and she clings to it obstinately. When all else fails, it is the bag that comes to her aid:

> [...] there is of course the bag. [*Turns towards it.*] There will always be the bag. [*Back front.*] Yes, I suppose so. (p. 148)

> There is of course the bag. [*Looking at bag.*] The bag. [*Back front.*] Could I enumerate its contents? [*Pause.*] No. [*Pause.*] Could I, if some kind person were to come along and ask, What all have you got in that big black bag, Winnie? give an exhaustive answer? [*Pause.*] No. [*Pause.*] The depths in particular, who knows what treasures. [*Pause.*] What comforts. [*Turns to look at bag.*] Yes, there is the bag. [*Back front.*] But something tells me, Do not overdo the bag, Winnie, make use of it of course, let it help you... along, when struck, by all means, but cast your mind forward, something tells me, cast your mind forward, Winnie, to the time when words must fail -[*she close eyes, pause, open eyes*]- and do not overdo the bag. (p. 151)

The bag is Winnie's only point of reference in a situation slowly destined for inexorable catastrophe and in a certain sense the story proves her right - even when she has sunk into the sand up to her neck, the bag stays beside her, a souvenir of the "good old days" when she could spend her days going through its contents.

But even when she has her arms free to "play", the warning she gives herself is not to overdo it. She must use the game sparingly because it must last as long as possible to bring her that unique comfort, which words one day will no longer be able to bring her, as the day will come when even these will fail. The thought of her incipient end is made acceptable by the permanence of the objects. Although they seem futile, derisory or collected arbitrarily, they have the faculty of consoling and keeping company, which gives all the characters the illusion of being real, while being conscious of void and nothingness.

Some of these objects recur often in Beckett's world and bear the stamp of clownish atmosphere: the often enormous bags and suitcases that clowns play at passing back and forth or dropping, the whistle of Hamm and in *Acte sans paroles*; bicycles (Hamm asks Clov to go and get him two bicycle wheels), the alarms and clocks (whether visible, like Pozzo's watch and Clov's alarm clock, or heard only, as in *Happy Days*), the umbrellas (Winnie bashes Willie over the head with one), the spectacles (in variations such as Winnie's magnifying glass and Clov's telescope). And then Pozzo's pipe and spray, the medicines of Winnie and Hamm, Hamm's gaff – all everyday objects that, outside of their normal context, can take on a comical quality.[13]

When the characters handle things, they create a crazy sentimental relationship with the objects, which are "loved" with almost fetishist passion. Turning inanimate objects into "compagnons muets et fidèles"[14] is an absurd, illogical mental process, which surprises us. Comic surprise is also created by these everyday objects when they are recontextualised in a setting that negates them. On a bare stage like that of *Godot* even a very common pipe becomes an alienating factor in its own right and a stage pretext for the characters' routines. Pozzo inexplicably loses his pipe after placing it in his pocket, provoking irreverent enjoyment in Vladimir and Estragon. Theirs is the revenge of the loser over authority, when it suddenly finds itself in trouble.

Food, in the best Rabelaisian tradition, is loaded with archetypal connotations - the poor man's hunger is insatiable and the demand for food continuous. All Beckett's texts contain so many references to food that one might speak of his personal gastronomy: Belacqua's lobster, burnt toast and gorgonzola; Estragon's chicken, turnips and carrots; Nagg's biscuit; Krapp's bananas; the carrot in *Acte sans paroles II*; Lipton's tea in *Play*; Watt's disgusting mush given to Knott, and so on. Some characters are so orally fixated that they recall very strongly the hunger of Pulcinella or Punch.[15] For Estragon food is an obsession, so much so that he begs carrots from Vladimir and leftover chicken abandoned by Pozzo, and Nagg's repeated requests for "me pap" irritate Hamm. Nagg reacts exclusively to basic physiological functions, hunger, kisses and calls of nature and offends the ascetic wishes of his tyrannical offspring. Meriting separate consideration, then, is Krapp, whose bananas allude to sexual and coprological obscenity.

The act of eating in Beckett, however, does not imply the joyous contact with the world found by Bakhtin in medieval comedy and in particular in Rabelais, though it does take the same exaggerated forms, whether in abundance (Mary's pantagruelian appetite in *Watt*, pp. 49-54) or penury (the obsession of Estragon and Nagg). While in Rabelais eating and drinking are demonstrations and expressions of the grotesque, where the body swallows and absorbs the world, incorporating it within, in Beckett the function of nourishment is always frustrated, disturbed and de-automatised. The act of eating is for Belacqua "almost a masochistic act, a furious fight against the dry and hard bread, a painful mastication";[16] Estragon eats joylessly, wishing for a carrot when all that is left is a turnip, and when he gets the chance to munch on something more consistent, Pozzo's chicken, his meal is overshadowed by the thought that the bones are destined for poor Lucky. Likewise, Nagg succeeds in getting his biscuit only as recompense for Hamm's blackmail, but the only kind left is too hard for his toothless mouth to chew on.[17] Krapp's passion for bananas is spoiled by his constipation, which is known to be aggravated by the fruit. Even the reference to Lipton's tea in *Play* contains melancholy disappointment: "personally I always preferred Lipton's" (p. 314).

If Beckett's starving characters make us laugh it is because, for them, hunger and food serve to "lower" the tone. Also because this physiological function is carried out in unexpected ways and contexts, creating an alienating impression of contrast with what is happening or being said on stage. But the relationship with food is just one of the symptoms of discomfort for these anomalous clowns and their general attitude towards the reality surrounding them gives us at the same time feelings of anguish and of comical detachment. Beckett's characters cannot handle the material, psychic and emotional spheres according to rational logic, in the usual way, but submit to life's currents as a necessary evil, to which they are condemned without hope of escape. In the spectator this alienation provokes a sense of restlessness and frustration, since they seem to be totally submerged in an inextricable muddle. Yet often this anguished perception slides into comedy and we find ourselves laughing at the human pain and unhappiness of these characters and, through them, at universal anguish. How does this shift occur? How can one laugh at human unhappiness?

The secret lies in the compresence of contraries, universal aspirations and material needs, seriousness and playfulness, tragedy and comedy – opposites that constantly bounce back and forth without ever reaching dialectic resolution. The clowning is functional to the existential torment and, vice versa, Beckett's humour has always something at the same time exhilarating and heartbreaking – his characters are never mere clowns. Their ineptitude is comical because it is clumsy and exaggerated, it involves every human manifestation indiscriminately and determines every action - their relationship with themselves, with the others, with the surrounding space and the complex interrelations of all these elements.

3.2. "J'ai naturellement pensé au pseudo-couple"

When characters in Beckett are involved with their fellow men they are, more often than not, one of a pair. The couple is the human relationship that best describes the links between Beckett's anti-heroes. Think of Vladimir/Estragon, complementary and conflictual like Hamm/Clov; of Pozzo/Lucky who with Hamm and Clov share the mixture of tyranny and servitude; of A/B in *Acte sans paroles II*, opposite and complementary (A refuses food and moves slowly, B eats and moves quickly), needing just interaction to become an authentic comic duo; of Winnie/Willie, of Nagg/Nell, of Mr/Mrs Rooney, sad old creatures of habit; of the young Krapp/old Krapp dichotomy that interprets the difference so strongly as to give the impression of an actual dialogue between two people. They are all various manifestations of the same relational mechanism - the couple. Or rather, the "pseudo-couple", as Beckett himself defines it in *L'Innommable* (p. 16). On that occasion Beckett, through the voice of the unnameable narrator, attributes the definition to the couple Mercier/Camier, protagonists of the novel. Specific terminology aside (not just a "couple" but a "pseudo-couple") this becomes a veiled admission that Mercier and Camier should be considered as the archetypal couple of his relational universe.

Coming shortly after the couple of servants in Watt,[18] Mercier and Camier repeat their physical and psychological patterns. *Watt* contains an exhilarating review of physical types employed as servants in the Knott household and we discover that Knott, the mysterious master, only allows two types of constitution around him, bony and plump:

> Vincent and Walter, they were very much your height, breadth and width, that is to say big bony shabby seedy haggard knock-kneed men, with rotten teeth and big red noses [...], just as I [Arsene] am very much Erskine's and Erskine very much mine, that is to say little fat shabby seedy juicy or oily bandy-legged men, with a little fat bottom sticking out in front and a little fat belly sticking out behind. (p. 57)

Further on we discover that these two types ended up serving together alternately - Vincent with Arsene and Walter with Erskine, that is, one bony and one plump servant at a time. The image that immediately comes to mind is that of Stan Laurel and Oliver Hardy, the most famous duo of comic cinema and Beckett's favourites. A probable reference to them occurs in the "Addenda" chapter at the end of *Watt*, in "hardy laurel" (p. 254). Indeed a type of laurel tree that does exist, it seems to us too close to the sound of the comics' surnames and coherent with Beckett's word-play found throughout the novel to be mere coincidence.[19] For Beckett these two actors were the true incarnation of his pseudo-couples and he would liked to have seen them as Didi and Gogo, because he admitted that they would have been ideal physically for the parts.[20]

The fat/thin model is used again for the *clochards* Mercier and Camier, being the former thin and the latter fat. Their description is given by monsieur Conaire, who is looking for them and asks for news of them from Georges, the innkeeper where they are lodging:

> un petit gros, dit monsieur Conaire. Rougeaud, cheveux rares, multiples mentons, ventre en poire, jambes torses, petits yeux de cochon. [...]
> Comment est l'autre? dit monsieur Conaire.
> Un grand maigre barbu, dit Georges, qui tient à peine debout.
> Il a l'air méchant comme une teigne. (pp. 84-85)

Right from the physical appearance of these archetypes we can glimpse the sense of that "pseudo" placed before the word "couple" - we are not dealing with identical elements nor with radically different ones, but with characters that are similar and opposite. Beckett's definition, in fact, would appear closer to that used in physics, when a couple of forces is a "system of two forces, equal and parallel but of opposite direction, which act on the same body".[21] The commonly understood sexual connotation of the term "couple", the union of a man and a woman, is rarely encountered, since Beckett's couples are generally formed of two men.

The couple in Beckett is conceived according to criteria of indissolubility and opposition, its poles are inspired by the compresence of differences. In this regard, physical and psychological connotations become mixed up and derive sense from mutual coexistence. It seems that the two poles of the couple must "encastrer physiquement l'un dans l'autre car leur relation est celle d'un vieux couple qui fonctionne sur l'*agglutination physique* en même temps que sur le *rejet*. Ils ont besoin l'un de l'autre, ne peuvent se séparer pour longtemps mais ne se supportent plus".[22] Like two sides of the same coin the components of the couple go back and forth in a mirror relationship, falsely perceived as identity. Thus in *Watt* Mr Hackett sees the affinities between Watt and Mr Nixon: "when I see him, or think of him, I think of you, and when I see you, or think of you, I think of him. I have no idea why this is so" (p. 17). His feeling cannot be explained through rational thought, but is strong and undeniable to perception, which glimpses identities, despite principally physical evidence of differences and contrasts.

Physical contrasts go beyond the actual body to include its outward bearing and its clothes. We might take the example of Vladimir and Estragon, or of Clov and Hamm, or in part Willie and Winnie, where the former are conceived as part of perpetual motion and the latter, of immobility. Vladimir and Clov walk with swift, short steps, while their alter-egos are bound to the earth and to stability. Estragon is lying on the ground when the curtain opens, struggling with his shoes, while Hamm is sitting in his wheelchair. Hamm and Clov are extremes of contrast in movement, both condemned irreversibly to their condition. Clov could not sit down even if he wanted to and Hamm is clearly paralysed: "chacun sa spécialité" (p. 25). The contraposition between Winnie and Willie is not so evident – the woman has absolutely no dimension of movement, while the man moves through space in short, circumscribed moments.

During preparation of his *Godot* for the Schiller Theatre in 1975, Beckett explained the link between Vladimir and Estragon in metaphorical terms, associating the one with the celestial dimension and concretely therefore with the tree, the other with the terrestrial dimension and therefore with stone. Iconographically, he wanted them to have complementary, opposite costumes: "Vladimir is going to wear black and grey striped trousers which fit him, with a black jacket, which is too small for him; the jacket belonged originally to Estragon. Estragon, on the other hand, wears black trousers which fit him, with a striped jacket which is too big for him; it originally belonged to Vladimir. [...] Similarly, Lucky's shoes are the same colour as Pozzo's hat, his checked waistcoat matches Pozzo's checked trousers, and his grey trousers match Pozzo's grey jacket".[23] As in their clothes, Didi and Gogo also complement each other in their words - their lines seem to come from remnants of the same monologue.

The tangible appearance of the couples is nothing more than a visualisation of their psychological and emotional interplay. The characters are connected to each other by ties of love-hate, by the impossibility of living with or without the other, in other words, by schizophrenic relationships they cannot do without. Perhaps sadistic is a better description, if a sadist couple signifies the forced combination of two *personae* that can be complementary but also opposed.[24] They suffer because they are driven both by repulsion and attraction at the same time or, they attract and reject each other from one moment to the next, eternally and with no apparent motive.

The stage model that immediately relates to such dynamics is that of the clown couple, especially the dialectic between *clown blanc/clown auguste*. This duo, which repeats the stereotypical master/slave from classical comedy and from the Commedia dell'Arte and would later be developed by music-hall and comic cinema with the stage function of comic/stooge, may be considered the prototype of Beckett's pairs.

The origins of the *clown auguste*, also identified as Augusto or Augustus, are unknown and concealed in myth - he apparently appeared "spontaneously" in about 1865 when, in the Renz circus in Berlin, or the Ciniselli circus in St. Petersburg, a drunken stable-boy called Auguste entered the ring during a performance, getting up to all kinds of tricks. He was an enormous success with the public who thought they were watching an exhilarating comic number from the programme. This tempestuous, over-romanticised beginning was adopted in its entirety by Chaplin in *The Circus*, with Charlot in the role of the romantic, clumsy circus assistant who becomes a much-loved clown, thanks to his unintentional disasters. But this apart, the role of the *auguste* had always existed among circus comic repertory, even before he officially became a myth. Even before the modern circus, the Commedia dell'Arte had already used servants as comic characters, eternally entangled by their own ineptitude and/or cunning (the Zanni, Pulcinella, Arlecchino and all their many European variants). The *auguste* portrays the subversive energy of the comic, corporality, animality and the uncontrollable force that escapes reason. Rationality, by contrast, is portrayed by the *clown blanc*, who returns things to normal, with his intelligent, *super partes* mockery. In Shakespearian terms this dichotomy might be illustrated by the nature of Caliban and the culture of Prospero. It can be easily classified as follows:

	CLOWN BLANC (culture, man)	***CLOWN AUGUSTE*** (nature, beast)
HAIR	thin, tidy, "hairiness" is hidden and disciplined	untidy and thick, or bald, "hairiness" is evident and unkempt
COSTUME	well cut, rich fabric, embroidered with sequins	too small or too big, exaggerated colours, dirty
SHOES	ballet shoes	excessively large
MOVEMENTS	elegant and in command	awkward
LANGUAGE	precise, total command of linguistic code and its meanings	ambiguous, uncultured, vulgar, playful
SYMBOL	of cultural normality, of rationality, of the hero	of cultural abnormality, of sensuality, of the anti-hero
BEHAVIOUR	adult, always appropriate	senile or infantile, but always inappropriate
STAGE ROLE	stooge	comic

The description of the *auguste* seems to describe the *clochards* of Beckett we have met – the untidy hair of Didi; Gogo and, initially, Lucky; Krapp who actually shows his animality by being unshaven; the protagonists of *What Where* with their "*long grey hair*" (p. 469), and Pozzo's baldness;

the mismatched clothing of Didi and Gogo that fits neither of them or Krapp's too-short trousers; the big shoes of Estragon and of Krapp; the clumsiness of all of them; their obscene, absurd ranting; the equivalence of senile and infantile behaviour in Nagg and Nell.

Up to this point Beckett's anti-heroes would seem a perfect match for their circus cousins, but in fact the former possess a complexity lacking in the latter. In the circus environment, the roles of mocker/mocked can be reversed and the law whereby the *clown blanc* makes fun of the *auguste* can be turned on its head, with the *auguste* not necessarily the object of abuse and trickery but the abuser.[25] In Beckett compresence of the *blanc/auguste* functions within the same character is the rule rather than the exception as in the circus. This generates a destabilising short-circuit both of rational logic and of the "parallel" logic of the clownish *ludus*.

In Beckett the alternation of the roles of comic and stooge is less clearly defined than in the circus. In the case of Beckett's characters one can generally say that a function of comic/stooge is portrayed by some couples: Clov stooge of Hamm (Hamm explicitly says so - Clov is there to give him the line),[26] Lucky stooge of Pozzo, Willie stooge of Winnie. The situation is more complicated in the cases of Didi/Gogo, Nagg/Nell and Mr/Mrs Rooney, where both functions alternate in both characters. It is possible to discern in these couples hints of dominant/passive character, but they are not clear or univocal enough to define the roles of comic/stooge. On closer inspection, in fact, their stage functions are always reversible.[27]

None of the repressive figures like Pozzo or Hamm, for example, ever maintain the coherence of the *clown blanc*. Though they may give the impression of being rational, law-abiding and authoritative, it can happen that the stage situation transforms them into derided victims of the *auguste*-characters who ironically find themselves taking on a coercive role. Didi and Gogo speak like educated people, with excellent use of language and cultural references, seeming almost academics, (when Vivian Mercier pointed this out, Beckett replied with the question, "who says they aren't?")[28] while maintaining a tramp-like appearance and infantile emotional state. Consider the change in fortunes between the first and second act of *Godot*. In the first act Pozzo is the dominating figure over all and is even able to maltreat Lucky with impunity, without paying any attention to Vladimir's protests. In the second, his weakness is obvious right from his stage entrance: he is blind and shabby, he stumbles, falls and when he asks for help from what he thinks are two passers-by, Didi and Gogo get their revenge by intimidating their former tyrant. But even in act 1 Pozzo had shown himself to be two-faced, for our first impression of tyranny towards Lucky is modified by the revelation (we will never be sure it is true) that in fact it is Lucky who is cruel and heartless towards Pozzo: "je n'en peux plus... plus supporter... ce qu'il fait... pouvez pas savoir... c'est affreux... faut qu'il s'en aille... (*il brandit les bras*)... je deviens fou" (p. 46). The cunning of the dominant character and the stupidity of the passive one are two completely reversible values.

Their psychological complementarity is revealed in the feelings of love shown by kisses and embraces and their opposite in outbursts of rage and in fighting. Both manifestations are based on a certain degree of aggression found in comic duos, the aggression of clowns, which is inoffensive. The clowns' expansive nature leads them to exaggerate every manifestation of emotion, which often implies violating the physical boundaries between people. The clown is allowed to go beyond the limits of discretion, of the individual and of respect for the other. He breaks the common social norms applicable in adult society and is allowed to do so solely because of his childish, animal, crazy eccentricity.

Body movement, in relation to acquisition of knowledge and of social role, can be divided into two basic attitudes – 1) ABSTRACT, associated with sight and 2) CONCRETE, associated with touch. The first implies movement limited to "demonstrating", to virtual behaviour and a a body considered as "expressive means of special thoughts and of acknowledgement of the objective rules of space", while the second implies the actual action of grasping, of real behaviour and a body used as "means of squatting a familiar or unfamiliar space, or in any case a space that is not interpreted".[29]

In the rational adult world human behaviour is regulated by the former. The individual applies his mental faculties to a reality from which he remains materially separated, and his efforts at understanding are entirely abstract and intellectual. In states of infantile and/or pathological irrationality, by contrast, it is permissible to bypass knowledge and to grab the object of desire. Those who live outside social boundaries, savages, children or madmen, do not recognise a space or a situation that requires abstract interpretative behaviour and they invade the space, grabbing, clutching, swallowing. Think of the joyous invasion of space by Harpo Marx, who not only carries around with him a world of accessories, but grabs any object or person he meets, with carnivalesque violence. It is no chance that Artaud, in *The Theatre and its Double*, cites the Marx Brothers as an example of his concept of actor, and he frequently uses the term "saisir" = to grab.

But these irruptions and their underlying aggression are never harmful - they break the rules of society but never cause physical harm. And even the social subversion is somehow authorised by the fact that we are dealing with eccentric, out of the circle individuals.

The certainty of subversion in Beckett is anything but reassuring, for the adult and child worlds are overlaid in a single, contradictory individuality, with the effect of overturning manifestations of love and hate. His characters are at the same time rational philosophers and silly clowns and when they come into violent contact with each other, their fights look like embraces and their embraces generate only frustration.

Among the effusions of affection, Nagg and Nell's kisses, the kiss alluded to from Willie to Winnie and Vladimir and Estragon's embraces should be carefully examined.

Shortly after appearing out of their dustbins, Nagg and Nell have the usual conversation:

> NAGG. - Tu dormais?
> NELL. - Oh non!
> NAGG. - Embrasse.
> NELL. - On ne peut pas.
> NAGG. - Essayons.
> *Les têtes avancent péniblement l'une vers l'autre, n' arrivent pas à se toucher, s'écartent.*
> NELL. - Pourquoi cette comédie, tous les jours? (p. 29)

The absurd, paradoxical situation that has brought them to live in rubbish bins does not stop Nagg from asking his elderly wife for a kiss. Her calm reply acknowledges the impossibility of doing so, but Nagg does not desist, so the pair try pathetically to lean out of their bins and bring their faces closer. No chance - Nell was right and she it is who stigmatises their clumsy attempt as "farce" (p. 99) played out by them every day. Their desire for tender physical contact is frustrated by the material impossibility and annulled by the surrounding context.

Of a different nature is the ambiguous allusion to a hypothetical kiss in Willie's final action in *Happy Days*. Winnie is sinking ever deeper into the sand and Willie goes up to her with a strange look ("don't look at me like that!" p. 167), whether to shoot her with the pistol or proffer a last sign of affection we do not know. Love and hate are intermingled in the same pseudo-action, in its polyvalent allusion to the realm of affection with countless shades of ambiguity.

The play containing most physical contact is *En attendant Godot*, where the characters touch, embrace, fall on top of and hit each other. Vladimir and Estragon's embraces are always somewhat uncalled for, an unexpected consequence that desecrates their sentimental value and emotional content. They either separate hurriedly because closeness has revealed the other's smell, or they clumsily lose their balance.

> ESTRAGON. - [...] Voyons, Didi. (Silence.) Donne ta main! (Vladimir se retourne.) Embrasse-moi! (Vladimir se raidit.) Laisse-toi faire! (Vladimir s'amollit. Ils s'embrassent. Estragon recule.) Tu pues l'ail!
> VLADIMIR. - C'est pour le reins. (p. 21)

Estragon's desire to console results in Vladimir softening up again, the two companions become friends again, but their proximity reveals the stench of Vladimir, so Estragon springs back swiftly, saying that his breath stinks. Each to their own, as Hamm would say, because "ESTRAGON. - Lui pue de la bouche, moi des pieds" (p. 65).

The two are linked in another embrace when, out of fear, they flee into each other's arms. This time Pozzo has unwittingly terrified them with his arrival and he finds them "*enlacés, la tête dans les épaules, se détournant de la menace, ils attendent*" (p. 28). Or at the beginning of act 2, Estragon abandons himself so completely to the embrace that he risks falling when Vladimir loosens his clasp:

> *Estragon lève la tête. Ils se regardent longuement, en reculant, avançant et penchant la tête comme devant un objet d'art, tremblant de plus en plus l'un vers l'autre, puis soudain s'étreignent, en se tapant sur le dos. Fin de l'étreinte. Estragon, n'étant plus soutenu, manque de tomber.* (pp. 81-82)

The violence indulged in by Beckett's characters, whether erotic-aggressive or conflictual, is of a clownish nature, in that its effect is always comical. Common actions of clowns include punches, kicks, falls and shoves, but they are of the kind that does not hurt, nor kill, at which, therefore, one can laugh. The clown's pistol shoots blanks or out pops a flag with "bang!" written on it. It is a weapon conceived not to kill but to deride. Likewise all the tumbling that produces joyful contact with matter and with the ground is never intended to seriously damage the other, only to make fun of him.

It was innocuous violence, of which Chaplin was very proud, praising the safety of his productions: "no member of my cast was injured in any of our pictures. Violence was carefully rehearsed and treated like choreography. A slap in the face was always tricked".[30] The actor, however, recognised the profound impact of psychological and social aggression, because "when you kick a portly gentleman there [on his bottom], you strip him of all his dignity".[31]

The conflicts we find in Beckett's theatre are of various kinds: from psychological violence, with guilt complexes, threats of abandon, cynical pressure, to verbal or actual physical violence. Verbal violence includes insults and shouting. There are characters that lose their patience and shout their exasperation at others (Vladimir at Pozzo who doggedly refuses to understand him, p. 43; Winnie at Willie to attract his attention, p. 139 et seqq.; the stationmaster in *All That Fall* to his subordinate, p. 180 et seqq.; Hamm to all his peers). Or there are those who impose their dominance on the weak (Pozzo to Lucky and Pozzo with all the rest; again, Hamm, the "great dictator" of Beckett's universe, towards all around him), manifesting their attacks on others even just with a peremptory, "military" tone of voice. Often, too, these outbursts of anger are accompanied by various insults. These insults for them are a type of aggression on the whole joyous and innocuous, though energetic. This is evident in the playful exchange of Vladimir and Estragon who "play at insults", which we give in the English version, as the French original has only the generic indication "*echange d'injures*" (p. 106):[32]

> ESTRAGON: That's the idea, let's abuse each other.
> [*They turn, move apart, turn again and face each other.*]
> VLADIMIR: Moron!
> ESTRAGON: Vermin!
> VLADIMIR: Abortion!
> ESTRAGON: Morpion!
> VLADIMIR: Sewer-rat!
> ESTRAGON: Curate!
> VLADIMIR: Cretin!
> ESTRAGON: [*With finality.*] Crritic! [...]
> VLADIMIR: How times flies when one has fun! (pp. 70-71)

Physical brutality can be divided into two types - staged and evoked. Several times in *Godot*, Vladimir refers to the beatings and ascertains, firstly, that Estragon was not a victim of them, then, the boy sent by Godot. These too are attacks we feel are harmless, since the supposed victims cannot remember them and are quite uninterested in recalling the hypothetical episodes. There are two kinds of bodily abuse - direct contact between individuals (kicks, punches, slaps and so on) and throwing of – more or less – blunt objects. The latter has its own specific nature, known in the circus but massively enlarged on in silent cinema.

In the world of American cinema at the beginning of the century the term "slapstick" came into use to indicate this particular type of clownish violence. By association slapstick began to be used for all acts of aggression involving throwing any kind of object at a human target –

and its most recurring image in silent cinema is the pie in the face.

A nice example of this might be Beckett's Winnie, who not only surprisingly spits, hitting an imaginary person with her own bodily liquids, but she strikes Willie, hidden behind the mound, with her parasol. Then she throws the empty medicine bottle at him. In the first version of the play (later modified during production) it hits Willie, drawing blood, but does not provoke a verbal reaction. Willie stays silent and what follows is pure pantomime:

> *she strikes down at him with beak of parasol* [...]. *She strikes again. The parasol slips from her grasp and falls behind mound* [...], *tosses cap and bottle away in WILLIE's direction. Sound of breaking glass.* [...] *Top back of WILLIE's bald head, trickling blood* [...]. (p. 141)

The physically inoffensive character of the violence of Beckett's clowns is well summed up in the Chinese torture suggested by the Spectator in *Eleutheria*. Armed with pincers and catheter (p. 142), the torture – clearly "Chinese" as in old vaudeville cliché – attempts to make Victor confess something that does not exist. His terror is simply ridiculous. The mere mention or threat of physical violence is enough to coerce him. This is a sadistic threat but on the whole objectively an innocuous one. The metaphorical allusions, however, are strongly subversive, recalling the cruelty of Artaud: "dans le droit fil du Théâtre de la Cruauté d'Artaud [...] l'on fait venir un tortionnaire chinois afin qu'il fasse subir à Victor un interrogatoire".[33] The connection with Artaud is mentioned elsewhere by Blin and Barrault. Roger Blin, Beckett's first director, was one of the few friends and supporters of Artaud when he was still alive. Blin admitted that the first Lucky he directed "devenait un personnage d'une cruauté formidable",[34] while Barrault firmly insisted that if Artaud had known Beckett he would have admired him greatly, since "le théâtre de Beckett est un parfait théâtre de la cruauté".[35]

As well as underlying psychological and emotional dynamics, this joyous, subversive violence also sets in motion spatial dynamics. Here we must turn our attention to an area little explored by critics of Beckett –

that of stage space. In this manifestation of comic gesture the characters not only bring into play the relationship with their peers, but also their perception of actual space and interrelation with this. The character, in his display of aggression, is no longer simply related to himself or to the others, but to his own body *within* space.

3.3. Banana skin

Beckett's characters move throughout space, although – and despite the fact that – this is often very constricted. There are rooms closed against an external menace (*Fin de partie, Krapp, Film*, but also *Footfalls, Rockaby, Eh Joe* etc.), a strip of ground which they cannot abandon (*Godot*) or actual cages of matter (the mound of sand in *Happy Days*, the urns of *Play*, Hamm's wheelchair. The space is claustrophobic, suffocating and apparently inhibits all movement. In reality the characters move around continuously, not only with actual gestures and movements in space, but also with allusions and evocations of speech. Consider, for example, the recurring mention of hanging in *Godot*: Didi and Gogo, wishing to make time pass as quickly as possible, are always trying to invent new games and pastimes. One of these is "playing at hanging themselves".

> ESTRAGON. - Si on se pendait?
> VLADIMIR. - Ce serait un moyen de bander.
> ESTRAGON (*aguiché*). - On bande?
> VLADIMIR. - Avec tout ce qui s'ensuit. [...] Tu ne savais pas ça?
> ESTRAGON. - Pendons-nous tout de suite. (p. 21)

The action is only verbally evoked, for the pair will never have their wish. Yet it is full of multiple references, first of all, to clownish violence, because hanging is in itself a "thème classique d'Entrée de cirque".[36] Hanging someone by the neck until he is dead is not seen for its destructive and irreversible aspects, but as a *ludus*, perhaps with an obscene aim. Indeed another of the references is to the obscene sphere of sex, or rather to solitary satisfaction of the instinct. When Estragon suggests the game to his friend, he is immediately delighted because hanging, one knows, provokes erection. Estragon is fascinated by the unimagined consequences of this game and remains obsessed by the idea the whole time, right until the final gag. The paradoxical connection between hanging and erection has a famous precedent in Joyce's *Ulysses*, where the characters get into an excited argument over capital punishment. But rather than considering its social or humane aspects, they concentrate on the particular effect hanging has on the nerve centres of the genitals:

> -There's one thing it hasn't a deterrent effect on, says Alf.
> -What's that? says Joe.
> -The poor bugger's tool that's being hanged, says Alf.
> -That so? says Joe.
> -God's truth, says Alf. I heard that from the head warder that was in Kilmainham when they hanged Joe Brady, the invincible. He told me when they cut him down after the drop it was standing up in their faces like a poker.
> -Ruling passion strong in death, says Joe, as someone said.
> -That can be explained by science, says Bloom. It's only a natural phenomenon, don't you see, because on account of the...[37]

And he continues with the scientific explanation of this phenomenon.

Carefree hangings, without the obscene ambivalence of Beckett and Joyce, can be found in Laurel and Hardy films. In *The Devil's Brother* (1933) and *Way Out West* (1937) Stan is obliged to hang Ollie, but this results only in comic effects and not in death, and in *Going Bye Bye* (1934) Stan says "aren't you going to hang him right away?" referring to a shady, threatening character whom he and his sidekick had had condemned to death. The logic underlying this idea is that which follows paths different from normal – rules of the game, childish or dissociative psychological processes. It is the parallel logic behind the actions of Vladimir and Estragon.

Their dissociative disorder is radicalised into obsessive manias, so Gogo never forgets the idea of this brilliant entertainment and mentions it several times, often in a roundabout way, especially when boredom seems to be winning over their ability to pass the time: ("ESTRAGON (*regardant l'arbre*). - Dommage qu'on n'ait pas un bout de corde. [...] Fais-moi penser d'apporter une corde demain", p. 74) or in the negative when Estragon does not remember the tree in Act 2 ("VLADIMIR. - Mais si. Tu ne te rappelles pas. Il s'en fallu d'un cheveu qu'on ne s'y soit pendu", p. 84).

Until finally, yet another suggestion of hanging at the end, even more ambiguous and pathetic because Godot has not arrived, provoking the trousers-down gag.

> ESTRAGON. - Viens voir. (*Il entraîne Vladimir vers l'arbre. Ils s'immobilisent devant. Silence.*) Et si on se pendait?
> VLADIMIR. - Avec quoi?
> ESTRAGON. - Tu n'as pas un bout de corde?
> VLADIMIR. - Non. [...]
> ESTRAGON. - Attends, il y a ma ceinture.
> VLADIMIR. - C'est trop court.
> ESTRAGON. - Tu tireras sur mes jambes.
> VLADIMIR. - Et qui tirera sur le miennes?
> ESTRAGON. - C'est vrai.
> VLADIMIR. - Fais voir quand même. (*Estragon dénoue la corde qui maintient son pantalon. Celui-ci, beaucoup trop large, lui tombe autour des chevilles. Ils regardent la corde.*) (p. 132)

The rope is too short to carry out the plan and Estragon gets to the end in a grotesque pose with his trousers round his ankles. This image contaminates a comic cliché with a pathetic *tableau* depicting failure, impossibility of action and the inescapability of cyclical time. In that tragicomic image the spectator recalls all the games, the pastimes and the conflicts that have taken place in the two acts without time having progressed at all, and perceives the sensation of the circular path of time-space. Estragon, frozen with his trousers down, proposing to separate from his friend ("si on se quittait?" p. 133) and admitting his weariness ("je ne peux plus continuer comme ça", ibid.) is a figure that is tragic and comic at the same time. Emotion and laughter mingle and act upon each other. The comical effect is no longer that of a cliché, but something different and bitter tasting. Something that is missing in Laurel and Hardy's *You're Darn Tootin'* (1928) where the act of pulling down the trousers of passers-by is repeated and developed ad infinitum, or in *From Soup to Nuts* (1928), where the waiter serves the salad in his underpants because he was asked for an "undressed salad". Nor is it found when Charlot loses his trousers while dancing in *The Gold Rush* (1925), or when the circus *auguste* loses his trousers when teased by his companions.[38] Beckett's characters express a bitterness and sense of frustration that is shared by the audience, together with the feeling that all is vain, both tears and laughter, never freeing themselves from the paradoxical necessity of carrying on, continuing with this mad life.

The action of hanging is only evoked, we do not see it on the stage, yet it maintains all its significance of gesture and when Didi and Gogo plan the game, a real pantomime arises before the eyes of the spectator, where the pair clumsily hunt for a rope, try the branch for strength, help each other to climb up and so on. Likewise in *Fin de partie* we see Nagg and Nell scratching each other's backs or scratching on the edge of the dustbin. There is no action, but their dialogue is so strongly evocative that is visualises the absurd scene.

> NAGG. - Tu peux me gratter d'abord?
> NELL. - Non. (*Un temps.*) Où?
> NAGG. - Dans le dos.
> NELL. - Non. (*Un temps.*) Frotte-toi contre le rebord.
> NAGG. - C'est plus bas. Dans le creux.
> NELL. - Quel creux?
> NAGG. - Le creux. (*Un temps.*) Tu ne peux pas? (*Un temps.*) Hier tu m'as gratté là.
> NELL (*élégiaque*). - Ah hier!
> NAGG. - Tu ne peux pas? (*Un temps.*) Tu ne veux pas que je te gratte, toi? (pp. 34-35)

The evolution of the dialogue creates an image of gesture, of movement and brings to life a virtual pantomime that will never actually be seen. We might imagine a faint attempt by Nagg to scratch himself on the edge of the bin, as the kiss asked for results in the characters actually leaning forward, but the actions remain unfinished, suspended in an eternal wish.

Beckett's theatre is rich in clear gestures, although their quality lies in a special energy, which is restrained and has countless nuances so the characters do not merely repeat clownish pantomimes but do them with an identical form and disconcerting effect. Being de-contextualised, the routines acquire much more significance than is found in the ingenuous performance of the clowns.

The gestures can be minimal and still maintain their pantomime comedy. For example, Winnie in Act 2 is stuck up to her neck in the sand and has little left to move, but she continues to use what remains of her body to keep herself company - she pokes her nose out, blows out her cheeks to look at them, makes funny faces that miniaturise the frenetic manual activity of Act 1 when, though immobile from her waist down, she gesticulated endlessly, using all the "toys" in her black bag. Or gestures can expand in actual space to the point of becoming authentic pantomimes. The majority of examples are found in *Godot* where, in a general effect of inaction, which serves to convey the waiting, there are several moments of activity. The macro-action of perpetual waiting is peppered with micro-actions and movements in space. Let us first consider simple movements in space, that is, pantomimes.

No fewer than three plays open with a long instruction concerning mimed action: *Eleutheria*, which contains two parallel actions in two separate stages, one of which is without dialogue, only pantomime; *Fin de partie*, where we find Clov busy about his daily activities while all is resting in the room; and *Krapp's Last Tape*, where old Krapp does an authentic gag with his bananas and tapes. We might also partially include *Happy Days* in this category, where Winnie marks her incessant flow of words with frenetic physical activity, making the best she can of every single physical possibility remaining. These movements may be clumsy, like those of Clov or of O in *Film*, or comical in contrast with the spoken dimension.

Other movements are more articulated in the space and the time of the plot, almost becoming *tableaux*. In *Godot* Estragon "*suce méditativement le bout*" of the carrot (p. 27) in a pose that is ridiculous and obscene at the same time, like that of Krapp, who "*meditatively eating banana [...], puts end of banana in his mouth and remains motionless*" (p. 216). Estragon and Krapp are laughable in this pose because they seem to waste too much of their intellectual energy in the simple act of feeding themselves. They seem to "meditate" on a mechanical action that only needs to be done instinctively. Their fixed pose is obscene in that it alludes to *fellatio*, since to a childlike mind bananas and carrots are associated with the male sexual organ.

In *Godot* the characters' gaze becomes comic when Didi, Gogo and Pozzo look at the sky contemporaneously and when Didi and Gogo scour the horizon. In both cases we smile at the clumsiness of their clownish movements and their incoherence with the unfolding of the drama. In fact the *tableaux* seem to block the development of the story with nuggets of movement that have their own value. Or rather, they have their function as elementary comment and illustration of the dialogue. Twice the three characters look at the sky and in both cases the gesture describes what the lines say. When Vladimir asks himself "la nuit ne viendra-t-elle jamais?" (p. 49), immediately "*tous les trois regardent le ciel*" (ibid.) and shortly afterwards, when Pozzo mentions the night, he asks his captive "audience" also to look at the sky whence night will descend: "ah oui, la nuit. (*Lève la tête.*) Mais soyez donc un peu plus attentifs, sinon nous n'arriverons jamais à rien. (*Regarde le ciel, sauf Lucky qui s'est remis à somnoler. Pozzo, s'en apercevant, tire sur la corde.*) Veux-tu regarder le ciel, porc! (*Lucky renverse la tête.*) Bon, ça suffit. (*Ils baissent la tête.*)" (p. 51).

Of another type is the gaze of Vladimir and Estragon towards the horizon in Act 2, when they stare at the audience looking for some kind of presence, as does Clov, less extemporaneously, with a telescope. When in *Godot* Didi and Gogo run across the stage in anxious agitation because they think someone was coming, they are two clowns, they are Laurel and Hardy who flee tripping over each other. "*il entraine Vladimir vers la coulisse gauche, le met dans l'axe de la route, le dos à la scène. [...] Il court vers l'autre coulisse. Vladimir le regarde par-dessus l'épaule. Estragon s'arrête, regarde au loin, se retourne. Les deux se regardent par-dessus l'épaule. [...] Ils continuent à se regarder un petit moment, puis chacun reprend le guet*" (p. 105). Although Clov is alone, he is no less clumsy than his colleagues, so the act of surveying the horizon with a telescope is transformed into a comic routine of going up and down the ladder and forgetting objects: "*il monte sur l'escabeau, braque la lunette sur le dehors. Elle lui échappe des mains, tombe [...]. Il descend de l'escabeau, ramasse la lunette, l'examine, la braque sur la salle [...]. Il baisse la lunette, se tourne vers Hamm [...]. Il monte sur l'escabeau, braque la lunette sur le dehors [...]*" (p. 45).

As a variation on the pantomime of gazing, we might consider the pantomime of concentration, for both involve the immobility, pretending to be deep in thought, of the *tableaux*, and ostentatious gesture. Pozzo forgets the subject of his discourse and asks the two tramps to help him find the thread of it, so "*tous les trois se découvrent simultanément, portent la main au front, se concentrent, crispés*" (p. 57). They all mime concentration in a somewhat elementary mode, using the cliché of the hand on the forehead. In the second act, this gesture is repeated by Vladimir and Estragon alone, but while the French version simply indicates "*ils réfléchissent*" (p. 91), the English one plainly refers to Act 1, as they remove their hats and think deeply:

> ESTRAGON: Let me see. [*He takes off his hat, concentrates.*]
> VLADIMIR: Let me see. [*He takes off his hat, concentrates. Long silence.*] Ah! [*They put on their hats, relax.*] (p. 60)

When watching this second pantomime the spectator recognises the identical image as in Act 1 and can interpret the action of Vladimir and Estragon as a recurring, prelogical routine. Taking off their hats to think better attributes their action to an infantile or clownish sphere, where relations of cause and effect are governed by anarchical, ludic logic, so better concentration does not merely derive from mental effort, but from freeing the head from any physical constriction. The elementary simplification of the thought process, which we would expect to be internal and internalised, is instead externalised with an inverted cliché - concrete for abstract – when we would expect the contrary.

Movements of the body in space can be found even in semi-immobile or concealed characters like Willie, who reveals his hidden activity by glimpses of the newspaper he is reading or by grotesque noises. Also, in plays without a comic dimension, like *Ghost Trio* and *Ohio Impromptu*, where, however, there are flashes of ridiculous pantomime. In the former, the man reacts clumsily to the female voice, in the latter, the reader obeys the blows of the listener and quickly scans the pages for the point mentioned.

A separate category is the pantomime of falling, tripping and losing one's balance, whose archetypal comic valence made these actions a commonplace of clowning and silent cinema. In cinema production, falls are considered as an authentic comic technique, known as pratfall, falling down on one's bottom. The stage technique has the broader meaning of physical imbalance. The body's equilibrium is a basic foundation of western culture and if it is disturbed this is "punished" by an emotional distancing that often provokes laughter. Beckett challenges this principle in various ways, not always through the use of comedy. His prose, indeed, is full of characters who prefer, instead of the upright position, the horizontal one of crawling or lying on the ground or on a bed, thus confounding the victory over animality obtained by *homo erectus*. The supine, horizontal body, in decomposition, opposes the hierarchy of face-high and body-low.[39] The comic body in itself contains a destabilising anomaly. When it encounters space, it always does so in dissociated ways, with its principle being that of imbalance.

The pattern of falling recurs often in Beckett, though in different ways. It ranges from a minimal degree of overbalancing to the flat-out fall or to actual tumbling. In the play fragment *Human Wishes*, later abandoned, we encounter a character who is dumb and expresses himself exclusively through gesture, Levett, who is introduced by the words of the other characters as a drunkard and shown on stage according to this description. He is the stereotype of the *auguste*, "reluctantly drunk, in great coat and hat, which he does not remove, carrying a small bag" (p. 299), whose movements are so unsteady that he risks falling: "he advances unsteadily into the room [...] emits a single hiccup of such force that he is almost thrown off his feet [...]. His unsteady footsteps are heard on the stairs" (ibid.). The comic effect of overbalancing is rendered grotesque by the cause, the drunkenness that makes him hiccup, so that the hiccup destabilises his already precarious balance.

We saw in *Godot* that Estragon, after embracing Vladimir, almost fell when his friend stopped holding him, but this is not the only point where one of the characters loses his balance. Indeed in *Godot* balance is constantly being threatened. The characters move clumsily and often trip, when engaged in their strange activities. Estragon, when showing his sore leg to his friend "*chancelle*" and "*manque de tomber*" (p. 94) several times. Shortly afterwards he and his companion, tangled together, bounce around the stage "*les corps emmêlés, ils titubent à travers la scène*" (p. 97). Thus we come to the final scene when they argue over the rope to hang themselves "*ils prennent chacun un bout de la corde et tirent. La corde se casse. Ils manquent de tomber*" (p. 133). Yet, as if conscious of this physical defect, Didi and Gogo had even tried to improve their balance by doing the tree yoga exercise, posture 52 of Hatha Yoga[40] – but even there, "*titubant*" (p. 108).

Clov, too, in a rash gesture nearly falls off the ladder because he loses his balance, "*lève les yeux au ciel et le bras en l'air, les poings fermés. Il perd l'équilibre, s'accroche à l'escabeau*" (p. 99), and Krapp saves himself at the last minute from one of the most stereotypical falls in Beckett's universe - slipping on a banana skin. Absolutely the most frequently used comic cliché in Hollywood cinema, it can be found with other variations as to the material slipped on, but with the banana skin it maintains its implied connotations to the obscene, alluded to by the shape of the fruit, and to the infantile. Harpo Marx threw banana skins on the road in *Horse Feathers* (1932) and circus clowns deliberately put them in each other's path to make fun of their antagonists. Banana skins are the joyous overturning of the vertical position, a childishly obvious prelude to the catastrophic consequence. Krapp's banana skin is part of an episode so tightly constructed dramatically as to form a micro-scene within surrounding events. He unpeels the first banana and throws the skin down by his feet, "*he treads on skin, slips, nearly falls, recovers himself, stoops and peers at skin and finally pushes it, still stooping, with his foot over edge of stage into pit*" (p. 216). When he then has to throw away the second banana skin, he throws it directly "*into pit*" (ibid.), this time cunningly, but the comic effect is the same as before, being a malicious reminder of the first one.

We might exclude as a pratfall Willie rolling down the mound within which Winnie is disappearing, for it is not quite a fall – his instability does not threaten a vertical position as he is already crawling on the sand. So pratfalls ending with bottom on the ground are mainly found in *Godot*.

Lucky's dance introduces a tragicomic dynamic that combines the various pantomime elements analysed so far. When Pozzo obliges Lucky to dance for Didi and Gogo, he performs a dance that is not described in the stage directions. We can guess at its movements from the title Lucky gives to it and the reactions to the performance from the improvised audience. Pozzo actually asks the two friends what they think was the title of what they have seen and they have different interpretations, given below both in the English and French versions, which are not the same:

ESTRAGON: La mort du lampiste	ESTRAGON: The Scapegoat's Agony
VLADIMIR: Le cancer du vieillard	VLADIMIR: The Hard Stool
POZZO: La danse du filet (p. 56)	POZZO: The Net. (p. 39)

The movements represent the dancer's convulsive attempt to free himself from a net in which he is imprisoned, but might also give the impression of an agony, as suggested by terms "cancer", "stool" and the unequivocal "agony", in substitution for the more anonymous "mort". The "lampiste" is rendered in English as the scapegoat, clarifying the allusion only possible in French where the lamplighter represents the lowest social level. In the Fifties there was a very common joke, transformed by other cultures with different butts, which divided human beings into men, women and a lamplighter. The use of the singular noun adds to the isolation of this already marginal figure of the humble profession.

The dance is followed by a second performance by Lucky, a monologue that provokes uncontrollable reactions from his spectators and an escalation of violence that turns against him. Pozzo has made him put on a hat, so he can think, the magic stage costume that marks the beginning of the show and Lucky is drawn out of his catatonia. While Lucky vomits his meaningless flow of words, the three spectators react with a counter-scene, at first rather surprised, then disappointed and protesting.

> *Attention soutenue d'Estragon et Vladimir. Accablement et dégoût de Pozzo. Premières murmures d'Estragon et Vladimir. Souffrances accrues de Pozzo. Estragon et Vladimir se calment, reprennent l'écoute. Pozzo s'agite de plus en plus, fait entendre des gémissement. Exclamations de Vladimir et Estragon. Pozzo se lève d'un bond, tire sur la corde. Tous crient. Lucky tire sur la corde, trébuche, hurle. Tous se jettent sur Lucky qui se débat, hurle son texte.* (pp. 59-61)

Their rage mounts gradually. The initial expectation and attention fades. Lucky's audience, both on and off stage, progressively begins to feel uncomfortable and this feeling increases as the unstoppable monologue continues and gains speed. The ever-faster rhythm, apparently without end, brings the listener to a state of hysteria, and finally to the physical necessity of somehow stopping Lucky. Pozzo tries to bring his slave to order as one would a runaway horse, pulling on the rope, but Lucky is unperturbed. They all start shouting and throw themselves upon him hoping he will stop, but the flow has started and it is not easily stemmed. Lucky continues to struggle and to shout out his speech. At this point, a brilliant idea - the hat, we need to take off his hat. Once again, cerebral activity is associated with headgear and if the flow is triggered by the hat, to stop it one must remove the hat. This is an infantile thought, which creates absurd relations of cause and effect between non-homogeneous elements.

The entire action is a slow progression towards an outburst of violence but again, this violence does not harm, being clownish aggression with paradoxical outcomes. In mime terminology the two movements would be called "slow-burn" and "chase". Slow-burn is an invasion of space by the character, done slowly, progressively and inexorably. Examples are the chase sequences in silent cinema that cover increasingly large spaces, spreading like wildfire throughout the whole town. Think of *Cops* (1922) where Keaton goes from one scrape to another, ending with the entire Los Angeles police force chasing him. Or consider how fights break out in westerns: one man hits his rival, who is defended by a third, who hits another and so on, until the entire saloon is destroyed, they fall out into the street and involve the whole town. This paradoxical procedure, based on exaggeration, often ends with a chase scene. Though Vladimir, Estragon and Pozzo are static and do not make free use of space as in the examples from cinema mentioned above, they follow the pattern of slow-burn, as their resentment and impatience gradually grow and are manifested in degrees of progressively violent reaction. They move from murmurs and facial expression, physical unrest and exclamations to the first aggressive interaction of pulling at the rope, shouts and finally bodily assault on Lucky. This last movement is the capture following the chase, but of the latter there remains only the final moment, its violent conclusion.

The gag is not over with the capture, but the comic effect is prolonged by Lucky falling under the weight of the other three and by Vladimir's fascination with the hat.

> *Vladimir s'empare du chapeau de Lucky qui se tait et tombe. Grande silence. Halètement des vainqueurs. [...] Vladimir contemple le chapeau de Lucky, regarde dedans. [Pozzo] arrache le chapeau des mains de Vladimir, le jette par terre, saute dessus. [...] Il donne des coups de pied à Lucky. [...] Estragon et Vladimir mettent Lucky debout, le soutiennent un moment, puis le lâchent. Il retombe.* (pp. 62-63)

The chase and slow-burn end with Lucky's pratfall. Meanwhile Vladimir and Pozzo ingenuously vent their anger on the hat, the former hunting for its secret concealed within, as a child studies a puppet to discover how it moves, the latter pulling it here and there. Lucky is on the ground, exhausted. To pull him up with all his luggage the three perform a classic clown number, which consists of holding up a dead weight that collapses when let go. This game is complicated by the fact that Pozzo, in an attempt to prepare Lucky for departure, tries to hand him all the baggage, which Lucky weakly lets fall. The image of the three men linked together, staggering, and Pozzo trying to overload a body that can hardly stand up is exhilarating and in Act 2 is repeated with a significant variation - Pozzo is in Lucky's place.

When Pozzo and Lucky finally leave, the comic play continues off-stage. Lucky has hardly left the stage when Pozzo pulls the rope to stop him. There is big crash of falling luggage and departure is delayed. Their appearance in Act 2 opens and closes in the same way, except they both finish on the ground. The "entrée" of Act 2 is a catastrophic event involving all the characters in a single, disastrous fall from which they are unable to rise immediately, remaining on the ground in an absurd pose, though this is not perceived as such by the characters. The stage directions for the pratfall divide the scene as follows: 1) Pozzo and Lucky fall on entering, 2) Pozzo asks for help, 3) Vladimir and Estragon consider the advantage to themselves of helping him, 4) Didi and Gogo also fall down heavily.

> *[Pozzo] s'agrippant à Lucky qui, sous ce nouveau poids, chancelle [...]. Lucky tombe, en lâchant tout, et entraîne Pozzo dans sa chute. Ils restent étendus sans mouvement au milieu des bagages. [Vladimir] essaie de soulever Pozzo, n'y arrive pas, renouvelle ses efforts, trébuche dans les bagages, tombe, essaie de se relever, n'y arrive pas. [...] Estragon tire, trébuche, tombe. Long silence.* (pp. 108-115)

A long dialogue follows in which the characters are lying on top of each other on the ground without apparently losing their impassiveness - Lucky says nothing, Pozzo only after a while begins to groan, Didi and Gogo chat happily. This grotesque image is tragic and comic at the same time, and unquestionably destabilising and alienating. We feel like laughing at the clumsiness of characters who seem to be clowns that never learn from their mistakes, but we are distressed by the pathos they inspire in us. We know that Pozzo is (has become?) blind and Lucky is (has become?) dumb and, hearing the pathetic cries for help of the former, we cannot help thinking of his tyrannical behaviour in Act 1. We have the impression of an inescapable irony of fate, which overturns human destinies transforming the powerful into weak and the weak into tyrants. And yet our distress is mocked by the characters themselves, who transform pathos into laughter, with their carefree behaviour that disorients us - are these characters foolish clowns or sad human remnants? They are, of course, both.

The clownery with its falls and overbalancing, its ragged aspect and staggering walk, is never without the bitter sense of a cyclicality from which there is no escape, of an irreversible consumption, of the impossibility of saying and acting and, despite everything, of the obligation of following the progression of this sick life for ever. The symbolic value of the clown's fall has a clear affinity with the principle of disintegration of matter.[41]

All the *entrées*[42] of Beckett's characters are often irresistible pieces, both in his drama and his prose. There are Nagg and Nell who appear in their dustbins, first timidly showing just their fingers, then cautiously raising their heads, or there is Watt who appears on stage bumping into a porter, falling on the ground with his hat and luggage and knocking over the porter's milk can. Both of these are "entrées comiques" that follow the technical rules of clown comedy, but with overtones that are original to Beckett.

The scene in *Godot* when the four fall down may be thought of as an *entrée* ("une brève exposition vient nouer l'intrigue d'ou découlera une cascade de péripéties et bien entendu la chute finale"),[43] with its complex, clearly defined structure and may be considered not only pantomime (movement of the body in space), but a gag (body moving *in* the action).

3.4. Body in-action: the gag

Beckett often uses the words "gag" and "to gag" with different meanings, or rather with some of the various meanings acquired by the word in its long history, which it may be useful to review.

The word "gag", as a noun, originally meant something forced into the mouth to prevent speech and as a verb, the act of doing this. It is not clear what influence or evolution led it to indicate a stage device in theatre, that of improvising part of the dialogue to cover a lapse of memory or any other event. This is the first meaning of "to do a gag" in the performing arts. In music-hall, however, it starts to indicate a deliberate, prepared, preordained improvisation, an effect or stage-play studied in detail, to give an effect of spontaneity and extemporaneity. From being just useful improvisation, in music-hall the gag starts to be for the first time a premeditated, aesthetic construction.

Like all the technical equipment of popular theatre, the term moved from British music-hall to cinema, where it reached great heights with new and different elements, becoming variable and elusive. So this is not a term invented by filmmakers, though they did give it precise technical connotations. It indicates a micro-narrative element that is simple, but complete, carried out in the succession of exposition/evolution/resolution and inserted into the main story of the film. The simple plot of early comic films was deliberately interrupted by brief, stand-alone scenes, isolated from the overall story - the gag destructured and restructured the cinematic dramaturgy.[44] The gag is a "structure dynamique et démonstrative dans laquelle, à un exposé objectif des données, succède leur exploitation dans une certaine direction, puis le détournement de cette direction dans un sens inattendu, ce qui entraîne la *chute*, véritable «résolution», qui serait impossible sans l'enchaînement logique et irréversible des prémisses au développement et du développement au terme du cycle".[45]

The gag should not be confused with simple comic effects (falls, pulling faces, tripping etc.) that occur naturally – for example, as an involuntary accident – and which only art can transform into an aesthetic technique. The gag does not exist in real life, but is a completely artificial product, result of maieutic activity that organises real facts and presupposes a degree of premeditation that is incompatible with reality, though inspired by it. The gag should be interpreted not using the instinctive reactions that naturally accompany simple comic effects, but using rational, aesthetic intelligence.

While simple comic effects derive from "what" (what happens, what is said, what is done…), those of the gag derive from "how" – it is not so important what happens as how it happens. A basic comic effect can be obtained, for example, by a passer-by that slips on a banana skin and falls down. The gag will transform this event into a little story where laughter is provoked by the various degrees of evolution of the action. The fellow who falls will take part in a sequence something like this: he is walking along and sees the skin on the ground, he avoids it, he turns back and has forgotten the banana skin he had walked round, he slips and falls. We might synthesise the difference between gag and basic comic effect by describing the former as a "paradigm", which functions by accumulating distinguishing elements (the "how" becomes more precise by adding more and more modes), and the latter as a "syntagm", which works by substituting elements (the "what" proceeds by exclusion).

The gag results in defamiliarisation of reality and revelation of absurdity and automatism. It is structured in either 3 phases (exposition/development/resolution) or 2 phases (exposition/defamiliarisation). Its significance comes from the associations it creates, from its context. A gag is not nonsense or absence of logic, rather a process of contradicting a logic that makes another logic absurd. It is not a revelation of the unknown, but a fresh look at the already known. *"The gag [...] consists minimally of two basic phases which in themselves need not to be either comical or absurd, but which begin to evoke the sense of absurdity and laughter at the moment of their encounter"*.[46] The gag is a particular phenomenon of defamiliarisation that reciprocally annuls the rational logics of reality and of art, creating a free space for paradoxical mixing: *"pathos is one of the basic themes of humour. Depathetication is one of the basic principles of humour"*.[47]

Nonetheless, the term 'gag' is commonly used with a certain amount of ambivalence and polysemy, due to its evolution in the field of cinema. On the one hand, it was used with its technical meaning, but on the other, it passed into common usage. As the culture of cinema became known to the masses, so a vast public, unfamiliar with the field, was able to learn and use the term 'gag', often incorrectly. So the 'gag' has come down to contemporary criticism as a double-sided medal, both technical and commonplace, ambiguous and specific. For a long time its meaning remained equivocal, without a clear technical definition. Since it was only known in practice on the comedy set or music-hall stage, its interpretations were varied and sometimes contradictory.[48] Even today we still find it used to describe comic improvisation, a comic situation in general or a funny joke.[49] Some Beckett critics have associated the gag with the *lazzo*, tracing the evolution of this comic technique in a line running from the Commedia dell'Arte to Hollywood cinema, maintaining that gag and *lazzo* are the same thing. Stan Gontarski found an "extensive use of the *lazzo*" in Beckett: "many of the comic activities Beckett includes in his drama reflect the theatrical tradition in which he works, music-hall and vaudeville, those modern vestiges of low comedy and improvisation epitomized in the Commedia dell'Arte in which stock characters improvised around a set routine, the *lazzo*. [...] The *lazzo* finds its way into modern drama chiefly through the early comic film".[50] Similarly, Edith Kern, exploring the relationship between Beckett and the spirit of the Commedia dell'Arte, assumes that *lazzi* and gags can be considered similar, both being comic fragments, extrinsic or intrinsic to the action, scattered throughout the broad lines of the plot, with the function of emphasising the theatricality of the stage event, undermining the desire or the expectation of verisimilitude.[51]

Beckett uses the word 'gag' in the English version of *Pochade radiophonique* (English title *Rough for Radio II*) with its original meaning of "bandage" (p. 275). In the English version of *Catastrophe*, which has the same title as the first French version, we find the word "gag" (p. 459) translating the French "baîllon" (=bandage, p. 77): the director has made as much use as he wants of the actor sitting on a bench and now wants him to be completely silent, so the assistant suggests putting a gag on him. In English the expression contains an ambiguity that could overturn the meaning of the suggestion - if the assistant is suggesting, instead of an object to keep him quiet, giving him "a line", the director's reaction to this must be read as a refusal of silence or of words: "for God's sake! This craze for explicitation! Every i dotted to death! Little gag! For God's sake!" (p. 459).

Elsewhere Beckett is aware of the use made by cinema of the word 'gag' as a technical term. Although *Acte sans paroles II* and *Fragment de théâtre II* were originally written in French, Beckett employs the English word – now in common use throughout Europe – to signify a "short scene" with a flavour of improvisation. In the former, stage directions read "gags lorsqu'il s'habille et se déshabille" (p. 105), while in the latter, B, tired of the routine with A, comments "pour moi, ce gag a assez duré" (p. 51), with a faint negative hint of "farce". Also, in the director's notes for *Krapp's Last Tape* at the San Quentin Drama Workshop, he defines Krapp's near fall on the banana skin as "gag with skin".[52]

Beckett, therefore, includes gags in his plays and wants "action", since the gag is action structured according to precise aesthetic and dramatic criteria. The idea that Beckett's theatre includes action may seem a new one, as it is commonly considered to be essentially static and inactive. Yet the body of the actor or character on Beckett's stage, rather than being dominated by inaction, seems to us to be a body "in action".

If "movement" is the changing of a position or state, a mere shift, a passing situation, "action" is doing something concrete with an intrinsic ability to produce effects. To act is to produce effects on the part of an agent and its synonyms are to operate and to work, concepts that link action with the semantic area of *labor* – effort. Actions are often organised around various movements, which use the peripheral movements of the body – gestures.[53]

In Beckett, a small number of physical movements is able to create a rich pattern of actions, thanks to constant allusion to movements that are not made but are imagined by the spectator, or by reducing movements to their minimum, all of which is not suppression or removal, but miniaturisation of movements. The energy is restrained, referred to, alluded to, deviated, but always present. The action does not lose its inherent, necessary solidity, but is transformed in clowning, where maximum physical precision accompanies maximum lack of logic. Action in Beckett does not proceed in a linear, univocal way, which is why it is not seen, not perceived as action. It is achieved through fragments, dispersion and multiplicity. The main action of the drama seems to make no progression towards a final point, since Beckett disdains the central conflict of traditional theatre. Instead, we have a multitude of parallel oppositions – simultaneous or successive – that create constant tension. The obstacle of the plot, traditionally consisting of a negative event to be overcome, in Beckett is perceived as positive, is sought after, desired by the anti-heroes (while heroes seek to overcome it) and its resolution is feared, felt to be a threat. This is why the action is not considered solely for its effectiveness, but for its duration, which allows the characters their stage time and ludic entertainment. Effective action in Beckett's plays has a unique aspect, that of length, rhythm and intrinsic meaning. The progression is horizontal-circular, rather than vertical-linear, i.e. it does not proceed *through* space-time, but *within* space-time.

We can also distinguish two types of action - micro-actions, constructed on limited movements in space-time on stage and with greater or lesser effect on the overall plan of the work, and the macro-action of the plot. A Beckett gag is a micro-action that interrupts the plot flow, but which is a metaphor of it, being both a disturbed and disturbing process. It is a *mise en abyme* of stage action, or rather a *scene en abyme*.[54]

Beckett is quite clear on this, in an interview granted to Charles Marowitz in 1962, when the director asked to meet him to discuss *Acte sans paroles II*, which he hoped to stage in April. Marowitz met Beckett at the Closerie des Lilas in Paris and described the meeting, with ample quotations from the writer's own words. Talking about *Acte sans paroles*, Beckett drew a clear distinction between mime, mere body movement and action, maintaining that "for Beckett (as for Le Coq), Mime is not sufficient unto itself. The term itself does not apply to either of his mime-plays for they are merely (as named) acts without words. 'With Marceau', says Beckett, 'I always feel the absence of words; the need for them'. In his own mime works, actions are self-sufficient substitute for language. As for Mime itself, he thinks the art-form is being stretched beyond its bounds. Being asked to do things it cannot do by itself and which language does it better [...]. His interest is not so much in Mime but in the stratum of movement which underlies the written word". This excerpt contains so much that it must be examined point by point.[55]

Beckett seems interested not so much in movement in itself, but in that underground current beneath the flow of speech, that parallel language of gesture. As a language, a complex of standardised relationships used to communicate, that of gesture cannot be compared to that of the word, because in so doing we would be asking mime to overrun its own boundaries and invade a territory that is not its own, that of the word. By competing, it would lose its intrinsic qualities and nature. Mime has its own rules, chief of which is not to ape the word, otherwise gestural expression would risk appearing as language that is imperfect, instead of specific, as in the mime of Marcel Marceau. For Beckett, Marceau "mimed" words, so the spectator felt the lack of verbal expression. Beckett's mimed actions, on the other hand, are acts without words, or actions that have their own meaning. Speech, any kind of speech, is in itself an act, an organised sequence of cognitive acts,[56] if we accept as true the definition of act established by philosophical tradition, from Aristotle to scholasticism, as that which brings into being, that which makes possible the transition from potential to existence. Marceau's mime assumes the absence of words, Beckett's substitutes them, creating not a fabric of gestures, but of actions. It is no chance that his "mimes" are entitled "acts – that is, manifestation of acting – without words", because his characters do not *mime* the actions, they *do* them. Le Coq also agrees that the mime is not important in itself, but the movement, through which "the word is saved".[57]

In the "literary cul-de-sac"[58] mentioned earlier where Beckett found himself at the beginning of the Fifties, he acquired an almost obsessive interest in mime, producing various types of work – with varying success – that were based on or contained mime actions. These not only included finished, published texts of "actes sans paroles", but also the pantomime *incipit* of *Fin de partie* (Clov with the ladder and the windows) and of *Krapp's Last Tape* (Krapp and the routines with bananas, tapes and keys), as well as abandoned projects, which I will refer to conventionally as "Ernest & Alice" and "Mime du rêveur A". The first consists of a brief unpublished excerpt[59] with two characters, Ernest and Alice, who very strongly recall the dynamics between Winnie and Willie, with their personal conflicts and inability to separate from each other. The dialogue between the couple is enhanced by a gauche micro-pantomime that is limited in space but rich in symbolic content, for Ernest is obliged to go on the cross and Alice busies herself in satisfying his requests with incoherent forms of comfort. The atmosphere between sacred and profane desecrates both categories of the spirit, the couple's human relationship, presumably of love, and the theological origins of their actions (the cross, the oil, the salt, Ernest called "mon petit Jésus" by his partner).[60] The gag plays on this blasphemous ambiguity.

"Mime du rêveur A",[61] also called "Dreamer's Mime", as its sole protagonist is a dreamer, is an unfinished study for a mime in which the dreamer searches desperately in his pockets for a pair of spectacles then used to examine the audience. This develops as a single chain of various gags, where the character loses his balance several times and "plays" clownishly with three objects (a photo, a match and a magnifying glass), which he cannot handle properly but which he makes interact in the final twist: he puts the photo on the ground and observes it carefully with the magnifying glass until he burns his fingers with the match in his other hand. The result was an "unusual amount of music-hall humour"[62] which evidently left Beckett unsatisfied, for he then decided not to finish what we might consider as the first *acte sans paroles*.

L'Acte sans paroles I adopts the structure of "Mime du rêveur A" and develops through a single sequence of gags with only one character on stage. His behaviour follows the deviant logic of clowns and he constructs a series of actions that appear without sense, being reactions to enigmatic and/or elementary stimuli. His stage entrance is decidedly clownlike - he is pushed violently on stage by a hidden force, staggers and falls, gets up, dusts himself off, reflects. This fall scheme is repeated obsessively several times in an identical manner, almost becoming a gestural tic of the character, who continues to be a victim of events beyond his control. A spindly tree descends from the sky and stops halfway, suspended in the air, and when the character sits in its shade it folds up like a parasol. When a water carafe descends he cannot reach it, nor are the various sizes of cube that appear any help, for he climbs up on them, overbalances and falls. In short, every time that, following reflection, he embarks on an action, this is vilified by his failure. Even when he tries to free himself from this perverse game by leaving the stage, "someone" or "something" throws him back on stage, hurling him like a dead weight or rag doll. The only action he manages is to cut his nails when a pair of scissors appears from above, an everyday act, more an activity than a real action. The character in *Acte sans paroles I* is a *clown triste* who does not register frustration and his face remains impassive in a fascinating and intense deadpan. He does not learn from his mistakes, continues to fall down and has to dust himself off, but he is not cast down by his failures. He tries and re-tries the most fantastic solutions, such as lassoing the carafe, interpreting "his" reality with a very infantile creativity. In the end he is totally defeated. After receiving and losing objects for no apparent reason, all the things he had "played with" up till now disappear, while he remains impassive, staring into space. He does not even react to the fact that the much-desired carafe is now accessible – the play is set in a desert – nor does he try to escape from the stage any more.

The final image is of a character sitting on the ground, on a stage now truly deserted, with no more objects, looking at his hands. This gesture had occurred already during the appearing/disappearing routine, but now in the ending it acquires special significance. The *tableau*, strongly positioned at the end of the play, acts as a metaphor of all the actions he has carried out/suffered -[63] we see the man immobile, staring at his hands, the part of his body most closely linked with action, with *labor*. His hands are inactive, palms upwards, observed in their inactivity, or rather in their inability to deliberately complete an action. All premeditation is in vain, the only action he manages to conclude is the unsolicited and superfluous one of cutting his nails in a desert. Here we recall the comic numbers already discussed of the clown Grock, who obtained results not from his always disproportionate efforts applied to action, but from unforeseeable chance. The actions given by Beckett to his character speak of the impossibility of taking action without representing it on stage, but putting it into action. He is Tantalus dressed as a clown, who never learns but suspends the action and is ready to repeat the same routine ad infinitum, like the characters in *Play*. Or like Krapp, who wishes to give us an impression of cunning with his banana skin thrown into the audience, after the first one had made him fall, but whose gesture simply refers again to the fall and not to acquisition of knowledge. The unfinished gag highlights the impossibility of taking action and of learning anything, even in a semblance of flaunted slyness, like that of Krapp.

We might note that the man in *Acte sans paroles I*, like other anti-heroes in Beckett, wavers between two different types of action - that which is done and that which is suffered. "Suffering" by definition excludes "action" (Lat. *patior*=to suffer, to be passive), but in this case we are in the presence of both forces. The man acts on the reality around him and is defeated, but at the same time he is "acted on" by a mysterious energy that pushes him with violence, which appears and disappears at will.

The same principle dictates the actions of the two characters in *Acte sans parole*.

The obscure force is no longer embodied by the sound of a whistle as in *Acte sans paroles I*, but by a goad, whose function is clearly to prod the characters into action. Though defined in Beckett's opening stage directions as a "mime" (p. 105), this too is an act without words. The two characters carry out their frenetic activity at different speeds, and this becomes an authentic gestural pattern, like the recurring tic in *Acte sans paroles I*. This activity is dictated by someone/something with the power of starting the action from offstage. The goad is almost a third character whose function is to proclaim the stage fiction, representing the hand of the creator, whoever he might be - the author, the director, God - who prods the character and corresponds to the whistle in *Acte sans paroles I*, to Winnie's alarm clock that daily obliges her to begin a new day identical to all the rest ("begin, Winnie", p. 138), as well as to the light in *Play*, which shines sadistically on the faces of the three characters. It is a creator without a universal design, who restricts himself to imposing actions. The lack of a clear, recognisable aim, integral to the general plot, makes these actions almost self-referential, were it not for the shifts into other logics that open to the spectator the possibility that this action might be inspired by "another" kind of feeling.

Beckett's gags use the aesthetic structure of any comic scene, but their contrast with the principal action, already used in cinema gags, is absurd in nature, that is, the spectator cannot see any connection of cause and effect, which in cinema had been present. In Beckett's hands, the subversive capacity of this mechanism spreads like wildfire, destabilising the entire structure of the play, but also of how we acquire knowledge and how we interpret things. For example, after enjoying the gags of Vladimir and Estragon, the spectator leaves the theatre feeling he has been duped, that he has laughed at what appeared to be elementary comic routines, but which perhaps are much more than that. Likewise the spectator who expects to see a tragedy and who interprets what happens and what is said on stage in this sense is similarly frustrated, since he too is applying the wrong interpretative tools to Beckett's paradox, whose objective is precisely to demolish certainties and introduce doubt. *Not to represent doubt*, as something still existential, but to actually practice it, refusing even to seek consolation in doubt as an element of negative thought - Beckett's actions are doubt of doubt itself, a total submersion of the human element.

The comic content of the gags, nonetheless, remains greatly enjoyable and indeed it is precisely their intense comic energy that makes Beckett's game work. Gags in Beckett can contain gestures, words or noises, but they all highlight the physicality of the body, of locution and of sound, often without clear confines between them.

They are structured around obsessive repetition of the same gesture or action that becomes increasingly imperative. There is the gag where Lucky keeps hold of the luggage the whole time. This follows a much-used circus cliché, a number that Rémy called "Load and unload" (from 1910), when the circus-master orders the *auguste* to load and unload the suitcases. Pozzo orders Lucky to bring him certain items and each time the servant patiently puts down the luggage, gives him the object requested and goes back to pick up the suitcases. This cruel depiction of reality can coherently be attributed to Pozzo, especially when he is relating to Lucky.[64] The final comic effect is spread across a sequence that is divided into fragments. These fragments, which follow on each other in a logical sequence, are amplified by this repetition. The progression ends when Lucky falls to the ground with all the luggage, no less than three times - at the end of Act 1 and at the opening and closing of Act 2. The action does not pass unobserved by the spectator, for it is pointed out by Vladimir's hints, when he *"annonce qu'ils sont tombés à nouveau"* (p. 127) and by Estragon, who asks why Lucky does not put the luggage down. Pozzo continues to ignore Estragon's question and the latter, with childish insistence, continues to ask the same question: "pourquoi il ne dépose pas ses bagages?" (p. 39), until his angry outburst when he shouts, trying to simplify his question, awkwardly miming the act of carrying a heavy weight and speaking to Pozzo as if he did not share the same linguistic code:

> ESTRAGON (*avec force*). - Bagages! (*Il pointe son doigt vers Lucky.*) Pourquoi? Toujours tenir. (*Il fait celui qui ploie, en haletant.*) Jamais déposer. (*Il ouvre les mains, se redresse avec soulagement.*) Pourquoi? (p. 41)

Gogo is exasperated and uses the ungrammatical, elementary code we use with children or strangers who do not understand our language, endeavouring to illustrate his words with the stereotypic pantomime of someone carrying luggage. The gag effect continues well beyond Pozzo's answer ("c'est pour m'impressionner, pour que je le regarde", p. 42), till when Pozzo, who has forgotten what he was talking about, asks the pair to help him remember and Gogo, who instead has not forgotten the exchange of lines about the luggage, inopportunely returns to the subject, suggesting that it was what Pozzo was referring to:

> ESTRAGON (*triomphant*). - Ah!
> VLADIMIR. - Il a trouvé.
> POZZO (*impatient*). - Et alors?
> ESTRAGON. - Pourquoi ne dépose-t-il pas ses bagages?
> VLADIMIR. - Mais non!
> POZZO. - Vous êtes sûr?
> VLADIMIR. - Mais voyons, vous nous l'avez déjà dit.
> POZZO. - Je vous l'ai déjà dit.
> ESTRAGON. - Il nous l'a déjà dit? (p. 57)

Clov alludes to the same clown number of "load and unload" when he throws on the floor all the objects he was carefully picking up. This has the effect of a gag, because it develops as follows: 1) EXPOSITION: Clov begins to pick up objects scattered over the floor, 2) EVOLUTION: he becomes frenetic and starts theorising about universal order and 3) RESOLUTION: when ordered by Hamm "*laisse tomber les objets qu'il vient de ramasser*" (p. 79). His desire for order, which had started off his first action of "fabriquer un pue d'ordre" (ibid.), is negated and overturned by the indifference with which Clov throws the objects back where they were and leaves them there, in their untouchable chaos.

The mechanism of the "spread out" gag, which develops progressively at different times during the main plot, was well known to Hollywood. A classic example might be Groucho Marx's gag in *Duck Soup* where, as head of the State of Freedonia, he often has to leave suddenly in a sidecar, which regularly takes off without him. This is not just repetition with variations, but a scene separate from the main plot, divided into brief fragments, which comes out "in instalments" during the story. In Beckett's theatre, this technique corresponds to the precise need to create a recurrence of significance and signifier that can at the same time convey the musicality of speech and the infinitely cyclical nature of thought. There are countless examples. When Winnie reads the writing on her toothbrush, it is with difficulty owing to her extreme short-sightedness, and with comic overtones because, once deciphered, far from satisfying Winnie's curiosity, it raises a question that turns out to be of an obscene nature. "Pure... what?" (p. 129): thus begins Winnie's action – unable to decipher the small letters, she looks for her glasses in her bag, puts them on and tries to read, but can only get a few more words "genuine... pure... what?" (ibid.). While she continues with her monologue, she takes a handkerchief, cleans her glasses and tries again: "guaranteed... genuine... pure... what?" (p. 140). It is still not enough. She tries cleaning the handle of the toothbrush: "fully guaranteed... genuine pure..." (ibid.), she starts to clean her glasses again. She then busies herself with other activities and seems to have given up the idea of reading her toothbrush, until she pulls a magnifying glass out of her bag and with great difficulty manages to decipher only "fully guaranteed... genuine pure... hog's... setae" (p. 143). We feel that Winnie, having praised the style, the good old style, of the phrase, has forgotten the whole thing, but she returns to the content of the phrase, wondering to herself what a "hog" is. The gag is reiterated until the end of Act 1, when Winnie goes back to reading all of her toothbrush handle with the same doubt as to "hog", but this time she decides to ask Willie, who replies laconically "castrated male swine. [...] Reared for slaughter" (p. 159), provoking delight in Winnie and chilling the spectator with the cruel image of the castrated pig ready for slaughter.

En attendant Godot is a constant interweaving of gags "in instalments". Then there is the obscene pantomime of Estragon watching Vladimir, who has gone into the wings to urinate, and inciting him as if he were a boxer ("*Vladimir sort. Estragon se lève et le suit jusqu'à la limite de la scène. Mimique d'Estragon, analogue à celle qu'arrachent au spectateur les efforts du pugiliste*" p. 20), which is taken up again when Pozzo appears with some variations that transform it from a simple comic effect into a gag. To understand the comic effect, one must know the joke about the two friends at the theatre, to which Beckett certainly refers: while at the theatre, one of them goes to the toilet but gets the wrong door and unwittingly finds himself urinating on stage. When he comes back to his seat his friend says, " what a pity, you missed such a hoot, a fellow came on and pissed on the stage". In *Godot* the gag starts when Vladimir goes off to urinate, Estragon watches him from onstage and calls Pozzo to show him the spectacle but Pozzo, slow to act, does not manage to enjoy the scene. The surprise ending, when Pozzo arrives late, goes back to a genuinely comic dimension with the punch line of the joke – Estragon to Vladimir: "*tu as raté des choses formidables. Dommage*" (p. 49).

Another gag of this kind is the gestural 'catchphrase' found throughout the play and which denotes in differing ways the principal characters - Estragon's routine with his shoes and Vladimir's with his hat. From the very beginning we discover the former struggling with his shoes, trying to take them off, clearly because they are hurting him. He will repeat this attempt several times until Act 2, which opens with Estragon's shoes on stage and their owner denying ever having owned them. Vladimir's hat has the same function and the same rhythmic cadence in the actions of the character. From the outset it counters the gag with the boots. While Gogo is intent on his footwear, Didi is the same with his bowler hat:

> *il ôte son chapeau, regarde dedans, y promène sa main, le secoue, le remet.* [...] *Il ôte à nouveau son chapeau, regarde dedans.* [...]

Il tape dessus comme pour en faire tomber quelque chose, regarde à nouveau dedans, le remet. [...] Estragon, au prix du suprême effort, parvient à enlever sa chaussure. Il regarde dedans, y promène sa main, la retourne, la secoue, cherche par terre s'il n'en est pas tombé quelque chose, ne trouve rien, passe sa main à nouveau dans sa chaussure [...]. (p. 12)

For an instant both friends find themselves looking inside their piece of clothing, trying to find the reason for their discomfort. And for a while they continue their parallel pantomime. That of Vladimir is to some degree taken up by Clov, who hunts for a flea in his trousers. The behaviour of the former is very like that of someone who has an insect, a flea in his hat, while the latter admits it openly and tries to remedy it. Once again Beckett uses the old comic cliché of the insect that makes the character scratch, until a clownish solution resolves the problem in laughter.[65] But yet again the *incipit* is contradicted by the unexpected consequences: "une puce! Il y a encore des puces? [...] Mais à partir de là l'humanité pourrait se reconstituer! Attrape-la, pour l'amour du ciel!" (p. 50), Hamm cries, anguished by the possibility that all of humanity might be reborn from the flea. Hamm's inverted idea is an exaggerated paradox leading to Clov's solution: "entre Clov, un carton verseur à la main. [...] *Clov dégage sa chemise du pantalon, déboutonne le haut de celui-ci, l'écarte de son ventre et verse la poudre dans le trou. Il se penche, regarde, attend, tressaille, reverse frénétiquement de la poudre, se penche, regarde, attend*" (pp. 50-51).

The two objects, hat and shoes, are then used in comic stage actions, for example the hat is the spark that sets off Lucky's monologue - when he wears it, he begins to perform, with the already-seen consequences. The bowler hat has a stage presence that almost makes it one of the characters. It is kicked by Lucky, inspected by Vladimir and "played" in the most comic routine in *Godot*. The hat gag in Act 2 has Didi and Gogo passing three hats, belonging to Lucky, quickly from hand to hand and on their heads:

Estragon prend le chapeau de Vladimir. Vladimir ajuste des deux mains le chapeau de Lucky. Estragon met le chapeau de Vladimir à la place du sien qu'il tend à Vladimir. Vladimir prend le chapeau d'Estragon. Estragon ajuste des deux mains le chapeau de Vladimir. Vladimir met le chapeau d'Estragon à la place de celui de Lucky qu'il tend à Estragon. Estragon prend le chapeau de Lucky [...]. (p. 101)

... and so on. The image is the familiar one of Harpo and Chico Marx in *Duck Soup* who switch hats in a clownish turn. But it also brings to mind the many circus routines that use headgear - there was "The Hat" (1925) which involved balancing a hat on the tip of the nose, a challenge interpreted by the *auguste*, inverting the order of balance (the nose on the hat instead of vice versa) and turning against himself the trick he had prepared for the *clown blanc*; or "The Squashed Hats" (1945) where the clowns play at bashing in each other's hats; or again "Puddings in the Hat" (1950), a trick where the *clown blanc* appears to make some puddings in a hat and when the *auguste* tries to do the same he fails miserably.[66] The circular movement of arms and hats is interrupted only when one of the hats is flung to the ground - the game is no longer amusing and it stops. They go on to another form of entertainment.

That Beckett may have drawn some inspiration from the Marx Brothers film is of no particular importance for the comic effect of the gag, which works independently. The same cannot be said for the cat and dog gag in *Film*, where it is the presence of Buster Keaton that brings a very special touch to the action, with his artistic charisma. According to the script, the sizes of the two animals were to inspire a comic atmosphere from the start. Beckett wanted them to be inverted compared with normal logic, where cats are smaller than dogs, so the cat should have been much larger than the tiny dog. This disproportion was used when the film was made, though it was not as strikingly obvious as the author would have liked. However, the exact, stylised scheme of entrances and exits was followed masterfully by Keaton. In the part of O, he was to take the animals out of the house one at a time and of course when he managed to get rid of the dog, the cat got back in and vice versa – all done without ruffling his stiff, awkward bearing.

3.5. Portrait of Beckett as a director

Thus far we have seen how much gestuality there was in Beckett's comedy and, through this, how much was written into the play itself, thereby discovering in this "playwright of the word" a universe that had remained hidden to those who thought he was fairly indifferent to the technical and material dimension of the stage. *Stage*, not dramatic literature. His work as a director and his proven knowledge of the theatre and cinema panorama show that Beckett was perfectly aware of the specific natures of the genres and media he used. He was both fascinated by their expressive potential and distressed by their specific mechanisms, as the difficulties in making *Film* and the television dramas show.

The theatre was, for Beckett, essentially a challenge. A linguistic one. Flinging himself into the uncharted realms of play-writing, he obliged his writing to leave behind the ways of the novel, short story and poetry and to explore the uncertain routes of literature for the theatre. In the Fifties he had experimented enough with the possibilities of expression of the above-mentioned genres, now his real challenge lay in the theatre, in the dual role of author and supervisor of stage production. The theatre offered a new language to put him to the test, with the same function as had had French for his prose and which would have the language of film, once he had become familiar with dramatic and stage communication. He faced this challenge fully aware of the facts and was able to learn from his first directors.

His first ever director, Roger Blin, acknowledged that "Beckett n'avait pas encore la très grande expérience théâtrale qu'il a acquise depuis; mais il possédait déjà une connaissance très précise du théâtre comme spectacle, c'est-à-dire comme un événement qui se déroule sur une scène".[67] Beckett followed the stage production of *Godot* that Blin had courageously agreed to take on, leaving maximum freedom to the director, but discreetly guiding its orientation. In return Blin taught Beckett the craft, not only on that occasion, but during the frequent work done together. Together with American director Alan Schneider, Blin had the most influence on Beckett's technical education as a director, acquired in the darkened theatre during rehearsal and in long sessions with the actors.

Beckett participated in the majority of the French and English productions of directors he admired (Jean-Marie Serrau, Donald McWhinnie, Anthony Page, Peter Hall, Deryk Mendel, Walter Asmus and Pierre Chabert) always alongside an official director that he requested and supported, but whom he tactfully directed and instructed. After years of "hidden" directing, Beckett began to direct in his own right, first with a work by Pinget, *L'Hypothèse* (Paris 18th October 1965). This was the only time in his career that he directed another author's text and from then on, he directed his own. In Germany he found the work environment most congenial to him. At the Schiller Theater Werkstatt in Berlin Beckett found the atmosphere, technical and human resources that were ideal for staging his dramatic work. The German actors, in particular, rigorous, disciplined and well trained, were the delight of Beckett as director. With them he was able to apply the method of working he had perfected, which was founded on attention to physical detail and negation of philosophical interpretations. Other actors tended to concentrate on the polysemy of Beckett's text, losing sight of its bare, concrete realisation. But as a director, Beckett wanted the actors only to let the text speak, *embodying* his images.

Over the years Beckett developed his own particular technique of directing. He went to rehearsals with a series of notes prepared beforehand, which he then ignored or substituted with new ideas. There, he changed the text, modified and perfected it into a version often different from the published one. *Endspiel* in 1967, for example, had to be re-published in Germany, so changed had the text been by Beckett's direction. Often he inserted technical improvements to make the stage play flow better, he toned down the comic and tragic hues and he reduced. Textual modifications made by Beckett when directing were essentially of three kinds: 1) improvement of technical-material effect of scenes; 2) balancing of tragic and comic tones; 3) reduction to the essential, or removal of too clearly autobiographical references and organisation of the material according to criteria of rhythm and musicality.[68]

His way of working seemed to convey an extraordinary charm, impossible to communicate, except with seemingly insignificant details such as his extreme concentration and maniacal attention to detail.[69]

Beckett placed himself on equal footing with the actors and, "forgetting" his own text, he seemed to discover it with the actors and learn it with them. In reality he knew his texts by heart, even the German translation, and had a clear idea of how his scenes were to be actually staged. He himself often demonstrated the interpretation or physical attitude, as when in the *Endspiel* mentioned above he personally showed the actor Horst Bollmann how Clov should walk, probably copying Jean Martin in Blin's *Fin de partie* – London, Royal Court Theatre, 1958 – who had got this walk just as the author wanted it and became a model for all future Clovs. Or consider the extenuating rehearsals with Billie Whitelaw, when Beckett sat in front of the actress, repeating with her the pauses, intonations and variations: "we would sit opposite each other and speak the words in unison, he in a whisper and me out loud".[70] Or again, Beckett's tape recording of "Lucky's Monologue" to which Jack MacGowran listened to learn and absorb the rhythm.

Beckett wanted "physical themes"[71] from his actors, concentration on physical tasks to super-connotate the character, always victim of some tic, or the action. Together with his negation of psychologism, this made Beckett a modern director. He often insisted on this negation, resisting both naturalistic and aesthetic psychologism. It is to the latter he was referring, as early as the Thirties, when he criticised the "snowball act",[72] where a character is gradually described by developing his traits in a strictly causal way, as a snowball rolls down the mountain to the valley getting bigger as it goes, as if the character was bound by a foreseeable and unquestionable connection of cause and effect. In his Trinity College lessons, the "snowball act" posed him the problem of the conflict between human experience and literary mechanism, resolved by him in his plays by discarding realist psychological drama. Against naturalism, the young Beckett, lecturing at Trinity College, praised Flaubert, Rimbaud, Dostojevskij, Gide and his "acte gratuit", and classical Greek drama that "doesn't pretend to be real –remains a work of art- is human beneath".[73]

Psychologism was driven from the stage at the pre-expressive level, at the moment of identification with the character and at the expressive level, in the general atmosphere of the performance. Beckett's indications to the actors would always be contrary to blind identification with the character and, paradoxically, the categorical imperative would be "don't act". His actors were not asked to abandon the more artificial tones of acting to take on more natural ones, not *to pretend*, but *to be* the character. The great difficulty was in keeping a psychological and emotional distance from the character to allow the text's ideas and emotions to come out, over and above theatrical convention. "His 'Don't act' instructions necessarily caused me some difficulty. Surgeons want to surge, actors want to act. An actor is usually hired precisely for the personal things he will bring to a piece".[74] The ambiguity of Beckett's instruction to Billie Whitelaw was amplified by the presence of characters who "are acting", who do not conceal the performing aspect of theatre, as does naturalistic pretence. Only "excessive" acting could coherently fulfil the sense of Beckett's narrative. As Roger Blin said, you cannot act Pozzo naturalistically, only theatrically, excessively "et de toute façon *il n'est pas possible de jouer Beckett naturel*".[75]

In addition to indications in the text, other key elements of anti-naturalism are Beckett's comments as director, including his unique concept of "Wartestelle", devised by him and used in his productions of *Warten auf Godot* (1975) and *Endspiel* (1967). The German term (warten=wait, stelle=point, place) means a "waiting point", a concept with spatial rather than temporal connotations.[76] For Beckett this is the moment and place where the stage action freezes into a fixed *tableau* with strong pictorial content, but used to underline a significance that should not be pathetic: the moment when "a character is interrupted in midaction and holds an awkward position for a brief tableau";[77] "these frozen silences are [in *Waiting for Godot*], as Beckett's German term for them indicates, tangible instances of waiting. They lead directly into four key references to waiting. The first two references define specific expectations. The last two register unfulfilment. [...] The series establishes the conditions, expectations, and disappointments that are central to the play".[78] To me this motionless space/time seems almost like deadpan action.

The anti-naturalism of this instant, not just a moment of pause but a real suspension of the action, is evident and does not seem particularly unusual, but for this very reason it is more significant. The effect of "Wartestelle", by emotionally distancing from the character and concentrating the action, is alienating and therefore, in Brecht's later definition, a "Verfremdungseffekt".[79] Here Beckett's theory of acting meets one of the high points of twentieth-century theatre - the practice and theory of Brecht. Brecht's distancing effect involved recognising as "strange" what we considered as apparently normal, so that events could be represented on stage as if they were new and unknown.[80] It is, therefore, a de-familiarisation, exactly like the "Wartestelle" and the comic that Beckett wanted on stage, with the difference that Beckett could not accept the sole interpretative key and focussed interpretation of Brecht.

Anti-psychologism was also to be a criterion for acting, for Beckett told his actors to forget the explanations and the whys and wherefores of the character and concentrate on the physical actions. This concept immediately brings to mind the attention paid by certain twentieth-century avant-garde movements following Stanislavskij to the corporeal dimension of the actor. Though Beckett was never a theatrical theorist like Brecht or Artaud[81] and though he expressed himself strongly against the various "Methods" that were experimenting with new forms of acting expression, we cannot ignore this aspect of his work as a director, which inevitably brings him into comparison with masters of contemporary theatre. He told Deirdre Bair that these Grotowskis and these Methods were not for him and that the best work of theatre he could imagine was one without actors, only text. He adds then that he is trying to write one of this kind.[82] This statement appears to contradict his own experiments with theatre and directing. Beckett's universe was increasingly evolving towards rarefaction, but this did not mean doing so to the detriment of the actor's body, mortifying it before the script. On the contrary, this process was achieved precisely due to the materiality of the actor's body. Beckett's work with actors, especially in the Seventies and Eighties, showed that the actor's physicality was essential and functional to his stage aesthetics and to the visualisation on stage of those rarefied atmospheres brought about by the texts. The ambiguity that has often led to misunderstanding is based on Beckett's paradoxical method - to embody surreal, oneiric atmospheres he uses the least immaterial part of the play, the actor's body, and through this he breaks through the barriers of matter itself. This repays the actor, not with disappearance of the Body under the aegis of the Word, but with catalysis of energy, so paradoxically the spectator's attention is held by its materiality, exactly because it is limited, circumscribed and frustrated. Consider Winnie's body that sinks, so that the spectator sees an ever-smaller part - the effect is identical to what cinema can obtain by zooming in, and in the end the close-up enters the body, the face of the actor.

Beckett's polemical tone in a letter to Bair towards new theories of theatre that work on the energy of the actor (Stanislavskij is clearly alluded to in the term "Methods") may be explained by Beckett's desire not to be associated with any form of theatrical dogma, or perhaps by a kind of mute hostility towards Bair's work which does not seem to have satisfied him. He reacted with annoyance when asked for an opinion on her biography.[83] In effect, some years before he had written to Christian Ludvigsen, the Danish translator of his texts "I dream of going into a theatre with no text, or hardly any, and getting together with all concerned before really setting out to write. That is to say a situation when the author would not have a privileged status as is the case when he arrives with a text already set, but would simply function as a specialist of neither more or less importance than other specialists involved…".[84] There are two possible reasons for these contradictory statements, either a change of opinion over the years by Beckett, or a personal approach that differed towards the two academics - in his reply to the American scholar we see a closure, without alternatives, while towards Ludvigsen his tone is the relaxed one of someone reflecting on his work and future projects. This latter possibility seems to me most likely, in line with Beckett's infinite availability to those he admired, see his great collaboration with his official biographer James Knowlson, who had the merit of being interested in Beckett's life in relation to his works and not as an event in itself. By contrast, he was unapproachable to those he feared guilty of misinterpretation. In any case, his aesthetic objective revealed to Ludvigsen, which precedes the other in time, seems to me particularly significant for its implications, which the Danish critic had already perceived. He replied in fact: "the latest point in your letter –about going into a theatre with no text, or hardly any, as you expressed it– might have some special interest in my case. I happen to know a pupil of Grotowski called Eugenio Barba who now has settled down with a little group of hardworking actors in a smaller town in Jutland. They work with authors nearly in the way you dream of".[85] It is significant the Beckett's work as a director and his aesthetic aim bring to mind the most recent theatrical experiments of our century.

For Jonathan Kalb, Beckett is an alternative to the Stanislavskij/Brecht axis, since his actor prepares himself in the same way, but without the satisfaction and full training of the latter method, only a sensation of continuous frustration.[86] They suffer psychic frustration, for they are interpreting doubt in itself, without help from ideologies, but also physical frustration, being constrained, caged in, imprisoned and subject to physical suffering (think of the "cage" in *Not I* or the urns in *Play*, or of Winnie). Beckett's actor has indeed a holy devotion to the stage and to psychophysical pain, "Beckett requires a 'holy' actor no less than Artaud and Grotowski"[87] and his practice is truly close to Artaud's cruelty. Physicality as an instrument of cruelty in theatre and anarchy, being outside of the normal and the avant-garde at the same time, are shared by Beckett and Artaud. But the two authors have many more affinities than we think. Artaud's "cruel" pages appear powerfully brought to life by Beckett's images of men who crawl and who carry with them physical or intimate purulent wounds, who are tired of going on and continue to drag on their wretched existence, while incapable of thinking, feeling and communicating.

The "cruelty" and tyranny of Beckett's writing and directing are paradoxically the instruments that liberate the actor, opening up new ways of expression. Imprisonment that liberates is the best metaphor for the acting Beckett requests. So the old cliché that Beckett wanted actors to be like puppets, a tyrant using actors at his will, is transformed into Beckett as a modern director, open to the actor's creativity, trying to direct its efforts towards precision of gesture. It is difficult here to avoid thinking of Barba and Grotowski. If an actor only finds his artistic freedom through discipline, Beckett's plays encouraged many actors to overcome their personal limits and reach new heights of virtuosity: "many [plays] carried actors to new heights of accomplishment".[88]

Walter Asmus, in evoking the friendly atmosphere of Beckett's rehearsals, maintained that the work went on without violating the actors' independence and that Beckett was able to establish with them a very special "communion de pensée et de sentiments",[89] by means of which he succeeded in pushing them beyond their own limits and the objective difficulties of the texts themselves. His taste for precise rhythm extended from the text, where all was intrinsically musical, the syntax, the assonance, the pauses, the movements, the gestures, to the stage setting, laid out in the stage directions and made concrete by his direction. Everything had to be extremely precise from the elocution to the stage business,[90] and this added considerable difficulties to the already challenging texts of Beckett. Conveying chaos with precision was often too confused a direction for the actors, not at all used to deal with tensions conflicting on several levels, not only those within the script, but also those affecting their own emotions. "Parce que le texte de Beckett et les mots choisis par lui comportent une certaine charge émotionelle, le comédien ne peut pas neutraliser complètement les intonations sans finalement trahir l'auteur", but Beckett wanted anti-psychologist and anti-naturalist acting, so the battle within was automatically engaged. Restraining one's own emotions and conveying the tensions of the script with a certain detachment present enormous difficulty, as "morphologiquement, un comédien ne peut jouer deux intentions opposées sans que dans le passage, aussi court soit-il de l'une à l'autre, sa voix ne se charge de l'une et de l'autre".[91]

On Beckett's stage the actor's body, bereft of all historical and psychological identity, is both distressed by the lack of traditional interpretative criteria and at the same time stimulated by the new task. Beckett radicalises the human body on stage and by intensifying the body's performance he strongly evokes its material energy. Even when absent the body has meaning: "the performance of animation moves beyond the bodies on stage: when the stage body ceases movement or when it disappears altogether, the material intensity it has evoked lingers in an animated gap in space, time, and discourse, a darkness that is phenomenally charged with energies drawn from both audience and actor".[92] Its energy is a language in itself, free of convention and tormented by its own physicality, "Beckett's troubling the body disengages it from what conventionally makes it 'mean' and by doing so, the performance of his work stages a condition that strips living to its essentials to ask what lies behind language's formulation of consciousness".[93] In other words Beckett emphasises "the irreducible physicality of human bodies in the spaces they actually inhabit".[94]

In torturing the actors' bodies Beckett grants them a valuable gift - the challenge against themselves and their own possibilities and capacities for expression. He also strengthens their physical capacities, emphasising the independent meaning of physical language on the stage. The suffering was an involuntary component, for Beckett obviously did not intend to physically torture his actors, but it was an essential component, because this very great psychophysical attention to detail and to organisation around difficult physical and vocal tasks quickly exhausted the delicate mechanism of the actor. Billie Whitelaw has often discussed the psychophysical pain of interpreting *Not I* ("the work was painful; my ribcage protested at having to take such little breaths. Like a singer, I had to work out exactly *where* I was going to snatch breath. I was hyper-ventilating like mad and often became dizzy, staggering round and round the stage. My jaws ached")[95] or the discomfort of playing Winnie ("being on stage as Winnie felt a bit lonely. [...] I felt I had to have something of my own in the mound. I filled it with all the rabbits I'd been collecting for thirteen years").[96]

This tortured body embodies Beckett's fantasies, the actor's body engaging in "exercises de reptation, de supination, de lévitation" and falls,[97] or succeeding in surprising us and itself by doing "une sorte d'équilibre-déséquilibre",[98] so as to act musically, to find and follow the rhythm of the piece, to act dancing and singing. The metaphors of song, dance and music are those most frequently used to explain the staging of Beckett's texts, even by the author himself. He wanted his characters to move as if in a ballet, with their gestures following precise choreography.[99] These metaphors of dance and song share the element of rhythm, represented on stage by stylised movements and by carefully delivering the punctuation of the text, thus creating refrains or variations in the vocal and gestural interpretation. Beckett's insistence on the musicality of the verbal and physical text was known to all the actors and directors who worked with him. A varied or repeated rhythm had to have meaning in itself, creating a score that was parallel to that of the drama and illuminating it with an ambiguous, ever-elusive sense. The musicality inherent in the texts was amplified on stage by repetition of the same sounds and gestures, by clever variation of tone of voice and by timing that marked the atmosphere between tragedy and comedy.

Comedy, for Beckett, was essentially a question of rhythm. The right choice of rhythm made the line, gesture or action work, or not. And the comic hue was never separate from the tragic one. In his productions, Beckett strove for the proper balance between both elements and, if necessary, even changed the original text. "Emphasize humour whenever possible" he used to say to Eva Katharina Schultz during rehearsals for *Glückliche Tage* in 1971, "don't play Winnie's psychology".[100] Billie Whitelaw had understood this even before she worked with Beckett and she perfectly delivered the rhythmic cadence of the mistress in *Play*, emitting that special mechanical and chilling laugh, which was funny and disconcerting at the same time: "in my script I find I've marked the actual *stresses* of syllables, to actually relish the syllables, to use them for rhythmic purposes. [...] I tried to think of the words not as carrying specific meanings, but as *drum-beats* - a sort of Morse code, I suppose. [...] The mistress in *Play* has to sound a particular laugh. One day a maniacal, robot-like automatic laugh came out of my mouth, going right up and down the scale - what I called my laugh button".[101]

The rhythm brought about the right balance between tragic and comic and sustained it coherently throughout the performance. The most difficult task was to find the correct musical tempo: "je crois que c'est essentiellement ce que nous avons fait pendant ce travail de répétitions. Trouver le dosage entre le rire et l'émotion, ne tomber ni dans la farce ni dans la chialerie".[102] The timing included gestures and words together, making them coherent internally and with the general atmosphere of the play. The spoken words are woven into the gestures like different notes on a single stave. The comic or pathetic effect depends exclusively on the key the score is played in. "Le comique naissait par le rythme et le minutage. Le comique venait de lui-même, sans qu'on en parle. Un minutage très précis. Beckett disait «Ils sont épuisés: plus lentement, parlez plus bas.» Et cela devenait pathétique".[103]

The comedy Beckett deprecated was that of easy effect, so he strenuously countered the actors' tendency to say the lines in a superficially comic way, just as he disapproved of a too overtly tragic interpretation of his works. The truth of Beckett's dramatic and stage texts lies in the confusion of the two planes, in the parallel delivery of both emotive and aesthetic dimensions. It was this very point of balance between tragedy and comedy that he appreciated in the productions of his plays. More than total fidelity, Beckett looked for adherence to the spirit of his text. Notoriously critical of those who wanted to stage his works, Beckett alternated between a desire for total control and the trust he granted to some of his interpreters. What he could never stand were productions lacking in harmony of sound and without a careful balance between tears and laughter.

His favourite actress, Billie Whitelaw, who best grasped the profound sense of his work, who was overcome by emotion without having to understand the reason for her own emotions and who blindly followed Beckett's instructions without rationalistic embellishment, also best expressed this key point: "[Beckett's works] are not plays *about* anything, they represent emotional states of mind", "what Beckett wanted was not the acting out of an internal thought, but the internal thought itself".[104]

Notes

1 See J. Pat Miller, who, according to Beckett was the best Lucky ever, and who was allowed to change his costume at the 1984 staging with the San Quentin Drama Workshop. McMillan-Fehsenfeld 1988, pp. 74-75.
2 Cronin 1997, p. 382.
3 Chaplin 1992, p. 145.
4 In the 1910s he bought and read the stories of Sexton Blake and his assistant Tinker, published in *The Union Jack*, his favourite comic (Knowlson 1996, pp. 30-31), as well as another children's weekly, *The Boy's Own* (Cronin 1997, p. 37). His knowledge of Walt Disney is documented. It is also curious to recall that Beckett had briefly considered resolving the technical difficulties of the dog and cat scene in *Film* by using a cartoon: "Beckett even entertained the possibility that the dog and cat routine should be an animated cartoon, but rejected the idea quickly on formal grounds" (Gontarski 1973, p. 108).
5 Doodles are found in the following manuscripts, among others: RUL MS3000/1; RUL MS1396/4/6; RUL MS3458/59/60 and in the manuscripts of *Watt* and *Malone meurt*, see photos in Lake 1984.
6 Knowlson 1996, p. 632, where he cites a conversation with Beckett during rehearsals for *Ghost Trio* in December 1976 (see p. 820, n. 101).
7 In *Dream of Fair to Middling Women* quotes Polichinelle (French version of Pulcinella or Punch, p. 20); in *More Pricks Than Kicks* we read: "like fantoccini controlled by a single wire they flung themselves down on the western slope of heat" referring to Punch and Judy (p. 100); in *Murphy* Beckett quotes Petrushka, (one of the European versions of Pulcinella, see Greco 1988 and 1990), and other *fantocci*: "all the puppets in this book whinge sooner or later, except Murphy, who is not a puppet" (pp. 6 and 86); in *Malone Meurt* we meet a puppet show (p. 201); in the poetry "Mort de A. D." (in *Poesie*, p. 35) Beckett uses the puppet as a space metaphor: "espace pantin".

8   Pirandello 1974.
9   For Gontarski (1985, p. 62) Krapp's red nose is unquestionably sign of a "drinker's snout". In *Watt* the protagonist has a red nose (p. 20) due perhaps to loneliness. Beckett sarcastically associates the emotional, existential dimension of inner loneliness with looking for "comfort" in drunkenness, a condition marked by a red nose. For Krapp, like Watt, owing to his long, forced, misanthropic solitude, this external sign has become chronic.
10 Countless examples of impassive faces can be found also in the novels and short stories, such as the exhilarating figure of Watt who reacts to all kinds of arbitrary abuse with an equanimity that is as enviable as it is improbable in real life: "the stone fell on Watt's hat and struck it from his head, to the ground. [...] Watt, faithful to his rule, took no more notice of this aggression than if it had been an accident" (p. 30).
11 Bergson 2002.
12 MS2932, p. 1.
13 In this sense there is no difference between Beckett's prose and his theatre – bowler hats everywhere; the umbrella in Murphy; the bicycle in *Molloy*, *More Pricks Than Kicks*, *Watt* and in the short story "XII"; the bag that mysteriously vanishes into thin air in *Mercier et Camier* and the sack in *L'image*.
14 Borrelli 1967, p. 49.
15 See Remy 1974. In the clown numbers created by the author we find turnips (p. 72), carrots (p. 76) and even a chicken (p. 240).
16 Oliva 1967, p. 157.
17 In the original version it is a "bisquit classique" (p. 24), which in English is substituted with a well-know brand of dog biscuits, "Spratt's medium" (p. 97). Nagg's disappointment is pathetic: "c'est dur! Je ne peu pas!" (p. 24).
18 Though only published in 1970, the novel *Mercier et Camier* was written between July and October 1946, shortly after *Watt*, begun in '41, taken up again in '43 and completed during the war. Knowlson 1996, pp. 333 and 360.
19 This suggestion was also made by Bair 1990, p. 63. More cautious, Hugh Kenner who frequently links Beckett's characters to those of

silent comedy but makes a special exception for the pseudo-couples in *Watt*, because for a certain period of time Arsene/Erskine (both plump) and Vincent/Walter (both bony) are found together. This exception to the Laurel and Hardy model, far from being a chance, negligible detail, is a further move towards chaos – no pattern is incontrovertibly linear, not even when it appears so. Kenner 1973, p. 76.

20 Beckett in an interview with Mel Gussow (1996, p. 41).
21 Dardano n.d., vol. I, p. 454 (my translation from Italian). Several critics have interpreted Beckett's world according to the criteria of contemporary physics. See Tagliaferri 1996, for whom Beckett gives aesthetic form to Heisenberg and Bohr's principles of uncertainty and complementarity. Also Henning 1988, where the cylinder in *Le Dépeupleur* is illuminated by the principles of thermodynamics.
22 Blin 1990, p. 161.
23 Extracts from the work diary of Walter Asmus, Beckett's assistant director, from McMillan-Fehsenfeld 1988, p. 137 (author's translation from the German).
24 Tagliaferri 1996, p. XIII.
25 Bouissac 1976, p. 176.
26 See pp. 79-80: when Clov asks what use he is to him, Hamm replies "a me donner la réplique".
27 There is a singular, dramatic exception in the couple in *Ohio Impromptu*, who are "*as alike in appearance as possible*" (p. 445). In this respect they resemble the four characters in *What Where* (monstruous re-duplication of the couple) described as "*as alike as possible. Same long grey gown. Same long grey hair*" (p. 469).
28 Mercier 1977, p. 46.
29 Celati 1976, pp. 49-54 (my translation from Italian).
30 Chaplin 1992, p. 188.
31 Ibid. p. 215.
32 For the insults in the first version (that of Blin, 1953) and for the criterion followed for the German productions see Aslan 1982, pp. 211-214.

33 McMillan 1990, p. 104. On the Theatre of Cruelty see Artaud 1958.
34 Blin 1990, p. 161.
35 Barrault 1990, p. 177.
36 Aslan 1982, p. 224.
37 Joyce 1986, p. 250.
38 Remy 1974, p. 233.
39 Memola 1982, p. 152.
40 Some scholars doubt the very clear association of the tree game with the yoga exercise – see States 1978 (pp. 16-17) who rather sees the Christological symbolism of the crucifixion.
41 See Henning 1988, p. 15.
42 From Manetti 1980 (pp. 243-244) we learn that "reprises" indicate the clowns' numbers during the interval, to allow the technicians time to change the equipment, while "entrées" are the clowns' specific numbers.
43 Levy 1977, p. 81.
44 Cremonini 1978, p. 20.
45 Coursodon 1973, p. 170.
46 Havel 1980, pp. 13-14. A similar view is held by Pasolini 1971, p. 36.
47 Ibid. p. 20.
48 See Coursodon 1973, who give a complete history of the term in cinema criticism, pointing out the contradiction and imprecision. He is among the few who to precisely reconstruct its etymology and technical definition.
49 Alvey 1952, p. 38 and Cauda 1936-1944, p. 328.
50 Gontarski 1977, p. 54.
51 Kern 1966.
52 RUL MS2101.
53 Richards 1997, pp. 85-86.
54 Borrowing the definition from Segre 1984, p. 51.
55 Marowitz 1962, p. 44. Pilling 1976 has a different opinion: "his comment on Marceau [...] can, in fact, be applied with much more justice to his own written mimes [...], which are strident and unsatisfying" (p. 108).

56 Greimas-Courtes 1986, p. 42.
57 Le Coq 1980, p. 201.
58 Gontarski 1985, p. 25.
59 RUL MS1227/7/16/2. Given the strong similarities, this is discussed as a preparatory text for *Fin de partie* by Restivo 1991 and Gontarski 1985.
60 RUL MS1227/7/16/2, p. 4.
61 The original conserved in RUL (MS1227/7/16/1) is reproduced in Gontarski 1985, pp. 193-198.
62 Gontarski 1985, p. 41.
63 Just as the final *tableau* of *Godot*, showing Estragon with his trousers down round his ankles, has the function of concentrating into a single tragicomic image the sense of the entire play.
64 Remy 1974, p. 25. In the number of "The Guitar", too, the *auguste* lets a big, heavy suitcase drop with a crash (see p. 221).
65 The flea is an insect especially beloved of clowns: see the magic of the flea tamer or the clown who finds a flea on his leg, takes it, tenderly sighs ("it has blue eyes"), squashes it and then cries over it (ibid. p. 225).
66 See the catalogue of clown numbers ibid. "The Hat" is on p. 83; "The Squashed Hats" p. 88; "Puddings in the Hat" p. 165.
67 Blin in Melese 1966-1969, p. 146.
68 For more information on development of the texts see Gontarski 1985, from whom we take a synthesis of how tragic/comic tones were balanced: in *Krapp* "Beckett carefully adjusted the tone of his play, deepening Krapp's pathos and simultaneously undercutting or undoing that pathos with comedy" (p. 63); in *Happy Days* Beckett added comic tones at the end to balance the pathos, but at the same time reduced the initial tendency to overload with comic tones, "the final effect remains serious predicament undercut with vulgar gesture" (p. 84).
69 See Knowlson 1990, p. 277.
70 Whitelaw 1995, p. 127.
71 Kalb 1989, p. 34.

72 McMillan-Fehsenfeld 1988, p. 25. From an interview with Irish actress Rachel Burrows (16th June 1982), who was a pupil of Beckett and still has her lesson notes.
73 Gontarski 1985, p. 11, quoting Beckett's lessons from Rachel Burrows' notes.
74 Whitelaw, p. 120.
75 Blin 1990, p. 163.
76 As we find, instead, in McMillan-Fehsenfeld 1988, p. 79 et passim.
77 Gontarski 1973, p. 88.
78 McMillan-Fehsenfeld 1988, p. 117.
79 Ruby Cohn not only finds an analogy between Wartestelle and Verfremdung but also posits an influence by Brecht on Beckett: "Beckett intends both audience and actors to be aware that the play is a play. Influenced, perhaps, by Brecht's *Verfremdungseffekt*, Beckett suggested that actors in *Godot* employ the trick of 'contrapuntal immobility'; lines like 'I'm going' were to be accompanied by 'complete stillness on the part of the speaker'" (Cohn 1962, pp. 218-219). But on the relationship –even if indirect- Beckett/Brecht see Gidal 1986, where (on p. 182) he highlights the peculiar paradox that results from the comparison: "Beckett enacts a Brechtian distantiation-effect".
80 Brecht 1964 and Artaud 1958.
81 Gontarski 1985, p. 2: "what aesthetics theory can be get from Beckett is usually culled from his early fiction and critical writing".
82 Bair 1990, p. 573.
83 Gussow 1996, p. 35. When the critic asked Beckett what he thought of Bair's biography, he replied shortly "there is nothing to say about it".
84 Letter from Samuel Beckett to Christian Ludvigsen on 8th December 1966, in Ludvigsen 1997, p. 73.
85 Letter from Christian Ludvigsen to Samuel Beckett on 12th March 1967, ibidem.
86 Kalb 1989.
87 Ibid. p. 147.
88 Gussow 1996, p. 9.

89 Asmus 1990, p. 350.
90 Many have emphasised that Beckett when directing insisted on precision; among these see Schneider 1990, p. 186; Greenberg 1990, p. 239; Seyrig 1990, p. 344; Asmus 1990, p. 356.
91 Both quotes from Blin 1990, p. 165.
92 Gray 1995-1996, p. 1.
93 Ibid. p. 10.
94 Connor 1988, p. 141.
95 Whitelaw 1995, p. 122.
96 Ibid. p. 154. I want, however, to recall that whenever Beckett realised that the actor could not manage the physical difficulty he was ready to make a – slight – change to the text: see *That Time*, originally conceived with only two blinks during the stare, which "would have caused an unbearable burden for the actor" (Gontarski 1985, p. 155) and which Beckett changed to eyes open and fixed only during the silences.
97 Simon 1990b, pp. 79-80.
98 Dort 1990, p. 228.
99 See Asmus 1990, p. 349 and McMillan-Fehsenfeld 1988, p. 258.
100 Both quotes are from Ben-Zvi 1990, p. 22. From personal notes of actress Eva Katharina Schultz.
101 Whitelaw 1995, pp. 78-79.
102 Blin 1990, p. 160.
103 Asmus 1990, p. 352.
104 Whitelaw 1995, the first quote is on p. 76, the second on p. 120.

* CHAPTER FOUR *

"TRAY BONG".
NOISE. RHYTHM. MUSIC

4.1. Only a manner of speaking

All those who worked with Beckett strongly emphasised his insistence on the musical delivery of his *pièces*. This was exemplified by the various contributions to the special edition of *Revue d'Estétique* dedicated exclusively to Beckett,[1] where directors, critics, actors, musicians, stage designers and artists all recalled his musical ear, "oreille de musicien. Mais aussi du poète".[2] Musicality was the genesis and form of all his artistic activities, the verbal fabric of prose and poetry, the balance between words and gestures and the harmony of all stage elements. Rhythm was the aesthetic principle of all his work, with its skilful blend of words, gestures and absence of gestures, immobility and silence. He was not striving for the trite harmony of similar elements, but for the organic alternation of harmony and dissonance, in order to create a meaningful progression that was independent of and parallel to simple communicative logic.

When Beckett was creating, he was thinking musically. In this way he constructed his "dream of consciousness"[3] of words, gestures, movements and sounds. He defined his works using musical terminology and directed his actors as a conductor directs his musicians. Musical metaphors are those most frequently used by Beckett's actors and directors in explaining his work, "for Beckett's trusted actors, the notion of such meticulousness in tone and tempo was familiar. Indeed, such actors recurrently use musical analogies when describing the experience of being directed by Beckett".[4] And indeed his criteria when directing undoubtedly constructed a musical structure similar to a stave. Antoni Libera summarised this as follows:

> Beckett's way of directing consists of the following elements:
> 1. approaching a play (both the text and stage activities) as if it were a musical score [...].
> 2. attempts at bringing out the melody and rhythm of the text. Treating each text as if it were poetry. Proper placing of logical accents.
> 3. a very precise designing of the stage movements, as if in a ballet [...].
> 4. the pace of the acting and speaking. The majority of the plays were intended to be acted or played quickly (allegro, presto). Playing Beckett's plays too slowly kills them [...].
> 5. bringing out the comic elements, which are a mixture of Irish humour and classics of the silent movies (Chaplin, Keaton).
> 6. bringing out sadness and lyricism [...].
> 7. the spirit of German romanticism [...].[5]

Music, ballet and design are all metaphors for a single concept - conveying rhythm in a precise form.

Transgression of this principle prompted those rare occasions when Beckett became intransigent and critical with directors who, in his opinion, did not understand this deeply essential aspect of his theatre and did not share his aesthetic sensibility. He complained to Charles Marowitz that "producers don't seem to have any sense of form in movement. The kind of form one finds in music, for instance, where themes keep recurring. When in a text, actions are repeated, they ought to be made unusual the first time, so that when they happen again -in exactly the same way- an audience will recognise them from before".[6] Verbal repetition and punctuation in the texts, if strictly respected, would suffice as a guide to Beckett's "score", but Beckett added to these textual instructions those of a musical director. The nature of the relationship between words and gestures in Beckett, that "inevitable sort of correspondence between words and movement"[7] was a fundamental component of the score and merits further clarification.

The corporeal dimension is the most immediate means of human, and more generally animal, expression, but it is not necessarily perceived only visually. To the visual experience we might add that of touch,[8] smell and hearing: a voice connects with the body of a speaker, a noise with one or more objects, music with a musical instrument. All these are sounds with precise connotations deriving from the materiality of their source, for example, the sound of a stone falling will be directly proportional to the size of the object. Or the perception of a body on stage may paradoxically be conveyed by the word, the *discours*. Some pieces of theatre – whether dialogue or monologue – evoke the material dimension of the body so strongly as to be considered part of gesture, rather than words. This is the case, as we have seen, for some of Beckett's pantomimes which, rather than actually taking place in material space, are merely indicated by the *logos*. But they do this so evocatively and with such a wealth of physical detail that they fall outside the dominion of "what is said", entering that of "what is done". In Beckett, the line between speech and action is so extremely subtle, with constant mutual interchange, that it is hard to separate them clearly. Gesture conveys an autonomous language, words a material gestuality. Beckett explicitly said as much to Marowitz when commenting on his "acts without words" and his interviewer understood this well, associating Beckett's mime more with Le Coq than with Marceau.[9]

Le Coq, with his mime that is no longer entirely silent, takes us into the universe of sounds, which are at last recognised as the bridge between word and gesture. The acoustic dimension is, in Beckett, the key to understanding the musicality of his creations and the play between words and gestures.

Sound is at the same time part of the gestural and the verbal elements. It is a sign or mark of an action or is assimilated with hearing, like words, though it has not yet their full significance, often being merely an incidental trace.

The original accidental nature of sound is, in an aesthetic dimension, transformed into focussed, deliberate meaning. Its repetition is always a complex sign. Like the other stage elements, sound refers to a network of meanings that, for its very nature, maintains a highly ambiguous aura. The presence of background sounds and noises in everyday life is almost imperceptible, given its continuous nature, but when transposed into a performance, it acquires an extra level of significance. This process takes places almost unconsciously, since the type of perception involved is pre-conscious.

Familiarity with a constant soundtrack and noises makes us almost forget their presence, unless they suddenly stop or create effects of alienation that are perhaps unexpected. In the latter case what strikes us most is surprise, as well as the contrast with what we were expecting. Much of clownish comedy uses acoustic effects to alienate and their routines are often noisy, full of rude, loud, funny or discordant sounds.

The place where, above all others, sounds, music, noises and words are the essential alphabet of communication is the radio.

In all of Beckett's writing there is a blind spot rarely entered by academics, but one that throws a different light on the complex, trans-medial nature of his experimentation. This is a surreal landscape where images are paradoxically generated in and by the dark and perceived through a rich network of subliminal emotions. These are the radio dramas that, together with those for television, represent the most obvious sign of Beckett's aesthetic restlessness. "Revolving around voices and sounds", these texts are "among Beckett's most revealing works. Here he deals with his own experience of the creative process both as a quest for fulfilment and release and as form of compulsion and slavery".[10]

It is not my intention to relate the story of Beckett's relationship with radio, which in any case has been so well told already by Clas Zilliacus,[11] but I would like to underline how, yet again, Beckett's flair was exercised on artistic genres with surprising technical knowledge, and how his comedy sometimes ran along hidden paths.

Beckett's interest for radio, already hinted at, arose at the end of the Fifties, when the BBC managed to stimulate his interest for the radio plays being broadcast on the Third Programme. The BBC "played a vital part in the creation of Beckett the radio dramatist",[12] actually giving him the opportunity to unfold his idea for *All That Fall*. This work was not commissioned but the result of an external stimulus, in line with the radio station's scheduling policy. The Third Programme occupied a strange, marginal position that often gave rise to contradictions - on the one hand it enjoyed considerable freedom within the BBC itself, but on the other it had to suffer the constant attentions of censorship. Of all British public radio programmes, it was certainly the most flexible and the most courageous in its choice of radio drama, but its relations with other government institutions were troubled and it was constantly under investigation by the Lord Chamberlain. In radio drama, the Third Programme was always ahead of its time and as early as the Fifties it had begun choosing avant-garde authors. It preferred works that were specially written for radio, rather than adaptations, and the producers often encouraged authors to make contributions of this type.

Beckett replied to pressing invitations from the BBC with his first radio play, *All That Fall*, which was written with surprisingly mature technical ability. Until that time, Beckett's experience of radio had been solely as a listener,[13] yet when he writes the radio play he makes full use of the medium's potential, with very few slips due to inexperience, inserting for example visual details that would be impossible to convey on the radio.[14] After the BBC production in 1957 of *All That Fall* there were other productions in English of *Embers* (1959) and *Words and Music* (1962). In 1963 the first French collaboration took place with *Cascando* for RTF, continuing with *Esquisse radiophonique* and *Pochade radiophonique*, which only later would be translated into English with the titles of *Rough for Radio I and II*.

In all of these productions Beckett concentrated his desire for rhythm and his tragicomic vision of the world. The result was radio plays thought unsatisfactory by their author, having been written too easily,[15] and unsuccessful with listeners, because obscure and gloomy. Not even the critics, sometimes, grasped the very delicate sense of rarefaction that permeates these plays and the delightful sense of comedy that constantly counterbalances, here too, the pathos. Nonetheless, Beckett's radio plays remain small masterpieces of verbal musicality, of suspense (although the story-telling was rather slow-moving if not inexistent) and of pure slapstick comedy, all carried out with an astounding sensibility for radio as a medium.

Beckett's focus in using all the performing media does not only throw light on his technical know-how. It also, even more significantly, indicates the precise direction in which Beckett's aesthetic had decided to travel.

Once we recognise the evolution or involution of Beckett's writing regarding forms of the spoken and/or visualised word, we also realise that in no way had it occurred by chance. The systematic and persevering manner in which Beckett explored the expressive possibilities of new communications systems, making increasingly extreme choices in his approach to the new and latest performing technologies (radio, cinema and television) was a clear sign of his aesthetic intention.

The literary word, flung out of the front door by Joyce's experimentation and negated by Beckett in way that was as polemic as it was ambiguous, came back through the window of rediscovered orality. When there was nothing more to say and no instrument for saying it, when what remained was to continue to talk of failure while daring to fail, then literature was dead. Out of its ashes Beckett's word arose, purged of the cumbersome presence of his master Joyce, and it learned to sing and to dance. According to Frasca, Beckett's experience can be associated with that of other authors, writing in English and other languages, caught up in the problem of a post-Joycean aesthetic. However Beckett distinguishes himself for the clear "evolution of the joycean «stream of consciousness» toward a sort of a gradually more resonant and simultaneous (from which the *necessarily* theatrical outcome) «stream of perceptions»".[16]

The musical and pictorial, or rather sculptural, quality of Beckett's *parole* was not limited to the implosion of discourse experienced by most twentieth-century avant-garde movements and by the Grand Master, Joyce. It invents a new creative universe, where literature can no longer be a mere hieroglyphic on a flat surface, but a graphic sign sculpting space and time. Beckett's word is no longer that of Joyce, modernist, trusting – despite everything – in the creative function of the author and the infinite malleability of the verbal fabric. It is, instead, a word made *flesh*, which acquires its fullest sense when spoken or acted. No longer written literature, read in solitude, it is text that becomes, as it is already during writing, music and images.

Beckett rediscovers an orality long lost to Western civilisation and, to do so, conquers the technological instruments offered by that civilisation. Beckett's encounters with mass means of communication, far from being chance infatuations, are for him the only possible direction for literature, a literature that becomes theatre, radio, cinema and television, surviving through the sensuality of these media.

The aesthetic sense is clear: words read according to modernist logic and current conventions can no longer survive, they must be read aloud to release their musicality and give form to the visual evocations of the text. This was the foundation of song and dance in Beckett's *parole*, and the origin of the difficulty or perhaps the impossibility of grasping the separation between word and gesture in Beckett, because the two poles were in constant dialogue.

4.2. Words and music

From childhood Beckett had a musical education, learning early on to play the piano and to sing. His days then, as throughout his life, were enlivened by piano playing and listening to records. There were already several other musicians in the family when the young Samuel began exploring his natural inclination for music. It was a passion that accompanied him all his days. He played Haydn, Beethoven, Chopin, Schubert and Debussy, as well as improvising accompaniments by ear. Stories are told of him pounding away at the piano at thronged London parties[17] and his country cottage, though bereft of home comforts, had to have a piano. He played for his own enjoyment, or rather for relief from spiritual anguish. In later years, he mostly played when alone and far from the city hubbub and he never played in his house in Paris.

He had considerable professional contact with musicians, who were often attracted towards Beckett's words for their inherent rhythmical quality that made them pieces of music in themselves. The French musician of Rumanian origin, Marcel Mihalovici, was one of these and one of the few who managed to carry out his projects with Beckett. Attracted by the musical resonance of the text of *Godot*, Mihalovici asked Beckett to write an opera libretto, which he would set to music. Beckett declined politely, but allowed him to set *Krapp* to music. The result, a work in which the "leitmotiv du silence donne lieu à des passages particulièrement beaux",[18] must have quite pleased Beckett, since he gave the musician a text he requested for a radio play commissioned by French radio station RTF and broadcast in 1963. This was *Cascando*, modelled on the almost-contemporary *Words and Music*, a radio drama produced by the BBC in 1962, both conceived and written within a short space of time in 1961.

The author's cousin, John Beckett, also collaborated on *Words and Music*, which was recorded with the composer conducting a twelve-piece orchestra. A different arrangement by Aric Dzierlatka was used for the production broadcast on Swiss French radio.

Music, for Beckett, was an all-inclusive aesthetic principle, inspiration and goal for all artistic expression. His affirmations in the article on Proust are particularly explicit and, although Beckett refers to the French author, he is giving his own personal aesthetic vision. In the final pages he dwells on the musicality of the word. After saying that an entire book might be written on this broad question in Proust, Beckett goes on to quote from Schopenhauer who in his *Die Welt als Wille und Vorstellung* wrote of the metaphysics of music. Beckett thought that the philosopher's influence on this aspect of Proust was incontrovertible and, for his part, he agreed with both that "music is the Idea itself, unaware of the world of phenomena, existing ideally outside the universe, apprehended not in Space but in Time only" (*Proust*, p. 92). Music is pure form, uncorrupted by the materiality that affects other forms of artistic expression. It is metaphysics in action, not perceived in space but in the flow of time. And perception, indeed, is the stumbling block of this art, since "This essential quality of music is distorted by the listener who, being an impure subject, insists on giving a figure to that which is ideal and invisible, on incarnating the Idea in what he conceives to be an appropriate paradigm" (ibid.). Music's perfection lies in being immediately understood and eternally inexplicable or, as Beckett defined it in *Proust*, "an art that is perfectly intelligible and perfectly inexplicable" (p. 92). It must be perceived im-mediately, that is to say, without rational intermediation. It is something that cannot be explained, as Jacques says in *Eleutheria*: "c'était clair sur le moment. Ce n'est pas une chose qu'on peut raconter. C'est un peu comme la musique" (p. 126). Music is a perfect art, but its weakness is revealed when its form is perceived by imperfect beings. The paradox of modern art – the impossibility of taking form and the urgency of giving form to this torment – finds its synthesis in music. It is no chance that when Beckett met Stravinsky in Paris in 1962 they had a passionate discussion about the dilemma of translating the abstract into plasticity.[19]

Music as an artistic genre and aesthetic principle permeates all of Beckett's work without exception. From the musical citations scattered throughout his writing we could even reconstruct his profound, attentive knowledge of music. He mentions classical and contemporary musicians and uses technical terms or metaphors taken from the semantic field of music.[20]

The text with most musical metaphors is *Dream of Fair to Middling Women*, where we find: "who said [...] that the best music (what did he know about music anyway?) was the music that became inaudible after few bars [...]" (p. 12); "the night firmament is abstract density of music, symphony without end" (p. 16); "the banquet of music" (p. 40); "[...] make it look like a sonata, with recurrence of themes, key signatures, plagal finale and all" (p. 49); "I think of his earlier compositions where into the body of the musical statement he incorporates a punctuation of dehiscence" (p. 138); "plane of white music, warpless music expunging the tempest of emblems [...]" (p. 181) and so on.[21]

But essentially the music is present within the texts, as regulative principle of the verbal structure or rhetoric figure. On this point, too, Beckett was surprisingly explicit. In a letter of December 1957 addressed to Alan Schneider, which became famous after the publication of *Disjecta*, Beckett states quite firmly: "my work is a matter of fundamental sounds (no jokes intended) made as fully as possible, and I accept responsibility for nothing else. If people want to have headaches among the overtones, let them. And provide their own aspirin" (p. 109). His tone does not admit contradiction - the sound is its own meaning, an autonomous language, and it is the only one sought by Beckett. All other interpretations may lead to a headache. His works are full of comic overtones in various ways. The comedy is brought about by different mechanisms but based on a common sound play. This is the key to interpreting "the «abnormal» punctuation, certainly less logical than it is declamatory"[22] of many Beckett texts even in prose, as Frasca shows, speaking of the novel *Watt*. The punctuation marks the rhythm of the text, in preparation for the diction.

Already in *Eleutheria* Beckett had begun experimenting with plays on alliterative words without paradigmatic meaning in the speech:

> VITRIER. - Où qu'il faut la mettre! Mais dans le... dans le... dans le truc, quoi, pas dans ton derrière, dans le... dans la DOUILLE, voilà, mets-la dans la douille, et gouille-toi, andouille. (p. 85)

Shortly after finishing *Eleutheria*, Beckett sat down to write *Godot* and there he put one of the most terrible and exciting pieces in the history of contemporary theatre - Lucky's monologue, based on a special play on words. Lucky's monologue might be defined as paradigmatic *grammelot*, that is, carnivalesque subversion on a paradigmatic level of the speech, leaving the syntagmatic level intact. On the surface, the speech appears coherently logical, being constructed according to the rules of syntax, but it does not result in coherence of meaning. Lucky's desperate gabble, similar to that of the mouth in *Not I* - also freed after being long constrained to silence - vomits disordered fragments of discourse that might be coherent on their own, but which are wrongly put together so that the meaning is made null.

Lucky makes references to elements of a fairly cultured nature, but as he goes on, something becomes less convincing. At the start it seems to be a lecture on any subject requiring a certain high tone and lofty vocabulary, perhaps parodying academic lectures, political speeches and religious sermons. As the performance goes on, the oration disintegrates before us - it is no longer a confused jigsaw of different dissertations, but pure onomatopoeic suggestion. Didi, Gogo and Pozzo – along with the audience – are brought to a vertigo that undermines the very functioning of verbal communication, of which Lucky is no longer capable, as our ears bear witness. The war between sound and words has been won by the former and it is sound that has got the upper hand and which transmits its alternative sense.

The entire monologue is a sublime piece of music, shocking and comical. The sense of embarrassment for Lucky's meaningless outburst of speech is countered by the grotesque reoccurrence of terms with an obscene sound or double meaning: "Acacacacadémie d'Anthropopo-pométrie de Berne-en-Bresse de Testu et Conard [...] de Testu et Conard [...] de Fartov et Belcher" (pp. 60-61).

Beckett constantly makes use in his work of rhythmic repetition of the same words or whole sentences, but not always with comic effects. When this happens, it may be for two reasons: non-homogeneity with the context or repetition for its own sake. The fact of a speaker repeating a refrain that torments his listeners is indeed cause for laughter. The Italian word for catchphrase, *tormentone*, conveys the notion even better: A *tormentone* is a recurring phrase that appears from nowhere and makes people laugh because they recognise it. Whoever encounters it is – after Bergson – caught in a mechanism that is faulty.

Tormentoni are very frequent in Beckett, beginning with the most famous one in *Godot*:

> ESTRAGON. - [...] Allons-nous-en.
> VLADIMIR. - On ne peut pas.
> ESTRAGON. - Pourquoi?
> ESTRAGON. - On attend Godot. (p. 16 and elsewhere)

This recurs like a real musical refrain that, after the first few times, provokes laughter from the spectator, who recognises the phrases and the ingenuity of the characters that continue to play the same games without ever learning the rules. When directing, Beckett insisted these refrains be spoken with the same, identical tone each time, to further emphasise their pounding repetition.[23] Recurring verbal themes in *Godot* turn out to be connected with the biggest issues of the drama. That of *Godot* is connected with waiting, that of the request for help with the harshness of destiny and Beckett himself records in his director's notebook the results of the cries for help: 14 are ignored, only 4 receive a reply, 1 attempt fails, 1 is unknown and 1 conditionally answered. Again in Godot, the word "*ciel*", meaning a natural element or Paradise, is actually underlined by the pantomime of the characters, in clownlike fashion, by looking upwards as if to make sure that the sky is still there. The phrase "qu'est-ce que je disais?" (pp. 41 et seqq.) acts almost as a *Wartestelle*, being always followed by a pause, before the forgotten subject can be found. The theme of "sleeping" often includes doubt as to whether sleeping and waking can be reversed, as Beckett himself underlines when directing in Germany.

At times the refrain torments the listener with foolish small talk, emptied of its original social function. There is repetition of the platitudes of everyday life, empty chatter filling the silences. A wonderful example is in *All That Fall*, where Mrs Rooney's weary march towards the station is peppered with the usual questions about health or whether the weather promises a perfect day for the horse racing. Mrs Rooney meets several acquaintances: Christy ("how is your poor wife? [...]Your daughter then?", p. 172), Mr Tyler ("what news of your poor daughter?", p. 174), Mr Slocum ("how is your poor mother?", p. 177). The old lady stops them all to discuss the health of their loved ones. But her kind concern is met with replies that verge on the evasive when the men describe their poor relations' health as follows: "no better, Ma'am [...]. No worse, Ma'am" (p. 172), "fair, fair. They removed everything, you know, the whole... er... bag of tricks. Now I am grandchildless" (p. 174), "thank you, she is fairly comfortable. We manage to keep her out of pain" (p. 177). They all, however, seem to be more concentrated on the races than on the tragic events in their own families: Christy, "nice day for the races, Ma'am" (p. 172), Mr Tyler, "divine day for the meeting" (p. 174) and later "lovely day for the fixture" (p. 184), Tommy, "nice day for the races, sir" (p. 179). We should remember that the first title of *All That Fall* was *Lovely Day for the Races*, discarded, perhaps because too similar to the title of the Marx Brothers film of 1947, *A Day at the Races*.[24]

The small talk, the clichés and the platitudes of everyday speech have a precise function, a phatic one, to verify effective contact between the sender and the receiver. These are stereotyped forms of discourse with a clear function and coherence within a social system, a function that is communicative, well structured and complex - to clarify, state and impose psychological, cultural and social relationships between speakers. In Beckett this mechanism is active only apparently, while in reality it has lost its original meaning and is used merely for the purpose of rhythm. This type of conversation is banalised to allow an expressive use of the phatic function, so the sense derives, not as before from the dynamics of relations between the speakers, but from musical repetition of the same platitudes. The language is not only impoverished, but also *deviated* into unexpected directions.

The same happens in Human Wishes, where polite chit-chat creates dialogues without communication and empty British politeness is made to explode by gradually increasing the friction between polite tone and aggressive content:

MRS WILLIAMS Knot on, Madam, knot on, or endeavour to talk like a sensible woman.
MRS DESMOULINS You wish to provoke me, Madam, but I am not provoked. The peevishness of decay is not provoking.
MISS CARMICHAEL Insupportable hag. (p. 296)

Eleutheria might be considered as an ideal continuation of this semantic structure. The same bourgeois setting, although in another century, is the scene for charming mutual insults, disguised as small talk:

MME PIOUK. - Violette!
MME KRAP.- Marguerite! (*Elles s'embrassent.*)
MME PIOUK. - Violette!
MME KRAP.- Tu m'excuseras de ne pas me lever. J'ai un peu mal au... peu importe. Assieds-toi. Je te croyais à Rome.
MME PIOUK *s'assied.* - Quelle mauvaise mine tu as!
MME KRAP.- Tu n'es pas très fraîche non plus. (p. 22)

Happy Days is entirely based on the ordinary common sense of a well brought up middle-aged woman ("did I brush and comb my hair? [*Pause*] I may have done. [*Pause*] Normally I do. [*Pause*] There so little one *can* do. [*Pause*] One does it all. [*Pause*] All one can. [*Pause*] 'Tis only human", p. 145). Her catchphrase is symptomatically "the old style", the stereotypical nostalgia for the good old days. The same melancholy, drawing room atmosphere, with the addition of bourgeois gossip, permeates *Come and Go*, where there are three Winnie-like figures in large hats in the first version, who in pairs hint at a mystery concerning the third woman who is off stage. Their light, society tones are ironically countered by the characters' physical constriction - while *Human Wishes* and *Eleutheria* were set in a real drawing room, *Happy Days*, *Come and Go* and *Play* have lost their natural drawing room setting. In *Play*, in particular, we are shocked by the acute conflict between tone of speech and actual physical condition of the characters. Their lines, taken on their own, would seem to be a parody on bourgeois drama constructed around a plot of betrayal. There are all the required clichés of plot, such as the love triangle, and of script, but these are destroyed by the paradoxical stage setting, for the three characters are sunk in urns with only their heads visible – they are a parody of the parody.

A completely different comic effect is obtained by the use of music in Beckett's texts. Not just the *musicality* inherent in the verbal structure, but actual *music*.

Some of Beckett's characters hum songs and melodies. Mrs Rooney listens to the notes of Schubert's *Death and the Maiden* coming from the house of an old woman living alone, but ruins the atmosphere with her tuneless singing (on arriving at the station she will do the same with a hymn that Miss Fitt has started to hum, angering this lady who is disturbed by the old lady's wail). Schubert's music at the beginning and end of the radio drama creates around itself an entire visual dimension. It deflects the main action from its course and goes straight into the house of the abandoned old lady, where there is a profound sense of melancholy and sadness, as suggested by the title and music itself. Mrs Rooney dissolves this heavy melancholy by humming the melody in her toneless way, adding a second level of grotesque counterpoint - in the background there is the loneliness of the solitary house, while on stage is Mrs Rooney who, though she is sorry for the old woman, makes a distinctly comical contrast with her awkward halting and humming. Our sadness as listeners for the lonely old lady does not last long and is soon directed towards Maddy's absurd behaviour.

Winnie, too, hums a tune, as it plays on her musical box. "[the musical box] *plays the Waltz Duet 'I love you so' from The Merry Widow. Gradually happy expression. She sways to the rhythm. Music stops. Pause. Brief burst of hoarse song without words -musical box tune*" (p. 155). The tune, which suits the image of Winnie, is *The Merry Widow* and she may be imagined at a ball surrounded by admirers. The result is pathos, because we sense how very far Winnie is from that ephemeral atmosphere, while at the same time noticing her comical doggedness in living in her world of dreams and optimism, albeit buried in the sand up to her waist.

In *Godot* and *Eleutheria* the songs themselves, in addition to occurring without reason, are comical, for they are vaudeville songs. The words are funny and they rhyme in an elementary way with obscene words and images. The second act of Godot opens with Vladimir who, at first timidly, then with satisfaction, sings a children's song whose rhythm, says Beckett, must be that of a military, mechanical march.[25] Almost at the end of *Eleutheria*, Dr. Piouk sings and dances "il a perdu son pantalon/ Tout en dansant le charleston" (p. 155), which alludes to the imaginary of music-hall, not only for its intrinsic rhythm, but also for the reference to dropped trousers. Both tunes are songs in the Brechtian sense: they create an effect of comic alienation, are "gestural" and connected with cabaret. All these musical interludes, be they songs, snatches of song or melodies, succeed in breaking the dramatic flow, never linear in Beckett, with another jerk. For the characters, they are one of many games used to pass the time, while for us spectators, yet another enigma to be solved. Until we discover that the enigma is not hiding a secret but a cleverly contrived mechanism of derision.

In the radio drama *Embers*, music is the source of a real gag. Protagonist is a music master and, according to the worst ever cliché, an Italian one:

MUSIC MASTER: [*Italian accent.*] Santa Cecilia! [*Pause.*]
ADDIE: Will I play my piece now please? [*Pause.* MUSIC MASTER *beats two bars of waltz time with ruler on piano case.* ADDIE *plays opening bars of Chopin's 5th Waltz in A Flat Major,* MUSIC MASTER *beating time lightly with ruler as she plays. In first chord of bass, bar 5, she plays E instead of F. Resounding blow of ruler on piano case.* ADDIE *stops playing.*]
MUSIC MASTER: [*Violently.*] Fa!
ADDIE: [*Tearfully.*] What?
MUSIC MASTER: [*Violently.*] Eff! Eff!
ADDIE: [*Tearfully.*] Where?
MUSIC MASTER: [*Violently.*] Qua! [*He thumps note.*] Fa! [*Pause.* ADDIE *begins again,* MUSIC MASTER *beating time lightly with ruler. When she comes to bar 5 she makes same mistake. Tremendous blow of ruler on piano case.* ADDIE *stops playing, begins to wail.*]
MUSIC MASTER: [*Frenziedly.*] Eff! Eff! [*He hammers note.*] Eff! [*He hammers note.*] Eff! [*Hammered note, 'Eff!' and* ADDIE's *wail amplified to paroxysm, then suddenly cut off. Pause.*] (pp. 258-259)

Although this scene is only heard, it suggests a classic image: the music master beating time, standing by the piano, where his unwilling, tearful pupil gives a poor performance. The master's anger and Addie's growing despair at being scolded are exaggerated to create a funny scene, achieved above all due to the mounting of the sound. The music is interspersed with their lines that almost rhyme, especially if one thinks of English pronunciation: "fa! what? eff! eff! where? qua! fa! eff! eff!". This may seem like a tongue-twister for children but it is actually the sequence of notes from Chopin's waltz and is interspersed by playing the waltz on the piano, creating ironic counterpoint between the serious music and its parodic conversion to the stave.

Even more than *Embers*, there is a group of radio dramas entirely developed around the interaction of words and music: *Words and Music*, *Cascando* and *Esquisse radiophonique*. The very title of *Words and Music* reveals itself to be enigmatic. Though it might seem to indicate a plot telling the story of a duel between words and music, just as appeared to be the case for *Film* and *Play*, this is not so. In reality, the noncommittal appearance of the title is giving us information about the performing genre involved. The medium of radio is by definition built on alternating words and music, so Beckett's title is revealed as circular tautology describing not so much the play's plot as the means of communication used by it.

The radio drama mechanism used both in *Words and Music* and *Cascando* is that of a gag where the action unfolds through an opening-and-closing mechanism. Music is one of the characters on stage, with its own language made up of notes, and it alternates with words in a struggle where first one, then the other is liberated. The conflict proceeds rather like Buster Keaton's cat and dog gag in *Film* - the door is opened and the cat thrown out while the dog slinks in and so on. In American cinema, something similar might be Harpo Marx's musical interludes that in all circumstances calm even the worst racket, which invariably starts up again when Harpo stops playing.[26] This play enables various types of relationship between words and music – accompaniment, conflict and presentation.

In *Words and Music* the music sometimes announces the words "comme le roulement du tambour, au cirque, annonce que l'acrobate va exécuter l'exercise le plus périlleux de son numéro, elle annonce un exercise de la parole".[27] The effect of the struggle might be comical because both types of sound are given humanoid dignity and behave like two of Beckett's clowns, in accordance with the rules of carnivalesque aggressiveness and absurd association.

In *Cascando* the "open-and-close" gag is even more explicit, with the presence of a character Ouvreur, who announces alternately the liberation of Voix and of Musique: "j'ouvre [....]. Et je referme. [...] J'ouvre l'autre. [...] Et je referme" (pp. 47-48 et seqq.). He who opens and closes the game at his will is a disturbing figure, an absolute demiurge, quintessence of an authorial presence. Here too, as in *Godot*, the ludic dimension is explicit and alienating, since we know that these strange characters are interpreting the parts of a game.

There is a similar mechanism of opening-and-closing in *What Where*, though here the play is on light-movements, when the auditory dimension is visualised by the presence of a human-sized tape recorder. From this issues the voice of Bam announcing his own game. "I switch on" is the command whereby the light switches on illuminating the other characters and their moments of stasis and of pantomime. "I switch off" is the command for dissatisfaction, a desire to close and start again. The tape recorder is the demiurge who likes to show his creative action, when on a command from his voice the stage is animated or disappears into darkness, into the void.

The music of *Esquisse radiophonique*, though inserted harmoniously and in a structurally coherent manner between the lines of Lui and Elle, in reality should be heard in the light of the opening lines:

> ELLE. - C'est vrai que ça joue tout le temps?
> LUI. - Oui.
> ELLE. - Sans arrêt?
> LUI. - Sans arrêt.
> ELLE. - C'est inconcevable. (*Un temps.*) Et ça parle tout le temps?
> LUI. - Tout le temps.
> ELLE. - Sans arrêt?
> LUI. - Oui.
> ELLE. - C'est inimaginable. (pp. 89-90)

With this premise, music and words become a dreadful phantasm, an inconceivable, unimaginable perspective, with their continuous, incessant flow. A stone guest who never fails to appear for the grim appointment, making a fine show of himself. *Esquisse radiophonique* is the most meta-reflexive of Beckett's three radio dramas that combine words and music, and it declares its own monstrous nature.

Music plays an active part in the action on stage, it *is* a character who speaks using its own code and provokes, if not the laughter, at least the perplexity of the listener, who is trapped in this game whose rules he thinks he knows, but realises he does not know how to play - a *ludus* that is perfectly intelligible and perfectly inexplicable.

4.3. Noise and silence

In 1969 Kenneth Tynan asked Beckett for a contribution to his review *Oh! Calcutta!* Beckett sent him an extremely enigmatic and shocking text entitled *Breath*, barely a page of stage directions that describe a disturbing atmosphere. The scene opens on the stage littered with indiscriminately scattered rubbish. The stage action consists of a faint light rising at almost the same time as a sound, then there is an interval of 5 cleverly conceived seconds, which gives the audience time to look around the stage and ask themselves what is happening. The very brief sound inserted by Beckett was intended to be the cry of a newborn child mingled with a death rattle, superimposing the instant of the beginning of life with its end. Simply trying to imagine this slow, fleeting breath overlaying life and death, beginning and end, yin and yang provokes a state of uneasiness, of embarrassment and of perplexity. The light following the rhythm of the breath and the immobile scene only serve to further focus attention on the breath, as Beckett in just 5 seconds of pure sound succeeds in disturbing the spectator and involving him in a rapid perceptive synthesis of the anguish of living.

Noise is a highly relevant component of any performance. This sound, in everyday life unhampered by laws and communication codes, in a performance becomes an alternative code and is transformed from pure acoustic signal into an element of expression. Noise is neither music nor words, and is not perceived by the ear as a harmonic, meaningful collection of sounds. Yet even noises can become *code*, that is, a collection of signals regulated by a law.

In the complex system of the theatre, any acoustic stimulus possesses its own meaning, but this function of expression and communication is exasperated even further by the new media - cinema, radio and, in part, television.

The importance of noise in cinema was clear from the days of silent film. With its origins in pantomime where the clumsy actions of the actor when he trips, falls, hits someone or so on are associated with noises, silent comedy began to allude to noises mainly through the live musical accompaniment. Even the sounds of words are soon visualised with the lip reading of which Lubitsch was fond, going beyond the – albeit brilliant – total silence[28] of Keaton, who did not mime the words, but thought them. With the coming of the talkies, comic cinema kept its moments of silence. Think of the Marx Brothers, uniting Groucho's logorrhoea with Harpo's dumbness, or of Laurel and Hardy, who alternated mute pantomime with dialogue. The latter employed an aesthetic of sound with allusive function - there was no need to see the fall, it was guessed at from the sound and from the face of the person watching the tumble. The effect was much more exciting. And the same occurs in *Godot*, with the falls offstage of Pozzo and Lucky.

The role of sound in radio merits separate discussion. This means of communication was based *on* sound in all its manifestations – words, music, noises, silences – and in all its functions, whether communicative, expressive or lyrical. Radio is the medium that completely exploits all the fascination of sound, its storytelling power and its stimulation of the imagination. As radio listeners we finds ourselves in a virtual world that exists independently in our own fantasy. We are completely absorbed because, in contrast to television, which must be watched, the radio broadcast follows us everywhere in our daily life and can be the background to it.

Sound is one of the most compelling elements of radio dramas, whose function is to substitute the visual perception of a stage setting.[29] It must construct an entire world around the words of the characters. The voices, too, of the actors contribute to the atmosphere with a well-defined characterisation of the part, coherent with the character being played. Attention and care regarding the form of sound was perhaps what attracted Beckett to radio - the form of the words, of the music, of the noises and of the silences. With this awareness, Beckett was very scrupulous in his use of sound and in choosing his cast. The actors were so carefully chosen that many of them went on to become Beckett actors *par excellence*. The cast of the first production of *All That Fall* (BBC 13th January 1957, directed by Donald McWhinnie) included Mary O'Farrell (Mrs Rooney), Gerard Devlin (Mr Rooney), Allan McLelland (Christy), Harry Hutchinson (Mr Barrell), Pat Magee (Mr Slocum) and Jack MacGowran (Tommy).[30] We find Magee and MacGowran in minor roles and they would shortly begin their career as Beckett actors and enthusiasts. The all-Irish cast with its very distinctive vocal connotations evoked a vision of the atmosphere of the Dublin suburbs, where the small railway station was the hub of social life for the inhabitants. Provincial human relations link them together, with tinges of bigotry (Miss Fitt), of charity (Mrs Rooney who asks after everyone's health), of convention, cynicism or gossip. The noises requested by Beckett caused not a few problems to the sound technicians. He wanted them to be stylised but not impersonated by humans or technology, taken from nature but anti-natural, in short, hyper-realistic. In the end, they decided on natural sounds used in an anti-realistic way - the animals that open the drama make their calls as if sharing a common aim of parody ("*sheep, bird, cow, cock, severally, then together*", p. 172), nature speaks – in a paradoxical and anti-naturalistic way – only when called upon, the wind blows twice when the characters' words mention it (pp. 181 and 194) and the station, destination of all of the characters, is only heard when the train finally arrives.

Beckett does not always use sound, or music, with a touch of comedy – think of the anguish and cruelty of *Breath* – but its repetition often creates unexpected, funny associations.

The opening scene of *All That Fall* is a perfect score, combining country sounds, human footsteps, music and voice: progression of country sounds/ silence/ human footsteps/ progression of music/ footsteps cease/ mrs rooney's line/ louder music/ footsteps/ music stops/ mrs rooney hums/ stop. After which the action begins with a sound announcing the arrival of Christy's cart. Each of these sound sections starts up when the previous one fades, in an acoustic wave that falls and rises with a different sign.

Mrs Rooney meets various people on her walk. All the characters encountered by the character and by listeners are associated with sounds of movement, beginning with the old lady who struggles on with her "two hundred pounds of unhealthy fat" (p. 191), and then Christy associated with the cart, Mr Taylor with the bicycle, Mr Slocum with the car, Tommy walking uphill, Mr Rooney with the train and the stick and Mrs Fitt walking downhill. In a play where nothing seems to happen all the characters are in motion.

The quality of sound chosen by Beckett is without doubt linked to the cliché - he takes the worst of stereotypes and makes it creative. Consider the constant sound of footsteps in *All That Fall* or of the sea in *Embers*, barely audible in the background that, unlike the sounds of nature in *All That Fall*, fills all the silences. These are clichés equivalent to the creaking door in a horror film. Their use in itself is nothing new, but what Beckett does with them is surprising. In *Embers*, as earlier in *All That Fall*, the constant background of the waves enables Beckett to increase the volume of other micro-sounds within the play, but this only happens when these are mentioned: "hooves" (pp. 253 and 257), "drip" (p. 255), "stone" (p. 260). Nature reacts to the human and takes on the role of antagonist and co-protagonist. Obviously, the image of nature as an active character creates the same surprise as the anthropomorphism of children's stories. This is one of the ways in which sound creates comedy. The others lie in the obscene and in rhythmic repetition.

Many of Beckett's characters insist on disclosing the baser functions of their bodies, instead of concealing them as social convention would demand. Mrs Rooney, Willie and Animateur (from *Pochade radiophonique*) blow their noses noisily; Mrs Rooney slaps herself violently to chase off a bee; Winnie spits: the man in *Play* sighs repeatedly: Didi and Gogo's movements are marked by sighs and sounds of effort (snorting, puffing, panting) as are those of Krapp, all of whose actions have an acoustic background (munching, turning pages, switching the tape recorder on and off, locking and unlocking the drawers). Krapp, in particular, is the protagonist of a real gag based on sound. Immediately after the tape has borne witness to the young Krapp's firm decision to stop drinking, the scene with the old Krapp contains the sounds of three bottles being quickly uncorked, one after the other: "[...] to drink less, in particular. [...] *Pop of cork. Ten seconds. Second cork. Ten seconds. Third cork* [...]" (pp. 218-219). Thus the sound emphasises the exaggerated tautology on which the character of Krapp is based - he is contemporaneously a clown and a drunkard, he is twice a fool, the first time for the very fact of being or seeming a clown, the second, for the fact of being drunk. Under the influence of alcohol the individual loses all inhibitions and becomes a child again, he then takes "pleasure in nonsense".[31] The clown, already a child by vocation, becomes doubly so in the stereotype of the drunkard.

Through the noises they emit the bodies of the characters are shown in their crudest, animal state. The resulting obscenity is automatically laughable, as clowns know well- for they regularly use these acoustic accompaniments.

Rhythmic repetition becomes funny when we see that the characters are not learning anything from their many mistakes and that, instead of changing strategy, they persist with the same routines. The singsong rhythm of *Play*, but also of *Not I* with completely different effects, and the recurring verbal motifs spoken with the same intonation every time go beyond the logic of learning and self-correction. The characters have no limits, are not obliged to adopt rules coherent with civilised society and can follow their eccentric, antisocial models. The contrast is actually strengthened by the fact that these characters still live within the structure of society and we laugh because we see the contrast between the situation and the characters' inappropriate behaviour. Beckett's super-principle of rhythm is here found used for comedy, but elsewhere, it is a basic criterion of the composition. One of the most interesting European productions of *All That Fall* took place in Denmark, directed by Søren Melson who used – after the manner of Beckett – a metronome to hold together the various elements of the drama, as Beckett had done for *Happy Days* with Brenda Bruce.[32]

More structured occurrences of comic sound are found both in theatre and on radio: in *Ohio Impromptu* we find the "open-and-close" gag, where the listener knocks imperiously on the table and the reader starts reading again at the acoustic signal. The mechanical, static nature of the exchange is so chilly that we are obliged to smile in embarrassment.

There are real sound gags in *All That Fall*, where the sound paradoxically constructs the visual element. We can identify at least three: the gag of the car, the hymn and the stairs. The latter two take place in the station before and after the train arrives. Miss Fitt, to pass the time, is humming a hymn. Mrs Rooney joins in clumsily, until the girl loses her patience and threatens to drop her ("MISS FITT. [*Hysterically.*] Stop it, Mrs Rooney, stop it, or I'll drop you!", p. 184). Then, when Mr and Mrs Rooney head for home, they begin their tiring, clumsy descent of the station steps, panting with the effort, dragging their feet and chattering noisily about the mysterious delay of the train. The automobile gag takes place during the journey to the station and is an irresistibly funny piece, exploiting the ambiguity of radio where one can only hear, not see. There are ambivalent phrases with a sexual innuendo ("MR SLOCUM: [...] I'm coming, give me time, I'm as stiff as yourself. [...] MRS ROONEY: Stiff! Well I like that! And me heaving all over back and front. [*To herself.*] The dry old reprobate!", p. 178) and similarly ambivalent sounds ("*effort* [...] *breathing hard* [...] *giggles* [...] *panting*", ibid.), which make the "mounting" of the fat old woman even more laughable. We guess from their dialogue that Mr Slocum, though driven by noble motives to offer a lift to Mrs Rooney, begins to lose his patience when he becomes aware of the unforeseen difficulties of the task. The fat, elderly lady is hauled up into her seat like a dead weight and it is doubtful whether she will ever be able to get down. After all this effort, the scene ends with the car not starting and when after more effort it does, they run over a distracted hen.

In the meticulous timing of the dramas (for theatre, radio and television) and of their production, silences play a fundamental part.
Clas Zilliacus, introducing a chapter on this specific subject, mentions the attitude of Western culture towards silence, oscillating between horror at the lack of words and desire for silence.[33] Beckett's silence in the theatre can be verbal or gestural, as in the frozen images of the *Wartestelle*. On radio it challenges the *horror vacui*, the fear of emptiness, intrinsic to this medium and has a fair variety of forms and meanings. It may indicate the disintegration of language, a character reflecting or a pause for comic effect. It may represent a physical action, but above all it is an instrument of anti-realism: "Beckett's dramatic dialogue [...] is manifestly different from spontaneous conversation. His sentences are meaningful, artfully polished wholes".[34] Beckett's use of silence, in short, is close to the use he makes of music – it *is* music. Beckett made a distinction between the intensity and length of his pauses and made full use of this for variety of expression. An example of a long, comical pause is found in *Godot*. In Act 2, Pozzo and Lucky enter and fall down one on top of the other noisily.

After long negotiation, Estragon decides to help Pozzo get up, makes several attempts but loses his balance and falls on top of him. To save his friend, Vladimir reaches out to him, but in pulling him up, he too loses his balance and falls on the others. After a vigorous exchange of lines and pantomime, there is a grotesque *tableau* on the stage: all the characters are centre-stage on the ground one on top of the other, with Lucky's luggage scattered round them. They remain immobile. The stage direction is "*long silence*" (p. 115). In that lapse of time when the action is frozen, we recognise the absurdity of the pose.

Early on, Beckett had revealed his ideas as to the significance of silences, in the form of a declaration of aesthetic. In *Dream of Fair to Middling Women* Belacqua-Beckett is uncharacteristically explicit:

> the experience of my reader shall be between the phrases, in the silence, communicated by the intervals, not the terms, of the statement, between the flowers that cannot coexist, the antithetical (nothing so simple as antithetical) seasons of words, his experience shall be the menace, the miracle, the memory, of an unspeakable trajectory. [...] I shall state silences more competently than ever a better man spangled the butterflies of vertigo. (pp. 137-138)

The experience of the reader, but also of the audience, must be *between* the sentences, not *in* the sentences. Readers and audiences must discern what is unsaid, in the intervals of the ceaseless flow of information.

The vertigo of silence captures them who abandon themselves to it and, paradoxically, brings them nearer to the truth. Which is always unspoken… "between the flowers that cannot coexist".

Notes

1. This excellent volume first appeared in 1986 as a "numéro hors-série", evidently to celebrate the writer's 80th birthday. It was republished in 1990, on his death, with bibliographical and chronological updates and some more articles. I refer to the latter version.
2. Arikha 1990, p. 4.
3. Gussow 1996, p. 10.
4. Bryden 1998, p. 44.
5. Antoni Libera in Oppenheimer 1994, pp. 108-109.
6. Marowitz 1962, p. 44.
7. Ibidem.
8. For stage examples see the erotic provocations of Living Theatre in the Sixties.
9. Marowitz 1962, pp. 44-45. On Le Coq see De Marinis 1993.
10. Esslin 1980, p. 150.
11. Zilliacus 1975. Other bibliographical material on the subject might be Worth 1981 and Esslin 1980.
12. Ibid. p. 11.
13. See ibid. p. 64.
14. Ibid., see the different versions of *All That Fall* and their development towards the text finally published.
15. Esslin 1961.
16. Frasca 1998, p. XXIII (my translation from Italian).
17. Edward Beckett interviewed by Mel Gussow (1996, p. 122). For more information on music in Beckett's biography see ibid. and Knowlson 1996. Bryden 1998 is specifically dedicated to Beckett's relationship with music.
18. Fournier 1990c, p. 245.
19. Bryden 1998.
20. See Knowlson 1996, who reconstructs his experience of music in relation to his works.
21. *Murphy,* too, contains a paradoxical linguistic metamorphosis when the acronym M.M.M., which stands for Magdalen Mental Mercyseat, becomes "music, music, MUSIC" (p. 161).

22 Frasca 1998, p. LIII (my translation from Italian).
23 See McMillan-Fehsenfeld 1988.
24 Zilliacus 1975 says that the original title "with its echo of the Marx Brothers, is suffused with an atmosphere of comic levity from the very beginning" (p. 39) which is perhaps why it was discarded.
25 See McMillan-Fehsenfeld 1988, p. 131.
26 See *A Day at the Races*.
27 Croussy 1971, p. 134.
28 As Fink calls it, 1980, p. 233.
29 See the principle of the "radiogenic" and indications for use of sound in Pradalie 1951.
30 In the French production (RTF 19th December 1959) there were actors who had already worked with Beckett: Marise Paillet and Roger Blin.
31 Freud 2002, p. 122.
32 See Knowlson 1996, p. 501. The Danish broadcast by DR was one of the first productions following the BBC one and was broadcast on 3rd January 1958. My acknowledgments go to Sigvard Bennetzen, DR for kindly allowing me to listen to the tape and to Professor Bent Holm for the information.
33 Zilliacus 1975, p. 154.
34 Zilliacus 1975, p. 166.

* CHAPTER FIVE *

"WORDS FAIL US". WORDS. SPEECH. TEXT

5.1. The betrayed tradition

As well as visiting the cinema and theatre and listening to the radio and concerts, another substantial part of Beckett's cultural education was the reading he did as a student or out of intellectual curiosity. This is the area most familiar and most explored by critics, because Beckett has mainly been studied as a writer.[1] Beckett was acquainted with a vast literary tradition, including a considerable amount of comic and humorous literature, once again demonstrating his specific, technical interest in the genre.

Any discussion of Beckett's techniques of written comedy necessarily requires a swift glance at that literary background on which he gazed, cross-eyed - in one direction he was looking at its models and forms, while in the other, he was trans-gressing from its teaching by trans-lating it into his own language. This twofold background looked both at literary and theatrical comedy, as well as on the wider literary panorama over which Beckett was to wield his hatchet of parody.

With these models Beckett formed a dialectical relationship of alternating refusal and acceptance, with the one state sometimes turning into the other. Consider, for example, his conflictual relationship with Sterne. Between 1932 and 1933 he read the work of the Anglo-Irish humorist and a few years later wrote to MacGreevy that he did not at all like *Tristram Shandy* (letter of 5th August 1938)[2] and this judgement was repeated whenever critics spoke too much of the – quite evident - similarities between the two authors. In the Sixties, however, Beckett "wrote to William York Tindall that he had a great admiration for Sterne and particularly for *Tristram Shandy*",[3] demonstrating the fact by including Sterne's name in a radio drama of the same era (ca. 1961), *Pochade radiophonique*, in an ironical line of Animateur: "connaissez-vous les œuvres de Sterne, mademoiselle?" (p. 76). The citation is clearly a tribute if we consider the other authors mentioned explicitly by Beckett, for Sterne appears together with his beloved Dante and few others. Beckett had read and studied Sterne over the years and his private library included two versions of *The Works of Laurence Sterne*: a 1780 edition in 7 volumes (Dublin, D. Chamberlaine: he had volume 4) and that of 1910 (London, Oxford University Press), which included *Tristram Shandy*.[4]

As well as Sterne, Beckett read a great deal from the whole literary tradition of irony. Diderot, Fielding and Swift (we know he owned *Gulliver's Travels* in the Oxford University Press edition of 1963 and volume 6 of the anthology, *The Prose Work of Jonathan Swift* by Bell and Sons from 1922)[5] were read by him in 1932-33. Stephen Leacock was a youthful passion (he was reading the Canadian humorist of English origin in 1915-23 with his schoolmate Geoffrey Thompson). He was fascinated by the humour of Pierre-Jean Jouve and even considered of doing his Ph.D. on him, though he decided on Proust (1926).[6] In 1935 he went on to study the authors of the picaresque novella and read *Don Quixote* by Cervantes (his notes for *Murphy* date from more or less the same period and include numerous quotations from *Don Quixote*, some in the original Spanish).[7] Shortly after, he read *Pantagruel* by Rabelais. Beckett bought a copy of *Pantagruel* in the Génie de France edition in July 1935 and probably read it immediately. It fired his imagination: no fewer than 23 pages of notes show the young Beckett "writing out quotations ranging from large sections to single phrases, as well as paraphrasing some of its more genial, uproarious moments". During the same period Beckett wrote the first 10,000 words of *Murphy*, which were profoundly affected by what he had just read. With its "blend of erudition and humour, wordplay and coinages [...], pleasure in the sound of difficult or archaic words"[8] it strongly recalls Rabelais' masterpiece.

As well as the prose humorists, there were also those of the theatre, upon whom Beckett would base his dramatic skills - Shakespeare who struck him for his musicality, Racine, whose complete works he owned in the Garnier edition,[9] Corneille, Ben Jonson (he certainly read *The Alchemist*), Molière's complete plays by Hachette and Maeterlink's *Théâtre* volume 1, edited by Fasquelle.[10]

To this range of "classics", he added the study of the literary world of Latin and Greek. In what is known as the "Whoroscope/Murphy notebook"[11] Beckett filled several pages with a chronological chart summarising the history of Greek literature by genre and gave a special place to comedy, divided into "ancient", "middle" and "new".[12] Under these categories he listed the respective authors, including Cratinus, Aristophanes and Menander, followed by brief notes on satire and its subject.

The Latin world was represented in this notebook by Horace, from whom he jotted down the opening of *Epistula ad Pisones* with some personal notes. It appears as follows in the manuscript:

Surrealism
Humano capiti cervicem pictor equinam
Jungere si velit, et varias in ducere plumas,
Undique collatis membris, ut turpiter atrum
Desinat in piscem mulier formosa superne,
Spectatum admissi risum teneatis, amici?
(opening of Epistola ad Pisonem [sic]) [underlined by Beckett][13]

This passage has several points of interest. On one level, the choice of author and work is interesting: the *Epistula ad Pisones*, otherwise known as *Ars Poetica*, is Horace's most significant statement of aesthetics and one of the key points on which the entire theory of classical literature was founded. Beckett's choice immediately places him in an aesthetic *milieu* nourished by classical literature. A second level of interest introduces us directly to a theory of comedy that I can here preview. From *Ars Poetica* Beckett chooses the *incipit*, with its strong, disturbing image describing the grotesque creation of a painter. This monstrous figure assembled by absurd and unreal logic is able to transform even the harmonious grace of a maiden into a horrendous monster. In its presence, we cannot hold back our laughter, indeed in its presence all people laugh (the vocative "amici" indicates not a single individual laughing, but a whole group sharing the same values). It is surprising that Beckett chose to copy out the opening passage of *Epistula*, while the rest of the treatise illustrates the Horace's concept of teaching and of enjoyment. Yet here, evidently, Beckett felt very strongly how much he had in common with Horace. He deliberately ignored the more famous and significant parts of Horace's work, which cast light on the precise aesthetic and cultural policy Horace was aiming for, to surpass the perfection of Greek models, and stopped at a passage normally considered as introductory to weightier subjects. What struck the young reader of Horace was not his Augustan classicism, but that strange description of a paradoxical, deformed creature. The grotesque figures that Beckett was creating and imagining in his own system of aesthetics had their classical origin in that principle of comic monstrosity - from Horace's viewpoint, as from Beckett's, the repellent figure of Belacqua provokes not mere repulsion, but a disgusted laughter. Beckett's extraordinary capacity for discerning profound connections between events and for interweaving different aesthetic movements suggested his title for the passage quoted: "Surrealism".[14] For Beckett, Horace's image has a surreal quality, a dreamlike element that transcends reality, like the images of his own fictional universe. In the passage from Horace, Beckett discerned the irrationality elevated to an aesthetic principle and the freeing of the unconscious of the Surrealist movement, while at the same time perceiving the consonance with his own, original sense of the grotesque and the surreal. Like Proust in the article of that name, Horace provided him with an excuse for discussing his own aesthetic, under cover of supposedly impersonal criticism. Behind his brilliant interpretation of the *incipit* of *Ars Poetica*, Beckett concealed the exuberance of his own creative fantasy that in the Thirties, the period when he quoted Horace in his notebook, could no longer be kept at bay, but was urgently pressing for ex-pression, at first in prose, later in drama.

Beckett used the classics as formal influences, more or less hidden, or through direct quotation. For example, many of his titles have a double meaning involving the classics. *All That Fall* is a direct quotation from Psalm 145:14, "The Lord upholdeth all that fall", from the King James Bible, Cambridge edition. This lofty quotation seems strange considering the plot, where all that fall just fall and remain desperate. *More Pricks Than Kicks* distorts the sense of Jesus' words to Saul "it is hard for thee to kick against the pricks" (Acts 9:5), turning the quotation towards an obscene, blasphemous meaning.[15]

Beckett's quotations, whether in the title or in the text, are always slightly alienating, either because they contrast with the context or situation or because the quotation is not exact or complete. The effect, in any case, is parody. These frequent citations are clear signs of Beckett's cultural points of reference. *Happy Days* contains a real avalanche of references: Winnie quotes from Verlaine, from *Hamlet*, from *Romeo and Juliet*, from *Cymbeline* and *Twelfth Night* by Shakespeare, from *Paradise Lost* by Milton, from *Ode on a distant prospect of Eton College* by Gray, from *Paracelsus* by Robert Browning, from "Down by Salley Gardens", from *To the Hawk's Well* by W. B. Yeats and even from a nineteenth century minor Irish poet, Charles Woolfe. Winnie lives in her own world where the good old ways still appeal and where the most basic of everyday actions is accompanied by mention of Ophelia's line "o woe is me/ T'have seen what I have seen, see what I see",[16] which is though transformed into "woe woe is me [...] to see what I see", spoken by Winnie as she cleans her glasses (p. 140). She quotes Romeo's words as she applies her lipstick. Even these lines are delivered in her own way: the highly dramatic "beauty's ensign yet/ Is crimson in thy lips and thy cheeks/ And death's pale flag is not advanced there"[17] becomes "ensign crimson [...]. Pale flag" (p. 142). Whenever Winnie refers to the old style of the classics, her memory gets it wrong or confused: from *Ode on a distant prospect of Eton College* by Thomas Gray "And moody Madness laughing wild/Amid severest woe"[18] becomes "laughing wild... something something laughing wild" (p. 150).

Winnie carries on regardless, filling her monologue with truncated, reworked, almost unrecognisable quotations but always enjoying the "wonderful lines" in perfect "old style". Beckett would in future have other characters use many quotations, but nobody with the same dizzy satisfaction as Winnie.

Hamm quotes Baudelaire announcing, "un peu de poésie" (p. 110)[19] and Shakespeare, transforming the famous phrase in *Richard III*, "my kingdom for a horse!"[20] into a blasphemous parody: "mon royaume pour un boueux!", in English "my kingdom for a nightman" (p. 103)!

Godot contains fewer quotations, briefly hinted at by a word (the "divine Miranda" on p. 59 of Lucky's monologue refers to Shakespeare's *The Tempest*) or by a subject. Didi and Gogo dramatise some extracts from the Scriptures, discussing the plausibility of some episodes. Particular animation is aroused by the theological problem of the two thieves, summarised by St Augustine in the maxim "do not despair, one of the thieves was saved; do not presume, one of the thieves was damned". Vladimir is inspired to reflect on this paradox: "un des larrons fut sauvé. (*Un temps.*) C'est un pourcentage honnête" (p. 13). His optimism at all costs makes him consider only the hypothesis of salvation, commenting that, all in all, a 50% chance is not a bad start. This mundane calculation applied to divine teaching plunges the originally serious tone of Augustine's words into the depths of comedy. And it is amplified by the indifference of Estragon who is not only unconcerned about the possibility of spiritual salvation, but also cannot remember ever having read the Bible.

The list of quotations could go on for ever, in *All That Fall* (from *Effi Briest* by Theodor Fontane and from Dante), in *Krapp* (from John Donne and *Othello*), in *Pochade radiophonique* (from Dante and Sterne), from *Come and Go* (the title may refer to Eliot and the situation, as well as the opening lines, to the witches in *Macbeth*), in *Words and Music* (from Yeats)[21] and so on. And one could add the quotations of proverbs and idioms from popular culture and biblical references from religion. It has indeed been a favourite hobby of Beckett critics in recent years to discover how much Joyce, how much Dante or how much Descartes and so on is contained in his works. The intention here is not to compile such a catalogue of quotations, but to reveal their essentially parodic function.

Beckett wove into his texts a network of links with classical tradition by means of quotations, but at the same time he undermined this mechanism by choosing the comic register. This comic overturning warns us not to take too seriously whatever makes us laugh, but the parody remains constrained by the model. In the parody, the classic and its comic overturning are both essential to each other. The "twisted clichés or quotations"[22] that Ruby Cohn identifies in all Beckett's work starting from *Whoroscope* are recurring parodies of Western knowledge and their frequency in his texts indicates a more general attitude.

The painter and good friend of Beckett, Avigdor Arika, summed up this eccentric idea of classicity very well: "l'œuvre de Beckett, par sa rigueur, sa juste mesure, est naturellement classique" and this does not exclude it also being experimental, "sans excès et jamais arbitrairement".[23] This classicity is met, therefore, in the rigour and just measure of the writing, with clever distribution of the elements, musical density and allusive images. It is an art reduced to the essential, without unnecessary excesses, where every syllable is justified, as indeed in Dante and in the Bible.[24] Or in Chekhov, where comic and serious tones are perfectly balanced.[25]

With a paradox typical of Beckett, Pierre Chabert attempts to define that borderland in Beckett's theatre where tradition and innovation intermingle: "la création théâtrale qui a toujours privilégié l'action, la fable, est profondément bouleversée [in Beckett], à certains égards inversée. Elle prend son origine [...] aux sources de la scène elle-même, de la poésie ou du langage dans l'espace-lumières, sons, mouvements, corps. La 'mise es scène', le langage spécifiquement scénique devient originaire, générateur de la pièce elle-même, d'une écriture scénique, analogue à la peinture, à la sculpture, aux images visuelles des rêves, dont la parole demeure certes un élément important, mais un élément seulement".[26] It is by inverting traditions that Beckett creates an original archetype of genre to apply to his theatre - he goes to the very origins of theatre and exploits its pure principles to paint and sculpt his space, bodies and sounds. This instrumental and/or parodic use of the classic does not prevent him from being, himself, classical.

On close inspection, the paths of tradition in Beckett run mostly along the paths of parody. His entire dramatic and literary production is a progressive, systematic questioning of the most established theatrical conventions, until he finds autonomous means of expression. In order to construct his own language Beckett first had to deconstruct existing possibilities, sweeping away all outdated conventions cluttering up his path. Only from the ruins of the defunct theatre building could Beckett's unique world be born.

If we consider Beckett's early work as a young man, before *Godot*, we have: *Le Kid*, a student parody or irreverent burlesque inspired by Corneille's *Le Cid*; "The Possessed", a parody of academic theatrical criticism in dramatic form (like "*Che Sciagura*", another polemical pamphlet written as a dialogue); *Human Wishes*, a dramatic fragment that basically makes fun of the comedy of manners with its didactic tone and unpleasing artificiality; and *Eleutheria*, a completely parodic comedy. It is significant that the latter, Beckett's first complete work for the theatre, was clearly structured as a parody, perhaps too much so and this is why it was rejected. At first sight, *Eleutheria* seems to mock bourgeois drama, the "*pièce bien faite*", which had evolved from the light comedies of the French stage where it began into intimate and tormented realist drama at the turn of the centuries. Held up to the light, *Eleutheria* reveals the forms of the Scandinavian tradition of Ibsen and Strindberg that, differences between the two authors aside, has the stereotypical setting of a drawing room and focuses on the psychological torments of the protagonist. Beckett knew Ibsen from his student days at Trinity College, seeing the Abbey Theatre productions of *Vildanden*,[27] *Et Dukkehjem*, *En Folkefiende* and *Peer Gynt*. The latter's fantastical, tragicomic tones "made the deepest impression"[28] on him. Otherwise, Ibsen's markedly psychologistic realism only provided Beckett with a negative model, to be denied or overturned. Doctor Piouk clearly personifies such a parody and is, not by chance, Scandinavian. Within a bourgeois drama that is crumbling in all directions there are other parodic allusions to the theatre. McMillan and Fehsenfeld have reconstructed the myriad of theatrical conventions cited in the work, thereby creating an authentic manual of theatre history. Hamlet and Oedipus are impersonated by Victor; Jarry by Victor's father who expresses himself in the "merdre" style of Ubu; Artaud is referenced in the torture scene; Molière by the trick of hiding under the bed (when Mme Meck is looking for Victor, Vitrier answers "il est sous le lit, madame, comme du temps de Molière", p. 74); Yeats, by the protagonist's existential torment; and there are other references to Sophocles, Shakespeare, Corneille, Shaw,

Zola, Ibsen, Hauptmann, Pirandello, to Symbolism, to Surrealism and to Socialist Realism.[29]

We might also add Aristotle, whose unities are systematically denied by the double action on two stages, as described in the lengthy opening instructions: *"cette pièce comporte, aux deux premiers actes, une mise en scène juxtaposée de deux endroits distincts et, partant, deux actions simultanées, action principale et action marginale"* (p. 13). The stage is divided between the main action, which takes place in a bourgeois drawing room where the characters have text and lines, and a marginal action, a pantomime set in the solitary little room of the against-all-odds hero, Victor. There is no dividing wall between the rooms, so Victor can slip from one to the other. The third act is set in Victor's room *"vue d'un autre angle. Côté famille Krap mangé par la fosse"* (p. 119). The Aristotelian unity of time-place-action is overthrown in a single blow - the simultaneous actions in different places and times contradict the very foundations of Western theatrical aesthetics.

The staging described in the directions poses practical complications with a stage that must somehow "rotate" ("a chaque acte, la chambre de Victor est présentée sous un autre angle, ce qui fait que, vue de l'auditoire, elle se trouve à gauche de l'enclave Krap au premier acte, à droite de l'enclave Krap au deuxième acte, et que d'un acte à l'autre l'action principale reste à droite", p. 14), its double stage settings, one of which very luxurious, and its 17 characters. All these elements made *Eleutheria* an experiment that remained – fortunately – isolated in Beckett's production. *Eleutheria* essentially is a *parodia*, not so unlike the theatrical tradition it appears to negate. But apart from the obvious limits of the text, which was clearly never finished or revised by Beckett, the drama contains many interesting elements and some brilliant, amusing points of playwriting.

Eleutheria already showed a sign that was to characterise all Beckett's work, that is, of "destroying the banality of the domesticated theatre with precisely the material that made it what it was".[30] But Beckett was still a long way from finding his own language. *En attendant Godot* is almost contemporary with *Eleutheria,* but the inspiration for the latter is not so well concealed as that of other works. One of the most interesting moments in the drama is, for example, the appearance on stage of a Spectator who tries to intervene in the stage action, because he is terribly bored. This dramatic element is not innovative, having often been used by the twentieth century avant-garde, yet it has its own value, not least of which is as an experiment that Beckett would develop enormously in subsequent works. The pulling down of the fourth wall in *Eleutheria* is complete and the naturalistic convention is not contemplated either in the stage setting, for there is no division between the two rooms, or in the relationship between stage and audience.

5.2. "...à moi de jouer"

The Spectateur in *Eleutheria* suddenly bursts in at the beginning of the third act, in a moment when the action is stagnating into unbearable immobility and boring repetition:

> SPECTATEUR, *debout dans une avant-scène* - Arrêtez! (*Il enjambe avec raideur le bord de la loge et descend précautionneusement sur la scène. Il avance vers le lit.*) Je m'excuse de cette intrusion. (p. 127)

In the best tradition of Pirandello, the pretence is revealed and declared, and the spectators (the real ones) are obliged to adapt themselves to different new conventions and interpretative codes. The meta-theatrical shifts are inserted early on in Beckett to disturb stage convention.

The fact that Beckett as a director insisted on the presence of and on conveying the illusion of the fourth wall might seem contradictory, but in reality only serves to exasperate his use of meta-theatre. Michael Haerdter's rehearsal diary for *Endspiel* contains some of the directions given by Beckett to actors during rehearsal: "there is a surprise when Beckett explains this by means of a principle of naturalistic theatre - 'the play is to be acted as though there were a fourth wall where the footlights are'"[31] or again "Beckett instructs his actors [...] to act as if in front of a fourth wall".[32]

While Walter Asmus maintains[33] that Beckett the director wanted to re-establish the fourth wall, acting also as Beckett the playwright, by eliminating those asides to the audience, for example for the production of *Endspiel*, I believe that the value of Beckett's fourth wall was confirmed by those very asides that he was trying to remove. "Both audience and curtain are incorporated into the play, for Beckett uses the convention of the fourth wall or breaks it at will",[34] and it is by consolidating the convention that he can make breaking it even more surprising and profane.

The fact remains that his dramatic works contain a large number of asides to the audience, as does his prose to the reader, and a high awareness of pretence on the part of the characters. The characters seem to be constantly aware of the linguistic code they are using and of the stage situation in which their actions are carried out. They know that they are *speakers* using a convention to communicate among themselves and they know they are actors who are playing their parts. They communicate this knowledge to the audience, leaving it perplexed as to its own identity and function within the theatrical convention. The Western audience is participating in a codified ritual when it attends the theatre. By purchasing a ticket it stipulates a pact with the actors and commits to believing in their fiction. This bourgeois codification has been challenged by avant-garde movements from the beginning of the century up to the present and Beckett simply adds his very personal and original contribution to this trend. Far from being in line with any avant-garde thinking, Beckett interprets the relationship between stage and audience in his own way and, conserving the convention of the fourth wall, renders the glimpses through that imaginary division more pungent and more meaningful. The reference is clearly to the very being of the characters, so strongly represented by the frontal view and by their awareness.

Eleutheria, more than *Godot,* is a mine of similar references – the characters discuss their own lines, the aim of a good *pièce* and even ask for the curtain. Monsieur Krap provokes Dottor Piouk by asking "je me demande à quoi vous allez servir dans cette comédie" (p. 40), to which Piouk replies "j'espère que je pourrai être utile" (p. 41); Vitrier scolds Victor "j'ai vu des amateurs, mai jamais personne aussi mauvais que vous" (p. 88), calling him a "dreadful amateur actor" (Barbara Wright who did the

English translation used the term "ham", p. 87); and later he complains about the lines Victor has just spoken, "ce n'est pas la ligne que j'aurais choisie" (p. 93); when Mme Meck asks what is the point of Victor playing at hiding under the bed, Vitrier replies that "c'est dans un but de délassement et de divertissement publics" (p. 74), revealing the aim of light theatre through the ages; at the end of the first act M. Krap himself asks for the curtain ("rideau", p. 67), while at the end of Act 2 Vitrier uses it as a threat – if no clarification is forthcoming he will be obliged to bring down the curtain , "ne voyez-vous pas que nous sommes tous en train de tourner autour de quelque chose qui n'a pas de sens? Il faut lui trouver un sens, sinon il n'y a qu'à baisser le rideau" (p. 111).

As well as words, the characters twice make explicit gestures towards the public, firstly, at the start of Act 2 when Victor walks up and down in agitation, "*il s'arrête près de la rampe, regarde le public, veut parler, change d'avis, reprend sa marche*" (p. 71), then, when Vitrier tells the Spectateur that he wants to leave the stage: "je m'en vais. Vous me remplacez, n'est pas? Auprès de lui, auprès (*geste vers le public*) d'eux" (p. 137). In the first case, Victor shows that he fully realises the existence of another dimension outside of the stage, of another gaze observing him, which remains outside, though emotionally involved in his torment. But this quintessential, inept anti-hero cannot decide to directly address the observer, so continues his frenzied toing and froing. In the second case, by contrast, the audience is called upon by Vitrier's words ("eux") and by his gesture towards the auditorium, to underline the mysterious reference to "them". An unspecified other presence of unknown beings is also found in *Catastrophe*, where the Metteur en scène expects his creature to be highly successful: "formidable! Il va faire un malheur. J'entends ça d'ici" (p. 80), or even better in the English version, "terrific! He will have *them* on their feet. I can hear it from here" (p. 461, my italics).

Another time Vitrier refers to the public, but this time in an unorthodox way, offensively calling them an audience of gawkers. He is sustained by the authority of an author, playing, in fact, at being a poet, declaring himself to be the author. He thus effectively functions as a bridge between the public and what is happening onstage. "le Vitrier, comme le régisseur dans *Six Personnages en quête d'auteur* de Pirandello, représente la présence de l'auteur. Il se trouve là en tant que médiateur entre le public et ce qui se passe sur scène. Il se dit poète".[35] It is in the name of this authority as demiurge that he ambiguously says he is the author of the play:

> DR PIOUK, *au vitrier*. - C'est vous, l'auteur de cette plaisanterie de lycéen?
> VITRIER. - Faut bien amuser les badauds. (p. 96)

This play has been written to amuse idlers who enjoy prying into others' business. We are "les badauds", the observers, poking our noses into what does not concern us. The critical remark hits home and the public receives a feeling of embarrassment and unease, though the dramatisation of the audience-function, the character Spectator, does not seem at all affected, perhaps annoyed the confusion on stage. Onstage, in the manner of Pirandello, a spectator appears complaining about the slowness of the action and trying to take an active part in the play. The movement of an actor hidden in the audience who cuts vertically through the auditorium to rush onto the stage destroys, in itself, the fourth wall. The subsequent interaction of spectators with the characters and the stage action destroys any credibility left to the convention. The same effect is achieved by the prompter (Souffleur) who suddenly leaves his box, protesting loudly:

> VOIX DE LA LOGE. - Assez déconné. Au fait, au fait. [...]
> La farce, la farce. Assez duré.
> Le souffleur sort de son trou, monte sur la scène, son texte à la main.
> SOUFFLEUR. - Assez! Fini! vous ne suivez pas le texte. Vous me dégoûtez. Bonsoir. (Il sort.). (p. 132)

We are totally at sea. There are no more rules of drama or of logic left to respect. The chaos is total and eludes the form, so that the entire play founders on the rocks of the non-completion. I am not surprised at Beckett's dissatisfaction with *Eleutheria*, nor at his obstinate refusal to publish or stage it (today both these wishes have been ignored):

its development does suffer from an elephantine structure unworthy of the author and from an underlying indecision as to what to do. Like his character Victor, Beckett is unable to decide, uncertain whether to choose the safe but outdated paths of parodic tradition, or to take a radical choice of life and art to extremes. *Eleutheria* suffers from this limbo, while *Godot* bravely faces the unknown of a very personal form of drama, destined to make an original contribution to the genre of Western comedy and drama.

To a greater degree in *Godot* we find the same attitudes towards the audience as in *Eleutheria*, but expressed with much softer tones. Here too, the characters are aware of the code and pretence and here too, as later in *Fin de partie* and *Catastrophe*, they often address the public.

Beckett's characters never use the linguistic code without awareness of the artificial nature of the locutionary convention and they show this in their meta-discursive references, now on the signified, now on the signifier of their speech. Didi and Gogo are aware that they are using words in an instrumental manner for their games. To make the time pass more quickly, they tell each other stories, jokes, they insult each other, they quibble over theology and then decide to change the subject if they are bored: "ESTRAGON. - Passons maintenant à autre chose, veux-tu? VLADIMIR. - J'allais justement te le proposer" (p. 118).

There is Krapp who savours the word "bobina" like a sweet delicacy, or gets stuck on the dictionary definition of the word "viduity" ("[*reading from dictionary.*] State -or condition- of being -or remaining- a widow -or widower", p. 219). Winnie wonders what the correct form is for indicating her hair ("Willie, what would you say speaking of the hair on your head, them or it?" p. 146). Then there is the spasmodic exchange between the mysterious A and B in *Fragment de théâtre II* ("B. - [...] Merde! Où est le verbe? A. - Quel verbe? B .- Le principal. A. - Moi je n'y suis plus du tout. B. - Je m'en vais chercher le verbe et laisser tomber toutes ces conneries au milieu [...]", p. 49). These are all examples of the same attitude of the characters, for whom the logos is one of their favourite games, so no wonder they sometimes lay their cards on the table.

But the characters are even more aware of the entire situation of performance. W2 in *Play* knows she is being watched and spied on, but instead of being bothered by this situation, it is what makes her very existence possible, indeed she embarrasses the audience with her pathetic request for attention, "are you listening to me? Is anyone listening to me? Is anyone looking at me? Is anyone bothering me at all?" (p. 314).

Some of the characters, too, play at being actors. This is done particularly by the two great showmen of Beckett's universe - Pozzo and Hamm. They both adopt bombastic tones and insist that the others humour them by listening to their tirades and passing favourable judgement on their performance. Pozzo wants to be certain of having an attentive audience and before starting his speech he makes sure of this, "tout le monde y est? Tout le monde me regarde? [...] Regarde-moi, porc!" (pp. 40-41); and then he asks for an audience reaction, "comment m'avez-vous trouvé? [...] Bon? Moyen? Passable? Quelconque? Franchement mauvais?" (pp. 52-53).

Hamm is just as bad - and of course his name hints at him being a 'ham actor' – obliging everyone to listen the same old story, to which he adds his own stylistic commentary: "ça va aller. [...] Joli ça. [...] Ça c'est du francais! [...] Un peu faible ça. [...] Ça va aller. [...] Je n'en ai plus pour longtemps avec cette histoire. (*Un temps.*) A moins d'introduire d'autres personnages" (pp. 72-75). Each expression of auto-criticism, Beckett decreed, was to be delivered by Hamm in a normal tone of voice, alternating with that of the story, and represented so many deviations from the conventional flow of the drama, according to the rules. They create a complex pattern of switches that have two functions – one, internal to the play, is to reveal the pretence, the other relates to the exchange of communication between stage and auditorium. The public becomes aware of the pretence and reacts to the surprise, often with a smile. The last line alludes to the presence of an author, capable of ending or continuing the story as he pleases. Hamm wants to have us believe that he detains the important function of absolute creator, but the truth is that, like everyone, he depends on the other characters to interpret his role. When Clov asks him "a quoi est-ce que je sers?" (p. 79), Hamm replies instantly "à me donner la réplique" (p. 80), to feed me the line. The two characters are tied to each other by the ruthless law of dramaturgy: everyone exists in relation to the others, dialogue is only possible with all its elements and the game only functions if everyone accepts the pact. Hamm will not give up at any cost. Clov implores him to be allowed to stop playing, "cessons de jouer!", but he is inflexible, "jamais!" (p. 102), until Hamm himself asks to stop, "c'est fini, Clov, nous avons fini. Je n'ai plus besoin de toi" (p. 105). We are at the end of the game, that moment in a game of chess when the final part is being played, not yet the end, but preparation for it. This stage had particularly stimulated Beckett's imagination as an expert chess player, as being the fulfilment of the end, though not yet a fixed point. The "fin de partie", in chess terminology the "endgame", is the concrete materialisation of the purgatorial moments in Beckett's drama, the end in progress. Clov and Hamm, like Beckett's other characters, are eternally playing this challenge and are always ready to begin – "à moi de jouer", my turn – or to end with a grand finale. Hamm is resigned to ending his part and his language becomes increasingly explicit, using technical acting terms: he is preparing an "aside" ("aparté" p. 102), "j'amorce mon dernier soliloque" (ibid.), or "rebondissements" ("pourvu que ça ne rebondisse pas!" p. 103), further "underplots" (p. 109), the final exit.

Fin de partie, from the very first line begins to create this dual imaginative level of pretence and revelation. Hamm's "my turn" would soon be echoed, firstly by Winnie with her "begin Winnie [...] Begin your day, Winnie" (p. 138), which starts the stage action, conscious of an external, observing eye ("someone is looking at me still", p. 160). Then there is the *incipit* of *Embers*, where Henry orders the action to begin, made dramatic by the sound of the sea, "on. [*Sea. Voice louder.*] On!" (p. 253). Vladimir and Estragon, for their part, are conscious of the difficulty of beginning, "c'est le départ qui est difficile" (p. 89), but then solve the dilemma by starting a game that only works if both of them play. And when enthusiasm for the game wanes, a little encouragement will spark it off again: "voyons, Gogo, il faut me renvoyer la balle de temps en temps" (p. 15). The *ludus* is not particularly conceived as a metaphor and the two companions actually do amuse themselves by playing, without hiding the fact. Indeed, all Beckett's characters declare openly "je raconte" or "je joue", with the double meaning of acting and playing.[36]

The "je joue" is revealed in a most obvious manner by meta-theatrical references to the public - for example, three times Vladimir and Estragon look towards the auditorium and make ironic comments on what they see. Clov does the same.

Didi and Gogo wait for Godot and pass the time by discussing the case of the two thieves. Estragon's judgement is quite categorical: "les gens sont des cons" (p. 16). Then he inspects the surroundings centre-stage, looks first to the back, then to the auditorium, goes forward *"jusqu'à la rampe, regarde vers le public"* and comments "aspects riants" (ibid.), pleasing outlook. Vladimir does not agree with his friend – when he turns his gaze on the auditorium he sees nothing but a desolate bog: "tout de même... cet arbre... (*ce tournant vers le public*)... cette tourbière" (p. 18). It is only towards the end of the second day that Vladimir sees something other than desolation in the direction of the auditorium. Overcome with agitation at the thought that he and his companion are surrounded by some persons or some danger, he reacts as follows: "(*Vladimir va le* [Estragon] *relever, l'amène vers la rampe. Geste vers l'auditoire.*) Là il n'y a personne. [...] (*Il le pousse vers la fosse. Estragon recule épouvanté.*) Tu ne veux pas? Ma foi, ça se comprend. [...]" (p. 104). In a similar way, Clov sees a mad crowd in the auditorium: "(*il descend de l'escabeau, ramasse la lunette, l'examine, la braque sur la salle.*) Je vois... une foule en délire" (p. 45). The comic effect here is amplified by the fact that Clov uses a telescope for his inspection, focussing this circus instrument menacingly on the audience and making fun of them, while the protagonist of *Mime du rêveur* puts on a pair of spectacles "in order to examine the audience more closely".[37]

The audience, who according to convention likes to retreat into the darkened auditorium to doze or watch voyeuristically, is shaken from its torpor. But these invasions of its space only partially destroy the fourth wall, which continues to impose its presence, and so the audience's interpretative codes remain unsteady. The Paris audience of the Fifties, accustomed to avant-garde provocation, on first seeing *Godot* knew they could or must decodify a work of art by applying codes parallel to and different from the traditional ones. But even this sophisticated public was thrown by Beckett, finding itself in a network of appearances that referred back and forwards to each other in a sequence of Chinese boxes. It appears that the actors ignore us, pretending to believe in the fourth wall, and it appears that the characters seek for contact with the public. In actual fact, more than seeking contact they attempt clownlike provocations, involving the audience with the aim of mocking them. The direct and unconditional insult reaches its target with little difficulty – see the open insult to the public in *Human Wishes*:

> MRS WILLIAMS. Words fail us.
> MRS DESMOULINS. Now this is where a writer for the stage would have us speak no doubt.
> MRS WILLIAMS. He would have us explain Levett.
> MRS DESMOULINS. To the public.
> MRS WILLIAMS. The ignorant public.
> MRS DESMOULINS. To the gallery.
> MRS WILLIAMS. To the pit.
> MISS CARMICHAEL. To the boxes. (p. 300)

The ignorant public infests the whole theatre, the gallery, the pit, the boxes, and the playwright only thinks of pleasing them, making the characters speak when there are no more words left and explain when there is nothing to explain. Beckett's biting irony attacks that somnolent theatre, which flatters an undemanding public, happy with a well-written, light, evening's entertainment, needing everything explained without effort, as Hamm says, "ah les gens, les gens, il faut tout leur expliquer" (p. 61). An ignorant public that remains ignorant, an uninspired author that remains mediocre - Beckett's meta-theatrical switches involve the entire system of theatrical production and open it up to a post-modern crisis.

The game of confirming and negating the fourth wall and the authorial attitude of the characters ("je joue", I act) have the effect of shaking the audience, interrupting the stage action. The same effect is obtained by the characters' vocation for storytelling. The "je raconte" stimulates an alienating effect every time it occurs in a performance because here we would normally expect a dramatisation of the events rather than a story. Beckett overturns this rule, making great use of "je raconte", of storytelling, in nearly all his plays and radio dramas.[38] Beckett's storytelling, with its flavour of Brecht, is an authentic dramatic epic mechanism around which the main and secondary actions are arranged. All the characters like to tell the story of their lives, amidst the indifference of the others and their own problems of memory and concentration. These moments break the dramatic flow but are necessary to its development. The funny stories and jokes of *Godot* and *Fin de partie*, Winnie's grotesque stories of the good old days, the betrayals of *Play*, even the logorrhoea of *Not I* are a necessary part of the main dramatic action involving the players. The storytelling acts as a long break in the dramatic process and gives an epic dimension, in Brecht's sense, to the tale. The characters never cease to be completely part of the drama, in fact they use their narration to release hidden dramatic and psychological tensions, as when Hamm obsessively repeats his story, despite the exasperation of the others, or as in the schizophrenic relationship between old Krapp/young Krapp.

The characters' joke light-heartedly, unperturbed by lapses of memory, play together and mock themselves and the others. We might think they derive emotional respite from their storytelling, indeed some have seen an effect of "redemption" therein.[39] But more than respite, in this case there is an obligation to narrate, an impelling need, just as for Beckett the creative process is driven by the urge to write. Like his characters, Beckett is slave to an uncontrollable drive to create of which he himself has spoken, with "nothing with which to express, nothing from which to express, no power to express, no desire to express, together with the obligation to express" (*Proust and Three Dialogues with Georges Duthuit*, p. 103). This process and its results do not console the spirit, but they are the only game possibile to get through the immobility, which is why much room is given to comic playfulness. The stories of Beckett's storytellers combine in a sole register the pathos of an unhappy life with the irony, sarcasm and aggressive mockery of the clown. Their apparent light-heartedness is simply a sense of detachment, enabling them to slide from the comic to the pathetic and vice versa.

Beckett's dramatic techniques are designed to affirm a strong awareness of pretence, which is also awareness of the creative process and of the stage-auditorium relationship. These techniques may all be defined as meta-theatrical, whether they effectively make use of the "theatre-within-the-theatre", or provoke switches outside of the stage pretence, like the "je joue" and "je raconte". The transgressive impact of this technique is one of the most common devices in European stage tradition from the 16th century onwards, a praxis used to heighten the audiences' arousal and interest.[40] Beckett, once again, positions himself in line of rigorous continuity with the theatrical traditions of the past, but in addition to reinterpreting them in his own manner, he does so from a transversal, squinting viewpoint. As far as meta-theatre is concerned, for example, he clearly has in mind, more than the practice of the Commedia dell'Arte, one of the most interesting dramatic experiments of our century, a model that is an exemplary embodiment of infringement of theatre's conventions.

Beckett and Pirandello: an obligatory comparison when discussing meta-theatre, artistic relationship and aesthetic harmonies of great import, meriting special discussion.

I mentioned above the spectator in *Eleutheria* who, Pirandello-like, tries to resolve the dramatic impasse with his own intervention, but I have said nothing on how much there is of Pirandello in all Beckett's work and aesthetic. This is tricky but rewarding terrain, rich enough to merit its own monograph, hitherto lacking in Beckett criticism.[41]

Many have conjectured as to Beckett's effective knowledge of Pirandello and this has been made more difficult by the former's refusal to admit the conscious influence of the latter. When Aldo Tagliaferri expressly asked him about this, Beckett's reply was unconditional: "I am not conscious of Pirandello's influence on my work".[42] Many of the hypotheses regarding Beckett's knowledge of the Italian playwright are proposed by exclusion: it would have been impossible for a university student of French and Italian, who had gone to Paris in 1926 when the city was raving about Pirandello's plays, who had travelled through Italy in 1927 and who was planning a study of Jules Romain, who both esteemed and declared his debt to the Italian writer, not to have known Pirandello.[43] One undeniable fact, however, is the strong personal and intellectual influence of Professor Walter Starkie on his student Samuel Beckett during the university years. Professor Starkie had made a detailed study of Pirandello and had written a monograph on him, published by London publishers, Dent, in 1926, entitled *Luigi Pirandello*. He it was who introduced the young student to

Pirandello's works: "Starkie [...] had some knowledge of the continental theatrical avant-garde and Beckett was to remember later that he introduced him to the work of Pirandello, which he read with some pleasure".[44]

Having established that Beckett did actually know this most European of Italian playwrights from the beginning of the century, we may attempt some textual and aesthetic comparison. Beckett's anti-heroes have already been likened to Pirandello's man without qualities. Their torments, expressed through a strange balance of laughter and tears, seem to partake of the same philosophy and the same aesthetic.[45] The authors' thoughts on dramaturgy and the stage and on humour seem to be surprisingly similar.

Like Pirandello, Beckett shared a struggle with language, transformed into practice on stage, for both writers became playwrights and, thence, directors. In Pirandello's case, a better definition would be *capocomico*, but for convenience we shall use the term "director", which would only later be used in Italy for the stage profession.[46] Both men battled with the blank page and the three-dimensional space. Both, over time, acquired knowledge of the stage, of which as young men they had only been spectators. And both adapted their aesthetic thinking to the new requirements they encountered when working in the theatre.

Beckett's non-fiction work was limited to a very early period when he thought himself destined for an academic career, while Pirandello continued his theoretical activity alongside that of writer-director. Beckett's aesthetic thinking, however, can be gathered from meta-discursive snatches in his prose, in his theatre or in rare instructions to actors, whether verbal or in his notebooks, as well as in interviews. His positions do not seem to have changed much, but to have moved towards ever-increasing awareness of the details of stage production and familiarity with the techniques. Pirandello, on the other hand, would never openly repudiate the idea of a theatre of the word, but around 1935 he includes in his theoretical writings a notable awareness of the theatrical theatre,[47] and at the same time he was equal to the great European directors in stagecraft.[48] Claudio Vicentini has pointed out that "[...] it was not just the opportunity to work with actors that enthralled Pirandello. It was also the fascination of the instruments of scene",[49] so much so that Marinetti, the founder of Italian Futurism, called him a "«devotee of the theater» suffering from a real «idolatry of the means of stage»".[50]

Similarly, Beckett was to maintain his positions already expressed in *Proust* or in studies now collected as *Disjecta*, for, in discussing other authors, Beckett conceptualises his own aesthetic. The theatre would never be simply *spoken* action, but action *done*. Stage experience would give him greater awareness of this and diminish his original lack of confidence in actors and directors and their approach to their work. Like Pirandello, with some of them he would create a special relationship, strengthened by a union that was both personal and professional.

As far as dramatic conventions were concerned, Beckett challenged that of the fourth wall as Pirandello had done so scandalously in the Twenties. Pirandello's actor literally attacks the spectator from behind, entering from the back of the stalls and horizontally smashing through the barrier between public and actors. He makes the actors and characters talk, thereby revealing a pretence normally kept tacit and lifelike by convention. He speaks of dramatic conventions actually in the theatre – this is meta-theatre. The effect on the public – especially the Italian one – in the Twenties is shocking: all the occult and concealed mechanisms of the theatre are put shamelessly on show, in a dialogue between reality and pretence, face and mask, which only words have the power to manage and recompose, or reconstruct.

Beckett absorbed Pirandello's teaching in all its fascination, but times had changed, as had the artist. The destruction of dramatic conventions in Beckett has none of Pirandello's European, modernist avant-gardism, of his faith in words to convey a strong meaning and emotional impact. So much so that exceptions to the rule of the fourth wall require rigorous respect of this convention - Beckett's characters refer to the audience in such a fleeting, circumscribed manner that this can only work when the convention is very fixed. Even the awareness that the characters have and demonstrate on stage does not result in the pretence overcoming the reality, as in *Sei personaggi in cerca d'autore*, in *Questa sera si recita a soggetto* or in *I giganti della montagna* (also partly in *Enrico IV*) Beckett's characters are imprisoned in a circle from which they cannot escape and the game, in both senses of *ludus* and acting, is the only way to get through this eternal human Purgatory a little more quickly. This potentially consoling effect of the passage of time and of the arrival, sooner or later, of a resolutive end is nullified by identical repetition of the same routines. *Play* is twice repeated entirely and identically, and the ending cuts short a third repetition that we imagine will be completed. *Come and Go* also repeats the same routines twice. *What Where* obsessively reiterates the same passage with slight variations. *Godot* remains enigmatic in the return of Pozzo and Lucky and the boy. Winnie sinks ever lower but never changes those rituals she can still carry out. All is a closed circle, space and time. The characters are in the centre, playing. They use a language that has lost all of Pirandello's certainties and has, itself, exploded into complete giddiness. It no longer conveys a rational choice of deconstruction, but itself contains the deconstruction. Pirandello's reliance in the word, able to shock, to divert, to move and to educate, in Beckett is transformed into a distant illusion, no longer practicable or imaginable. It is the word itself that brings chaos. It *is* chaos.

Beckett and Pirandello meet most closely in their idea of the comic, which for both of them has a "humorous" quality. In his study on humour,[51] Pirandello reconstructs the etymology and history of the term, linking it to the black humour and bile of northern European origin. Having shown that it is not restricted to the literature of Northern Europe alone, he unfolds his own interpretation of humour. Of the well-known distinction between "perception of the contrary" (provokes instinctive laughter) and "feeling of the contrary" (laughter is accompanied by sym-pathy and reflection), Pirandello prefers the latter. Tragedy and farce are, for him, inseparable from each other and every smile is wiped by the tragic awareness of human life. With one grotesque image Pirandello succeeds in unfolding his theory on humour:

> an old lady whose hair is dyed and completely smeared with some kind of horrible ointment; she is all made-up in a clumsy and awkward fashion and is all dolled-up like a young girl. I begin to laugh. I perceive that she is the opposite of what a respectable old lady should be. ... [T]he comic consists precisely of this perception of the opposite. But if, at this point,

reflection interferes in me to suggest that perhaps this old lady finds no pleasure in dressing up like an exotic parrot, and that perhaps she is distressed by it and does it only because she pitifully deceives herself into believing that, by making herself up like that and by concealing her wrinkles and gray hair, she may be able to hold the love of her much younger husband - if reflection comes to suggest all this, then I can no longer laugh at her as I did at first, exactly because the inner working of reflection has made me go beyond, or rather enter deeper into the initial stage of awareness: from the beginning perception of the opposite, reflection has made me shift to a feeling of the opposite. And herein lies the precise difference between the comic and humor.[52]

Beckett, with fewer "existentialist" tones, maintained and practiced an identical mixture of tragic and comic. He did not expressly prefer the tragicomic model, corroborated in Pirandello by an illustrative relationship between art and reality, where art "illustrates" the torment of living, but it enacts chaos in texts and scene. Everyday suffering is not *acted*, but *presented* by the body and the word.[53]

Both can be interpreted within the Freudian understanding of humour, *Witz*: the psychic means of overcoming a perceived emotional and psychological obstacle. According to Freud humour emerges in order to turn painful experiences into pleasure: "where a tendentious joke is employed, pleasure is produced, then it is reasonable to assume *that this gain in pleasure corresponds to the saving in psychical expenditure*".[54] While Pirandello conveys this miscellany of pathetic and comedy through words that are often absurd, but always traced to an overwhelming logic, Beckett develops the elements of "dark humour", leaving both his characters and his audience in jeopardy.

The effect on audiences is completely different. Valerie Topsfield maintains that the two authors are altogether alike in "their use of comedy in manipulating the reactions of the audience".[55] The English academic finds that Pirandello's moralist aim, his revelation of the miserable face of reality beyond the mask of the theatre and of the everyday, was inherited by Beckett, whose public experienced the same uneasiness as that of Pirandello: "the same difficulty is experienced by Beckett's audiences, but this mixture of laughter and tragedy, and their evanescence, is a conscientious attempt to tell us that that is what existence is about".[56]

So, no difference between the public of *Sei personaggi* and *Godot*? And yet we feel that much has changed. Though Beckett and Pirandello used the same, indissoluble link between tragic and comic, as well as similar stage and dramatic techniques, they achieved very different aesthetic results. Beckett leads his spectator into a maze of suggestions with multiple levels of interpretation, without ever giving him the map to find his way out. Nor are Pirandello's *logos* or logical consequentiality saved - the absurd attacks both verbal expression and the logical categories of knowledge of reality. Beckett's spectator is lost, sharing the same bewilderment as the characters he sees on stage and from whom he deludes himself he is distant, safely behind that imaginary wall that separates him from the stage. In this sense Beckett's attack on the convention of the fourth wall is even more traumatic than Pirandello's. Although the stage impact of Pirandello's destruction seems more incisive, since it creates a complete dramaturgy around itself, that of Beckett is infinitely more destabilising, because it no longer has the safety net of word-rational mind.

Beckett certainly considered Pirandello as one of his masters of the twentieth century, but he took him to extremes and extended his boundaries to the heights of dizziness.

5.3. The speaking clown

If we follow the history of clowns up to its most recent developments, we realise that, in a time and place shrouded in mystery and by a mythological aura typical of the circus, the clown who descended from ancient pantomime suddenly, magically, began to speak. I do not refer to the *clown blanc*, always depicted with normal attitudes and so always in command of an appropriate linguistic code, but to the *auguste* who continued to express himself above all using his body, thus contaminating the adult locution.

What in circus terminology is called the "speaking clown" uses deviated and deviant verbal expression, always closely linked to the body's material animality. His means of communication are language as sound, or joint expression of word and gesture, which may describe or contrast each other. Also, because his use of the *logos* is childlike, he very often uses vocabulary from the semantic field of the body, particularly if obscene or embarrassing. In short, his function is destabilising and subversive.

Beckett's clowns are no exception to this rule and they dress, gesture, manage the space with its objects and people and make noises like circus clowns, as well as speaking like them.

In effect, this is the part of Beckett's comedy that till now has received greater attention from critics, since Beckett has been essentially interpreted as a playwright of the word. The first study of Beckett's comedy, that of Ruby Cohn, starts from the premise that, of Bergson's three categories used in her analysis, language is the element that is most fundamental to Beckett's comedy: "of the three domains, situation, character, language, it is mainly upon the last that Beckett's comic effects depend".[57] Comedy of word, so much so that Beckett uses action to underline the destabilising effects of language: "Beckett uses action to help him undermine language".[58] Cohn's analysis takes gestuality into account only as and when it is conveyed by the *logos* or supports the verbal. The comic is studied as an instrument for understanding Beckett's work as a whole, given that "an analysis of his humor therefore traces an attitude that is pervasive in his work, at its complex core, and an understanding of that humor may elucidate the core".[59]

The rhetorical figures of verbal comedy used by Beckett, though very varied, have in common the fact of being founded on contrast and on logical subversion. The words of Beckett's clown bring disorder, an irresolvable chaos that pervades man's faculties of interpretation and logic, a chaos that characterises the emotional and psychological relations between human beings and their communication. The battle with the word is not only aesthetic, where the artist seeks for words that escape him, but also everyday, experienced day by day as a real impossibility of communicating.

The speeches of Beckett's characters are vomited like an unstoppable flow or held back with the suffering of stipsis. In both cases the dynamics of communication are pathological. The words seem illogical, where they are instead a-logical and paradoxical, for they are not without meaning, only this is constantly deviated, absurd and far away from "normal" logic. The effect is of an upside-down world where madmen or clowns or children decide the rules of the game.

The a-logical elements are particularly evident when speeches of several characters collide with each other, calling into question both their linguistic knowledge and the psychic relations beneath their personal ties.

Cross-talk, a type of fast, witty dialogue, is very frequent in Beckett's work, especially in the theatre, where the lines undergo considerable rhythmic acceleration due to the quick succession of short verbal exchanges. In *Godot*, one of many examples is based on a misunderstanding between Vladimir and Estragon:

> ESTRAGON. - Qui?
> VLADIMIR. - Comment?
> ESTRAGON. - Je ne comprends rien... (*Un temps.*) Engueulé qui?
> VLADIMIR. - Le Saveur.
> ESTRAGON. - Pourquoi?
> VLADIMIR. - Parce qu'il n'a pas voulu les sauver.
> ESTRAGON. - De l'enfer?
> VLADIMIR. - Mai non, voyons! De la mort.
> ESTRAGON. - Et alors?
> VLADIMIR. - Alors ils ont dû être damnés tous les deux.
> ESTRAGON. - Et alors? (p. 15)

The psychological relationship between speakers becomes a strange mixture of contrasting elements. The state of conflict is not so much latent as manifest in the intolerance that he who refuses to understand shows towards him who cannot explain himself. In effect, the urgent rhythm of the cross-talk creates a pre-conscious level of conflict, long before we discover the reason for the resentment. And yet, even when war has been declared, the unbreakable tie of affection remains strong, so that sometimes Vladimir and Estragon seem to overlap their lines as if they were part of the same monologue. It is the pseudo-couple speaking. They are both different and separate, but so complementary that they often give the impression of being one single macro-character, speaking with different voices but following one line of discourse. Another example from *Godot* might be the wordplay on the identity of Godot and his promise to keep the appointment:

> ESTRAGON. - Et qu'a-t-il répondu?
> VLADIMIR. - Qu'il verrait.
> ESTRAGON. - Qu'il ne pouvait rien promettre.
> VLADIMIR. - Qu'il lui fallait réfléchir.
> ESTRAGON. - A tête reposée.
> VLADIMIR. - Consulter sa famille.
> ESTRAGON. - Ses amis.
> VLADIMIR. - Ses agents.
> ESTRAGON. - Ses correspondants.
> VLADIMIR. - Ses registres.
> ESTRAGON. - Son compte en banque.
> VLADIMIR. - Avant de se prononcer. (pp. 23-24)

Sometimes the cross-talk combines affirmations that contradict each other, or the speakers disagree and maintain the opposite, but even here they seem to be in line with a pre-arranged script, in a game agreed in advance, that shows them to be two faces of the same coin. Didi and Gogo provide various examples of this, too, after that of the music-hall and the circus, where they offer two different points-of-view in a mechanical manner, without ever coming together in true dialogue, on parallel lines:

> VLADIMIR. - Ça fait un bruit d'ailes.
> ESTRAGON. - De feuilles.
> VLADIMIR. - De sable.
> ESTRAGON. - De feuilles. (p. 87)

Cross-talk, already present before *Godot* in *Eleutheria* and *Human Wishes*, becomes pitiless in *Fin de partie*, where the tensions between Hamm and Clov explode in words, since they cannot use the corporal dimension given the physical immobility of three-quarters of the characters. The victim-executioner relationship between the two characters finds an outlet in aggressive repartee and so their tight dialogue is often coloured by a dreadful cynicism.

Wherever dialogue occurs in Beckett there is cross-talk, even in *Play*, a drama entirely constructed around the mechanism of repartee although its characters never speak directly with each other. The rapid accumulation of lines sounds like cross-talk and follows its general principle, but the character's speeches never collide with each other, remaining as monologues or soliloquys embedded between them. Beckett explodes the mechanism of this figure of speech from within, though he has used it and played with it up till that very moment. Incommunicability is a cage, just like the urns in which the actors are trapped, from which there is no escape. The only way is through soliloquy - to which no-one listens, except the theatre audience. Beckett's last dramatic work, *What Where*, is, like *Esquisse radiophonique*, entirely constructed on prolonged cross-talk, apparently senseless, and on its obsessive repetitions.

The musical quality of this technique can be easily recognised: the tight rhythm of the lines going back and forth from one character to another and the reiteration of the same verbal motifs create a sonorous repetition that provides the musicality of Beckett's text. Ruby Cohn has researched and catalogued[60] different kinds of these verbal repetitions. Her criterion was to consider the number of repetitions: "doublets", "triplets" and so on, up to an authentic refrain, a *tormentone* that marks the entire text. Within these, one can find sub-categories, depending on their position in the text: 1) "simple doublets", where a word or phrase is spoken immediately after the first time; 2) "interrupted doublets", the listener interrupts the speaker who repeats the word/phrase he was enunciating; 3) "distanced doublets", repetition takes place at too much distance to be immediately perceived especially in a play; 4) "echo doublets", a character repeats the words of another changing the tone. The same also goes for the "triplets": some can be "simple", generally sarcastic in tone, leading to a climax that is impossible with "doublets", while others are "echoes", the same word/phrase bounces between two or three people.

Beckett's characters play with the words, although these escape them, and weave a net of incongruous switches from the signified to the signifier and vice versa.

The misunderstanding, for example, which is founded on the contrast between what the character understands and what he or she finds out in the end, is based on a comic effect released by the discovery of the misunderstanding. Reality is deceiving and the character finds out the folly of it.[61] The misunderstanding in Beckett is often due to a literal interpretation of a figurative expression. Classified by Bergson and defined by Cohn as "misplaced literalism",[62] this type of misunderstanding is very common in clownish comedy, as indeed in all comedy from the Commedia dell'Arte up to stand-up comedy. I believe it was especially the comedy of cinema that gave Beckett his model, taken from the linguistic battles between the educated Groucho and the infantile Harpo in the Marx Brothers, and above all from Laurel and Hardy's repartee. The violence running between the lines of "misplaced literalism" derives from the disparity of comprehension of the two speakers who, though they think themselves equal, in practice discover they are incapable of really communicating. Reminiscences of Laurel and Hardy had already been noted by Kenner[63] who had made the connection between some lines from *Way Out West* (1937) and the ending of *Godot*:

HARDY: Get on the mule.
LAUREL: What?
HARDY: Get *on* the mule.

VLADIMIR: Pull on your trousers.
ESTRAGON: What?
VLADIMIR: Pull on your trousers.
ESTRAGON: You want me to pull off my trousers?
VLADIMIR: Pull ON your trousers.

(The quotation from *Godot* is in English to underline the similarity; p. 88). The combination of one sharp and one foolish character enables numerous misunderstandings to arise, as the latter stupid one tends to interpret figures of speech literally, to simplify the complex view of language and reduce it to the lowest terms of body and survival. The foolish clown is ignorant of the abstract symbolism necessary to the convention of figures of speech, therefore his speech is always of a poor, limited nature. In Beckett the process is not automatic as in traditional comedy, since his characters represent functions of speech, and more generally of psychology or drama, that are not homogeneous. The role of the cunning and the stupid player is totally reversible between them. Vladimir and Estragon, for example, (but I could also cite Pozzo/Lucky, Clov/Hamm, WInnie/Willie and so on) are not always coherent with only one of the two models - the former is not always wise and the second is not always stupid. Misunderstandings fill the speech of the one and the other. Also, the dynamic between the literal and the metaphorical can be overturned. We find both the literal interpretation of the figure of speech and vice versa, the metaphorical can be used to contrast the literal. In order to illustrate the former I can quote from *All That Fall*, when Mrs Rooney sighs "what will Dan say when he sees me?" to which Mr Slocum replies "has he then recovered his sight?" obliging the woman to specify "no, I mean when he knows" (p. 178).[64] Beckett's characters tend to carry the literal meaning to abstraction: when Pozzo says "je suis aveugle", Estragon comments "peut-être qu'il voit clair dans l'avenir" (p. 119). In both senses – literal (blindness) vs. metaphorical (seeing in the future) and metaphorical vs. literal – the effect can be comic, for it reveals the speakers' inadequacy.

A misunderstanding can occur in a dialogue, due to dissociation of meaning: in the English version of *Godot* for example, Estragon, replies "what" to Vladimir's question on "how":

VLADIMIR: How's the carrot?
ESTRAGON: It's a carrot.
VLADIMIR: So much the better, so much the better […]. (p. 21)

The spectator's surprise arises from realising the indifference with which the receiver accepts the deviated reply of the the other: instead of being surprised by Estragon's shift of conceptual cathegory, Vladimir accepts it as normal, even with some degree of satisfaction and continues the dialogue.

Misunderstandings can arise from any kind of friction between signified and signifier, made possible by countless figures of speech. In Beckett they may be engendered by paronomasia, that is, a pun, using two words with a similar sound, by polionomasia, that is, the tendency to confuse words,[65] or by spoonerism, that is, confusing the first letters of two different words.[66] Misunderstandings derive from the switch between an everyday sense to a universal one (Pozzo asks "qui êtes vous?" and receives the answer "nous sommes des hommes", p. 115; or Hamm orders the flea's death because "à partir de là l'humanité pourrait se reconstituer", p. 50. They also happen when different subjects overlap ("ESTRAGON. - Si on essayait avec d'autres noms? VLADIMIR. - J'ai peur qu'il ne soit sérieusement touché. ESTRAGON. - Ce serait amusant. VLADIMIR. - Qu'est-ce qui serait amusant? ESTRAGON. - D'essayer avec d'autres noms [...]", p. 117). Another cause is *Volksetymologie*, that is, the tendency for the speaker to construct his own etymology of a word whose meaning is unknown to him. This last term is borrowed from linguistics, where it means an etymology based on similarity of form or sound, activated when a speaker encounters a semantically obscure term whose form he changes to make the content clearer. An unknown element of the phrase or the word is altered, in order to be connected to a lexical family known to the speaker. According to linguistics, this is a procedure for modifying the signifier while maintaining the basic meaning and introducing the term in a new network of relationships, familiar to the speaker.[67] An example of this might be the frequent distortion of the name of Pozzo (Bozzo, Gozzo, pp. 29-30) and of Godot ("Godet... Godot.. Godin", p. 39) or Winnie's quotations.

Much more often the signified (the mental image) of a phrase contrasts with its vocal or sound signifier, that is, the line is not accompanied by a suitable tone or modulation of voice. *Play* is built entirely around this friction - the subject matter is pathetic and sentimental and might move us, were it not spoken by the actors in a monotone that flattens the sentiments into a monstrous litany. The fast, linear tone cancels out the amorous torments of the three characters in one single, indistinct flow, where the insults, the prayers, the story, the happiness and the disappointment are indistinguishable. The contrast of the tone with the content is so strong that at first the spectator loses track of the story, at the expense of his general understanding of the drama. The effect, desired and intended by Beckett, is once again of tragicomic bewilderment.

Another source of comedy is the contrast between normally irreconcilable registers - the colloquial and the erudite levels are constantly active in Beckett. Mutual metamorphosis is always possible, especially when we least expect it. Many Beckett characters incoherently alternate between proper and elegant speech, more like erudite academics than *clowns blancs*, and the foolish babble of the true *auguste*. Didi and Gogo, Mercier and Camier, Murphy, Watt, Hamm and Clov all do it and so, in his very own way, does Krapp. Because he listens to his own voice on the tape, Krapp plays on the difference in expression between the young and the old Krapp, the former, a promising young man and educated speaker, the other, disenchanted and a vulgar, boorish speaker.

The former expresses himself using language correctly and following a logical-emotional sequence, the other gabbles, expresses himself with indistinct sounds and the words he used as a young man have suddenly become incomprehensible, so he has to seek help in the dictionary. The distance between them is made evident by listening to the tapes.

Hamm is another schizophrenic speaker who alternates colloquial tones (the orders to Clov or daily needs, like medicine, the dog) with stately, rhetorical ones (the story), or pathetic tones with menacing ones (shouted orders, curses). But above all Hamm seems to act his part inside and outside the stage pretence, for the ham actor accumulates contradictions and unstable states of mind, and often his tone is in contrast with his line. When he asks for pardon from Clov, he does so "*froidement*" and in the face of the other's impassivity he actually shouts his excuses "(*Un temps. Plus fort.*) J'ai dit pardon" (p. 21). Cynicism gives these funny contrasts a black hue, turning them into black humour.

An expert in play on contrasting tones is Winnie, who alternates attention to her lowest bodily functions (brushing her hair and her teeth, cutting her nails, gargling) and cultured quotations and tales of high society. She talks to herself in a normal voice, but then varies the tone of her words and speech:

> Something says, Stop talking now, Winnie, for a minute, don't squander all your words for the day, stop talking and do something for a change, will you? [*She raises hands and holds them open before her eyes. Apostrophic.*] Do something! [*She closes hands.*] What claws! [*She turns to bag, rummages in it, brings out finally a nailfile, turns back front and begins to file nails. Files for a time in silence, then the following punctuated by filing.*] There floats up - into my thoughts - a Mr Shower - a Mr and perhaps a Mrs Shower - no - they are holding hands - his fiancée then more likely - or just some - loved one. (p. 155)

The tale of Mr and Mrs Shower then continues, marked by filing of her nails. Winnie here introduces another type of contrast present in all Beckett's texts – that between word and context.

The contrast in atmosphere involves the speech register and that of the situation together, as when a pompous tone is not justified by a suitable setting. A good example is that of Winnie chatting politely while she is sunk in the desert up to her waist, or of the love triangle in *Play* whose amorous adventures are dissected while imprisoned in the urns, or of Nagg and Nell who are even able to indulge in nostalgia from their dustbins. Other cases include Vladimir and Estragon, Pozzo and Lucky or Krapp, who in appearance are tramps but are refined in speech.

They all share a fair dose of eccentricity and refusal of reality. They all live in a parallel world, indifferent to the incongruities in which they are the players, open to our amusement or to our perplexity. It is not uncommon, indeed, for their gestures to be dissociated from their words (Estragon points the way to Vladimir without a hint of gesture: "(*sans geste*) Par là", p. 10) or for their dialogues not to follow a logical course. What appears to be jumping from one topic to another, a disorderly succession of incoherent arguments, is actually a way of organising thought – and therefore speech – according to a different concept of normality - and the underlying rule of Beckett's dialogues concerns association and emotion. Rather than replying to the other's verbal stimulus, Beckett's character reacts to a feeling provoked in him by the other person, so the (dis)ordering rule is the speaker's interior world, not the superior law of rationality. It is the logic of Shakespeare's fool, who is allowed to overturn an unquestioned and established order because of his folly. It is the infantilism of clowns who, just like children, are authorised to make mock of adults, justified by their ingenuity, which, in the case of clowns, is a pretence. Just as the fool is the only one allowed salacious irreverence towards the king, the clown is the one in the circus who can physically attack the spectators, sitting on them, touching them, shoving them, pushing past in an overbearing way, or verbally with swear words, offensive allusions, or simply by involving an adult – the involvement of children has a very different tenor and effect – in a game that tests his or her shyness with children. Beckett's clown/fool has no inhibitions and his fantasy can range freely through a-logical thought.

The a-logical and analogical associations open the way for unlimited possible outcomes of the speech and Beckett's clowns could carry on talking for ever, following their "schizophasic" dissociations. The "simultaneity of the possibles, the pathogen of the 'this and that'»"[68] allows for continuous development of the *logos*. This assumption, rather than comforting man with faith in language, has the opposite effect, because the driver of the *logos* is not going vertically, straight in a definite direction – it turns back upon itself in an infinite, vicious circle. Some characters are terrified of the moment when words will finally fail: Winnie is afraid of "the time when words must fail" (p. 151), in *Human Wishes* it is said with certainty "words fail us" (p. 300), and Clov shouts despairingly at Hamm "j'emploie les mots que tu m'as appris. S'ils ne veulent plus rien dire apprends-m'en d'autres. Ou laisse-moi me taire" (p. 62), but even the opening lines of *Godot* ("rien à faire", p. 9) and of *Fin de partie* ("fini, c'est fini", p. 15) can be read in the sense of the complete failure of gnoseology (and therefore also of speech).

Sometimes the irreconcilability of tone derives from the use of hyperbole that is so exaggerated as to be unacceptable to a logic that is not absurd. Or the use of litotes, where understatement – although its opposite – ends up having the same effect as hyperbolic exaggeration. Also signs of exaggeration are the unmotivated bursts of anger of the tyrannical characters, Pozzo and Hamm, but partly also of the victim-characters. Their tone of speech changes without warning from a tranquil talk to a ferocious harangue or violent scolding. The motive normally is not known, nor do the other characters ask themselves the reason. These excesses are for them coherent with the violence of clowns, which does no real damage, which makes a great show but is soon forgotten to make room for the next game. A character who blows his top is a sight not to be missed by the others, who are completely unconcerned by the consequences of his raving, as they know there will be none. In any case, the role of the braggart bullying the weak is a consolidated cliché of comedy. Hamm's behaviour towards Clov is no different from that of the father towards his son in the Karl Valentin's sketch "Confirmation Day": "If I had not been there, having compassion upon you, nobody in the world would have been a godfather for your Confirmation!".[69] Apart from the reference to confirmation, this line might have been spoken by Hamm to Clov when he begins to suspect that the little one in the story adopted by him is in fact Clov.[70] The feeling throughout the story is that the young boy should be grateful to his master-as-father-figure who has ensured his survival when the natural father was unable to provide for his needs. But Hamm's psychological cruelty is much more aggressive than that of the father of the confirmed, because the prospect of a world without pity for his son does not refer to the past, already remedied ("If I had not been there"), but to an apparently desolate future: "oui, un jour tu sauras ce que c'est, tu seras comme moi, sauf que toi tu n'auras personne, parce que tu n'auras eu pitié de personne et qu'il n'y aura plus personne de qui avoir pitié" (p. 54). In both cases, those destined for this world without pity display a childish indifference that leaves them impassive or throws them into fits of hysterical laughter. Beppe, the son in Valentin's sketch, just like Clov, cannot help bursting into fits of apparently unmotivated giggles.[71] In the world of clowns, cruelty hurts neither body nor soul.

Gianni Celati defined some of Beckett's verbal comic techniques as "verbal gags". Although Celati was analysing only Beckett's non-dramatic works, his observation can be applied also to the theatre. The verbal gag is essentially based on a hysterical relationship between speaker and listener. The latter "has a comic value to the extent that articulates the language in chains of manic-depressive movements from unpredictable bursts of rage of null outcome; has comic value as it becomes producer of verbal gags recited in front of us as a display of maladjustment or inappropriate reactions to circumstances".[72] Like the gestural form, the verbal gag appears to be developed on progressive levels, leading from an opening phase to the final resolution, with the explosion of contradictions or tensions or a simple punch-line. There are various examples in *Godot*, like the dialogue between Pozzo and Estragon that proceeds by superimposed contradictions (Pozzo seems to be offering spiritual assistance, Estragon accepts material help, Vladimir refuses charity and the apparent state of tramps, Estragon lowers the asking price, pp. 53-54). There is Pozzo's offer of money in exchange for help in getting up: this help is cruelly and paradoxically subordinated to a monetary offer and the unfortunate victim of the fall is ignored by the two friends who carry on talking. Then there is the wonderful gag with the watch. Pozzo can no longer find his watch and Vladimir suggests it might still be in his pocket:

> POZZO: - Attendez. (*Il se plie en deux, approche sa tête de son ventre, écoute.*) Je n'entends rien! (*Il leur fait signe de s'approcher.*) Venez voir. (*Estragon et Vladimir vont vers lui, se penchent sur son ventre. Silence.*) Il me semble qu'on devrait entendre le tic-tac.
> VLADIMIR. - Silence!
> *Tous écoutent, penchés.*
> ESTRAGON. - J'entends quelque chose.
> POZZO. - Où?
> VLADIMIR. - C'est le cœur.
> POZZO (*deçu*). - Merde alors! (p. 64)

From the initial situation of looking for the watch, the development leads the characters to the hunt, but the final resolution is twice disturbed by unexpected, deviant outcomes. Firstly, Vladimir destroys any hopes raised by Estragon by confirming that the tick-tock is "only" Pozzo's heart and that latter, instead of being reassured by the physiological normality of his body, exclaims "merde!" in disappointment. The hunt has been in vain. The resolution of the gag is emphasised a second time, when Vladimir and Estragon, frozen in a *tableau* against Pozzo's chest, are chased away by him because of their abominable smell.

Again in *Godot* we find a variant very commonly used in vaudeville, circus and comic cinema, where the gag begins with one speaker talking in a foreign language that is not understood by the other. This gag only appears in the English version, as it plays on the insertion of a phrase in French:

ESTRAGON: Que voulez-vous?
VLADIMIR: I beg your pardon?
ESTRAGON: Que voulez-vous?
VLADIMIR: Ah! que voulez-vous. Exactly. (p. 60)

"Exactly": Vladimir's incoherent reply shows he has not in the least understood the meaning of the phrase used by his friend, but he pretends with highly amusing, cool indifference to be completely at his ease.

Examples of verbal gags are found in the repartee between Hamm and Clov, in Mrs Rooney's ambiguous allusions and in the dialogue between Winnie and Willie – everywhere, that is, where demented repetition is set into the verbal structure with absurd consequentiality.

Finally, there is an isolated but highly enjoyable instance in *Godot* of an invented, non-existent word, whose real meaning is mysterious and fascinating to a first-time listener. "Alors j'ai pris un knouk" (p. 45, "knook" in the English version, p. 33), says Pozzo, for a moment firing the imagination of Vladimir who is suddenly distracted from gazing at the sky, "un knouk?" (ibid.), but lacks the courage to enquire further because Pozzo, acting as if it was something well known, continues to describe the details, "il y aura bientôt soixante ans que ça dure" (ibid.). The most mysterious object of discussion is left in its inscrutable mystery, setting off a verbal gag confronting ignorance with knowledge that has a very long and tested history. The exotic word (amplified in English by the strong assonance of the phrase "I took a knook", p. 33) inflames the imagination, but curiosity is held back by the assumption of being the only person not to know what the word means. This game of exclusion is totally effective on Vladimir, who does not dare to admit his ignorance.

5.4. "I was merely cursing"

Mr Tyler is cycling slowly along a quiet country road. He is following old Mrs Rooney, who struggles on towards her destination. She is a loquacious, grumbling old woman, but Mr Tyler chats with her, putting up with the tedium. Suddenly the monotonous journey is shaken - Mr Tyler has punctured the front tyre that he had carefully blown up before starting out, he reacts with disproportionate disappointment, politely and courteously explained. Mr Tyler curses under his breath: "nothing, Mrs Rooney, nothing, I was merely cursing, under my breath, God and man, under my breath, and the wet Saturday afternoon of my conception" (p. 175). His tone is still that of polite chat and the climax of the blasphemy contrasts with the normality of his delivery. In reality Mr Tyler is bringing down an enormous curse that includes all of Creation, in its spiritual, material and individual elements. Mr Tyler, however, is not the only one to use offensive bad language, indeed one of the chief pastimes of Beckett's clowns is the game of swear words.

Beckett expresses obscenity in various ways, by means of turpiloquium or by allusions to the embarrassing aspects of the body.

Of the latter, there are countless examples both in the drama and in the prose, obeying Rabelais' rule of lowering the tone. In Western culture, which exalts intellectual capacities and denigrates those of the body, the corporal hierarchy places the head (the mind) at the top and, at the bottom, the feet, the sexual organs, the anus and the mouth. Apart from the mouth, these parts are all found below the belt and concern "low" activities, rather unedifying although essential for survival, which our culture conceals as much as possible from both hearing and from sight. These parts are not spoken of, not mentioned in conversation and certainly never shown. If they are, the resulting effect is scandal and/or comedy. The mouth is included in this category when it greedily swallows solids or liquids (food, alcohol) or expels them (vomit, saliva, breath), or when it is symbolically associated with the anal orifice.

In opposition to this culture of concealment, we have that of exhibition - that of Rabelaisian carnival, of the world of childhood, of clowns and of comedy in general. One of the most exhilarating comic outcomes is provoked by this mechanism. In Beckett we have an authentic comic epic about mud, an element corresponding to a double parody of "high", adult culture, "tendance scatologique, quelle régression infantile au stade anal".[73] The scatological, being easily effective and highly improper, has always been the precinct of popular culture or of other viewpoints such as that of children, who have not yet learned to recognise and respect the corporal hierarchy, or of madmen, because their world is upside-down. Not rarely, however, has the scatological dimension been used in our century by cultured writers with the aim of lowering the tone to comic effect, backed in this by Freud's analysis of the theme of excrement.[74] Joyce and Beckett were particularly attracted to the scatological and both used it as a flippant metaphor of the creative process - defecation as the expulsion of the contents within and artistic creation as the expulsion of spiritual detritus were similar activities. The effort and the in/out process are the same. Joyce and Beckett "repeatedly use images and metaphors of bodily fluids and elimination; and both authors [...] link these images of urination and defecation to the process of artistic creation",[75] but while in Joyce the mind flows like the bodily functions, in Beckett the characters are constipated, constrained, metaphorically or really unable to move. The mental and physiological flow becomes difficult, de-automated, think of the physical and creative constipation of Krapp: "with Krapp, neither crap nor thought moves freely, through mere words do; in both cases, only gas flows. Constipated physically, Krapp is constipated intellectually, for the results of his thought [...] do not circulate".[76]

Beckett's clowns show their obscene bodies without shame and without inhibition. Sometimes their apparent good, bourgeois manners make them opt for a daring metaphor or a circumlocution so awkward in its desire to demonstrate auto-censorship, like that of the malicious Miss Carmichael in *Human Wishes*, who describes the bottom as "what will not dry black and what was never white" (p. 297), with an expression so colourful that it is no less obscene than the word itself. The double meanings are fruit of this false inhibition, false because the speakers can say more than would be possible in plain speech. The double meaning slides from literal, innocent interpretation to another level of interpretation, generally alluding to the sphere of sex. So the ravings of Victor in his sleep in *Eleutheria*, for example, seem dreadfully obscene to the listener:

> VICTOR [...] mer basse... profonde... profonde, onde profonde. (*Silence. Entre le vitrier. Il va vers le lit.*) Là les yeux... mille navires... les tours... circoncises... feu... feu... (*Silence.*)
> VITRIER. - Les tours circoncises feu feu! Eh bien, c'est du joli! (*Il secoue Victor.*) Debout, cloaque! (p. 119)

Vitrier does not hesitate to insult one whom he believes to be lewd with counter-obscenity, "cloaque", thereby returning the compliment.

An obscene double meaning, ambiguous and highly doubtful, is given by Krapp and is repeated twice. Young Krapp, on tape, is relating his love story with Bianca and the episode of their boat outing: "I asked her to look at me and after a few moments -[*Pause.*]- after a few moments she did, but the eyes just slits, because of the glare. I bent over her to get them in the shadow and they opened. [*Pause. Low.*] Let me in" (p. 221, repeated word for word on p. 223). The scene is one of seduction, with the girl lying on the bottom of the boat. The easy, intentional association eyes/vagina, amplified by the ambiguous "let me in", tinges the whole episode with sensuality. Young Krapp, like young Victor, is still tormented by the passions of the flesh, but while the latter unconsciously releases his energy when asleep, Krapp does not hide his use of prostitutes and onanism. "Fanny came in a couple of times. Bony old ghost of a whore. Couldn't do much, but I suppose better than a kick in the crutch. The last time wasn't so bad. How do you manage it, she said, at your age? I told her I'd been saving up for her all my life" (p. 222).

Sexual obscenity is also alluded to in Godot, with Vladimir and Estragon's idea of provoking an erection by hanging themselves and with the reference, only legible in the English version, to the clap, a sexually transmitted venereal disease: "VLADIMIR: [*Conciliating.*] I once knew a family called Gozzo. The mother had the clap" (p. 24, while in French we read "la mère brodait au tambour", p. 30). Obscene double meanings also underlie some of the best passages from *All That Fall*, aided by its being a drama for radio. Listening, not only to words that can be interpreted in opposite ways, but also to sounds that can be ascribed to completely different contexts, creates numerous opportunities for lewd meanings. Mrs Rooney's first meeting is with Christy, travelling with a mule that suddenly stops, refusing to go on. Mrs Rooney's reaction to the whipping of the poor beast is of sadistic pleasure, "harder! [...] If someone were to do that for me I should not dally" (p. 173). The second wayfarer is even more indecent, asking the old woman if he can put his hand on her shoulder, but Maddy's reply clearly shows her prurient interpretation, "I am tired of light old hands on my shoulders and other senseless places, sick and tired of them" (p. 175), refusing his advances. The lewd reference to the "other senseless places" of her body opens up our imagination as listeners, for hitherto we have thought of Maddy Rooney as a poor, very pious old woman and instead we now discover her racy side, which eventually explodes into a request on the verge of indecency. She and Mr Tyler are still walking along side by side, he trying to convince her to get on his bicycle, despite the flat tyre, as the train is about to arrive. Mrs Rooney begs him to stop tormenting ("being tormented" p. 176) and molesting her ("will you get along with you now and cease molesting me?" ibid.). Mr Tyler, offended, mounts his bicycle and rides off from the woman who suddenly, bothered by her "cursed corset", bellows after Mr Tyler to come and unlace her, "Mr Tyler! Mr Tyler! Come back and unlace me behind the hedge!" (p. 177), then, realising how daring she has been, bursts into wild laughter.

Mrs Rooney seems almost conscious of the dual interpretation of her words and sometimes seems to calculate the tone deliberately, like a naughty girl who enjoys these games. The gag of her "mounting" into the car and the similarities she finds with surrounding nature are another example. Mrs Rooney compares herself to the mule, to a "big fat jelly out of a bowl" (p. 174) to a "roll of tarpaulin" (p. 185) to be propped up against the wall; Miss Fitt takes her for a "big pale blur, just another big pale blur" (p. 183) and Mr Rooney defines her very unromantically as "two hundred pounds of unhealthy fat" (p. 191). Each of these associations lowers the human being to the level of animal or object, to an indistinct blur – and this is even funnier when the speaker is referring to himself or herself. Here there is a latent masochism of self-offence, a comic indifference to one's own personal dignity. Moreover, the other term of comparison refers to a visceral, symbolic materiality: the turned-out jelly, the pale grey blur, the fat, the mule, initially associated with dung ("CHRISTY: I suppose you wouldn't be in need of a small load of dung?" p. 173) and with farting ("MRS ROONEY: [...] Mercy! What was that? CHRISTY: Never mind her, Ma'am, she's very fresh in herself today" ibid.), are all references to the semantic field of excrement.

Beckett's clowns seem to suffer from real coprolalia, from the exaltation of verbal references to excrement. By analogy, we can extend the category to include all the physiological debris expelled by our body: the nail cuttings in *Acte sans paroles I* and *Happy Days*; spitting in *Eleutheria*, *Godot* and *Happy Days*; Winnie's perspiration ("I used to perspire freely" p. 152); the prostate mentioned in *Eleutheria* introducing Vladimir and Hamm peeing, both with urinary troubles; the farts in *Godot*, *All That Fall* and *Fragment de théâtre I* ("A. - Faites un bruit. B en fait un. A tâtonne, s'immobilise. B. - Vous n'avez pas d'odorat non plus? A. - C'est la même odeur partout" p. 30); the "identifying" smells of Vladimir and Estragon ("ESTRAGON. - Lui pue de la bouche, mois des pieds" p. 65); the vomit in *Godot* ("j'ai coulé toute ma chaudepisse d'existence ici" p. 86, beautifully rendered in English, "I've puked my puke of a life away here" p. 57) and in *All That Fall* ("oh no coughing or spitting or bleeding or vomiting" p. 181). The identikit of Beckett's anti-hero includes all kinds of disgusting detail. The body is shown in its most obscene, repellent aspect.

The characters' words are often marked by a taste for the macabre, not only concerning death, but all images evocative of the disintegration of matter. They indulge in dreadful descriptions, like that of pus used as a metaphor by Estragon, "on ne descend pas deux fois dans le même pus" (p. 84), and by Vitrier in *Eleutheria* who says to Victor "vous êtes là comme une sorte de... comment dire ça? comme une sorte de suintement. Comme une sanie, voilà" (p. 84). Note the crudeness of the term "sanie" (also the title of two poems in English, *Sanies I* and *II*),[77] which literally means "pus", in medicine a viscid discharge, product of inflammation. Or, the shadow of death is called up by associations with decomposition: tapeworms (Vitrier's son is accused of being hungry because he has parasites: "DR PIOUK. – Il a sans doute des parasites. VITRIER.

– Tu entends? Tu as des parasites" p. 102). There is also accidental castration (in *Fragment de théâtre II* A tells B the story of a certain Dubois "soi-disant qu'il avait perdu les parties dans un accident de chasse" p. 57, and even more explicitly in English – where the very common surname is translated as Smith - "reputed to have lost his genitals in a shooting accident", *Rough for Theatre* p. 247).

The macabre sometimes does not derive from the words used or images evoked, but from the absurdity of the situation. In *Eleutheria* for example, the passing of Victor's father is done as a clown's gag. The agitation is not catalysed by the actual, sad event, but by a superficial linguistic level: can the man coherently be called dead?

> MME KRAP. – Où est-il? (*Silence. Mme Krap s'affole.*) Il n'est pas mort? (*Silence.*) Il est mort! Il est mort!
> VITRIER. – Il ne l'était pas il y a cinq minutes, quatre minutes, pas ce que les vivants appellent mort.
> MME KRAP. – Il vit!
> VITRIER. – Le cœur bat, c'est certain. (p. 100)

In *Human Wishes* there is a similar play on death. After an irreverent exchange on the death of Dr Goldsmith, Mrs Williams says she is sorry for his passing, as he owed her money: "so was I, Miss, heartily sorry indeed to hear it, at the time, being of the opinion, as I still am, that before paying his debt to nature he might have paid his debt to me. Seven shillings and sixpence [...]" (p. 300). Her scant respect for the deceased, complaining about the insignificant debt, is comical: death is one of many pastimes that fill up the day, not feared as the end of existence, but sighed for, as a game for clowns. It is part of that violence which does not destroy but only joyously overturns. It is the same mechanism that regulates physical and verbal violence between the characters, who frequently insult each other without ever permanently damaging their good relations. Also, the mechanisms of the unexpected outcome (out of sadness for someone's death one would expect a sincere sentiment of affection, not venal interest), of disproportion (there is no proportion between the pecuniary level and the biological one of life/death) and of hyperbole (an unimportant episode – a negligible sum is owed, a few shillings – becomes a vital question), taken together, make the situation a comical one.

Insults result from hostile feelings towards others and so are effective signs of profound psychological and emotional feedback between the speakers. They are, in fact, very common in the plays where interaction between characters is or is intended to be lively: in *Human Wishes*, *Eleutheria*, *Godot*, *All That Fall* and *Play*. In the first and last, the obscenities appear to be mitigated by bourgeois politeness, while actually being bitter insults to the antagonist. The particular situation of emotional tension in *Play* justifies W1's insults to W2 ("pudding face, puffy, spots, blubber mouth, jowls, no neck, dugs you could- […] calves like a flunkey", p. 310) and what the man is thinking of his wife, or women in general, while saying something completely different to her: "God what vermin women. Thanks to you, angel, I said" (p. 311).

The insults in *Eleutheria*, like those in *Godot*, are highly inventive and make instrumental use of the sense of the macabre. See the following exchange between Mr and Mrs Krap:

> M. KRAP, *sortant un rasoir de sa poche*. – Aide-moi à me lever. (*Mme Krap recule.*) J'aurais préféré (*il essaie de se lever*) te laisser à ton cancer. Tant pis. (*Il se lève à moitié.*)
> MME KRAP, *reculant vers la porte*. – Tu es complètement fou! […] Espèce de vieil impotent! (*Revient vers lui.*) Dire que tu m'as fait peur un instant!
> M. KRAP, *se laissant retomber*. – Pas commode de se mettre sur son séant, même pour tuer sa femme.
> MME KRAP. – Crapule!
> M. KRAP. – Moi aussi?
> MME KRAP. – Fumier!
> M. KRAP. – D'ailleurs, tu ne prends rien pour attendre. Je t'égorgerai cette nuit, pendant que tu ronfleras. (pp. 58-59)

Personal insults alternate with threats, the tension is typical of married quarrels, done in the manner of the violent hyperbole of clowns, with no real outcome. The couple attack each other endlessly, without giving way despite clear signs of aging, for both have problems moving, or the absurdity of such exaggerated violence.

Of a similar tenor, with homosexual undertones, are the verbal battles between Vladimir and Estragon. Their sparring vividly recalls that of a couple tired of married life. And they themselves contribute to this impression: we find them "la main dans la main" on the Eiffel Tower (p. 11) in Vladimir's melancholy memory, and on honeymoon at the Dead Sea in Estragon's plans ("la mer Morte était bleu pâle. […] Je me disais, c'est là que nous irons passer notre lune de miel. Nous nagerons. Nous serons heureux" p. 14). Didi and Gogo love and hate each other at the same time. They know they cannot live without each other, so their insults are only a game to pass the time or an attempt at human contact. But like unruly children, they insult their peers when provoked: when Lucky kicks him, Estragon comes out with "le salaud! La vache!" (p. 44), confirming the impression of stupidity that the two had received of him at first sight. "VLADIMIR. – C'est peut-être un idiot. ESTRAGON. – Un crétin" (p. 34). And they have no problem in verbally and physically assaulting Pozzo, when at last they find him in difficulty:

VLADIMIR. – C'est encore ce salaud de Pozzo!
ESTRAGON. – Dis-lui de la boucler! Casse-lui la gueule!
VLADIMIR (*donnant des coups à Pozzo.*) – As-tu fini? Veux-tu te taire? Vermine! (p. 116)

Beckett's characters adore turpiloquium and even when alone find an excuse to curse. Krapp has noone to insult because he is alone, yet struggling with the tapes he "*curses*" (p. 217) and flings everything on the floor.

The transgressive quality of insults, of the obscene and of the macabre is clear, in a type of speech that is conservative by nature, that is, which adheres to current social norms. A fundamental rule of civil society is good manners, and this convention is transgressed by insults and curses. But this is just one of the instruments used by Beckett's characters for transgression - their entire use of the linguistic code has this effect. Moreover, their ludic approach to words makes us wonder whether they might even be aware of their break with the rules and might be deliberately using comic techniques in their speeches. Consider Mrs Rooney's meta-linguistic pause, when she reflects on her own way of speaking: "do you find anything… bizarre about my way of speaking? [*Pause.*] I do not mean the voice. [*Pause.*] No, I mean the words. [*Pause. More to herself.*] I use none but the simplest words, I hope, and yet I sometimes find my way of speaking very… bizarre" (p. 173).

Maddy Rooney puts forward the problem of an eccentric function of language and she tells us she is doing this, just as the meta-linguistic switches of other characters inform us of their awareness of the code being challenged even in its function. All Beckett's speakers know they will get a laugh when, pretending to be innocent, they play with the words, and they wickedly insist on using these mechanisms.

A final observation on obscenity with sexual innuendo concerns its link with the pun and with the joke. Though these two terms are often used as synonyms, in reality they are two different figures of comic speech. A pun, in French *calembour*, is strictly speaking a play on words, while a joke is a funny story. Ambiguity may arise if the joke is based on a play on words, becoming even more complicated when the play on words includes sexual obscenity. In this case, although quite distinct, the three dimensions fit inside each other like Chinese boxes – the obscenity fits into the play on words, which is inside the joke.

The pun, especially if rude, is one of Beckett's favourite techniques for introducing his characters. The majority of their names are built around puns, often obscene. In Eleutheria we have the surname of the Krap family (almost the same as Krapp, later) alluding to 'crap', that of Mr and Mrs Piouk sounds like 'puke', while Miss Skunk is self-explanatory. We should remember that the play was written in French, so the parody in these verbal games crosses both languages, short-circuiting them together. Of the same kind are the surnames discussed by the three women in *Human Wishes*: Mrs Winterbotham (winter-bottom or bother), Mr Pott of the Fleet (pot, fleet), Rev. Okey (okay or hokey – in the meaning of corny, phony) and Miss Tout (stout). Other examples might be found in *Godot* (Estragon – French for tarragon, Lucky – self-explanatory, Pozzo – Italian for well), or in *Fin de partie* (Clov – clown, or *clou*, French for nail, Hamm – Hamlet or hammer, Nagg – *naegel*, German for nail). More examples occur throughout the prose, but I will limit myself to citing Celia, in love with Murphy in the novel of that name, a play on the English pronunciation of the French expression "ce l'y-a" and with the Italian spelling of "celia", a hoax. Every time Beckett needed to name a character, he used a play on words or clownlike assonance. In the rarefied atmospheres of his later works, however, his characters were christened simply using letters of the alphabet or their stage functions (in *Play* they are indicated as M=man; W1=woman 1; W2=woman 2; in *Film* O=object, E=eye), or with abbreviations (in *Come and Go* the pun is cut short by abbreviation: Vi for violet, Ru, originally Ro for rose and Flo for flower).

Lucky's monologue is a real catalogue of puns and because of these and other figures of comic speech it has been studied and analysed in detail by critics.[78] From the start it seems to us absurd - treating cerebral activity as a physical exercise to be shown off and called up on demand is beyond all rational logic, being closer to the demonstrations of skill on which many clown numbers are based. The clowns' prank is usually based on a challenge where one clown has to show the others his skill in some field, often having boasted about this. The resulting situation has a "demonstrator" who acts and the others who watch, until the final prank is played on him. Lucky's monologue follows the same structure, without the intended prank at the *entrée*, but which is evoked by physical aggression at the end to silence Lucky, who is unstoppable.[79]

The lofty *incipit*, serious and academic in tone, makes it an exaggerated parody that during the course of the monologue becomes increasingly fragmented as it moves towards the dispersion of any unified sense and the destruction of syntax, until it becomes a mere accumulation of incomplete terms or snatches. The names mentioned are all puns or comic allusions: Puncher (English version -p. 42- from the original Poinçon, p. 59) is a pun on Mr Punch; Wattmann is perhaps an internal reference to Watt; Acacacacadémie and Anthropopopométrie play on the scatological "caca" and "popo"; the second part of Berne-en-Bresse perhaps alludes to breast, while the English version gives Essy-in-Possy, assonant with pussy; Testu and Conard allude to male genitalia, Fartov and Belcher are self-explanatory. The frequent alliteration and obsessive repetition of the same word create the rhythm of a speech that becomes increasingly fast and less rationally controllable. The obscenity of the names is echoed by other salacious images: food and faeces are assimilated in a consequential list, "les progrès de l'alimentation et de l'élimination" (p. 60), other terms are used for their double meaning: "la conation" (p. 60) refers to an effort but also suggests the retching as in a *conatus* preceding vomit; and "riding" implies both equitation and sexual intercourse.

The whole monologue is constructed according to the absurd logic of a-logical association, and the apparently serious tone is in contrast with the lack of internal coherence.

Obscene puns are not only used as a comic base for inventing names of places or or people, but also in the lines of the characters. In *Fin de partie* Hamm actually seems conscious of the double meaning:

> HAMM. - Coïte! Coite tu veux dire. A moins qu'elle ne se tienne coite.
> CLOV. - Ah! On dit coite? On ne dit pas coïte? (p. 51)

and in English:

> HAMM. - Laying! Lying you mean. Unless he's *lying* doggo.
> CLOV. - Ah? One says lying? One doesn't say laying? (p. 108)

"Coïte" for "coït"=coitus/ "coite"=tranquil and "laying"/ "lying" sound the same. Although Clov cannot hear much difference between the two sounds, they indicate a straightforward meaning and an obscene one.

In this sense we can understand H. Porter Abbott's opinion on the function of the pun, defined as an act of recycling the meaning, and cultural and linguistic heritage of the speaker. This function in his opinion requires three kinds of reading: 1) normalisation (even if the text struggle against it); 2) centrifugal escape (no control over the text); 3) sound and suggestion (assonance repeats similar sounds).[80] These categories are all found in Beckett's structure of text. The normalisation, rendered evident by recourse to the parodic model or to citations, reacts schizophrenically to any real attempt at reduction to the norm, and the language, free from conventional logic can express itself through the evocative function of its sonority. The pun creates ideological tensions within the discourse, opposite and contrasting tensions, centrifugal and centripetal, while fascinating us with the musicality of the assonance it uses.

In Beckett the connection running through pun-obscenity-joke is often what vivifies the funny stories told by the characters – their jokes.

5.5. "It had never been a good joke"

Beckett's delight in jokes is recorded at various levels of his life and his work. Jokes fill the speeches and actions of his prose and theatre characters, as they do the life of the author himself.

I have already mentioned Beckett's letter to MacGreevy where he tells his vaudeville joke about the centipede. But the same happens on other occasions for a variety of reasons. During rehearsals for the production of *Play* at the Ulm Theater in 1963, for example, Becket was directing alongside Deryk Mendel. The actor playing Man was desperate, he could not understand the text, he asked a lot of questions of himself and of Beckett, who avoided answering, saying that they were irrelevant questions. Since he persisted with his requests, Beckett replied in his own way with an elliptical allusion. He commented on the actor's need for logical interpretation by quoting the punch line of a joke also known to the Mendel: "Beckett said to Mendel with a smirk: '*The Absolute Camel*'. This referred to a joke both were familiar with which goes something like this: if an Englishman writes about a camel, he will use the title *The Camel*; a Frenchman will call it *The Camel and Love*; and a German, *The Absolute Camel*".[81] The joke is used here to summarise in a sarcastic manner the German actor's error, in search of metaphysical explanations when his job required physical actions and rhythm.

A joke with an explicative function is alluded to in *Watt*, though the enigmatic nature of the allusion led to an amusing diatribe among critics. Jacqueline Hoefer, in an article on *Watt* that appeared in *Perspective* in

1959,[82] maintained that the ladder mentioned by Beckett in the novel should be interpreted as that of Wittgenstein (*Tractatus Logico-Philosophicus*) and she supported this affirmation with an ample critical, comparative analysis. The question is rather complex, but I shall summarise it as follows. In *Watt* there is a ladder, from which Mr. Hackett falls and which anticipates Watt's symbolic fall from the ladder of knowledge after his time working for Knott. Later Watt loses all logical and gnoseological certainties. Arsene said that Watt changed after that experience, "what was changed was existence off the ladder. Do not come down the ladder, Ifor, I haf taken it away" (p. 42). The latter is the "incriminated" line, which, according to Hoefer, refers to the following passage of the *Tractatus*: "he [the individual] must so to speak throw away the ladder, after he has climbed up on it".[83] And in her opinion, Beckett's line is a phonetic rendering of a German speaking English, yet another reference to Wittgenstein. Some time later, John Fletcher decided to check the critic's opinion with the author himself and a very different explanation came to light: "unfortunately this interpretation [of Hoefer] is quite erroneous. Mr. Beckett told me in 1961 that the 'ladder' is a reference to 'a Welsh joke' (but he did not specify which)",[84] so that strange pronunciation which seems German should actually be interpreted as a Welsh accent. Beckett's reticence in revealing the Welsh joke makes identification impossible, but more significant is the blow to academia: not only did he not confirm the – plausible – intellectual interpretation of Hoefer, he substituted a popular joke. Moreover, we might note the conceptual use, or rather theoretical function, by Beckett of the structure of the joke itself and its plot.

Elsewhere Beckett, to give an idea of James Joyce's humour, mentioned one of the jokes he remembered best: "Beckett remembered Joyce on one occasion telling a story about a man who was having a bowl of soup in the dining room of a hotel. The waiter, who is looking out of the window, remarks, 'Looks like rain, sir'. To which the diner replies, 'Tastes like it too'".[85] Cronin, witness to this citation of Joyce by Beckett, commented that the two authors, both Irish, shared the same sense of humour, typically Irish - uncompromising, cruel, sometimes farcical. O'Casey, too, had said that "the Irish people are very fond of turning a serious thing into a joke".[86] A national prerogative, therefore, Irish humour, almost like another kind of humour that is mentioned when discussing Beckett's jokes or puns: Jewish humour. Though geographically and emotionally very far apart, the Irish Catholic and Jewish cultures have strong points of contact in their ways of laughing and mocking. Both share an often self-conscious guilt feeling, besides elements of megalomania. Freud, analysing jokes, made great use of "Jewish jokes" that he knew and loved: "the jokes made about Jews by outsiders [*Fremden*] are mostly brutal comic anecdotes, in which [the effort of making] a proper joke is saved by the fact that to the outsider the Jew counts as a comical figure. The Jewish jokes originating with Jews admit this too, but they know their real faults [...]. I do not know whether it often happens in other instances that a people should make fun of its own nature to such an extent".[87] Self-irony is a big part of this game and is interpreted by Jewish and Irish humour in the same way, with overtones of cruelty and black humour. Examples of this could be O'Casey, Synge, Joyce and Beckett, along with a vast assortment of Jewish comedians: the Marx Brothers, Woody Allen, Moni Ovadia, the Cohen brothers, Zero Mostel and many others.[88]

Ruby Cohn and Adorno pointed out some time ago that the tailor's joke in *Fin de partie* was a Jewish joke,[89] with its ferocious irony on the divine creation of the universe.

Regardless of definitions, this is one of the jokes found throughout Beckett's works and has various points of interest. This is how Nagg tells it:

> Un Anglais - (*il prend un visage d'Anglais, reprend le sien*) - ayant besoin d'un pantalon rayé en vitesse pour le fêtes du Novel An se rend chez son tailleur qui lui prend ses mesures. (*Voix du tailleur.*) «Et voilà qui est fait, revenez dans quatre jours, il sera prêt.» Bon. Quatre jours plus tard. (*Voix du tailleur.*) «Sorry, revenez dans huit jours, j'ai raté le fond.» Bon, ça va, le fond, c'est pas commode. Huit jours plus tard. (*Voix du tailleur.*) «Désolé, revenez dans dix jours, j'ai salopé l'entre-jambes.» Bon, d'accord, l'entre-jambes, c'est délicat. Dix

jours plus tard. (*Voix du tailleur.*) «Navré, revenez dans quinze jours, j'ai bousillé la braguette.» Bon, à la rigueur, une belle braguette, c'est calé. [...] Enfin bref, de faufil en aiguille, voici Pâques Fleuries et il loupe les boutonnières. (*Visage, puis voix du client.*) «Goddam Sir, non, vraiment, c'est indécent, à la fin! En six jours, vous entendez, six jours, Dieu fit le monde. Oui Monsieur, parfaitement Monsieur, le MONDE! Et vous, vous n'êtes pas foutu de me faire un pantalon en trois mois!» (*Voix du tailleur, scandalisée.*) «Mais Milord! Mais Milord! Regardez - (*geste méprisant, avec dégoût*) - le monde... (*un temps*)... et regardez - (*geste amoureux, avec orgueil*) - mon PANTALON!» (pp. 37-38)

The joke requires an actor who is particularly good at modulating and characterising the various voices, that of the narrator, the Englishman and the tailor, as well as at cleverly calibrating the pauses. The story, developed according the structure of presentation-development-resolution, might be defined as a gag, were it not that a gag must contain action, while a joke can be entirely verbal. Its vivacity, like that of other jokes in Beckett, enables us to visualise the entire scene and even to reconstruct sound details of the atmosphere through the various voices.

Beckett so loved this joke that he took it for the title of his article "Le Monde et le pantalon", on the art of the Van Velde brothers.[90] The joke's development is the classic one of its genre, based on repetition varied over time of the same action-situation-repartee: the tailor postpones delivery of the trousers several times with the approval of the ingenuous client. As the pattern is repeated the listener is put on guard - sooner or later the pattern will be broken and the punch line will arrive. The storytelling shortcut ("enfin") tells us that we have got to Easter and that the tailor is still putting his client off. The latter understandably reprimands him, mentioning the divine creation: if God made the world in six days, three months for a tailor to make trousers are a bit too much! This daring paragon paves the way for the punch line: "but sir, look at the world and look at my trousers!". The juxtaposition of world/trousers is daring and exaggerated, as is the whole act of divine/profane creation by God/

the tailor. The entire joke brings in a series of opposites that cannot be logically reconciled. Our laughter derives from these, and from the underlying blasphemy.

The divine creator, the supreme being above all others, source of all existing good, is associated with a miserable, lazy tailor, who declares he is a demiurge better than God - the semantic shift is enormous. And there is an even more blasphemous connotation: the comparison is not limited to association – surprising in itself – of what is un-like, but concerns the divine and profane *actions*. If, in theory, the fruits of the divine creation are wonderful and unsurpassable, in practice, according to the tailor, this world has not been made as well as his trousers, which far surpass in quality the imperfect, chaotic world, even if of divine origin.

Blasphemy is also found in the funny story in *More Pricks Than Kicks* that mentally sustains Belacqua when dying, making him cry – as always – laughing. Beckett seems to particularly enjoy offending Christian bigotry and gives the whole joke of which Belacqua was fond. The protagonist is a parson,

> who was invited to take a small part in an amateur production. All he had to do was to snatch at his heart when the revolver went off, cry 'By God! I'm shot!' and drop dead. The parson said certainly, he would be most happy, if they would have no objection to his drawing the line at 'By God' on such a secular occasion. He would replace it, if they had no objection, by 'Mercy!' or 'Upon my word!' or something of that kind. 'Oh my! I'm shot!', how would that be?
> But the production was so amateur that the revolver went off indeed and the man of God was transfixed.
> 'Oh' he cried 'oh... ! BY CHRIST! I AM SHOT!' (p. 184)

The macabre joke is as blasphemous as the one in *Fin de partie* and both indicate Beckett's attitude towards religion and towards humour - he uses the latter with a function of aggression-punishment against certain tenets of the Christian faith. Laughter reveals the imperfection of the servants of God (despite his apparent scruples, the parson actually blasphemes) and of the Father himself, whose imperfection is reflected in his creation. A joke has the power to show reality as it is, in its crudeness and in its misery. And the worse the taste, the more effective it is. Murphy's theory on bad jokes finds numerous examples in Beckett's texts. In *Dream of Fair to Middling Women* the jokes are "done", visualised or simply said. Sometimes it is enough to simply mention the pattern of speech of the joke, as in the exchange between Belacqua and Alba: "'You know what the rose said to the rose?' No, she did not seem to have heard that one. 'No gardener has died within the memory of roses'" (p. 175).

In *Fin de partie* the whole joke is told, from beginning to end, as happens in "Avant Fin de partie" with the demential pun on the "end" of the sausage that "has two".[91] In *Godot*, however, the logos embodies an incomplete joke, which is just hinted at.

The pretext for the analogy is the word "calme", whose English pronunciation "câââm" recalls the obscene French "con" (prick).

> ESTRAGON (*avec volupté*). - Calme... Calme... (*Rêveusement*). Les Anglais disent câââm. Ce sont des gens câââms [=they're pricks]. (*Un temps.*) Tu connais l'histoire de l'Anglais au bordel?
> VLADIMIR. - Oui.
> ESTRAGON. - Raconte-la-moi.
> VLADIMIR. - Assez.
> ESTRAGON. - Un Anglais s'étant enivré se rend au bordel. La sous-mâitresse lui demande s'il désire una blonde, une brune ou une rousse. Continue.
> VLADIMIR. - ASSEZ! (p. 20)

The joke is interrupted by Vladimir's roar and leaves an atmosphere not of happy relaxation, but of emotion and dramatic tension. Lowe[92] has reconstructed two possible endings to the tale, taken from the most popular jokes about brothels. The first version, already suggested by Ruby Cohn, has a homosexual basis. When the client is asked what colour of hair he prefers for the prostitute, he replies that he would prefer a boy, so the angry madam threatens to call the police and the client, ingenuous in the face of her anger, says "oh no, policemen are too gritty". The second version sees the Englishman choosing between various physical attributes of the prostitutes, opening door after door. Finally he opens the door announcing "big breasts" (in French, "grands cons") and he finds himself on the street. The story has its own aura that can be perceived before it is narrated, anticipated by the wrong pronunciation of "calm" and at the end of the play, when Vladimir asks the boy the colour of Godot's beard: "il a une barbe, monsieur Godot? [...] Blonde ou... (*il hésite*) ... ou noire?" (p. 130).

The bad taste almost makes it a dirty pub joke and in fact Beckett had defined the whole play as a "dirty joke".[93] It matches the more polite joke put on by Vladimir and Estragon in Act 1, which is turned into a real gag. It is the story of two friends who go to the theatre and one of them pees on stage: Beckett "incorporates a well-known joke into the action of the play, so that the joke is not told but enacted by the characters".[94]

In *More Pricks Than Kicks* the punch line is in the story itself, in the description of Belacqua's final act - his death, just as that of Murphy in the novel of the same name is narrated with the structure of the last line of a joke.[95] The action itself becomes a joke.

But in the broad panorama of funny stories, Beckett distinguishes two kinds - those that are really funny and "bad jokes". His spokesman on this is Murphy, who formulates an authentic theory on the subject.

The first category includes without doubt "pub jokes" and Murphy tells one:

> "Why did the barmaid champagne?" he said. "Do you give it up?"
> "Yes," said Celia.
> "Because the stout porter bitter," said Murphy. (p. 97)

Murphy also mentions another, which remains ambiguous and mysterious and whose subject is summarised briefly. We can guess that it is as silly as the one Murphy has just told, which he thinks to be such a laugh "and one other concerning a bottle of stout and a card party" (p. 98).

The subjects and settings both play on a semantic area typical of the Anglo-Irish pub. We have barmaids, champagne, stout and bitter.

But the whole pub atmosphere undergoes a metamorphosis of meaning provoking hilarity, untranslatable in other languages. This is perhaps why the joke was cut from the French version, translated by Georges Perolson with the active collaboration of Beckett, and which perplexes the reader who continues reading after the cut, with Celia's cold reaction and Murphy's sniggering. The French reader is surprised by this inexplicable reaction from the characters, lacking the part with Murphy's joke even in clumsy translation.

The joke is clearly based on similar-sounding words, on ambiguity, therefore, of meaning: "champagne" sounds like "sham pain"; "stout" can also mean "fat"; "porter" can be someone who carries luggage, though another type of pronunciation might bring it closer to "porto" ("port wine"); "bitter" might be "beat her" or "bit her". Interpretations can be multiple, but mostly move around the pub and drunk environment of many jokes.

Apparently Murphy's witticism generates what Freud would define as a typical acoustic joke,[96] a wordplay based on a diverse semantic use of the same word ("stout" as kind of beer or as character trait). More properly, it should be defined as *calembour*, a modest wordplay, in which the two different words recall each other acustically or hold a vague resemblance or association to each other. Murphy's *pun* plays with the sound of the words, in contrast to their meaning, leaving to the omophony the comic effect.

As a reaction to this pun Murphy bursts in a convulsive laughter, while Celia remains impassible looking at what almost seems a bad seizure:

> this was a joke that did not amuse Celia, at the best of times and places it could not have amused her. That did not matter. So far from being adapted to her, it was not addressed to her. It amused Murphy, that was all that mattered. He always found it most funny, more than most funny, clonic [...]. (p. 98)

But as we continue with the analysis of this laughter, we discover that it is not only the joke in itself that Murphy enjoys, but the grotesque visualisation of the entire scene. Murphy imagines the barmaid with a horse's head. Here Beckett is perhaps thinking of Horace's image from *Ars Poetica*, recopied into his Murphy notebook, which I discussed above:

> On the one hand the barmaid, fresh from the country, a horse's head on a cow's body, her crape bodice more a W than a V, her legs more a X than an O, her eyes closed for the sweet pain, leaning out through the hatch of the bar parlour. On the other the stout porter, mounting the footrail, his canines gleaming behind a pad of frothy whisker. (p. 98)

The picture conjured up by the story is more than poor Murphy can stand. His laughter turns into actual convulsions and he rolls on the ground until the attack passes, as suddenly as it came.

Murphy's taste for jokes also extends to bad ones and, just as the "good" ones make him laugh, the "bad" ones make him hysterical and aggressive. As chance would have it, what he takes to be a bad joke is simply a telling-off from his beloved. While Celia is removing all obstacles to him successfully finding work, Murphy is busy inventing excuses for not working, until Celia thinks she has found a surefire way to convince her fiancé: when he finds work, she at last can stop being a prostitute and dedicate herself entirely to Murphy, "then there will be nothing to distract me from you" (p. 48). This is corny line to which Murphy reacts.

> This was the kind of Joe Miller that Murphy simply could not bear to hear revived. It had never been a good joke.
> Not the least remarkable of Murphy's innumerable classifications of experience was that into jokes that had once been good jokes and jokes that had never been good jokes. What but an imperfect sense of humour could have made such a mess of chaos? In the beginning was the pun. And so on. (p. 48)

A "Joe Miller" was a second-rate, outdated joke. The French translation uses "plaisanterie", which in English is simply "joke", suggesting considering a "Joe Miller" as synonym for the latter word.

The reference to the old English comedian, metonym for bad jokes, is particularly compelling and influences our perception of the entire passage. Joseph (or Josias) Miller, born in 1684 and died in 1738, was a comic actor at Drury Lane Theatre in London, where he played from 1709 until his death, specialising in "Irish brogue" and in telling jokes. His jokes were for the most part awful and based on the aggressive mechanism of making fun of others: about stupidity, insolence and insults.[97] The actor, though illiterate, was able to play scripted parts read to him by his wife and was largely responsible for the success in London of William Congreve's comedies. He must have been very successful in his day, for his name was used as the title of a collection of jokes, compiled by John Mottley (a name surely too reminiscent of 'motley fool'[98] to be authentic) and entitled *Joe Miller's Jests: or the wit's vademecum*, published in 1739, after the actor's death. It seems that, of the collected jokes, only three[99] actually belonged to Miller, while all the rest were falsely attributed to this famous character or were the kind of jokes he used to tell. Walter Redfern, however, proposed a theory that Miller was used as a metaphor for stupidity, having been, in life, a kind of dull idiot when he was telling his funny stories to others. In support of this Redfern notes that the anonymous preface to the 1846 edition of *Joe Miller's Jests* maintained that the attribution to Joe Miller was by antiphrasis.[100]

Early example of deadpan, or synonym for old chestnuts, Joe Miller is a recurring obsession for Beckett and the phrase "life is a Joe Miller" is even found in the Murphy notebooks,[101] later to be elaborated into Murphy's impatience for jests bearing that name. But if life is a "Joe Miller", Murphy's intolerance for "Joe Millers" goes far beyond mere aesthetic judgement.

It is strange that Murphy's anger attributes the status of joke to Celia's very serious proposition. Celia does not intend to utter either a *good* or a *bad joke*, but her recipient (Murphy) decodes it –surprisingly for the reader- in a semantic distortion. Perhaps Murphy's laughter is a Freudian defence against suffering: Murphy does not *want* to read in Celia's words a painful truth, and escapes the embarassment by labelling the woman's utterance as a *joke*, or even worse, a *bad joke*. The triviality of Celia's concerns (work, home, everyday chores) clashes absurdly with Murphy's abstract thought. Murphy's gross pleasure for jokes and jests is in this situation inhibited. The Freudian saving of psychical expenditure does not activate any pleasure: Murphy is a victim of psychic inhibition that he is not able to release. Probably because Murphy's inhibition reaches its peak, as his joke reaches the top of the jokes' hierarchy. Freud defines as tendentious the joke to which he attributes the higher level of the jokes' hierarchy. According to Freud "the highest stage of joking, the tendentious joke, frequently has two kinds of inhibition to overcome, those opposing the joke itself and those opposing its tendency [...]": Celia clearly opposes the liberating tendency of the joke.[102] Funnily enough (no pun intended), Murphy reacts to his psychic constriction by uttering a joke and by expressing his anger toward a specific kind of joke, the Joe Millers.

Murphy cannot bear to hear repeated the corny jokes of the English comic and detests the predictability of those stories, those un-funny jokes. They have never been funny and, what is more, have caused universal chaos, while the universe, instead, is regulated by a precise classification of origin. "In the beginning was the pun." For the Bible, in the beginning was the Word. But in Murphy's cosmogony, the holy Word is replaced by the pun, the *calembour*, the play on words. The pun is Word, but a word that rebels against order and that recreates a different structure founded on overturning, on comic and aggressive inversion. This word is very different from the unique, sacred, unchanging and inviolable Word of the Bible. It is a word that negates, that annuls certainties and that generates a vital chaos, which in its turn generates. And so on, until the end of our days.

Notes

1 Knowlson 1996, but see also Pilling 1976.
2 Knowlson 1996, p. 295 gives his vivid opinion of the novel: "irritated me in spite of its qualities".
3 Ibid. p. 762, no. 168. Letter of 15th January 1963.
4 Ibid. p. 845.
5 Ibid. p. 846.
6 Ibid. pp. 165; 41; 75-76.
7 RUL MS3000/1.
8 Both quotes in Knowlson 1996, p. 217.
9 Ibid. p. 845.
10 Ibid. p. 844.
11 RUL MS3000/1, pp. 73-76 (the numeration, however, is not Beckett's but of the Archive).
12 Ibid. p. 75.
13 Ibid. p. 64. For an English translation see Horace 2005:
"What if a Painter, in his art to shine,
A human head and horse's neck should join;
From various creatures put the limbs together,
Cover'd with plumes, from ev'ry bird a feather;
And in a filthy tail the figure drop,
A fish at bottom, a fair maid at top:
Viewing a picture of this strange condition,
Would you not laugh at such an exhibition?"
14 Decoding this written manuscript required considerable research. Librarians at RUL were consulted as well as experts on Beckett's manuscripts, Julian Garforth, letter to the author, 30th October 1998. John Pilling is also in agreement with the interpretation.
15 But see Cohn 1962, pp. 26-28, for a more detailed analysis of the title.
16 Shakespeare 1994, p. 670 (III, 1, 163-164).
17 Ibid. p. 364 (V, 3, 94-96).
18 Gray 1966, p. 9.
19 He quotes from the sonnet "Recueillement", distorting it as fol-

lows: "Tu appelais - (*Un temps. Il se corrige.*) Tu RECLAMAIS le soir; il vient - (*Un temps. Il se corrige.*) Il DESCEND: le voici. (*Il reprend, très chantant.*) Tu réclamais le soir; il descend: le voici" (pp. 110-111).

20   Shakespeare 1994, p. 220 (V, 7, 7).
21   Pilling 1976, p. 102.
22   Cohn 1962, pp. 27; 40; 76-77.
23   Arika 1990, p. 3.
24   Ibid. p. 4: "son écriture par sa densité, par sa justification de chaque syllabe, est évidemment l'héritière de Dante, des classiques du XVII et XVIII siècles anglais, mai plus encore d'une écriture originelle [...]: la Bible".
25   See Schneider 1990, p. 182.
26   Chabert 1990a, p. 17.
27   Cronin 1997, p. 183.
28   Pilling 1976, p. 153, tells of Beckett seeing Ibsen productions at the Abbey Theatre (pp. 152-153).
29   McMillan-Fehsenfeld 1988, p. 31.
30   Pilling 1976, p. 92. And we might note that he is referring to *Play*, i.e. to the mature phase of Beckett's theatre.
31   In McMillan-Fehsenfeld 1988, p. 204.
32   Ibid. p. 238.
33   See Kalb 1989.
34   Guicharnaud 1967, p. 248.
35   McMillan 1990, p. 107.
36   See Ubersfeld 1990, pp. 67 and 69.
37   Gontarski 1985, p. 28.
38   Revelation of narrative pretence is also found in Beckett's prose, where he establishes a direct relationship with the reader, entering and leaving the convention. See all the *Thrilogy*.
39   Foster V. 1993, p. 26: "in both Beckett's and Shakespeare's late tragicomedies lives of suffering are finally redeemed by the aesthetic pleasure of the stories that can be told about them".
40   Taviani 1997, p. 36.

41   Uwah Okebaram 1989, already mentioned, does not fully examine the implications of the relationship between the two authors. Otherwise see Chemi 2006.

42   Letter from Samuel Beckett to Aldo Tagliaferri, Paris, 9th February 1984 (RUL MS4090).

43   All likely suppositions, unsupported by actual facts, are in Uwah Okebaram 1989, p. 5.

44   Cronin 1997, p. 63. But also Topsfield 1988, p. 26 mentions and Bair 1990, p. 59 confirms an interview with Beckett on 13th April 1972 (p. 77, no. 25).

45   Topsfield 1988, p. 26.

46   For a history of directing in Italy see Meldolesi 1984.

47   See AA.VV. 1986.

48   Taviani 1997, p. 96.

49   Vicentini 1993, p. 122, my translation from Italian.

50   Ibid. p. 123, my translation from Italian.

51   Pirandello 1974.

52   Ibid., p. 113.

53   As confirmation of the difference between the two playwrights, see their unlike relationship with the mask-function, underlined by Pilling 1976, p. 68.

54   Freud 2002, p. 116.

55   Topsfield 1988, p. 26.

56   Ibid. p. 27.

57   Cohn 1962, p. 22.

58   Ibid. p. 208.

59   Ibid. p. 7. However, in the years following publication of this study, the American academic would turn her highly intelligent attention specifically to the stage dimension of Beckett's theatre with her numerous, most brilliant contributions.

60   Cohn 1980, p. 98. But on repetition as an aesthetic principle of all Beckett's work see also Connor 1988.

61   Celati 1975, p. 116.

62   Cohn 1962, p. 13.

63   Kenner 1973, pp. 24-25.

64   A similar series of misunderstandings regarding the senses is found in scenes by Karl Valentin: "ANNI. Yes, I hear you I hear you, but you do not see you. SIMMERL. I well believe it! What you want to see in the dark? ANNI. Why, then, in the dark you hear" (in Valentin 1980, p. 81, my translation from Italian). Sight and hearing are in a comical short-circuit.

65   For Busi 1980 Gogo and Sancho Panza share this defect, which "serves more than comic purposes: it allows the reader to penetrate the various levels of linguistic and psychological perspectives offered by the author" (p. 20).

66   Cohn 1962, p. 75 finds this in *Watt* and it should be noted that it is one of the most common verbal techniques of clowns, see Remy 1974.

67   Bruni 1987, p. 87.

68   Frasca 1998, p. XII, my translation from Italian.

69   Valentin 1980, p. 142, my translation from Italian.

70   See pp. 53-54.

71   See Valentin 1980, pp. 135-137.

72   Celati 1975, p. 160, my translation from Italian.

73   Simon A. 1983, p. 96.

74   Freud 2002.

75   Brienza 1992, p. 117. But on the eschatological interpretation of artistic activity in Beckett also see Celati 1975, p. 182.

76   Dukore 1973, p. 352.

77   *Poesie in inglese*, p. 86 (with English text besides).

78   Cohn 1962, id. 1980; Dutton 1986; Kern 1977, id. 1966; Orr 1991.

79   For types of clowns' numbers see Remy 1974 and Bouissac 1986.

80   Abbott 1994, pp. 117-119.

81   Ben-Zvi 1990, p. 24.

82   Now in Hoefer 1965.

83   I give here the English translation of the passage as quoted by Hoefer (ibid. p. 75).

84   Fletcher 1964, pp. 87-88, no. 1.

85   Cronin 1997, p. 101.

86   Davoren's line from *The Shadow of a Gunman*, see O'Casey 1957, vol. I, p. 126.

87   Freud 2002, pp. 108-109.
88   But see also a wide range of studies of Jewish humour, including: Telushkin 1992; Berger P. 1997; Berger A. 1993; Grotjahn 1970.
89   See Cohn 1973 and Adorno 1961. Redfern 1998, maintains that "the tailor-joke [...] is naturally commandeered by Jewish experts on humour as one of their own".
90   Written at the end of the war in French for an art journal. Now in *Disjecta*, pp. 118-131.
91   See already mentioned and discussed Cohn 1980, p. 177.
92   Lowe 1995.
93   Cit. in Cohn 1986.
94   Lowe 1995, p. 14.
95   See Cohn 1973, p. 22.
96   Freud 2002.
97   See Redfern 1998, who also associates this type of comic mechanism with the superiority theory of humour by Thomas Hobbes.
98   Ibid.
99   WBE 1977, p. 468.
100 Redfern 1998.
101 RUL MS3000/1, p. 20 (page numbers in pencil by archivist).
102 Freud 2002, pp. 168-169.

* CHAPTER SIX *

ALL THAT *LAUGH* ACCORDING TO BECKETT

6.1. Comic Beckett?

Some Beckett critics and a part of his public have expressed doubts and perplexity as to the presence of comedy in Beckett.[1] The existential anguish he expresses, the pain of living and the encounter with our most agonising and traumatic inner experiences seem to deny any possible comic dimension. Others have been unable to deny that Beckett's game and the spectator's enjoyment lie in just that schizophrenic alternation between comedy and tragedy, in the mingling, the superimposition and the dialectic between comic form and tragic content.

My progression through the biography, texts and stage productions of Beckett has brought to light the comic component of his universe that, even when it has been recognised by critics, has then been relegated to the wings.

But how can we say, with certainty, that Beckett is comical? The presence of laughter might be one possible sign, as a sort of physiological indicator of the comic. Laughter is undoubtedly confirmation of success in transmitting comic forms – not necessarily voluntary or conscious – from a sender to a receiver, the audience, in a given cultural context.

Although the concepts of comedy and laughter are almost perennially bound together, they are very different from each other and it is possible to separate them. If all that is laughable is comical, we cannot say the same vice versa, for what makes us laugh is not necessarily, deliberately comical. Many examples can be found in treatises on theories of laughter,[2] but consider the most hackneyed of all, and one that never fails: a stranger walking along the street who suddenly trips and falls causes us, in the majority of cases, to laugh instinctively, in direct proportion to the circumstances of the fall. If the person who falls is not a stranger, but a very important personage, if the fall is particularly sudden or acrobatic, or if the victim is not seriously hurt, our laughter issues forth freely and heartily. The accidental fall is a typical example of involuntary comedy, while true comedy occurs following deliberate provocation of that gasping breath from the diaphragm, which we call laughter.

As a rhetorical device, comedy has a conscious aesthetic structure comprising a subject (the playwright, the actor who creates his own gags, or the friend telling us a joke…) who deliberately makes fun of a subject (a person, a situation, a vice, a category of people…) in front of an audience and in a given cultural setting. Without this triangle of communication and this cultural sharing, comedy does not emerge. Or it shouldn't. Just as without a precise motive – even accidental – laughter does not emerge. Or it shouldn't.

In reality, in Beckett we find a more complex and less straightforward situation. In his world, characters often burst out laughing for no apparent reason, while his texts and productions contain comic techniques that do not necessarily elicit laughter. And the laughter provoked always has a rather dirty, ambiguous, embarrassing and grotesque quality.

How, then, can we discover – if it exists – the comic in Beckett, if the process of cause/effect or the known conventions of comedy no longer apply? If comedy is no longer followed by laughter, can we call it comedy? And can that stifled snigger still be defined as laughter?

We shall approach the question with order and a clear plan, well aware of the doubts that Beckett himself raised on the subject. We shall not look at the comic as comedy, that dramatic genre with historical origin and diachronic development over the ages, of which Beckett said "ça commençait mal et ça finissait bien" (in *Nouvelles et textes pour rien*, p. 134). We shall rather consider the comic, instead, as a complex system of rhetorical norms and techniques from a synchronic viewpoint, within which we can identify some universally valid elements. These elements can be combined together in various ways and with different degrees of intensity, to produce different comic effects and then, the comic reaction – laughter. Different comic categories produce different types of laughter.

If the laughter has a dissociated, de-automatised quality, then we must observe it more closely, and where better than on the faces of Beckett's characters, to see where, why and how much they laugh, and on those of the audience? The latter is perhaps the most elusive element. The emotional, psychophysical and intellectual reactions of audiences are certainly the most mysterious and least studied component of performance. Audience reaction is subject to so many variables that it appears impalpable and yet some factors of perception and interpretation of a performance are stimulated by the characteristics of the performance itself. Below, Beckett's audience will speak through the voices of excellent readers and spectators and through analysis of the suffocated laughter of this audience.[3]

Last but not least, textual evidence of a theory of comedy or humour in Beckett's texts will be reviewed. By extrapolating the most significant passages from Beckett's prose, poetry and drama where he discusses his concepts of comedy and by reorganising them into a single, coherent story, it is possible to reconstruct Beckett's very eccentric theory of the comic.

6.2. "Rien n'est plus drôle que le malheur"

It is surprising how much Beckett theorised about comedy in his works. Surprising, because Beckett was always shy and reluctant to explain his aesthetic or ideology and, when asked for explanations, often gave misleading and deviating interpretations. On the one hand, Beckett supplied countless details on the facts, people or sources behind his texts but, on the other, he was decidedly hostile towards "an exegesis of his overall work".[4]

Yet if we look closely, as far as comedy is concerned Beckett gave extremely generous indications.

His prose, poetry and theatre are scattered with thoughts that, though unsystematic and unplanned, make up a sort of authentic theoretical *corpus*.

Laughter is often the opportunity offered to/by characters to introduce problems of tragedy and comedy, happiness and unhappiness, tears and laughter or possible connections between the two. A guffaw or a sly smile are the pretext for changing the subject, what was once an incontrovertible sign of joy and enjoyment is merely sound, just a signifier without its conventional signified. The new, different signified added in the context of Beckett is that of doubt - we can no longer immediately recognise a state of mind, but the sense slides towards a universal dialectic. Scatological meditations that are left in the limbo of the unfinished (of saying, communicating, explaining, developing) and of the ambiguous (where all opposites are equal and create a short-circuit), seeming all the more unexpected when we consider their source. Whether the speaker is Beckett's un-authoritative narrator or whether the word is spoken directly by the character, the effect of alienation is the same, as both figures are untrustworthy, unreliable and equivocal. As far as the narrator is concerned, I shall look more closely in the following paragraphs at how much he undergoes "deflation".[5] As for the characters, we can easily understand the reader's/spectator's doubts concerning them. Their physical appearance is sufficient - they are *clochards*, clowns, drunken tramps, human relics, crawling creatures, vague semblances of humanity. All of them love to discuss the universal questions of existence, of human destiny, of Man's place on earth, of happiness and unhappiness. These human effigies are obsessed by very real distress and their appearance of walking ghosts does not prevent them from tormenting themselves with endless questions without answer.[6] Their laughter is a sign of doubt, it is Winnie's bell that marks the start of another "happy day", or the start of a new show, the staging of the debate on happiness and unhappiness.

In this interpretation, the prose and theatre texts reflect the same model, with a continuity not uncommon in Beckett. There is, however, a fundamental difference: in the theatre the pattern is dramatised, so it permeates not only the speeches of the characters but also their actions.

Happiness that turns into unhappiness – and vice versa – is never completely sad for them, for they never lose their self-irony, nor for us who observe them, so that the whole dynamic is constantly turned into a game.

In *Mercier et Camier* and in *L'Innommable* laughter is associated with melancholy and regret, and in the end it is suppressed, thinking that after all tears are preferable. In the first novel the narrator gives a long description of that particular "spleen" suffered while waiting for the night to bring counsel, which may turn into a long wait and which recalls an annoying intertwining of regrets (p. 150), in the face of which one should fall about laughing, if only one were still capable:

> il est cependant une sorte de spleen difficilement conjurable. C'est l'attente de la nuit qui portera conseil, car ce n'est pas toutes les nuits qui possèdent cette propriété. Cela peut durer des mois. C'est l'entre-deux, la longue, la mièvre, la lassante mêlée des regrets, des derniers avec les résolus, on y est passé mille fois, c'est tordant mais on n'arrive pas à se tordre, à se dissoudre dans le sourire mille fois souri. (pp. 189-190)

The smile smiled a thousand times fails. It is blocked, stuck. Perhaps in the same awareness of the Unnamable, that to cry out of nostalgia is better than laughing:

> on se retourne, l'autre aussi, on le pleure, il vous pleure, c'est du plus haut tragique, ça vaut mieux que de rire. Quoi encore, des jugements, des comparaisons, ça va mieux que de rire, tout aide, ne peut qu'aider, à franchir la mauvaise passe. (p. 191)

The suggestion of the unnameable protagonist-narrator, however, seems to fall on stony ground, or on the indifference of a universe that in any case resounds with laughter. Even in *L'Innommable*, strange sounds are heard, including laughter that resembles groans, which mingle together and are superimposed. The suggestion of tears rather than laughter becomes ironic if placed among all the laughter of Beckett's characters, but it introduces the question of the meaning of life and of happiness.

Joy is mentioned, again, in *Mercier et Camier* and an attempt is made to define what happiness is. Beckett, with one of his most telling images, gives us an interpretation of this everyday hell we must endure, associating it with the torments of the thirsty in the desert:

> la joie par cuillerées à sel, comme l'eau aux grands déshydratés,
> et une gentille petite agonie à doses homéopathiques. (p. 130)

Such is all of life - a slow, inexorable, sweet agony, relieved by tiny amounts in homeopathic doses of good moments. Joy is inflicted upon us slowly, like water to the truly parched. Note the allusions to the desert in the French: the "salt spoon", with its syntactic connection with the image of the parched, adds to the literal meaning of the phrase an atmosphere of thirst and drought. The agony that homeopathically cures agony, over and above the ironic effect, is a key point of Beckett's thinking. The principle of giving the patients small amounts of the substances that caused their illness is associated here with the whole course of human life, in which joy is compared with agony. Agony in small doses (medicine) cures the eternal agony of human life (illness) and the supporting therapy is joy, also taken in homeopathic doses.

But what then is happiness? "En quoi consiste le bonheur sur terre, c'est-à-dire le bonheur? Oh, je ne les épargnais pas",[7] no-one seems to know, not even the one asking the question. Notwithstanding, "il poussa un rire strident et sauvage",[8] and we do not understand the reason for the laugh, which precedes the obscene lines that follow shortly: "potopompos scroton, bander mou et boire sec".[9] The secret of happiness is inscrutable, meanwhile, all one can do is to burst into strident laughter or savage scurrility. Life consists in progressively *losing* something: hair, teeths, ideals. We are alive as long as we breathe and, in the monotonous repetition of biological needs, we change: "nous respirons, nous changeons! Nous perdons nos cheveux, nos dents! Notre fraîcheur! Nos idéaux!"[10] Everything changes for the worst, all is inevitably consumed, therefore resisting pain assumes a quality of vital persistence. In *All That Fall* Mrs Rooney asks Mr Slocum how his poor mother is and he replies, "thank you, she is fairly comfortable. We manage to keep her out of pain" (p. 177): being quite well means suffering the least possible.

In such a gloomy, seemingly desperate atmosphere, the two clowns Mercier and Camier seem to contradict Mr Slocum's gloom with their clowning. It is from desperate anguish, says Beckett, that the most touching sense of happiness originates. Only thus can happiness occur and find its form. Mercier says so plainly:

> quant tu crains pour ton kyste, songe aux fistules. Et quand tu trembles pour ta fistule, réfléchis un peu aux chancres. C'est un système qui vaut également pour ce que d'aucuns appellent encore le bonheur. Prends un type par exemple qui ne souffre de rien, ni au corps ni à l'autre truc. Comment va-t-il s'en sortir? C'est simple. En pensant au néant. Ainsi dans chaque situation la nature nous convie-t-elle au sourire, sinon au rire. (pp. 91-92)

It is very simple. An infallible, very simple recipe that overturns the theory of the lesser evil. Ordinary common sense sees the secret of a quiet life in choosing the lesser evil. Mercier overturns this point-of-view, advising Camier to always think of the greater evil. And when there is nothing wrong either in the body or in that other thing some call the soul, there is always the thought of nothingness to assist us. In any event, nature gives us the chance to smile, if not to laugh. So another "happy day" is guaranteed. Mercier's apparent ingenuity is the same as Winnie's, who cries joyfully "another heavenly day" even in her desperate situation (p. 138) and who passes her day eternally grateful that things have got no better, but no worse either. Her inexorable fall into the sinking sand is scattered with joyful references to spiritual contentment that are difficult to believe from a nice-looking middle-aged woman being sucked into the sand. This incredibly alienating effect serves to further emphasise affirmations such as "marvellous gift" (p. 139), "wonderful lines", "can't complain", "great mercies" (p. 140), "what I find so wonderful" (p. 143) and so on, through to the paranoid repetition of her catchphrase "oh this is going to be another happy day!" (p. 142). What Winnie finds most exciting and comforting is discovering her well-known points of reference. The slow, gradual disintegration of matter reassures, rather than upsets her. Her joy on awaking is guaranteed by the same old routine of always. Things are neither worse nor better - what a happy day!

Winnie certainly does not share our point-of-view as external observers, nor the rational logic to which we are so tied. To us, Winnie is the personification of irrationality and our good sense is riled - how can she be so stupidly optimistic when the earth is swallowing her up? When we realise that Winnie's joy is not an attitude, but an authentic way of life, or survival, then we protest. But Winnie stays there in front of us, continuing to sink and to exclaim "oh les beaux jours!" The French version suggests a further connection between texts, recalling the last part of *Molloy*, when Winnie checks her gums. In the original version in English, Winnie repeats several times, with evident contentment "ah well [...] no worse [...] no better, no worse [...] no change [...] no pain" (p. 139 et passim). Her joy is based on the simple assumption that no change means no pain. If we re-read the line in French, the connection with *Molloy* seems even more evident: "enfin [...] pas pis [...] pas mieux, pas pis [...] pas de changement [...] pas de douleur" (p. 14) and concludes "oh le beau jour encore que ça va être!" (p. 20). The assonance is too great not to bring to mind the epilogue of *Molloy*: "mon genou ne va pas mieux. Il ne va plus mal non plus [...]. Ça ira plus vite. Ce sera le bon temps" (p. 271). Malone's gangrenous knee – like Winnie's gums – is not better, nor worse. On the other hand, the body's general deterioration "ça ira plus vite" and happy days will arrive.

Once again, our view of happiness is overturned, shaken at its apparently unshakeable foundations. The fall, and its variations of sinking, crawling, deteriorating brings no pain, but a certain euphoria of loss, a delirium of omni(im)potence. If the end of mind and body is near, then so is the end of eternal torment. And so the characters experience real exaltation in the fall, understood as a metaphor and as reality – which is one of Beckett's favourite images. *All That Fall, Cascando* (poetry and radio drama), *Echo's Bones, and Other Precipitates*, as well as *Catastrophe* and all other titles that mention an "end" (*Fin de partie, Malone meurt, Pour finir encore et autres foirades, Ends and Odds*) are all part of the same semantic field indicating a fall, a slip, a plummeting down, a final catastrophe, an end of game.[11] A vertigo to us incomprehensible, but for them, the characters, it is joyful and ingenuous, the only pipe dream in their daily struggle to live.

"Quand je tomberai je pleurerai de bonheur" (p. 109) reflects Clov in his "endgame", "when I fall I'll weep for happiness" (p. 132). The fall is certainly the best solution to his usual condition, for him, who has passed his life waiting for an improvement and who does not know if he has ever been happy. When Hamm asks him to go and see if his parents are still alive in their dustbins, Clov checks Nell who shows no sign of life and Nagg who is crying:

> CLOV. - Il pleure. [...]
> HAMM. - Donc il vit. (*Un temps.*) As-tu jamais eu un instant de bonheur?
> CLOV. - Pas à ma connaissance. (pp. 84-85)

Tears are a physiological reaction that undoubtedly proves the existence of life, *fleo ergo sum*. But they also bring back memories of happiness that has passed. Clov's laconic reply does not only deny he has been happy in the past, it questions the very idea of happiness. With an inversion common in Beckett, our attention is captured by the word itself and its referentiality. It is no longer the general sense of the discourse that creates meaning, but the meaning itself of the word: "pas à ma connaissance", "I don't believe so", "not that I know of" or better "from what I know of happiness probably not". The problem, for Clov, is to define what is meant by happiness. Not a new problem in Beckett's universe, and one shared by other characters.

In *En attendant Godot* all the characters have an opinion on happiness. All except Lucky, whose name speaks for itself, but whose condition of complete slavery is an oxymoronic superimposition. The others all express precise opinions. Estragon declares clearly that he is unhappy, even though he cannot remember since when ("ESTRAGON. - Je suis malheureux. VLADIMIR. - Sans blague! Depuis quand? ESTRAGON. - J'avais oublié" p. 70), indeed the only opportunity he has to be happy is when he sleeps ("je rêvais que j'étais heureux" p. 127). His incapacity is cause of resentment when faced with Vladimir's contentment – he manages to be content despite the melancholy:

> ESTRAGON (*tristement*). - Tu vois, tu pisses mieux quand je ne suis pas là.
> VLADIMIR. - Tu me manquais - et en même temps j'étais content. N'est-ce pas curieux?
> ESTRAGON (*outré*). - Content?
> VLADIMIR (*ayant réfléchi*). - Ce n'est peut-être pas le mot. (p. 82)

Happiness wells up at the same time as melancholy for his absent friend. Vladimir finds the combination unusual and immediately doubts the word he has just used: "content" might not be the right word. During his first encounter with the boy, Vladimir had openly admitted he did not know if he was happy or unhappy, just like Godot's young messenger:

> VLADIMIR. - Tu n'es pas malheureux? (*Le garçon hésite.*) Tu entends?
> GARÇON. - Oui, monsieur.
> VLADIMIR. - Et alors?
> GARÇON. - Je ne sais pas, monsieur.
> VLADIMIR. - Tu ne sais pas si tu es malheureux ou non?
> GARÇON. - Non, monsieur.
> VLADIMIR. - C'est comme moi. (p. 72)

Although at first Vladimir seems shocked by the boy's lack of awareness and indeed continues to press him with questions, in the end, he himself admits sharing the same lack of knowledge, which in English is even more explicit, "you're as bad as myself" (p. 50), introducing a value judgement that is strongly self-critical.

Finally, it is Pozzo's turn to express his view of happiness and he does so with a paradox: just as the tears of the world are unchangeable, so there is always the same quantity of laughter, so if one person begins, another stops.

> [...] Les larmes du monde sont immuables. Pour chacun qui se met à pleurer, quelque part un autre s'arrête. Il en va de même du rire. (*Il rit.*) Ne disons donc pas de mal de notre époque,

elle n'est pas plus malheureuse que les précédentes. (*Silence.*) N'en disons pas de bien non plus. (*Silence.*) N'en parlons pas. (pp. 44-45)

Like a true ham actor, Pozzo ends his tirade with a memorable sentence, which I believe relevant to quote in English too: "The tears of the world are a constant quantity. For each one who begins to weep, somewhere else another stops. The same is true of the laugh. [*He laughs.*] Let us not speak ill of our generation, it is not any unhappier than its predecessors. [*Pause.*] Let us not speak well of it either. [*Pause.*] Let us not speak of it at all" (p. 33).

His eloquence has got the better of him and the speech heads for involution, towards the affirmation of aphasia. All things considered, his harangue is not so different from the widespread confusion of happiness and unhappiness of the other characters. Not even he manages to define a smile without comparing it with its opposite, a tear. Not even he shows strong certainty about his own state of mind.

The protagonists of *Godot* are not the only ones to experience and express doubts on the concept of happiness. Didi, Gogo and Pozzo are in good company in their confusion and uncertainty as to the nature of their own sentiments and how to describe them in words.

In *Human Wishes*, the fragment abandoned by Beckett, there is a wonderful long scene where the main subject of discussion is mirth. We are in an elegant drawing room in 1781 (precisely on the evening of April 4th, a Wednesday!) and on stage sit three women, intent on various occupations. Mrs Williams is meditating, Mrs Desmoulins is knitting, Miss Carmichael is reading and then there is the cat, Hodge, who sleeps, "if possible".[12] The drawing-room chatter one would expect turns towards very measured scurrility and thence to mirth:

MRS D. To be called a loose woman would not move me to mirth, for my part, I believe. (Sits down).
MRS W. And to be called the daughter of a loose woman, would that move you to mirth, Madam, for your part, do you suppose?

MRS D. It would not, Madam, I believe.
MRS W. But what would move you, Madam, to mirth, do you suppose, for your part?
MRS D. To mirth, Madam, for my part, I am with difficulty moved, I believe. (Silence)
MRS W. Madam, for mirth, for my part,
      I never had the heart;
      Madam, for my part, to mirth
      I have not been moved since birth. [...]
MRS W. You say you are not merry. Very well. But who is merry in this house? You would call me merry, Madam, I suppose?
MRS D. No, Madam, you are not what I would call merry.
MRS W. And Frank, Madam, would you call Frank merry?
MRS D. No, Madam, I would not.
MISS C. Except when drunk.
MRS D. The gross hilarity of ebriety is not merriment, Miss Carmichael, to my mind.
MRS W. And Levett, Madam, would you call Levett merry?
MRS D. I would not call Levett anything, Madam.
MISS C. Not even when drunk.
MRS W. And poor Poll, here, Madam, is poor Poll here what you would call merry?
MRS D. She was taken into the house to be merry.
MRS W. I do not ask why she was taken into the house. I ask is she merry or is she not merry.
MISS C. I was merry once, I think.
MRS W. (Loudly). What is it to me, Miss, that you were merry once? Are you merry, or are you not merry, NOW?
MRS D. She was taken in to enliven the house. I do not feel myself enlivened, for my part.
MRS W. What you feel, Madam, and what you do not feel, is of little consequence.
MRS D. I am aware of that, Madam.
MRS W. I am not merry, you are not merry, Frank is not merry-
MISS C. Except when drunk.

MRS W. Silence! Levett is not merry. Who remains?
MISS C. The cat.
MRS W. (Striking the floor with her stick). Silence! (Silence)
MRS W. The cat does *not* remain. The cat does not enter into the question. The cat *cannot* be merry. (Silence)
MRS W. I ask, who remains? (Silence)
MRS W. (Loudly). I ask, who remains, who might be merry?
MRS D. Who was taken into the house to be merry.
MRS W. (Striking the floor with her stick). Silence! (Silence)
MRS W. I ask, who remains, who might be merry, and I answer (pointing her stick at Miss Carmichael), *she* remains. (Silence)
MRS W. Is she merry? (Silence)
MRS W. (At the top of her voice). IS SHE MERRY?
MISS C. (Softly). She is not. (Silence)
MRS W. (Softly). Nobody in this house is merry. (pp. 296-299)

The passage, packed with potentially different interpretations, can be read on several levels. The three women immediately show their social and cultural extraction through their marked colloquial formality. The comic effect derives from the alienating contrast created by this conventionalism with the scurrilous contents ("loose woman", Frank's hinted at, disgusting, drunkenness) and from the conflicts among the women. The scene is dominated by the despotic figure of Mrs Williams who grows increasingly angry until she reaches the final, subdued consideration. She is desperately trying to find out if anyone in her house is happy. This proves a difficult task, as those present give her evasive or laconic replies. Mrs Desmoulins says she is with difficulty moved to mirth, but finds it hard to specify what she means by happiness or by a happy person. Mrs Williams presses her, determined to get to the bottom of the question and combats any attempt at evasion by Mrs Desmoulins. Poll was brought into the house to make her merry, but this is not what the hostess asks, can one at least say that Poll is merry? The girl replies, again evasively, that she has been so in the past, but this is not what Mrs Williams is asking. She lights on the definitive dialectic weapon: if Miss Carmichael was brought into the house to be happy, then she must be the only one left on the list.

This momentary relief, however, leads to the final resolution; Miss Carmichael, to the explicit, authoritarian request to express herself, replies in the third person that she is not happy. "Nobody in this house is merry". End of discussion. They move on.

The strange sensation of confusion remains. The energetic verbal fencing of the three women on merriment creates delicious cross-talk and introduces a series of sense switches worthy of note. The cat, who may be asleep on stage, is involved in the diatribe as one of the possible partakers of the mirth under discussion. Surprise at the short-circuit between animal and human is immediately felt by Mrs Williams, who points out that the cat does not count because she cannot be happy - animals, it is known, do not share our passions. Only human beings are subject to joy. There are, however, some beings between the animal and the human universe, the drunkards Frank and Levett, and they too are excluded as "the gross hilarity of ebriety is not merriment".[13] Only human beings, who conform to ethical and social conventions, have this privilege. Yet it seems that not even they manage to enjoy this spiritual state: no-one is happy.

But if merriment is impossible, why do Beckett's characters continue to laugh and keep their sense of humour and self-irony even in situations that are apparently critical? Perhaps because the secret of this joy derives precisely from the unhappy awareness of man.

Winnie continues to giggle – with or without Willie – because of her solemn devotion to laughter: "how can one better magnify the Almighty than by sniggering with him at his little jokes, particularly the poorer ones?"[14] Laughter is a question of faith, and its function is to honour the Almighty. And it is God himself who pushes us in this direction, peppering the world with his little jokes. The image of God as a practical joker, even stronger in the English version given the implications of the word "joke", strikes us and leads us almost imperceptibly towards the blasphemy of the "poorer jokes". For Winnie, the mystery of Creation is an unbroken series of divine jokes, some good, some bad, at which one cannot help but laugh: "laughing wild... something something laughing wild amid severest woe".[15] The quotation Winnie cannot remember comes from *On a distant prospect of Eton College* by Thomas Gray[16] and reads "And moody Madness laughing wild/Amid severest woe":[17] even more offensive to the Creator, whose divine work is glossed as "moody Madness".

It is in the light of a thought like Winnie's that Murphy's theory on jokes takes on a pragmatic consistency, which the classification in itself does not, nor intends to have. For Winnie it is a way of living, while for Murphy it is part of his habitual activities of ordering his thought. Indeed Celia's romantic words, themselves in ironic contrast with her profession of prostitute and catalogued by Murphy as a "Joe Miller joke", lead into Murphy-Beckett's theoretical disquisition on jokes and the imperfect sense of humour. For Murphy, Celia's is "une énorme bêtise", similar to the passage in *Eleutheria* (p. 48), where Monsieur Krap points out what nonsense Docteur Piouk has just come out with, and enlarges on his opinion. What the doctor said was a lot of nonsense "car il faut sourire de son sourire" (ibid.). The same definition might be used for Murphy's "Joe Miller joke" - a load of nonsense that makes us smile at its very smile.

The "bêtise" as a source of laughter can be better understood by reading some passages from *Fin de partie*. As can the entire comic universe of Beckett. In one of Beckett's most explicit extracts, Nell agrees with the very essence of his humour and asserts the intimate connection between comedy and unhappiness. When Nagg laughs at Hamm's unhappiness, Nell replies

> NELL. - Il ne faut pas rire de ces choses, Nagg. Pourquoi en ris-tu toujours?
> NAGG. - Pas si fort!
> NELL. - (*sans baisser la voix*). - Rien n'est plus drôle que le malheur, je te l'accorde. Mais -
> NAGG. - (*scandalisé*). - Oh!
> NELL. - Si, si, c'est la chose la plus comique au monde. Et nous en rions, nous en rions, de bon cœur, les premiers temps. Mais c'est toujours la même chose. Oui, c'est comme la bonne histoire qu'on nous raconte trop souvent, nous la trouvons toujours bonne, mais nous n'en rions plus. (pp. 33-34)

The connection between unhappiness and comedy is further explained: it is not just superimposition or a casual mixture, but a real direct descent. The comic *derives from* the "malheur" (unhappiness, woe, misfortune, infelicity). Though Nagg is shocked to hear such shameless theorising on the reason for his laughter, Nell continues with her thesis, which of course is also Beckett's. How much this was Beckett's perception of the world and of the comic was shown by his suggested indication as a director, to be repeated several times over the years, during the preparation for the Berlin performance of *Endspiel* in 1967 when "he felt that the most *important* sentence is Nell's 'Nothing is funnier than unhappiness'. And he directed to display the fun of unhappiness".[18] Nothing is funnier than unhappiness, indeed it is the most comical thing in the world. Our life, therefore, will unfold in a chain of unhappiness that will make us laugh heartily, but the more we laugh, the more familiar this unhappiness will become, and so our enjoyment will not be the same. Like the tale that was once a good joke for Murphy but which we now do not wish revived,[19] Nell's "bonne histoire" continues to be a good story, but does not make us laugh.

This is the peculiar descent of Beckett's characters, with their funny anomalies, their handicaps we are unable to weep over and their misfortunes that do not appear to bother them: ugliness and deformation do not move us. This is the origin of the pitiless gaze of the author and of the public, the former creating and the latter observing the wretched mishaps of the *clochards* on stage. From this originate most of the comic effects used by Beckett: obscenity, foul language, physical and verbal violence and blasphemy are all descendants of the same laughable unhappiness.

>en face
>le pire
>jusqu'à ce
>qu'il fasse rire.[20]

The worst stands in front of us until it makes us laugh. It might be the epigraph of Beckett's comedy. It references the frontal dimension of the subject, often used by Beckett on stage - Winnie stands "en face" of us, just as Didi and Gogo, Clov and Hamm and Krapp are always conscious of being watched from the auditorium, not to mention O in *Film*, literally obsessed by the eye watching him.[21] But it also contains that "pire", the worst, an indeterminate, fatal show that goes on until it gets the desired result – laughter. That "jusqu'à ce" contains all the effort, the slow, gradual invasion of laughter that inevitably comes, while "fasse rire" suggests resistance to laughter, that imposed reaction, which urges us but we try to deny, which the object demands but the spectator refuses. The object of comedy is the worst, the tyrannical subject is an unidentified natural force and the public is just a puppet at the mercy of this fatal, universal disorder. It is the worst that makes us laugh, willing or not. Frontality, in this dimension, finds its ultimate meaning, redefining the meta-theatrical insertions with their alienating and anti-naturalist effects. The character "facing" us is the one who does not allow audience identification, the one who brashly shows he is part of a stage pretence. The pathos that sometimes touches the character is constantly counterbalanced and neutralised by the emotional distance of the spectator and the resulting laughter is in turn related to the pathos, in a strange mixture that makes the difference of Beckett's comedy.

This is what generates the laugh of laughs, the *risus purus*: the laugh without happiness.

> Of all the laughs that strictly speaking are not laughs, but modes of ululation, only three I think need detain us, I mean the bitter, the hollow and the mirthless. They correspond to successive, how shall I say successive...suc...successive excoriations of the understanding, and the passage from one to the other is the passage from the lesser to the greater, from the lower to the higher, from the outer to the inner, from the gross to the fine, from the matter to the form. The laugh that now is mirthless once was hollow, the laugh that once was hollow once was bitter. And the laugh that once was bitter? Eyewater, Mr. Watt, eyewater. [...] The bitter laugh laughs at that which is not good, it is the ethical laugh. The hollow laugh laughs at

that which is not true, it is the intellectual laugh. Not good! Not true! Well well. But the mirthless laugh is the dianoetic laugh, down the snout -haw!- so. It is the laugh of laughs, the *risus purus*, the laugh laughing at the laugh, the beholding, the saluting of the highest joke, in a word the laugh that laughs -silence please- at that which is unhappy. (pp. 46-47)

In this very dense passage from *Watt*, the author seems to reveal the deepest meaning of his humour, or appears to, because just when everything seems clear to us in Beckett, we find something that again confuses our ideas, insinuating post-modern doubt. We are, however, enlightened, for here we find elements of all the comic that was to follow and of that already in literary form. Beckett began writing *Watt* in Paris in February 1941, but he actually finished most of it when in hiding at Roussillon during the war years.[22] He wrote because he was unable to read, he had brought with him very few books and had few possibilities of procuring others. Above all, he wrote to stay alive, to conserve the mental clarity that was easily threatened in times of war. "He wrote, he said later, as a stylistic exercise and in order to stay sane, 'in order to keep in touch'".[23] The result was an exhilarating grotesque novel that made fun of Western rationalistic knowledge, undermining the capacities and possibilities of interpreting reality. More than Murphy, Watt is obsessed by a desire to catalogue, which he tries to apply to a reality that continues to escape him. Watt is the eternal question of the child trying discover the world of senses – WHAT? He trusts the ordered reason of grown-ups, although this trust is continuously frustrated and negated - his master, Knott, is the living negation of his efforts, NOT.

Cataloguing laughs is a concern of Watt, but it is not Watt speaking here, in fact the ironic asides of Arsene, the speaker, address him as listener. Of all possible laughs, Arsene chooses what could not really be defined as laughter, being similar to ululation, and of these chooses only three. These, the only ones worth mentioning, correspond to different degrees of intensity, to "successive excoriations of the understanding" (p. 51). So the intellect is excoriated, scratched, traumatically marked by these ululations, but in progressive degrees. The oppositions mentioned by Arsene are small/large, lower/higher, outer/inner, gross/fine and matter/form. So the lowest level (the bitter) has smaller dimensions, lower value, is superficial, mediocre and material, while the highest (the mirthless) is its exact opposite, having large dimensions, superiority, interiority, refinement and attention to form. The passage from one to another is rigidly and perfectly determined, creating a hierarchy with a surprise ending: if the laugh now mirthless was once hollow and that now hollow was once bitter, what was once the bitter laugh? "Eyewater", Mr Watt, tears. Going back upstream to the source of laughter, what we find is pain distilled into little drops of suffering. Or perhaps the "liquefaction of the self", from the too-perfect similarity of *eyewater* with *I-water*, which recalls the "deliquescence [of ego] in the very moods of existence".[24] Characters seem to melt as Surrealist artefacts in a Dalí painting.

But Arsene does not stop at going back to the origin of laughter – he starts to define each level of intensity. The bitter laugh, sour and distasteful, is the one that laughs at that which is not good and therefore involves the ethical sphere. The hollow laugh, false and misleading, is the one that laughs at that which is not true and therefore belongs to the intellectual sphere. The mirthless one, joyless, melancholy and sad, laughs at the laugh itself. In defining the latter, Arsene uses a very calculated crescendo, with intensifying emotion that culminates in the word "unhappy", in position of emphasis at the end of the tirade and preceded by a theatrical pause (silence please). It is the melancholy laugh of laughs, the pure laugh, the contemplative one, that which honours the highest joke – in a word, the dianoetic laugh. Aristotle defined the dianoetic virtues as those regarding the intellectual part of the spirit,[25] distinct from the moral ones, which concern sensibility, affections and their relationship with reason. Dianoia, the knowledge of discursive thinking, had already been defined by Democritus as the faculty for developing certain premises to the necessary conclusions by means of rational processes. This generates authentic knowledge, as opposed to that of the senses. The dianoetic laugh is rational in its capacity to grasp the connections between events, while the hollow laugh in intellectual and the bitter one sensual. They all originate in a tear.

The following summary may be proposed:

PROGRESSIVE STAGES OF LAUGHTER	OBJECT OF LAUGHTER	DEFINITION
1. [EYEWATER]		[tears]
2. BITTER	what is not good	ETHICAL
3. HOLLOW	what is not true	INTELLECTUAL
4. DIANOETIC	unhappiness	MIRTHLESS
5. [RISUS PURUS]	the laugh	HIGHEST JOKE

There are numerous examples of dianoetic laughter in Beckett's universe, the majority of the characters' laughs occur when they perceive a suffering which is ineluctable. Nell lucidly says that nothing is funnier than unhappiness, and her laughter arises from observation of deformity and monstrosity. The ugliness and deformation - Aristotle's basis for comedy - that do not provoke suffering mingle with the humour of Pirandello, the "dirty laugh" of the twentieth century that descends from ancient roots linking Beckett to Swift, Kafka and Cervantes, associating pathos (*"feeling* of the contrary") with comedy (*"perception* of the contrary").[26] Yet the cathartic effect of Freud's laughter, as a release of hidden inhibitions, in Beckett has vanished, contradicted by the total collapse of all certainties.

One of the protagonists of *Nouvelles et textes pour rien* tells of drowning several times and of finding it quite amusing, or at least so it seems:

> la mer aussi [...] je m'y suis même noyé à plusieurs reprises, sous diverses fausses appellations, laisse-moi rire, si seulement

> je pouvais rire, tout disparaîtrait, quoi, qui sait, tout, moi, embarqué. (pp. 162-163)

When recalling the drowning episodes, the narrator apostrophises the listener "let me laugh", laugh about pain, because if only he could laugh everything would disappear, even the pain. The hypothetical catharsis, though, is annulled by the hyperbole of the dissolution: the pain would go, but so would everything else around, the self and all the rest. A positive effect, that of eliminating something negative like pain, becomes a negative one, as its disappearance destroys everything indiscriminately. But not even the certainty of total death remains for the speaker, also cancelled by the probabilism of "qui sait". The catharsis that had overcome both Aristotle's rationalism and Pirandello's sentimentalism is nothing but a momentary illusion. The effect of arousal of laughter resuscitates for a brief moment but then leaves us worse off than before, like the "successful laughs" in *Comment c'est*: "rire réussis de ceux qui secouent un instant ressuscitent un instant puis laissent pour plus mort qu'avant" (pp. 170-171).

"The laugh laughing at the laugh" is the "sourire de son sourire" met in *Eleutheria*, an expression even closer to *Watt* in the English translation by Barbara Wright "laugh at our laughter" (p. 42). This smile is conscious of itself and of the unhappiness from which it originates. It is the awareness of laughing at what is unhappy and of unhappiness itself. So the highest joke (with all the many meanings of the word) honoured by our dianoia is a cruel hoax, perhaps a funny story about a fiasco:

> je me pris à songer à la cruauté, la riante. [...] Ce que je voyais c'était un homme chauve en costume marron, un diseur. Il racontait une histoire drôle, à propos d'un fiasco. Je n'y comprenais rien. Il prononça le mot escargot, limace peut-être, à la joie générale. Les femmes semblaient s'amuser encore plus que leurs cavaliers, si c'était possible. Leurs rires aigus crevaient les applaudissements et, calmés ceux-ci, fusaient toujours, par-ci par-là, et jusqu'à troubler l'exorde de l'histoire suivante. Elles [...] lançaient leurs cris de joie, vers la tempête comique, quel talent. (pp. 45-46)

This is the protagonist of "Le calmant" speaking, a novella included in *Nouvelles et textes pour rien*. He tells of seeing a sudden tempest of comedy, provoked by a chance *diseur*, so common in the public parks of Paris or London. An insignificant, bald little man, dressed in brown, tells a funny story about a fiasco, not better specified. It provokes a wave of unruly, turbulent joy. Quel talent, notre diseur! His secret was simply to evoke the cruelty (shades of Artaud!) that laughs, a cruelty that stimulates laughter rather than tears, but which derives from tears and is mixed with tears.

Unhappiness generates tears, tears generate the bitter laugh, from this comes the hollow laugh, from this the mirthless laugh, which laughs at unhappiness. The circle closes. The chain is complete. Quel talent, notre diseur!

6.3. "Pourquoi en ris-tu toujours?"

Given that in comedy the spectator's laugh hardly ever coincides with that of the characters, in fact the funniest character is the one who remains impassive in the face of his misadventures, we find in Beckett a particular deviation, if not subversion, of this general rule of comedy: his characters laugh, they laugh a lot and everywhere, they fill the pages and the stage with a reaction stolen from the audience. It is not always clear why or at whom or what they are laughing. But they carry on laughing, in different ways, with different laughs.

The laughs are mostly without apparent motivation and in inverse proportion to the laughs from the public. It is well known that Beckett asked for as many laughs as possible ("let's get as many laughs as we can out of this horrible mess")[27] for the London production of *Endgame* in 1964. Moreover, scattered throughout Beckett's texts and underlined in his own productions are significant comic elements, showing us how much he wanted to public to laugh. As indeed is shown by his comment to Christian Ludvigsen: "let the people laugh by all means, and then be reminded it is no laughing matter".[28]

The critic Wolfgang Iser, observing the theatrical productions done by Beckett himself, noted that the more the characters laughed, the less did the audience. He began to wonder if "as many laughs as we can" referred to the characters on stage rather than to the reaction of the public. Witnessing all these apparently pointless laughs creates in the spectator an enigma that remains unresolved, as well as a very deep sense of frustration: "the laughter produced on stage shows that the play does not seek to unfold a comic situation but uses the representation of a comic reaction to signalize something different, the side effect of which is to deprive the spectator of his chance to liberate himself (through laughter) from the critical situation in which he finds himself".[29]

The quality, at this point, of laughter of characters and public would seem to combine into a common, uniform state of hysteria that, for Styan, does not merely imitate the forms of mental disorder, but strongly suggests its actual presence.[30] The laughter of the characters is like that of Beckett himself and Rosette Lamont notices the analogy, "Beckett's laugh, or that of his many clown-heroes, is a grimace, somewhere between soundless merriment and mute sobbing".[31]

In all his literary genres, his characters laugh with desperate laughter, creating for us an enigma to be solved: why? who are they laughing at?

For Martin Esslin[32] Beckett's characters are *not* laughing (sic), they are quite unaware of their tragic destiny and the spectator delights in their funny and ridiculous presence. They lack dianoia, the ability to see through the appearance of pain, transforming it into a source of laughter. The spectators, by contrast, are gratified by the funny sadness of the events before them, since they possess dianoia. For Esslin the possibility of abandoning oneself to laughter depends upon dianoetic awareness. And the fact that the public laughs at characters who are unaware of being laughable and who never laugh might remind us of the deadpan gazes of the tragic comic heroes of Hollywood silent film. In reality, Beckett's pages are littered with characters who laugh with various degrees and durations of laughter. His intentions as a director emphasise this point several times as, for example, the exchange about the uproar following Lucky's monologue, between the American director, Nichols, and Beckett, as told by Gussow: "Nichols: What did you mean by 'general outcry?' Beckett: I meant general outcry. Nichols: With laughter? Beckett: Preferably".[33]

Beckett, particularly attracted by grotesque figures and by their possible comic implications, had early on begun to reflect on materials based on the connection between the grotesque and laughter.

I recall the already-mentioned passage from Horace[34] showing men and women contaminated by the animal kingdom, monstrous in appearance and consequently the object of laughter of those who saw them.

In *More Pricks than Kicks* there is a special association between the character's grotesque appearance and his, and the others' laughs. Beckett himself says provocatively that his Belacqua, despite his outrageously grotesque aspect, did not at all provoke laughter. A different fate awaited the protagonist of "La fin", similar in appearance to Belacqua, but who inspired such healthy laughter: "je prêtais toujours à rire, de ce rire robuste et sans malice qui est si bon pour la santé" (pp. 84-85). Belacqua shares with this character the same worn clothes, obscenity and neglect but, while one makes the observer laugh, the other does not. We find Belacqua several times with other characters, but his grotesque monstrosity passes unnoticed, despite the fact that it often makes him laugh himself:

> [...] the entry of his grotesque person would provoke no comment or laughter. (p. 15)

> [...] his grotesque exterior had long ceased to alienate the curates and make them giggle. (p. 43)

With his funny and repellent aspect, suffering from impetigo, covered in pustules and scabs, with his uncertain gait and paranoid behaviour, Belacqua should have provoked in whoever met him a mocking smile, yet those accustomed to him had stopped sniggering. Out of habit perhaps, or more likely because Belacqua flaunted an indifference for his own little defects that leaves us perplexed. Belacqua carries on with his usual activities without noticing their maniacal quality, he continues to prepare his breakfast according to fixed, unchanging rules, to divide his passion between Dante and lobster and to have an exuberant love life despite his repellent aspect and his character unsuited to the role of ladies' man. The other characters do not laugh at Belacqua, but he himself laughs loudly on various occasions. While his fiancée is desperately looking for him, together with a series of other characters, Belacqua is safely "in Taylor's public-house in Swords, drinking and laughing in a way that Mr Taylor did not like" (p. 36), a laugh of satisfaction that he has escaped danger, because he has managed to make a fool of them all by getting away. This laughter had a precise motive, quite different from that "memorable fit of laughing" that "incapacitated him from gallantry" (p. 25) whose precise cause we are unable to identify. The reader is only told that this uncontrollable reaction became memorable and that it caused its hero – later – certain psychophysical problems. But Belacqua's most unforgettable laugh is on the point of death, provoked by a blasphemous joke about a priest at amateur theatricals, a joke, which always made him laugh till he cried:

> [...] an angel of the Lord came to his assistance with a funny story, really very funny indeed, it always made Belacqua laugh till he cried [...]. It was a mercy that Belacqua was a dirty low-down Low Church Protestant high-brow and able to laugh at this sottish jest. Laugh! How he did laugh, to be sure. Till he cried. (p. 184)

Apart from the protagonist, *More Pricks than Kicks* is full of the smiles and laughter of the characters. Belacqua's aunt laughs at her nephew's ingenuity concerning the live lobster (p. 16), the O.P. laughs at a joke of unclear ownership (p. 82), Hairy is mocked by the bystanders with "laughter and jokes" (p. 147), Otto Olaf laughs unrestrainedly and hysterically with a reaction retarded by about five minutes (p. 159), the "Aschenputtel" laughs happily at his own sadistic behaviour (p. 185) just like the nun (p. 186) in the same hospital, Una bboggs is almost on the point of literally dying laughing:

> even Mrs bboggs could not refrain from joining in the outburst of merriment that greeted this fatuity. Una in particular seemed certain to do herself an injury. She trembled and perspired in a most fearful manner. [...] But Nature takes care

of her own and a loud rending noise was heard. Una stopped laughing and remained perfectly still. Her bodice had laid down its life to save hers. (p. 138)

Hearty, belly laughs, though sometimes rather cynical, resounding without inhibition. These are the most common laughs of Beckett's characters. They are found in Watt (Arthur laughs heartily at an aphorism-cliché, Mr de Baker guffaws until he is crying from laughter), in *Mercier et Camier* it is mostly Camier who laughs at the profound sayings of Mercier,[35] in the *Trilogy* the hearty laughter is limited but is there (Moran laughs at the joke about the soup, the photographer laughs at Malone, among Worm's noises is also laughter), in *Comment c'est* the high proportion of laughter does not correspond to the tone – anything but carefree – of the whole text: we find silent laughter, mad laughter, happy laughs, sad laughs, laughs like panting and an exhortation to laughter.

Hearty laughter that resounds across the stage in an even more preponderant way, where the guffaw is not only alluded to, narrated, described and imagined, but is there before us, assailing our ears with incomprehensible and enigmatic hilarity. Although these laughs appear arbitrary, an indirect metaphorical element can be noted - the heartiest of them, in fact, occurs when the characters make universalistic and existentialist reflections. The laugher is not, then, the response to a stimulus of cause/effect, but an indicator of discomfort, a marker of alienation, used according to a logic of analogical but significant superimposition.

In *Godot* Vladimir, Estragon and Pozzo all laugh, at different moments, but which have some similarities. When Vladimir suggests that his companion repents, Estragon asks him if we should repent that we were born. Vladimir finds the reason for repentance funny and laughs heartily:

Vladimir part d'un bon rire qu'il réprime aussitôt, en portant sa main au pubis, le visage crispé.
VLADIMIR. - On n'ose même plus rire.
ESTRAGON. - Tu parles d'une privation.
VLADIMIR. - Seulement sourire. (*Son visage se fend dans un*

sourire maximum qui se fige, dure un bon moment, puis subitement s'éteint.) Ce n'est pas la même chose. (p. 13)

Pozzo reacts with a "rire énorme" when he thinks that Didi and Gogo might belong to the same human race as him, of divine origin. Pozzo's pride in the species, which is also the narcissistic illusion of being somehow unique and unrepeatable, "the species of Pozzo", is disturbed by the realisation that such very imperfect beings as Didi and Gogo might be part of the same human category. This common belonging, far from comforting Pozzo, embarrasses and shakes a proud spirit such as his. His laugh is pompous but without joy and full of angry, repressed embarrassment:

> POZZO (*s'arrêtant*). - Vous êtes bien des êtres humains cependant. (*Il met ces lunettes.*) A ce que je vois. (*Il enlève ses lunettes.*) De la même espèce que moi. (*Il éclate d'un rire énorme.*) De la même espèce que Pozzo! D'origine divine! (p. 30)

Pozzo's laugh seems to question his words and it seems absurd to him that he must share his divine origin with tramps like Vladimir and Estragon. The arrogance of the man of power doubts one of the cardinal foundations of all monotheistic beliefs – that all men are descended from one single Father and Creator. The laugh of the powerful man mocks at humanity. Humanity, like Vladimir's laugh, partakes of a universal theme - being born, dying and belonging to the same species. The reason for Estragon's laugh is also of an existential nature. Pozzo, now blind, asks them if they are friends and this provokes in Estragon an instinctive, hearty laugh and a comical misunderstanding that extends the laugh from the character to the spectator. Both are laughs that laugh at human beings and their humanity:

> POZZO. - [...] mais êtes-vous des amis?
> ESTRAGON (*riant bruyamment*). - Il demande si nous sommes des amis!
> VLADIMIR. - Non, il veut dire des amis à lui.

> ESTRAGON. - Et alors?
> VLADIMIR. - La preuve, c'est que nous l'avons aidé. (p. 119)

Pozzo laughs haughtily in the first act, when he is at the peak of his strength and can arrogantly attack those he sees as inferior beings. In the second act, however, when he arrives blind and shabby, it is the two *clochards* that make fun of him, as they had already hinted at doing when Pozzo lost his beloved pipe: Estragon was delighted at Pozzo's stupidity and laughed noisily, after exclaiming "il est marrant, il a perdu sa bouffarde!" (p. 48). It was the first and last time that anyone laughed openly at the terrible Pozzo and the mockery resulted in punishment, very rare in Beckett. The crumbling values do not allow laughter to keep its social function of highlighting social defects, their isolation in a laughable universe, their punishment and expulsion for the current system of values. In *All That Fall* Tommy's embarrassed giggle, with sly, punitive intent, aimed at Mr Tyler's conventional platitudes, is in turn punished with a blow in the stomach: "MR TYLER: Lovely day for the fixture. [*Loud titter from* TOMMY *cut short by* MR BARRELL *with backhanded blow in the stomach. Appropriate noise from* TOMMY.]" (p. 184).

Returning to *Godot*, despite Estragon's small victory over Pozzo, it is generally Pozzo who laughs last, even though this isolates him from the other characters. Pozzo's laugh is mainly an expression of autistic self-satisfaction and isolates him in a *grandeur* that he enjoys alone. Pozzo laughs, alone, at his joke when Estragon, to justify Vladimir's bad temper, tells him that on that day everything looked black to him. Pozzo replies dryly "sauf le firmament" (p. 50), then laughs with satisfaction at his good joke.

Pozzo is satisfied with his reactive intelligence, though his actions constantly contradict the high opinion he has of himself, just as his pride in his creature, Lucky, is belied by the disappointing performance of the phenomenon. The "rire bref" (p. 55) that betrays Pozzo's pleasure in presenting the abilities of Lucky is the satisfaction of the ringmaster introducing his exceptional new number, and that of the *magister* presenting to the public his conquests of indoctrination, only to discover the *magister/puer* relation is in reality overturned and it is Lucky who has taught

Pozzo everything, or at least this is what Pozzo wants us to believe.

Pozzo's self-satisfaction devoid of critical sense excludes any irony towards himself. How different from the strongly self-ironic version of Mrs Rooney and of Krapp! Old Mrs Rooney, protagonist of *All That Fall*, shows profound self-irony when she uses a wild laugh to underline the obscene double meanings that she accidentally uses or hears:

> MRS ROONEY: [...] Mr Tyler! Mr Tyler! Come back and unlace me behind the hedge! [*She laughs wildly, ceaces.*] [...]
> MR SLOCUM: Is anything wrong, Mrs Rooney? You are bent all double. Have you a pain in the stomach? [*Silence*. MRS ROONEY *laughs wildly. Finally.*] (p. 177)

In the same way, old Krapp laughs at his young self, or rather at his good intentions, never put into practice, constantly betrayed by his dissolute, slothful behaviour. With hindsight he laughs bitterly at that promising young man:

> [...] Hard to believe I was ever that young whelp. The voice! Jesus! And the aspirations! [*Brief laugh* in which KRAPP *joins.*] And the resolutions! [*Brief laugh* in which KRAPP *joins.*] To drink less, in particular. [*Brief laugh* of KRAPP *alone.*] [...] Closing with a -[*brief laugh*]- yelp to Providence. [*Prolonged laugh* in which KRAPP *joins.*] (My underlining, p. 218)

This extract also brings in the subject of the musicality of Beckett's laughs. Those of Krapp, indeed, seem to follow a precise, pre-established rhythm, significant for itself rather than for the reason behind the laughter. The musical scansion follows a strict pattern within which the laughter of young Krapp and old Krapp seem to dance a ballet of counterpoint and harmony. Twice the tape laughs on its own and the live character follows it, then he laughs alone, then the tape alone, then they finish together in the grand finale with a prolonged laugh. The pattern is:

1. YOUNG KRAPP (TAPE)→OLD KRAPP (LIVE)[short]
2. YOUNG KRAPP (TAPE)→OLD KRAPP (LIVE)[short]
3. OLD KRAPP (LIVE) [short]
4. YOUNG KRAPP (TAPE) [short]
5. YOUNG KRAPP (TAPE)→OLD KRAPP (LIVE)[prolonged]

Laughter and monologue alternate, interweave and sometimes contrast each other, following a model also found in *Fin de partie* where Clov, however, accompanies his laughs not with a flow of monologue but with gestures. His initial pantomime is marked by enigmatic laughs, "cold and non-communicative laughter, which reveals itself as black humour, lucid awareness of a desperate condition that refuses the tragic".[36] Krapp and Clov share the same autistic behaviour but express their discomfort in different ways - one through the *logos*, the other through the *gestus*. Their laughs have the same effect of impenetrability and ambiguity.

When the curtain opens we find Clov occupied in activities whose sense and point escape us, and our perplexity increases with the repeated short laughs that accompany his actions.

> [...] *Il descend de l'escabeau, fait trois pas vers la fenêtre à gauche, retourne prendre l'escabeau, l'installe sous la fenêtre à gauche, monte dessus, regarde par la fenêtre.* <u>Rire bref.</u> *Il descend de l'escabeau, fait un pas vers la fenêtre a droite, retourne prendre l'escabeau, l'installe sous la fenêtre à droite, monte dessus, regarde par la fenêtre.* <u>Rire bref.</u> *Il descend de l'escabeau, va vers les poubelles, retourne prendre l'escabeau, le prend, se ravise, le lâche, va aux poubelle, enlève le drap qui les recouvre, le plie soigneusement et le met sur le bras. Il soulève un couvercle, se penche et regarde dans la poubelle.* <u>Rire bref.</u> *Il rabat le couvercle. Même jeu avec l'autre poubelle. Il va vers Hamm, enlève le drap qui le recouvre, le plie soigneusement et le met sur le bras. En robe de chambre, coiffé d'une calotte en feutre, un grand mouchoir taché de sang étalé sur le visage, un sifflet pendu au cou, un plaid sur les genoux, d'épaisses chaussettes aux pieds, Hamm semble dormir. Clov le regarde.* <u>Rire bref.</u> (My underlining, pp. 14-15)

This short, nervous laugh recalls that of Krapp. But Krapp is an old man lost in his memories and stories of times gone by, which conserve of the young Krapp a need of words and their fascination. Clov, instead, is a servant who cannot sit down, completely wrapped up in his practical activities. Krapp is a man of words, Clov of actions. So the rhythmic laughs are inserted, in the first case, in the flow of words that evoke past events and, in the second case, in the pragmatic routine, concentrated on mere everyday survival. Different backgrounds but the same rhythmic function of the laughs.

To these two may be added the logorrheic Winnie, who marks her monologue and gestures with laughs and smile, alternated with sad facial expressions. *Happy Days* contains a perfect architecture of these elements, constructed by Beckett. In 1971 Beckett himself directed the German version of the drama, *Glückliche Tage,* for the Schiller Theater in Berlin. As preparation for his work as director, he reviewed the translation by Elmar Tophoven, memorised it and the stage directions in German and made a series of notes on staging which he recorded in an 85-page director's notebook, written in English.[37] In the notes on Winnie's emotions and their external manifestation, Beckett lists three different facial expressions for Winnie and counts the repetitions: 31 smiles, 5 happy expressions, 8 sad expressions.[38] The smiles – broad, fading, restrained or childish – mark like a metronome Winnie's frenetic physical and verbal activity while she sinks inexorably. The sound of these trills and the sight of the soundless smiles or mere expressions or happiness have significance within the general structure, apart from the fact that they interpret a feeling of joy. If the smile is commonly understood as a sign of happiness, Winnie's is something more. Its almost mathematical repetition makes it a dramatic element in itself, with the function of marking the passage of time, slipping away, always the same. These are sonorous and visual reminders of a time that appears frozen in eternal suffering, which the individual tries to ignore or exorcise by immerging himself in narcotic hyper-activity. It is with this unconscious intention that Winnie smiles, delights or actually laughs. Only once, in fact, does Winnie indulge in laughter and, on closer examination, this is a particularly significant phenomenon.

In the first act of Happy Days, Winnie is delighted by the double meaning of "fornication" she finds in the mispronunciation of "formication", provoking a game of laughs between herself and Willie. Willie is the first to laugh quietly, followed immediately by Winnie, who soon finds herself laughing alone, as does Willie for a moment:

> WILLIE: Formication. [...]
> WINNIE: [*Murmur.*] God. [*Pause.* <u>WILLIE *laughs* quietly. After a moment *she joins* in. *They laugh* quietly together.* WILLIE stops</u>. *She laughs on a moment alone.* WILLIE *joins in.* <u>*They laugh* together</u>. *She stops.* <u>WILLIE *laughs*</u> *on a moment alone. He stops. Pause. Normal voice.*] (My underlining, p. 150)

This strange alternation of laughing together and laughing alone[39] raises the doubt that they are not actually sharing the same joke and that their joined laughter happens by chance. This doubt is raised a few lines on by Winnie herself: "were we perhaps diverted by two quite different things?" (p. 150). Poor, lonely Winnie is desperately searching for contact with the world and receives only surrogate human relations. Ingenuously Winnie pretends to believe in this pretence, but sometimes she cannot help harbouring "unhealthy" doubts, unhealthy because they would destroy her illusion. The episode of the laughs almost gives us the impression of a real emotional, psychological and physical contact between the two, but when it ends we are overcome by frustration and our fleeting first impression is transformed into the awareness that we have watched a sort of solitude duet.

Already in 1959 Beckett had tried a similar dramatic situation, where the laughs and smiles, shared or otherwise, indicated a deep chasm in human relations, especially between man and woman. The radio drama *Embers* is sunk in an oneiric atmosphere from which images of ghosts emerge that could be memories or real people. In this ambiguity, Henry, the protagonist, meets Ada and they share in a game of laughs similar to that of Winnie and Willie:

ADA: [...] [*She laughs*. *Pause*.] Laugh Henry, it's not every day I crack a joke. [*Pause*.] Laugh, Henry do that for me.
HENRY: You wish me to laugh?
ADA: You laughed so charmingly once, I think that's what first attracted me to you. That and your smile. [*Pause*.] Come on, it will be like the old times. [*Pause*. *He tries to laugh, fails*.]
HENRY: Perhaps I should begin with the smile. [*Pause for smile*.] [...] Now I'll try again. [*Long horrible laugh*.] [...] I live on the brink of it! Why? Professional obligations? [*Brief laugh*.] Reasons of health? [*Brief laugh*.] Family ties? [*Brief laugh*.] A woman? [*Laugh in which she joins*.] (My underlining, pp. 257-258)

The pattern is made even more complex by the express request for a laugh and the unsuccessful attempts at laughing. The cadence of individual and joint laughs hint at the later pattern in *Happy Days*: Ada laughs alone, Henry tries to laugh (alone), then laughs and she imitates him (they laugh together). Here, however, unlike in *Happy Days*, the repetition is barely noticed in the face of the absurd request for laughter. Laughter is by definition an instinctive reaction to a stimulus, but in Beckett the characters laugh even without stimulus or without a recognisable stimulus.

No surprise, then, if some request a laugh "on command". In *Fin de partie* Hamm had tried to impose a laugh by authority but his "on ne rit pas?" had been condemned by Clov with a "je n'y tiens pas" (p. 25). Later, however, it is Nagg who makes Nell laugh on demand with just a look: after having told the joke about the tailor "[...] *il fixe Nell restée impassible, les yeux vagues, part d'un rire forcé et aigu, le coupe, avance la tête vers Nell, lance de nouveau son rire*" (p. 38).

In *Embers* Ada tries to relive the good old days when Henry's smile elicited tender fascination, asking Henry to laugh once more as he used to do. The result is disastrous. She starts to laugh to encourage him in the task, but her first attempt fails. So Henry suggests they substitute the laugh just with a smile, a level inferior to the former and evidently easier to do, but even this attempt fails, this time in a "long horrible laugh". It is when Henry has stopped concentrating on the result that he manages some short laughs, which mark his desperate monologue and are finally shared by Ada.

Laughter and smiles are no longer the domain of spontaneity – something is spoiling and disturbing them, even in their collective dimension. In private, they underline the impossibility of emotional communication, in society they undermine the social structures based on personal relations. Polite smiles, for example, are the fruit of reigning social conventions and the associated social hierarchy. In Beckett these, too, are completely arbitrary and the object of sarcasm. In *More Pricks than Kicks* Belacqua got "such a pleasant smile" from the fishmonger that he commented positively how this could illuminate one's day:

> a little bit of courtesy and goodwill went a long way in this world. A smile and a cheerful word from a common working-man and the face of the world was brightened. And it was so easy, a mere question of muscular control. (p. 17)

In reality, these pleasant considerations conceal Beckett's irony, for he presents the smile as a muscle to be consciously controlled in function of daily social relations. It is a manifestation totally devoid of spontaneity but full of unbearable formalism and conventionalism, probably very British. Another striking example of a social smile is in the encounter between Power and Louit in *Watt*, where the smile corresponds to a greeting, much like removing one's hat. This habit is necessary to the smooth running of social relations: Louit smiles at Power who replies by raising his hat but, Beckett warns us, if they did not both follow this empty but necessary ritual, their normal routine would be disturbed and they would go "each on his way, Louit down, Power up, the one unsmiling, and the other covered" (p. 196).

Laughter is no longer the same, something has gone wrong in the automatic generation of effect from cause. Manifestations of laughter – private or collective – are governed by the principle of non-correspondence.

In the novel *Company* Beckett seems to describe one of those repetitions of smiles that we have seen in *Happy Days*, *Embers* and *Krapp*:

"when he chuckled you tried to chuckle too. When his chuckle died yours too. That you should try to imitate his chuckle pleased and tickled him greatly and sometimes he would chuckle for no other reason than to hear you try to chuckle too" (pp. 53-54). The smiles alternate and become a laugh which, instead of being healthily contagious, is a sterile, deliberate imitation, here too a muscle under control and used with judgement. Yet after a few lines the same smile is no longer returned, "the violet lips do not return your smile" (p. 56) and again "the ruby lips do not return your smile" (p. 58). By now the "deterioration of sense of humour"[40] is in motion and irreversible. The smile is there still, but not so much, less intense, less often, less important. It shines with a feeble light that persists despite its weakness: "autant dire que le sourire si c'en est un y est toujours. Ni plus ni moins. Moins! Et cependant plus le même. Rien de changé à la bouche et cependant le sourire n'est plus le même. Vrai que la lumière fausse. [...] Ce même sourire établi les yeux grands ouverts n'est plus [...]".[41]

In all three novels of the *Trilogy* (*Molloy, Malone meurt, L'Innommable*) there are stifled laughs similar to panting, while the faces of those laughing remain impassive, not in the least touched by the joy that should accompany laughter. Moran, the protagonist of the second part of *Molloy*, tells of being able to laugh without showing it: "et à l'idée des sanctions que Youdi pouvait prendre contre moi un énorme rire me secouait, sans que le moindre bruit se fît entendre ni que mon visage exprimât autre chose que la tristesse et la calme. [...] Rire étrange s'il en fut et qu'à bien y réfléchir je n'appelle ainsi que par paresse peut-être, ou par ignorance" (p. 251).

Nor is Malone shaken by any emotion, "sans rien exagérer bien sûr, en pleurant et en riant tranquillement, sans m'exalter" (p. 8). Laughter cannot be recognised from external signs, it is an intimate experience not communicated nor shared with the outside. Nothing in the expression, or on the face, no sound clearly indicates laughter, even the unmistakeable sound of laughing is confused with laments, so "ce sera le même silence que toujours, traversé de murmures malheureux, de halètements, de plaintes incompréhensibles, à confondre avec des rires".[42] After all, there is an irremediable confusion between tears and laughter, so that the two opposites can be arbitrarily exchanged, as we have seen with *Murphy*.

Laughter and tears even sound similar. The motivation that prompts man to react with one or the other is lacking, or is vague and indistinct. The individual can choose arbitrarily one of the two reactions, which once were spontaneous and governed by the principle of causality. Chance dominates Beckett's universe. It is a chance decision whether a character laughs or cries: "je crus qu'elle allait pleurer, c'était le moment, mais elle rit au contraire. C'était peut-être sa façon à elle de pleurer. Ou c'était moi qui me trompais et elle pleurait réellement, avec un bruit de rigolade. Les pleurs et les ris, je ne m'y connais guère".[43]

This confusion between tears and laughter means it does not matter whether one reacts with one or the other, as if the alternative between the two opposite physiological reactions were not in contrast, a sort of learned helplessness. "Belacqua snatched eagerly at the issue. Was it to be laughter or tears?" (p. 175). Belacqua is quite uninterested in the solution to the dilemma, since tears and laughter overlap and merge into one laugh that cannot be defined as such. Already in *Molloy*, Moran had defined that strange reaction as "laughter", admitting that this might be a wrong definition, although he would use it just the same out of laziness or ignorance. So when Belacqua finally decides on his reaction, Beckett intervenes ironically, distorting the final resolution of his character. For Belacqua, reactions that are by definition instinctive and irrational are fruit of a rational and clearly arbitrary decision.[44] Belacqua after many doubts sees clearly: "he would arm his mind with laughter, *laughter is not quite the word* but it will have to serve, at every point [...]. Smears, as after a gorge of black-berries, of hilarity, which *is not quite the word either*" (my italics, p. 182).

How can we define that grimace or that monstrous sound we incorrectly call laughter?

A laugh that can hardly be called such and which embodies the above-mentioned monstrosity is the smile of Watt. It is an often indecipherable sign, repellent and ambiguous in appearance and it appears through the coincidence between intention (doing what we commonly mean by smiling) and result (a deformed, frightening grimace):

> Watt smiled [...]. Watt had watched people smile and thought he understood how it was done. And it was true that Watt's smile, when he smiled, resembled more a smile than a sneer, for example or a yawn. But there was something wanting to Watt's smile, some little thing was lacking, and people who saw it for the first time, and most people who saw it saw it for the first time, were sometimes in doubt as to what expression exactly was intended. To many it seemed a simple sucking of the teeth. Watt used this smile sparingly. (p. 23)
> Watt's smile was further peculiar in this, that it seldom came singly, but was followed after a short time by another, less pronounced it is true. In this it resembled the fart. And it even sometimes happened that a third, very weak and fleeting, was found necessary, before the face could be at rest again. (p. 25)

The smile like a fart has an effect on the reader that is exhilarating and embarrassing at the same time. It is the same sensation received from Murphy's laugh. He too is a grotesque character, who enjoys old jokes that make no-one else laugh. Following a joke told by himself, Murphy starts to laugh so heartily that his reaction resembles an epileptic fit: "he staggered about on the floor in his bare feet [...] overcome by the toxins of this simple little joke [...]. The fit was so much more like one of epilepsy than of laughter that Celia felt alarm", but when the girl goes to help him "the fit was over, the gloom took its place, as after a heavy night" (p. 98).

This laughter has something puzzling, and certainly does not leave behind a good feeling - Murphy feels exhausted, with a melancholy taste in his mouth like after drinking too much.

Can it be that all natural behaviour has gone for ever? What is implied by the confusion of stimuli and their effects? What does this mean?

The questions, as always with Beckett, all maintain their question mark and, if anything, provoke more questions. One can, nonetheless, go more deeply into the question, continuing our analysis of the smiles of Beckett's characters. We are particularly assisted by the theatre, where the monstrous smiles are seen on stage, transforming into sight or sound what could only be imagined in the prose.

In *Fin de partie* Clov laughs without knowing what he is laughing at, so dissociated is the reaction from the stimulus, so he cannot identify the reason for his laughter, one is as good as another:

> HAMM. - [...] (*Clov rit*) Qu'est-ce qu'il y a là de si drôle?
> CLOV. - Une place de jardinier!
> HAMM. - C'est ça qui te fait rire?
> CLOV. - Ça doit être ça.
> HAMM. - Ce ne serait pas plutôt le pain?
> CLOV. - Ou le petit. (pp. 81-82)

Clov's laughter, rather than being unmotivated, has a whole selection of motives, which are superimposed and equivalent.

So the laughter we hear on Beckett's stage cannot appear like a normal laugh, but will always have something anomalous and alienating about it - a brake. Restrained laughter can appear in various forms, one of which is the laugh that decreases in intensity during the dialogue. This happens in *Fin de partie* where Nagg and Nell remember the accident in the Ardennes and laugh more and more quietly, "*ils rient.* [...] *Ils rient moins fort.* [...] *Ils rient encore moins fort*" (p. 31).[45] Or, when Hamm is about to commence his monologue, Nagg can barely restrain his hilarity and, instead of laughing heartily (in French we only read "ils rient" p. 70, while in English "they laugh heartily" p. 116) gives only a "stifled laugh", as Beckett's own translation says. From an instinctive, unstoppable laugh, Nagg passes to enforced repression, as decreed by authority, Hamm. Similarly in *All That Fall* Mr Barrell "*stifles a guffaw*" (p. 186) and in the English *Godot* Vladimir gives a "stifled" laugh (p. 20).

Beckett's characters experience the same embarrassment as the public and reader at these laughs and they restrain them as does Beckett's theatre audience. One might even doubt, like Vladimir and Estragon, that laughing was not allowed any more. Perhaps we have lost our right, perhaps it is forbidden:

> *Rire de Vladimir, auquel il coupe court comme au précédent. Même jeu, moins le sourire.*

VLADIMIR. - Tu me ferais rire, si cela m'était permis.
ESTRAGON. - Nous les avons perdus?
VLADIMIR (*avec netteté*). - Nous les avons bazardés. (p. 24)

But what is the sound of a stifled laugh? How does a stifled laugh sound?

I would like to suggest that the stifled laugh might sound like the "faint laugh" (p. 280) that disturbs the spectator in *Rough for Radio II* (English version of the original French *Pochade radiophonique*) or the "faint laugh" that in *Play* acquired the attribute of "wild" (p. 307). This is a wild, guttural sound, that comes from a hidden depth and that stays concealed even after it appears. It is laughter that fades out, dematerialises and seems to come from a mysterious, elusive other place. A ghost guffaw.

If the characters of the early novels or the early dramatic experiments manage occasionally to laugh openly, those of the later productions increasingly take on an indefinite nature between material and immaterial, so that their ever-paler smiles do not communicate joy or happiness, nor do they give clear indications as to their essence. The oneiric atmosphere (dream or nightmare?) of the later Beckett dissolves in its horribly compelling elusiveness all material solidity of the characters. And yet these damned souls, eternally condemned to this limbo, keep the flavour of past life. Or of the life that will always be. Or always in the balance.

6.4. Angelic smiles and satanic guffaw

A separate chapter in Beckett's "pleasant outlooks"[46] are the smiles of Dante and the blasphemous laughs of certain characters. The significance and apparent unethicality of these two elements are worth further investigation. .

Beckett's love for Dante accompanied him literally all his life - even in the nursing home where he spent his last months, he was reading Dante in Italian in a school edition of the *Divina Commedia*.[47] Beckett had certainly read *De Vulgari Eloquentia*,[48] *Vita Nuova* and *La Divina Commedia*.[49] He returned to the latter many times, studying it in more than one version in the original language and in several English translations.[50] He read and reviewed the critical article on Dante by Giovanni Papini (*Dante vivo*, Florence, Libreria Editrice Fiorentina, 1933) translated by Eleanor Hammond Broadus and Anna Benedetti.[51] And to Dante he dedicates a part of his first non-fiction work, entitled "Dante… Bruno. Vico..Joyce" and published for the first time in 1929 in *Our Exagmination Round His Factification for Incamination of Work in Progress*, a collection of articles wanted by Joyce to discuss his latest work, *Work in Progress*, which became *Finnegans Wake*. In Beckett's first prose work, the collection of stories *More Pricks Than Kicks*, the protagonist is named Belacqua from Dante and the first story is entitled "Dante and the Lobster". Elements of Dante's imaginary are found throughout Beckett's prose and in the last dramatic works. Beckett's figures of the damned, eternally tormented by the same sufferings, vividly recall Dante's infernal – or perhaps better, purgatorial – punishments. In fact Beckett did not particularly like Paradise, but nourished a real passion for Purgatory, particularly the Anti-Purgatory, without either the farcical comedy of Hell or the serious mysticism of Paradise. In *Pochade radiophonique* the two lower cantos are the source of an ironic gag:

> Animateur. [...] Vous avez lu le Purgatoire, mademoiselle, du divin Florentin?
> Dactylo.- Hélas non, monsieur, j'ai seulement feuilleté l'Enfer.
> Animateur (*incrédule*).- Pas lu le Purgatoire?
> Dactylo.- Hélas non, monsieur.
> Animateur.- Là tout le monde soupire, Je fus, je fus. [...] Curieux, n'est-ce pas?
> Dactylo.- En quel sens, monsieur?
> Animateur.- Eh bien, on s'attendrait plutôt à «Je serai», non? [...]. (p. 72)

And in *Eleutheria* an allusion to Hell gives rise to an auto-ironic joke by Monsieur Krap that plays on the meanings of "*cercle*" – when his wife accuses him of behaving as if he were at the club with his friends ("il se croit au cercle", p. 29), he replies with comic misunderstanding, "j'y suis. Au neuvième" (p. 30). This appears even more sarcastic if we remember that Dante's 9th Circle was that of traitors! Or again in *All That Fall* the damned are ironically compared to the protagonists: "MR ROONEY: [...] The perfect pair. Like Dante's damned, with their faces arsy-versy. Our tears will water our bottoms" (p. 191).

Some curious documents in Beckett's own hand – these have been partially discussed in a recent article by Mary Bryden entitled "Beckett and the Three Dantean Smiles" - note some smiles in Dante.[52] These three undated postcards were filled by Beckett with quotations from the *Divina Commedia* and his notes from reading Dante's text. The cards are conserved in the Beckett Archive, Reading, as part of his collection of Dante, which he donated to the Archive.[53] In these postcards Beckett recopies the words of Dante that he finds interesting and notes his own observations in the margin. The quotations are all from Purgatory and concern various moments of the journey: the excommunicated, the slothful, the listless, the negligent, those who died of violent death, Pia dei Tolomei. There are three notes on the smiles that Dante, the character, gives or receives from some repentant souls.[54]

The first shade that smiles at Dante is Casella ("1st shade to smile"), singer and musician, his contemporary and friend, who probably set to music Dante's poem "amor che ne la mente mi ragiona". We are in Canto II of anti-Purgatory and Dante watches the first entrance of the spirits into the other world, souls that have not yet fully realised their new state and that are still deeply tied to earthly memories. Because of their strong link with materiality, they appear so vivid that they almost seem still alive, deceiving the poet himself. And so Dante meets Casella:

> Io vidi una di lor trarresi avante
> per abbracciarmi, con sì grande affetto,
> che mosse me a far lo somigliante.
> Ohi ombre vane, fuor che ne l'aspetto!
> tre volte dietro a lei le mani avvinsi,
> e tante mi tornai con esse al petto.
> Di maraviglia, credo, mi dipinsi;
> 83 per che *l'ombra sorrise* e si ritrasse,
> e io, seguendo lei, oltre mi pinsi.

> 85 *Soavemente disse* ch'io posasse;
> 86 *allor conobbi chi era*, e pregai
> che, per parlarmi, un poco s'arrestasse.⁵⁵

The italics indicate the phrases recopied by Beckett on the card. Beside them are his comments: Beckett's attention is held by the deceptive physicality of Casella's spirit and he underlines the unchanged sensuality of his voice, which is still the same as when he was alive, so he can sing a heartbreaking love song even in a refuge of penitent souls.

The second soul, too, who smiles at Dante has vivid physical characteristics. This is Manfredi, son of Emperor Federico II, who died in a battle against the papal troops in Benevento in 1266. Manfredi is one of the few souls to be described by Dante in such physical detail as to be surrounded by an aura of sensuality.

Casella, too, seems still alive, but his fascination emanates essentially through the sound of his voice. But Manfredi's entire physical appearance is striking. It was perhaps this corporeal quality that interested Beckett. Also, the episode of Manfredi taken together with that of Casella establishes a model of repetition noted by Beckett (and written in his notes), which concerns the connection between the smiles of the souls and their still worldly materiality. Dante meets Manfredi in Canto III of Purgatory:

> Io mi volsi ver' lui e guardail fiso:
> 107 *biondo era bello e di gentile aspetto*,
> ma l'un de' cigli un colpo avea diviso.
> Quand'io mi fui umilmente disdetto
> d'averlo visto mai, el disse: «Or vedi»;
> e mostrommi una piaga a sommo 'l petto.
> 112 Poi *sorridendo disse*: «Io son Manfredi,
> nepote di Costanza imperadrice [...]».⁵⁶

Here too the italics refer to Beckett's quotations and he comments "2ⁿᵈ shade to smile, 1ˢᵗ Casella", underlining the classification of the smiles (first Casella, second Manfredi) and the clear link between the two situations. Both share the same atmosphere of still very earthly appearance, although the episode of Manfredi is clearly quite unique: "Manfredi is the only character for whom Dante describes his physical details, emphasising their extraordinary beauty", says the comment Beckett copied on the same card, evidently from the Italian edition he was using at the time.

In the third and last smile noted by Beckett, we find hints of the worldly essence of Dante the character, in contrast with the other-worldly souls, hints at the secular dimension of the first and second smiles. The situation in Canto IV to which it refers, however, is completely different. This time it is Dante who smiles, not a shade. Beckett copies no quotation from the *Commedia*, only a laconic, yet particularly significant note: "122 Dante smiles (at Belacqua) D's 1st smile?", referring to:

> Li atti suoi pigri e le corte parole
> 122 mosser le labbra mie un poco al riso.[57]

This is where Dante meets the indolent Belacqua whose laziness even in speaking ("le corte parole") elicits from him a brief ("un poco") smile. Beckett's note is anomalous - the first part, "122 Dante smiles (at Belacqua)", is written by hand in the same ink as the other notes on the card, but the words that immediately follow, "D's 1st smile", are in different ink. They are also followed by an ambiguous question mark. This punctuation, given the famous obscurity of Beckett's writing, on first glance appears to be an exclamation mark, but on closer inspection becomes a question. Considering the two different pens used, we might imagine two different times of writing and, consequently, of interpretation of the text: Beckett compiled the list of quotations that interested him from the *Divina Commedia*, but later, going over his notes, asked himself "is this the very first smile of Dante? when Dante smiles at Belacqua?" ("D's 1st smile?"). The question he asks himself seems to be in search of further confirmation of the fact that here in verse 122 was the first real smile of the Florentine poet. His constant returning to these smiles, and in particular the one directed to Belacqua, is another indication of his slow metabolisation of the passage and its particular difficulty. It is no chance that of Dante's heroes Beckett prefers the one who wrenches from the poet one of his very rare smiles. Belacqua would remain for Beckett a character associated with smiles and laughter: in 1984 he wrote in a private letter "bien, le bonjour de ma part au cher vieux luthier, avec un sourire fraternel".[58]

But what has provoked this smile and what does it provoke? Dante laughs because he discerns the same lazy attitude in Belacqua even after his death and because he senses his own emotional distance from this listless timewasting. Belacqua is eternally waiting without ever being moved to action. Dante, by contrast, anxious to reach the top, is keen to pursue his journey according to the scheduled stages. The dramatic contrast between the two attitudes of Dante and Belacqua is a metaphor of opposition between eternal time, that of the souls where nothing changes, and human time, that of Dante who must hasten because the time at his disposal is limited. Belacqua, that figure beloved of Beckett and ever-present in his writing, says to Dante:

> [...] «O frate, andar in sù che porta?
> ché non mi lascerebbe ire a' martìri
> l'angel di Dio che siede in su la porta.
> Prima convien che tanto il ciel m'aggiri
> di fuor da essa, quanto fece in vita,
> per ch'io 'ndugiai al fine i buon sospiri,
> se orazïone in prima non m'aita
> che surga sù di cuor che in grazia viva;
> l'altra che val, che 'n ciel non è udita? ».[59]

The words are those of an indolent impenitent, so sure of his own inaction as almost to mock those, like Dante, who are anxious to act. For some Dante experts,[60] Belacqua is the comic caricature of the lazy man who makes fun of those with too much faith in human striving for knowledge, which is revealed as useless because misleading. In Belacqua's eyes, even Dante's quest is a useless, ephemeral effort, so he returns the poet's critical smile by mocking him. Belacqua succeeds in showing Dante the reasonability sometimes hidden by indolence, in the slowing down. Benedetto Croce maintains that this awareness is the reason for

Dante's smile: "Hence Dante's lips move in *a tiny smile*: who ever one laughs at if not at ourselves, even when it seems that one laughs at others?".[61]

Dante's smile at Belacqua recalls the stifled laugh that Beckett elicits from his reader and Dante's Belacqua is entirely coherent with Beckett's countless lazy characters, prisoners of eternal time down here on earth. Beckett's characters serve their sentences even before death and their punishment is to endure the same routine without hope of change, in a flux of time that seems to mirror the unchanging quality of divine eternity.

But apart from Belacqua, how and when does Beckett use his notes on Dante's smiles? This is difficult to discern, given the impossibility of dating the postcards and therefore of envisaging any textual progression. However in some places Beckett seems clearly inspired by the smiles on his postcards.

His imagination is particularly struck by that first smile from Dante. While he merely alludes to the smiles of Casella and Manfredi in *Mal vu mal dit*, as those of the damned ("d'ici le rire des damnés", p. 72), we find that of Dante in *Company* and in *Le Dépeupleur*.

In the first short novel Dante's image of the indolent lutist is a visual association that synthesises the surreal journey followed by the reader from the start. It is an itinerary without a road, a movement without motion and everything seems to happen in perfect immobility. The nameless character travels seated while crouching in the dark:

> so sat waiting to be purged the old lutist cause of Dante's first quarter-smile and now perhaps singing praises with some section of the blest at last. (p. 85)

The journey of immobility in *Company* has been analysed by Enoch Brater, who was also the first critic to note that strange smile of Dante that seemed to want to say more than it did.[62] Despite this, Brater does not pursue this line of enquiry, nor does he note the profound link with that in *Le Dépeupleur*, where Dante's pale smile visualises Beckett's perspective. Beckett is, in fact, constructing his own surreal and infernal architecture and has reached the description of the non-seekers, those who wait unmoving in eternity. Beckett immediately makes the connection with that Belacqua who wrenched from Dante his only, sudden smile:

> ceux qui ne cherchent pas ou non-chercheurs assis pour la plupart contre le mur dans l'attitude qui arracha à Dante un de ses rares pâles sourires. (pp. 38-40)

These Dante-like smiles almost seem to approve Belacqua and his immobility. While Dante's text seems to manifest mockery at Belacqua's lack of faith and hope, Beckett's raises the doubt that it may be true that "sedendo et quiescendo anima efficitur sapiens".[63] This affirmation, a blasphemy in the ideological universe of Dante, is entirely coherent with that of Beckett. Beckett uses Dante's smile just as he uses the sacred Scriptures, to overturn their sense in parody. He attacks the unwavering faith of a knowledge without doubts, through the very elements of this knowledge. This intention of parody is the key to reading some allusions, more or less overt, to Dante, especially to Dante in Paradise, not particularly appreciated by Beckett. The "parler des étoiles c'est par mégarde" found in *Molloy* (p. 19), the "voir les belles choses que porte le ciel, et revoir les étoiles" in *Textes pour rien* (p. 196), the "cheminée au bout de laquelle brilleraient encore le soleil et les autres étoiles" in *Le Dépeupleur* (p. 44), all recall the luminosity of Dante's Paradise and the last verse of the *Commedia*:

> l'amor che move il sole e l'altre stelle.[64]

These references to Dante, although inspired by sincere admiration for the divine poet, have a sometimes imperceptibly unnatural quality. Dante's words, images and effects seem to be snatched violently from their narrative and ideological context and attacked mercilessly by parody. Beckett's aesthetic admiration for Dante did not extend to the Catholic faith that inspired his works, so what Beckett does is to recover, on the one hand, poetic forms and images and, on the other, deconstruct with parody. Dante's universe is condensed into a few effective visions, then inserted into a situation that contradicts its essential elements. The effect is of alienation, the sense slips into a parodic copy that destroys the pretended univocal nature of the signification: the significance is reflected in an interpretative prism that multiplies the possibilities to infinity.

When Dante speaks of the stars, it is a poetic metaphor to affirm the goodness of Christ's message and to educate in his ideology. When Dante's stars enter Beckett's universe, it happens distractedly, by chance, without that precise divine plan that makes sense of all of Dante's otherworldly voyage. Beckett distorts Dante's meaning by placing it comically in an unlikely *milieu*, in a whirl of different meanings that often verge on blasphemy.

Beckett, opposed to all ideological fundamentalism and all fallacious certainty of thought, many times makes fun of religious belief and its adepts who never doubt. His mockery, a playful but radical attack, focuses on religious fanaticism but also on religious institutions. In the novella "La fin", in *Nouvelles et Textes pour rien*, a character appears of whom is said "cela devait être un fanatique religieux [...]. Il s'était peut-être échappé du cabanon. Il avait une bonne tête, un peau rougeaude" (p. 113). The irony directed at this fanatic is amplified by the fact that his fervent speeches are anything but religious in character, citing Marx, capital, union and brotherhood. For Beckett, religion does not exclude the lay sphere but is above all a mental attitude, a kind of behaviour, almost humanistic, so whoever yells blindly like that must of necessity be a religious fanatic.

Sometimes, on the other hand, blasphemy originates from clever theological aggression that derives its profound knowledge of Christianity from observance and its unbridled violence from swearing. God, "le tout-impuissant, le tout-ignorant",[65] the "divine prick"[66] is hailed in several disrespectful ways: in *Company* he is the "crawling creator" (pp. 72 and 73) who poses the metaphysical problem "God is love?" but is no longer able to reply positively: "God is love. Yes or no? No" (p. 73) continuing with the parody of theological reasoning: "can the crawling creator crawling in the same create dark as his creature create while crawling?" (ibid.). Whatever reply one may give to such doubts, in the end the result will be that none of the replies is sacred and inviolate: "and many crawls were necessary and the like number of prostrations before he could finally make up his imagination on this score. Adding to himself without conviction in the same breath as always that no answer of his was sacred" (pp. 73-74). All in all, "God has tormented me all my life", as Beckett wrote precociously in the Thirties[67] and would continue to do so for the joy of Beckett's obscenity.

His irreverence is so extreme as to verge on blasphemy. Mercier and Camier blaspheme "mais avec courage" (p. 152), and the protagonist of *Premier amour* associates the figure of Christ and defecation in a single image:

> c'est l'anxiété qui me constipait, je crois. Mais étais-je réellement constipé? Je ne le crois pas. Du calme, du calme. Et pourtant je devais être, car comment expliquer autrement ces longues, ces atroces séances aux cabinets, aux water? Je ne lisais jamais, pas plus là qu'ailleurs, je ne rêvais ni ne réfléchissais, je regardais vaguement l'almanach pendu à un clou devant mes yeux, on y voyait l'image en couleurs d'un jeune homme barbu entouré de moutons, cela devait être Jésus, j'écartais mes fesses avec mes mains et je poussais, un! han! deux! han!, avec des mouvements de rameur, et je n'avais qu'une hâte, rentrer dans ma chambre et m'allonger. (pp. 14-15)

The figure of Christ occurs frequently in Beckett and always in irreverent situations. In fact Jesus is one of the favourite targets of Beckett's blasphemy, which extends to all Christian religious culture. As a good atheist, educated according to the strict principles of Irish protestant fundamentalism,[68] he knew the Holy Scriptures by heart, along with the related theological questions, and he uses these to parody and desecrate. Religious mysteries have a strange flavour in Beckett, linked as they are to the dogma of the existence of God and its corollaries. The word "God" is the subject of irreverent allusions, perhaps being too similar to "dog", when read backwards.[69] There is nothing new in the interpretation of Godot as God, or the waiting of the two *clochards* as a divine epiphany that always disappoints, but is always renewed in its expectations.

But more that God the Father, in Beckett's imaginary we have God's Son, the Lord's Anointed who sacrificed himself for us but who, inevitably is delayed, "est venu tard".[70]

In one of the fragments of preparation for *Fin de partie* the characters appear in an opening tableau like an iconographic stereotype of Calvary: Ernest "renversé sur sa croix" and Alice "assise sur une chaise au pied de la croix".[71] The Christological metaphors continue with Alice affectionately calling Ernest "mon petit Jésus!"[72] and Ernest asking for oil (a clear liturgical reference) from his spouse.[73]

Christ reappears in *En attendant Godot* where he is offensively used by Estragon in comparison to himself and recalled by Vladimir in the story of the two thieves. Both situations create alienating comical detachment, since the characters make two different allusions to the New Testament, with openly ironic levity. In the first case Estragon's conviction in comparing himself to Christ, despite Vladimir's scandalised reaction, does not prevent him from ending the argument with an ironical twist concerning the habit of using crucifixion as punishment:

ESTRAGON: - Jésus l'a fait.
VLADIMIR. - Jésus! Qu'est-ce que tu vas chercher là! Tu ne vas tout de même pas te comparer à lui?
ESTRAGON. - Toute ma vie je me suis comparé à lui.
VLADIMIR. - Mais là-bas il faisait chaud! Il faisait bon!
ESTRAGON. - Oui. Et on crucifiait vite. (p. 73)

In the second case the irreverence is more subtle. It is not a grandiloquent blasphemy but a slight theological doubt expressed by a down-and-out to his companion. It is not so much the doubt in itself that is offensive as the situation it occurs in: Vladimir says "Un des larrons fut sauvé" and Beckett's irony immediately gives him the overtly ingenuous comment "c'est un pourcentage honnête" (p. 13). The blasphemy occurs when Didi and Gogo speak of the Bible as an unimportant book of which they remember the coloured illustrations of the Holy Land, when they flicked through it distractedly: "VLADIMIR. - Tu as lu la Bible? ESTRAGON. - La Bible... (*Il réfléchit.*) J'ai dû y jeter un coup d'œil" (ivi).

The worst blasphemy seems to be the characters' attitude towards the divine, rather than the actual imprecation: in *Fin de partie* Hamm blurts out the notorious "le salaud! Il n'existe pas!" (p. 76), but a believer might be offended not so much by this epithet attributed to God as by the fact that this shout comes after an unanswered prayer. Hamm prepares to pray and tyrannically compels Clov and Nagg to pray also, if they want to have some biscuits, then when he realises that his petition has not worked, he explodes into sacrilege. This passage was one of the most tormented during preparation, as Restivo's study[74] of the manuscripts has shown, and the troubled composition shows Beckett's connection with a passage that he evidently considered particularly significant. It is therefore understandable that he strenuously defended the final result against the attacks of censorship. When Endgame was to be performed in London in 1957, the Lord Chamberlain refused his permission because of this phrase, which Beckett had translated into English as "the bastard" He doesn't exist!" (p. 119). A long, extenuating negotiation followed, as Beckett would not hear of eliminating the line. When the Lord Chamberlain suggested the word at least be substituted with "bastard", Beckett suggested "swine" and inexplicably it was accepted! The English performance continued with the change, but for the Faber edition, Beckett insisted the original term be reinstated.[75]

In the final monologue, then, Hamm uses a particular form of blasphemy. He associates the form of expression of the Christian liturgy with an obscene reference: The peace is no longer in our hearts, according to the original formula, but "à nos... fesses" (p. 110).

But the most incisive blasphemy is the ambiguous one, heard among the laughs of some characters. Ambiguous, because hidden in the folds of a contrasting speech or situation. Blasphemous, because simply alluding to the divine provokes an explosive laugh, to us incomprehensible. The satanic laughter of these characters bursts out suddenly and violently, and surprises us for its suddenness and force, whose mystery we are unable to understand. "And they say there is no God, said Mr. Case. If circumstances strongly contradict any optimistic faith in a divine presence, or if life reveals it to be a "bad old bugger", then the characters' bursting out laughing is understandable. Unshakeable faith, in a world without certainties, has the effect of a funny joke.

The same happens in *All That Fall*, with the title itself introducing the pun on Psalm 145 (where David praises the Lord), which is quoted by Mrs Rooney and makes Mr and Mrs Rooney burst out laughing together:

> "the Lord upholdeth all that fall and raiseth up all those that be bowed down." [*Silence. They join in wild laughter*] (p. 198)

The laugh is wild, like the "good laugh" of Mouth in *Not I* at the mere mention of divine mercy. The text of *Not I* is delivered quickly and the listener does not immediately notice the link between the laugh and the phrase spoken, partly because the connection is analogical and profound. The first short laugh interrupts the phrase, which ends with a good, resounding laugh. Mouth laughs at faith in the divine and at its mercy: "brought up as she had been to believe... with the other waifs... in a merciful [*Brief laugh.*]... God... [*Good laugh.*]" (p. 377). The idea of mercy provokes laughter, but what unleashes hilarity is the idea... of God!

Those smiles that seemed so angelic in Dante, in Beckett have become instruments of the devil. From the angelic smiles of the *Divina Commedia* we have sunk into the abyss of blasphemous laughter, diabolical ways of distancing oneself from the divinely revealed truth and instruments of violent aggression towards all absolute beliefs. These laughs fully exploit the whole subversive quality of the comic and aggressive quality of laughter, managing to shake even the firmest, most unassailable systems. Satanic laughter, completely enslaved by its fascination for the divine.

6.5. The suffocated reaction

Beckett's characters laugh, they laugh a lot, often, heartily. Sometimes their laughter is rather sadistic, a little macabre. Yet they carry on laughing, and sometimes accompany their outbursts with considerations on laughter, on happiness and on the comic. These are, of course, the considerations of Beckett. But his public? His readers?

When the courageous French editor Jérôme Lindon first laid his hands on a manuscript by the still unknown Samuel Beckett, it took only a few lines to induce an outburst of unstoppable laughter and to convince him immediately to publish the strange book. It was *Molloy*, and Lindon recalled the event, during an interview with James Knowlson:

> I took it away, I took *Molloy* under my arm to go for lunch and in the Métro I started to read it. And as I changed trains at La Motte-Piquet Grenelle, in the lift [...] I burst into hoots of laughter. And I thought 'people are going to think I'm crazy' [...]. So I stopped reading, naturally, and stood with the manuscript behind my back... and people looked at me as I carried on laughing like a fool. They couldn't understand why I was laughing since I was clearly doing nothing. Then I came back to the office, finished reading the manuscript within the day and, that same evening, wrote to Suzanne to tell her 'Yes, I'll take the book, there's no problem'. And a few months later, I published *Molloy*.[76]

It is 1950 and Paris was the scene of a cosmopolitan ferment among the young that was unparalleled. At that time, a group of intellectuals of various origins, who had chosen to live in Paris, decided to found an English-language magazine inspired by ideals of cultural tolerance, freedom and broadmindedness - *Merlin*. The Merlin juveniles, when they began to be interested in an unpublished text by Samuel Beckett, had already for some time been attracted by this new author who, like them, was an English-speaker but had decided to live in the French capital. In autumn 1952, *Merlin* had published the very first literary criticism of Beckett - Richard Seaver's "Samuel Beckett: an Introduction".[77] After that date, the editors had been curious to discover that Beckett had a novel, written in English, still unpublished. They started to hunt down the untraceable, shy author to ask his permission to publish an extract of the novel in their magazine. Puzzled by the lack of response, they were still not ready to give up the project when one day they had a nice surprise:

> [...] one rainy afternoon [...], a knock came at the door and a tall, gaunt figure in a raincoat handed in a manuscript in a black

imitation-leather binding, and left us almost without a word. That night half a dozen of us -Trocchi; Jane Lougee, *Merlin*'s publisher; English poet Christopher Logue and South African Patrik Bowles; a Canadian writer, Charles Hatcher; and I- sat up half the night and read *Watt* aloud, taking turns till our voice gave out. If it took many more hours than it should have, it was because we kept pausing to wait for the laughter to subside.[78]

The stage quality of the prose text in *Watt*, even funnier when spoken, read aloud, and the exhilarating character of the reading was noted even by the scholar Wayne Booth, saying "my friends and I gather to read Beckett's *Watt* aloud to each other [...] enjoying the whole show".[79] The same concept has often been underlined by Gabriele Frasca, who gives us one of the funniest images of the reader – in his case reader-translator – of *Watt*, "if ever the reader should wish to imagine the work of the translator of *Watt*, it would be more or less this the way of picturing him: his left eye to the text and the right eye to the screen, the right ear to the language of the other one and the left ear to his own, his hands never still, feverishly consulting vocabularies and dictionaries, and his body shaken by the most authentic, tasty, dianoetic laughter of his life".[80]

From the prose, I will go on to examine Beckett's theatre, where the reactions are more easily identified by laughs. This time the collective laughter, no longer the intimate, silent laugher of readers, show some variations. The experiences mentioned above tell of readers unable to hold back their laughs, but we should note carefully the kind of readers to which they refer. These are intellectuals of all kinds, writers, translators, editors and researchers, who meet in small groups to share common ideals in a proto-theatrical setting. A public, therefore, ready for the nonvisual aspect of the text, a public that interprets Beckett's writing, deliberately ambiguous, in comic key. But how to approach the much more varied theatre public?

In 1953, Beckett was performed for the first time in theatre. The audience of the tiny Théâtre de Babylone in Paris was to get a shock that for some would change the course of their lives, as happened to Ruby

Cohn. The American scholar was carrying out research into the theatre in Paris when the first production of *Godot* was staged. Intrigued by the poster, she went along to watch this strange performance, which was to focus her professional career on Beckett and his themes.

Although Paris in the Fifties was not new to artistic experiments of all kinds, the Godot-event exploded unexpectedly with a beneficent, regenerating fire. Word spread quickly around town of a play where nothing happened, where the characters were awaiting an unknown person who would never arrive… a performance with a mixture of tragedy and embarrassed giggles. "A bout d'une dizaine de jours de représentations, le bruit avait couru dans Paris qu'il se passait quelque chose au 38, boulevard Raspail [address of the Théâtre de Babylone] et la salle fut pleine tous le soirs. Il nous fallait emprunter des chaises au café à côté, pour les spectateurs en retard ou en surnombre. Nous avons tenu six mois et nous avons recommencé la saison d'après".[81] The first spectators of *Godot* were delighted and perplexed and the laughter soon faded into pale smiles or frowns.

> Laughter did not ring out through the little Théâtre de Babylone, as in performances I saw later. Rather, chuckles faded into smiles or frowns.[82]

A stifled, frustrated laugh, without the courage or necessary strength to come out. But still a laugh. Later, in November 1957, prisoners at San Quentin Jail in California joined their laughter to that of all the other spectators of *Godot*, when Herbert Blau staged it with his San Francisco Actors' Workshop. This time the laughs were no problem, "ce public fut immédiatement conquis, pris, fasciné. Le rire spontané est très vite venu. Et lorsque nous en sommes arrivés au monologue de Lucky, il y eut une telle ovation qu'il fallut attendre un bon moment avant de pouvoir continuer".[83] A hearty, seemingly liberating laugh, in the face of something well-known and suffered personally every day. A superficially joyous outburst, but deeply rooted in the suffering of the prisoner who reacts with sympathy to the endless wait of Vladimir and Estragon.

Other critics have emphasised the tragicomic connotation of the laughter provoked by Beckett's texts, recognising that it comes from the throat, rather than from the mouth of the stomach, as does hearty laughter.[84] We should indeed ask ourselves which laughter we are speaking of. It would in fact seem clear that the stifled laugh spoken of by Iser[85] is not that of the first readers of *Molloy* and *Watt* or of the prisoners of San Quentin, recalled by them as an unstoppable, disorderly impulse. Or so it would appear. On close examination, we find a certain embarrassment in Lindon ("I thought 'people are going to think I'm crazy' [...]. So I stopped reading [...] and people looked at me as I carried on laughing like a fool")[86] and in Cohn's account.[87] And although one might repute as generally valid Iser's theory of "stifled laughter", since we effectively find in the public and in the characters the psychological processes analysed by the critic, this is not the only interpretation possible of Beckett's laughter.

Beckett deliberately involves his spectators in a mechanism of alienation and frustration, but they react to the different types of comedy used by the author as dramatic or narrative strategies. The spectator, therefore, can decode different comic stimuli, to each of which corresponds a different kind of laugh: the snigger, the smile, the stifled laugh, the laugh, the giggle, the laughing fit to burst and so on – all different reactions to a corresponding, different stimulus. Each type of comedy has its own kind of potential laugh, which can be elicited or not, depending on variables of the actual production, such as the actor's artistry in interpreting the scene or comic line, the skill of the director and the overall quality of the production. Given the variety of comedy in Beckett, we are no longer surprised at the coexistence of definitions like the "satanic laugh" of Tagliaferri[88] beside the "childish laugh" of Julie Campbell,[89] apparently irreconcilable. On close inspection, both dimensions appear connected by different but coexistent causes and effects. The seemingly contradiction of different kinds of laughter can be partly explained by that fact that critics have hitherto analysed only parts of Beckett's composite comic universe, so they were only able to have a partial, restricted view of its aesthetic forms. Consequently, we have the coexistence – not at all conflictual or contradictory – of interpretations, definitions and analyses that differ greatly, symptoms of a rich text rather than of poor criticism.

Iser, in his work *The art of failure: the stifled laugh in Beckett's theatre*,[90] analyses the laughs elicited in the public by Beckett's plays and those of the characters in the text, taking as examples *En attendant Godot* and *Fin de partie*.

He noted among the public sudden bursts of laughter and a certain embarrassment caused by this instinctive physiological reaction. The laugh burst out unexpected and sudden, but the state of mind it left was neither of liberation nor of joy. As unexpectedly as it comes, it goes, ending up restrained by a sense of unsuitability, producing neither contagion nor happiness. Although the laugh takes place in a communicative system that by definition and practice is *collective*, that of the theatre, within which basic social norms must be shared, it seems that this "collectivism" is not upheld, apart from in the convention of the spectators' presence at the same time and place. Beckett's theatre creates no solidarity between the group of spectators, making pointless even the common acceptance of rules and social conventions, because the social confirmation produced by liberating group laughter does not happen. Beckett's laugh is stifled by the individual, alone and isolated in his solitude, repressed by a terrible sensation of impropriety.

The most similar image to this embarrassed reaction is that of the adolescent, already aware of social and hierarchical conventions, obliged by a figure of authority to behave properly when instead he cannot help laughing. In the same way, Beckett's spectator stifles this hilarity in his throat, where it arises. And just as the adolescent is scared by his inability to deal with a higher system of values, so the sense of frustration in Beckett's spectator overpowers that instinctive desire to laugh that he really feels.

But whence comes that feeling of discomfort? The function of comic mechanisms is, by definition, that of dialectic opposition (to the serious) and of overturning (of the serious). The spectator, therefore, in a certain sense is alerted by the instability of comic situations and expects a dynamic situation. So, in itself, the comic cannot justify our sense of frustration in front of Beckett's scenes. Indeed psychoanalytical theories on humour emphasise the very liberating effect of laughter: "by laughing we free ourselves from entanglement in a situation that otherwise we could not cope with [...], our very attitude turns [...] into one that is not to be taken seriously, thereby freeing us from an overstrain to which we have been subjected".[91]

In Beckett there is a double process of negation: the effect of unmasking the comic loses its indisputably dialectic character and, vacillating, disorientates the spectator, who finds himself in an unexpected cognitive situation outside of the schemes he is accustomed to use. The system of comic contrast (the sense derived from two opposing elements: serious/comic, tall/short, old/young etc.) crumbles with the mutual negation of the opposites. As we no longer have two precise situations that oppose and exclude each other, we consequently lose the interpretative security that comes from recognising aesthetic or cultural categories or any logical opposition, including a comic one. The "effect of mutual toppling positions"[92] affects the processes of interaction between different positions and more in general the entire semantic and communicative process. The spectators, who have lost all their normal points of reference, feel trapped and frustrated and react with a special type of laughter that, resulting from cognitive disorientation, dies on their lips, leaving them perplexed. This laughter is the response to a crisis situation, deriving from the failure of our cognitive faculties, which have proved unable to control the circumstance we have before us.

It may seem the negation of comedy, but in reality Beckett is radicalising the genre, taking its limits to extremes, constantly disappointing our expectations and suddenly surprising us with an unexpected surprise. "In comedy we naturally expect the unexpected, but the surprises we anticipate are only related to that which we are given to observe and comprehend, and which is therefore related to subject matter; we do not expect surprises in relation to our own faculties of observation and comprehension".[93]

The liberating nature of laughter, according to Freud able to neutralise our inhibitions, in Beckett brings no catharsis. For Freud, the pleasure we derive from laughter comes from a discharge of psychic energies that, unutilised, can be liberated. This process occurs spontaneously when the comparison of two different expenditures of energy creates an evident, perceivable disproportion, releasing an outburst of laughter.

Freudian laughter, therefore, may be defined as conflict that has been eluded but not resolved. The different ways of activating this process of elusion depend on the type of comedy used and result in different types of laughs. Take, for example, the comedy of the clown. According to Freudian analysis we are disposed to understand the movements of the clowns as exaggerated and illogical, because we compare their lavish expenditure of energy with the "normal" saving of energy: this difference in energies end up with laughter.[94] We find the clowns' actions liberating because their ingenuity and limited intellect generates in us a feeling of superiority when compared with them.

So why do Beckett's clowns not trigger this cathartic process? What holds us back?

Iser believes that we stifle our laugh because the superiority we feel in comparison with Beckett's characters behaving like ingenuous clowns is an inappropriate feeling of superiority. When we realise this, our instinctive reaction of laughter dies on our lips. We begin to doubt our own intellectual and interpretative faculties, because what we thought were clowns no longer seem naïve and innocuous. The characters' indifference towards their main task, for example waiting for Godot, makes us doubt their naivety, as we think their actions may have a motive we are unable to grasp. "Whenever the diverse and apparently nonsensical actions seem to converge unequivocally into clowning, the characters suddenly relate once more, with detailed and often weighty allusions, to the overall plot line [...]".[95] And vice versa, when we are convinced of their main task and that they intend to carry it out, they surprise us with a clumsy, unproductive clowning action. In any case, we quickly realise that they are completely indifferent to carrying out any task. And so on, in an eternal (purgatorial) repetition of motives and dramatic structures.

Our sensibility and our intelligence are shaken by this. And our frustration deepens when the characters start to laugh among themselves.

Every aesthetic system creates a complex, non-linear signification, because there is always a hidden meaning to be deciphered. Figures of speech themselves, so necessary to all artistic expression, must be decoded by the user. According to Freud, in a similar situation a complex psychic process is obviously triggered, through the individual's more or less repressed inhibitions. This psychic working is easier at certain moments of our lives, such as in dreams or when laughing, in short, when the effort of repression is replaced by the relaxation of energy. So laughter is a saving of energy that would normally have been used to produce or control an inhibition.

This complete and satisfying pleasure of Freud is denied to the spectator of Beckett. Our process of signification, rather than being complex, as aesthetic norms or conventions would decree, has an additional difficulty - the reciprocal tottering of interpretative levels. The spectator of *Godot*, for example, is shaken by the constant contradiction of the two different actions – the repetition of failed actions and the hopeless waiting. When we start believing the Vladimir and Estragon are just clowns, we are immediately reminded by the characters themselves of their main task of waiting for Godot. When, on the other hand, we start to be convinced that they actually do have a final task, then the hopelessness of the waiting is revealed together with the lack of any salvation or hope for mankind. This mutual distortion of two behaviours shows us that it is our own interpretations that are inappropriate and that our own intellectual faculties are unreliable - the comedy *happens* to the spectator.[96]

Beckett's spectators, experiencing this contradiction for themselves, laugh with an embarrassed laugh that they try to repress, always constrained by a sense of inappropriateness. Instead of Freud's dis-inhibiting laugh, Beckett's creates in everyone their own inhibitions. It is therefore understandable why it is an isolated, not contagious laugh, for it occurs according to the character and intensity of the individual's inhibition - it depends on the different "timing of the toppling effect".[97] At this point the chain reaction of inhibitions is set off. The spectators who realise they are laughing alone feel even more embarrassed and restrain their laughter, which they are unable to share joyfully with one another.

Bridled by this eternal frustration, they become the subjects of the comic contradiction and begin to harbour the doubt that perhaps the characters they would like to laugh at are actually laughing at them.

Some critics agree with Iser's analysis, although with differing forms and definitions.

Henning, for example, speaks of a muted, reduced, weakened laugh, that makes no sound, although its traces are found at the level of style and structure. This "muted laughter"[98] seems like an interior laugh, an internal backfiring, not consciously understood from the first moment. A restrained impulse rather than a real action. Notwithstanding, for Henning this laughter continues to have an aggressive quality, indeed it is the main weapon against all oppressive and closed thoughts. The internally dialogised (for Henning carnivalesque) laugh fights "against the monologic tendency of official forms".[99]

The images brought to mind by this type of laugh also derive from a semantic field indicating physical, as well as psychic and emotional discomfort: mutism, suffocation, physical repression. Adorno agrees with the suffocating effect discussed by Iser and sees in it a general deterioration of the same category of humour: there is nothing ingenuous left to use as object of laughter, so the laughing subjects have neither the place nor the time, nor the aesthetic category to abandon themselves to this joyful reaction. And if the impulse, despite everything, is felt, it suffocates the laugher.[100] The same confusion of tragic and comic but with opposite effects on the spectator is found in Verna Foster who, after affirming that the comic does not necessarily produce a laugh, attributes to the comic in Beckett – and in this finds perfect correspondence in Shakespeare – a consolatory function (sic) that comes from giving the suffering a sort of meaning or frame.[101]

In reality the laughter of Beckett's spectator or reader seems to us closer to Iser's analysis and his "stifled laughter". The laughter elicited by Beckett is bitter, fruit of repression and source of repression. It is laughter without joy that mingles tears and laughter. It is laughter – Rosette Lamont reminds us[102] - of the grotesque, which Beckett calls "risus purus" and Baudelaire "comique absolu".[103] It is mixed with weeping, "laughter and tears come to the same thing in the end".[104] It is what the public shares with Beckett's characters. It is, in the end, the dianoetic laugh conjectured by Beckett. In the loss of certainties and values, comedy finds its postmodern function: the mediation of the purest intellectual faculties and human strengths. Comedy that turns in to tragedy or that springs from tragedy and tragedy that does not convey desperation but human distress have often confused critics and audiences. The tragicomic paradox has then directed critics' and audiences' interpretations towards the image of Beckett as a pessimist and misanthropist. In reality both his artistic intention and his life demeanour were far from this gloomy picture.

To conclude I wish to quote Irish actor Jack McGowran, in an interview with Mel Gussow that indeed emphasises the real Beckett temperament: "[Beckett]'s written about human distress not human despair. Everything in his work ends with hope. I've never met a man with so much compassion for the human race".[105]

In this essential humanity and courage I believe resides Beckett's modernity and relevance for the 21st Century. Hope that is not afraid of meeting distress, and the steadfast will of going on, "as no other dare fail".[106]

Notes

1. One source, for all, Simon R. K., already cited, 1987, p. 90.
2. Ferroni 1974.
3. Iser 1989.
4. Tagliaferri 1967, p. 37, my translation from Italian. Tagliaferri's comment on prose can be referred to the drama: "the crisis of identity has become the crisis of the interpreter" every time the interpreter decides to be a creator, to indulge in creation as a novelist (ibidem).
5. See Bishop L. 1989, but also Tagliaferri 1967, Locatelli 1984 and 1990a, Pringent 1993.
6. We are reminded of Dante and the souls in Purgatory that had fascinated Beckett so much. Casella, Manfredi and Belacqua also share the strongly sensual quality mixed with disembodiment of the penitent souls, who are eternally damned. They resemble Beckett's ghosts who struggle on earth (is it indeed the earth?), damned to an eternal cycle of the body constantly decomposing and the mind questioning without replies.
7. *Mercier et Camier*, p. 60.
8. Ibidem.
9. Ibidem.
10. *Fin de partie*, p. 25.
11. Remember the famous opening lines of *En attendant Godot* ("rien à faire" p. 9) and of *Fin de partie* ("fini, c'est fini" p. 15).
12. *Human Wishes*, in Cohn 1980, p. 295. The entire introduction to the play is a parody on the dramatic convention of stage instructions: the obsessive precision of the date, the women's attitudes, the cat mentioned as a protagonist and also intent on his activity which he hopes will be possible are all signs of the author's active participation right from the composition of the text. Note the ironic allusion, similar to that of the cat, to *Krapp's Last Tape*, when the tape describes a bucolic scene where two lovers play with a dog and then reflects "moments. Her moments, my moments. [*Pause.*] The dog's moments" (p. 220).

13 *Human Wishes*, in Cohn 1980, p. 298.
14 *Happy Days*, p. 150.
15 Ibidem.
16 The indication is from Paolo Bertinetti, curator of the notes in TC, p. 848.
17 Gray 1966, p. 9.
18 Cohn 1973, p. 154. Beckett also emphasised that this should be considered the most important phrase of the drama to Gussow (1996) and to Ludvigsen (conversation with the author 17th August 1998).
19 The English version uses "revive" with its double meaning of "reanimate" but also of "bringing back into fashion". Here we have the entire life of a comic line, born at a certain moment, repeated many times, until it is consumed and finally decays.
20 *Mirlitonnades*, in *Poesie. Poèmes suivi de Mirlitonnades*, p. 42.
21 For the problem of image-action/image-perception in *Film* see Deleuze 1983, pp. 85-90.
22 Beckett was in hiding, with Suzanne Dumesnil, wanted because of his activism in the Paris Resistance. Knowlson 1996, p. 297.
23 Ibid. p. 333. The source is an undated interview by Lawrence Harvey with Samuel Beckett (Dartmouth), see Ibid. p. 768, n. 50.
24 Both quotations in Frasca 1998, p. XXXVII.
25 Golden 1976 (eventually also AA.VV., *Enciclopedia Garzanti di Filosofia*, Milano, Garzanti, 1981, p. 210).
26 Pirandello 1974, p. 113.
27 Cohn 1973, p. 152. Said by Beckett, when directing actor Patrick Magee during rehearsals for *Endgame*, to help him enter into the true spirit of the performance. The actor was better at the tragic, rather than the comic lines.
28 Ludvigsen 1997, p. 41. Beckett's letter to Ludvigsen, Paris 1st May 1956.
29 Iser 1989, p. 176.
30 Styan 1968, p. 223.
31 Lamont 1987b, p. 63.
32 Esslin 1986a.

33 Gussow 1996, p. 98.
34 Taken from MS3000/1.
35 See p. 96 "Lorsque les causes m'échappent, dit Mercier, je ne suis pas à mon aise", and p. 154 where Mercier breaks into philosophical-existential considerations.
36 Restivo 1991, p. 206, my translation from Italian.
37 This information and description of contents of the *Regiebuch* are in Cohn 1973, pp. 185-193.
38 Ibid. p. 187.
39 The pattern is: 1. Willie laughs alone; 2. They laugh together; 3. Winnie laughs alone; 4. They laugh together; 5. Willie laughs alone. Note that when one joins the other in laughing, the other stops. So the model is in fact more complex than shown here.
40 "détérioration du sens de l'humour", *Comment c'est*, p. 27.
41 *Mal vu mal dit*, p. 66.
42 *L'Innommable*, p. 178.
43 *Molloy*, p. 54.
44 Watt behaves in the same way when, after his profound ruminations on human life, he is led "to decide not to smile after all" (p. 201).
45 In *Watt*, too, there is a similar dissolution, except there is no involution but a choice between open or weak laughter: Watt "[...] would have smiled, if he had not been too weak, or laughed outright, if he had been strong enough to laugh, outright" (p. 221). Weakness prevented the laughter. The result was a pale reminder of pale smiles.
46 Godot, p. 16: "aspects riants".
47 Gussow 1996, p. 60.
48 Pilling 1976, p. 134.
49 Knowlson 1996, passim.
50 He certainly owned *La Divina Commedia* with comments by C. T. Dragone (Alba, Edizioni Paoline, 1960) and an English translation by Revd. Henry Francis Cary (London, Bell and Daldy, 1869). This information is given by Knowlson 1996, p. 841, who inspected all of Beckett's private library in Boulevard St-Jacques in Paris (letter from James Knowlson to the author, Reading, 6th November

1997). These volumes can be seen in RUL, as Beckett donated them to the Archive.

51   The review appeared under the title "Papini's Dante" in *The Bookman*, Christmas 1934, now in *Disjecta*, pp. 80-81.

52   Bryden 1995, pp. 29-33.

53   Three undated, unsigned postcards, cm. 10, 5x14, RUL MS4123. All quotations from this Beckett manuscript refer to this collocation.

54   This is postcard no. 1, numbered by the archivists in pencil, written on both sides.

55   *La Divina Commedia*, ed. by Giuseppe Giacalone, Roma, Signorelli, 1975, Purgatorio, Canto II, 76-86, pp. 27-28. My italics. Numbers are reported as Beckett does in the postcards. From a recent online version of the *Divine Comedy* owned by Beckett (Dante 2005) I have the following translation of the quoted passage:
"Then one I saw darting before the rest
With such fond ardour to embrace me, I
To do the like was mov'd. O shadows vain
Except in outward semblance! thrice my hands
I clasp'd behind it, they as oft return'd
Empty into my breast again. Surprise
I needs must think was painted in my looks,
For that the shadow smil'd and backward drew.
To follow it I hasten'd, but with voice
Of sweetness it enjoin'd me to desist.
Then who it was I knew, and pray'd of it,
To talk with me, it would a little pause".

56   Ibid. Canto III, 106-113, pp. 45-46. My italics. From Dante 2005 I have taken the following translation:
"I tow'rds him turn'd, and with fix'd eye beheld.
Comely, and fair, and gentle of aspect,
He seem'd, but on one brow a gash was mark'd.
When humbly I disclaim'd to have beheld
Him ever: "Now behold!" he said, and show'd
High on his breast a wound: then smiling spake.

«I am Manfredi, grandson to the Queen
Costanza: [...]»".

57 Ibid. Canto IV, 121-122, p. 64. The following translation is from Dante 2005:
"His lazy acts and broken words my lips
To laughter somewhat mov'd; when I began".

58 Letter from Samuel Beckett to Gabriele Frasca, Paris 14th December 1984.

59 Canto IV, 127-135, p. 65. The following translation is from Dante 2005:
" [...] My brother, of what use to mount,
When to my suffering would not let me pass
The bird of God, who at the portal sits?
Behooves so long that heav'n first bear me round
Without its limits, as in life it bore,
Because I to the end repentant Sighs
Delay'd, if prayer do not aid me first,
That riseth up from heart which lives in grace.
What other kind avails, not heard in heaven?"

60 See the already-mentioned edition of the *Commedia* commented by Giacalone 1975 (pp. 66-69) and Marchese-Rossi 1982.

61 Comment by Benedetto Croce, in *La poesia di Dante*, Bari, Laterza, 1921, p. 104 (my translation from Italian).

62 Brater 1983, pp. 156-171.

63 The real Florentine lutist Belacqua is said to have quoted these words from Aristotle, in reply to criticism of his slowness, according to Anonimo Fiorentino, quoted by Giacalone 1975, p. 63, n. 105. "Sedendo et quiescendo" was the title of a story by Beckett from the Thirties, later absorbed into *Dream of Fair to Middling Women*. The protagonist, obviously, was Belacqua.

64 Paradiso, Canto XXXIII, 145. The following translation is from Dante 2005:
" [...] the Love impell'd,
That moves the sun in heav'n and all the stars".

65 *L'Innommable*, p. 100.

66 "Con divin", *Nouvelles et Textes pour rien*, p. 170.
67 From *Dream of Fair to Middling Women*, p. 82.
68 See Bair 1990, Knowlson 1996 and above all Cronin 1997 for "fundamentalism" in Irish Protestantism.
69 American novelist Paul Auster (who openly admits the strong influence of Beckett on his writing) suggests the play on words: "[God] is a funny word to me. When you put it backwards, it spells dog. And a dog is not much like God, is it? Woof woof. Bow wow", in Auster 1988, p. 20. But the metathesis dog-God has also been interpreted by critics as mocking the master-slave relationship (see Jacquart 1990, p. 141) or as proof that the metaphor of the dog is one of Beckett's favourite elements of comparison in describing his characters (Pilling 1976, p. 62).
70 In two typewritten pages conserved at Trinity College Dublin (MS4663) we read "Le Christ est venu tard", see Restivo 1991, p. 41 and Gontarski 1985, p. 45. But see Pilling 1976, p. 120 for invective against Christ.
71 RUL MS1227/7/16/2, p. 1.
72 Ibid. p. 4.
73 Ibid. p. 5. Also for contextualisation of this fragment in the development of *Fin de partie* see Restivo 1991, pp. 43-44 and Gontarski 1985, pp. 26-27.
74 Restivo 1991, p. 103.
75 More details in Knowlson 1996 (pp. 448-451) and Lake 1984 (p. 98).
76 Interview by James Knowlson to Jérôme Lindon, 13th July 1989, in Knowlson 1996, p. 377.
77 *Merlin*, I, Autumn 1952, pp. 73-79, now in Federman-Graver 1979, pp. 79-87.
78 Seaver 1976b, p. XV.
79 Booth 1974, op. cit., p. 265.
80 Frasca 1998, p. LIII (my translation from Italian).
81 Blin 1990, p. 164.
82 Cohn 1973, p. 128.
83 Mandell 1990, p. 201.

84 Laughter in Beckett for Federman "starts somewhere in your throat", in Beckett 1971, p. 11.
85 Iser 1989.
86 Knowlson 1996, p. 377.
87 Cohn 1973, p. 128.
88 Tagliaferri 1993, pp. 771-792.
89 Campbell 1997.
90 The article appears in *Prospecting: From Reader Response to Literary Anthropology* (Iser 1989, pp. 152-193).
91 Iser 1989, p. 157.
92 Ibid. p. 155.
93 Ibid. p. 161.
94 Perniola 1976, p. 7.
95 Iser 1989, p. 166.
96 See Ibid. p. 169.
97 Ibid. p. 172.
98 Henning 1988, p. 3.
99 Ibid. p. 2.
100 Adorno 1961 (see particularly pp. 674-675).
101 Foster V. A. 1993, p. 16.
102 Lamont 1987b, pp. 56-70.
103 Beckett's expression comes from in *Watt*, p. 47. That of Baudelaire from "De l'essence du rire et généralement du comique dans le arts plastiques" (Baudelaire 1976).
104 Lamont 1987b, p. 65.
105 Gussow 1996, p. 21.
106 "Three Dialogues" p. 21.

* REFERENCES *

This book makes use of an extensive bibliography, here divided into texts *by* Beckett, a critical bibliography *on* Beckett, with special attention to the themes of comedy and humour, and finally a general bibliography that collects texts used in building knowledge on the broader themes of comedy, theatre, cinema and radio. The purpose of this reference list is to offer the Beckett reader the necessary tools for further research.

* TEXTS BY SAMUEL BECKETT *

All the references listed below are clustered in thematic categories. The first one indicates the texts and manuscripts by Samuel Beckett that have been consulted in the present monographic research. Published texts are divided into collections and individual works, grouped in genres: 1) prose, essays, poetry and theatre and 2) broadcasting (radio, TV, film). Because in the course of the present study the Italian versions have been consulted and compared to the English and French versions, I also refer to these volumes. The criteria chosen are chronological, based on the first edition of the first publication. As is known, Beckett used to translate his own works from and to English and French. Quotes in the present book consistently use the language of the first edition. If not indicated, all the translations are by Beckett. If the volume referred to is different from the first edition, it will be indicated in square parenthesis [...].

Collections are quoted as following (see below for full reference):

CDW: *The complete dramatic works*, London-Boston, Faber & Faber, 1986
COM: *Comédie et actes divers*, Paris, Les Editions de Minuit, 1972
PAS: *Pas suivi de quatre esquisses*, Paris, Les Editions de Minuit, 1978
CAD: *Catastrophe et autres dramaticules*, Paris, Les Editions de Minuit, 1986
TC: *Teatro completo* (notes by Paolo Bertinetti, trans. to It. Carlo Fruttero), Torino, Einaudi-Gallimard, 1994

In-depth bibliographic information and full lists of theatre performances in: *Revue d'Estétique* 1986 and 1990, Knowlson 1996; Federman-Fletcher 1970; Davis R. J. 1979.

Manuscripts

The acronym RUL refers to the "Samuel Beckett Collection" consulted at the Reading University Library Archives, Reading (UK). Descriptions, titles and page numbers in the manuscripts report the criteria applied by the Archive, or otherwise indicated with (*). Twice I quote manuscripts that are not *by* Beckett but are relevant to the present research, the reader will find them in square parenthesis [...].

GD stands for German Diaries, Beckett's travel log from the Thirties, when he travelled to Germany. They are collected at the RUL.

[RUL MS1227/1/2/16]
    McCormick(*), letter by John McCormick to James Knowlson, 7.10.1970.

RUL MS1227/1/1/7
    Letter(*), letter by Samuel Beckett to Colin Duckworth, Paris, 15.9.1965.

RUL MS1227/7/4/1
    Eleuthéria, photocopy of the typed version of the play in 3 acts in French, copy of the typed version owned by A. J. Leventhal, 1947 ca., 20x21cm., 133 sheets.

RUL MS1227/7/16/1
    Mime du rêveur A, photocopy of the typed version with manuscript addenda by Samuel Beckett, s.d. [early Fifties, according to Restivo 1991, p. 42], 27x21 cm, 4 sheets; sheet 1 "for Reading University Library. Sam Beckett"; sheet 4 "Original in Lawrence Harvey Baker Library Collection donated to Dartmouth" [U.S.A.]. Reproduced in Gontarski 1985, pp. 193-198.

RUL MS1227/7/16/2
    Ernest & Alice(*), untitled typed version, with manuscript addenda by Samuel Beckett, in French, 1956 ca., 25x21 cm., 9 sheets; sheet 1 "for Reading University Library. Sam Beckett".

RUL MS1227/7/17/2
    Letter/interview(*), letter/interview by James Knowlson to Samuel Beckett with manuscript replies by Beckett, 10.1.1971.

RUL MS1396/4/6
    The Gloaming, original manuscript, December 1956, 21x17 cm., 16 sheets.

RUL MS2101
    Notes for Krapp's Last Tape, notes by Samuel Beckett for the staging of *Krapp's Last Tape* by San Quentin Drama Workshop, n.d., 2 pp.

[RUL MS2898]
: *The first mirror*, letter by Erika Tophoven to James Knowlson, attaches a photocopy of an Irish folktale.

RUL MS2915
: *Act without words II*, typed version, 2 pp. followed by a drawing by Beckett showing the three positions for A and B, 21x27 cm.

RUL MS2929
: *Chamfort*(*), postcard with no date or signature, manuscript by Samuel Beckett, 7 quotes from Chamfort, 15x10 cm.

RUL MS2932
: *Unpublished play fragment*, undated manuscript, probably 1952, 3 pp., 21x25 cm.

RUL MS3000/1
: *Whoroscope/Murphy Notebook*, manuscript notebook, red cover with manuscript block letters "WHOROSCOPE", s.d. [from the 1930s], 11x17 cm.

RUL MS3056
: *The Possessed*, unsigned article, in *T.D.C.: A College Miscellany*, March 12 1931, p. 138.

RUL MS3458
: *Human Wishes*, typed version with manuscript addenda by Beckett with black ink and blue pencil, with "doodles", s.d. [1936-37; cfr. Bryden 1992a, p. 47], 15 sheets, 27x21 cm.

RUL MS4090
Letters(*), letters by Samuel Beckett to Aldo Tagliaferri, Paris, 9.2.1984 [on Pirandello] and 21.1.1985 [on Camus].

RUL MS4123
: *Dante's postcards*(*), 3 postcards, no date, manuscripts, 10,5x14 cm.

GM
: *German Diaries*, manuscript diaries, Thirties, several measures (notebook 6: 21x16 cm.).

Prose, essays, poetry

"Dante...Bruno. Vico..Joyce", in *Our Exagmination Round His Factification for Incamination of Work in Progress*, Paris, Shakespeare and Co., 1929 [in *Djsiecta*, pp. 19-33].

"Che Sciagura", in *T.C.D.: A College Miscellany*, XXXVI, November 14 1929, p. 42.

"Hell crane to startling", in *The European Caravan. An Anthology of the New Spirit in European Literature*, compiled and edited by Samuel Putnam, Maida Castelhun Darnton, George Reavey and J. Bronowski, New York, Brewer, Warner & Putnam, 1931, pp. 475-476.

"Casket of pralinen for a daughter of a dissipated mandarin", in *The European Caravan. An Anthology of the New Spirit in European Literature*, compiled and edited by Samuel Putnam, Maida Castelhun Darnton, George Reavey and J. Bronowski, New York, Brewer, Warner & Putnam, 1931, pp. 476-478.

"Text", in *The European Caravan. An Anthology of the New Spirit in European Literature*, compiled and edited by Samuel Putnam, Maida Castelhun Darnton, George Reavey and J. Bronowski, New York, Brewer, Warner & Putnam, 1931, pp. 478-480.

"Yoke of Liberty", in *The European Caravan. An Anthology of the New Spirit in European Literature*, compiled and edited by Samuel Putnam, Maida Castelhun Darnton, George Reavey and J. Bronowski, New York, Brewer, Warner & Putnam, 1931, p. 480.

Whoroscope, Paris, The Hours Press, 1930 [in Cohn 1962, pp. 303-306].

Proust, London, Chatto and Windus, 1931 [*Proust and Three Dialogues with Georges Duthuit*, London, John Calder, 1965].

More Pricks Than Kicks, London, Chatto & Windus, 1934 [London, Calder and Boyars, 1970].

Echo's Bones and Other Precipitates, Paris, Europa Press, 1935 [cfr. It. *Poesie in inglese*].

Murphy, London, Routledge and Sons, 1938 [London, John Calder, 1963; *Murphy*, Paris, Les Editions de Minuit, 1965].

Molloy, Paris, Les Editions de Minuit, 1951.

Malone meurt, Paris, Les Editions de Minuit, 1951.

L'Innommable, Paris, Les Editions de Minuit, 1953.

Watt, Paris, Olympia Press, 1953 [London, John Calder, 1963].

Nouvelles et textes pour rien, Paris, Les Editions de Minuit, 1955 [Paris, Les Editions de Minuit, 1958; *The Expelled and Other Novellas*, London, Penguin Books, 1980].

"From an Abandoned Work", in *Trinity News*, vol. III, n. 4, 1956 [cfr. It. *Teste-morte*].

Anthology of Mexican Poetry, translated by Samuel Beckett, compiled by Octavio Paz, Bloomington, Indiana University Press, 1958.

Comment c'est, Paris, Les Editions de Minuit, 1961.

Imagination morte imaginez, Paris, Les Editions de Minuit, 1965 [cfr. It. *Teste-morte*].

Assez, Paris, Les Editions de Minuit, 1966 [cfr. It. *Teste-morte*].

Bing, Paris, Les Editions de Minuit, 1966 [cfr. It. *Teste-morte*].

Têtes-mortes, Paris, Les Editions de Minuit, 1967 [cfr. It. *Teste-morte*].

Poèmes, Paris, Les Editions de Minuit, 1968.

Sans, Paris, Les Editions de Minuit, 1969 [cfr. It. *L'immagine Senza Lo spopolatore*].

Mercier et Camier, Paris, Les Editions de Minuit, 1970.

Premier amour, Paris, Les Editions de Minuit, 1970.

Le Dépeupleur, Paris, Les Editions de Minuit, 1970 [cfr. It. *L'immagine Senza Lo spopolatore*].

Still (It. trans. L. Majno), with illustrations by Stanley William Hayter, Milano, M'Arte Edizioni, 1974 [with original version in English].

All Strange Away, New York, Gotham Book Mart, 1976 [cfr. It. *Quello che è strano, via*].

Collected poems in English and French, London, John Calder, 1977.

Poèmes suivi de Mirlitonnades, Paris, Les Editions de Minuit, 1978 [cfr. It. *Poesie. Poèmes suivi de Mirlitonnades*].

Company, London, John Calder, 1979 [London, John Calder, 1980].

Mal vu mal dit, Paris, Les Editions de Minuit, 1981.

Worstward ho, London, John Calder, 1983 [Frankfurt am Main, Suhrkamp Verlag, 1989 (German version by Erika Tophoven)].

Disjecta. Miscellaneous Writings and a Dramatic Fragment, London, John Calder, 1983.

Collected Shorter Prose 1945-80, London, John Calder, 1984.

L'image, Paris, Les Editions de Minuit, 1988 [cfr. It. *L'immagine Senza Lo spopolatore*].

Stirring Still, New York and London, Blue Moon Books and John Calder, 1988.

Comment dire, Paris, Les Editions de Minuit, 1989 [cfr. It. *Qual è la parola*].

As the Story was Told: uncollected and late prose, London, John Calder, 1990 (posthumous).

Dream of Fair to Middling Women, Dublin, The Black Cat Press, 1992 (posthumous).

Theatre and broadcasting (radio, tv, film)
Individual works

En attendant Godot, Paris, Les Editions de Minuit, 1952.

Fin de partie, Paris, Les Editions de Minuit, 1957.

All That Fall, London, Faber & Faber, 1957 [in CDW].

Acte sans paroles I, Paris, Les Editions de Minuit, 1957 [in COM].

Krapp's Last Tape, London, Faber & Faber, 1959 [in CDW].

Embers, London, Faber & Faber, 1959 [in CDW].

Happy Days, London, Faber & Faber, 1962 [in CDW; *Oh les beaux jours suivi de Pas moi*, Paris, Les Editions de Minuit, 1963-1974].

La manivelle: The old tune, by Robert Pinget, English adaptation by Samuel Beckett, in AA.VV., *New Writers II*, London, John Calder, 1962.

Acte sans paroles II, in *Dramatische Dichtungen*, Band I, Frankfurt, Suhrkamp Verlag, 1963 [in COM].

Cascando, in *Dramatische Dichtungen*, Band I, Frankfurt, Suhrkamp Verlag, 1963 [in COM].

Words and Music, in *Evergreen Review*, vol. VI, 1963 [in CDW].

Play, London, Faber & Faber, 1964 [in CDW].

Come and Go, London, Calder and Boyars, 1967 [in CDW].

Eh Joe, London, Faber & Faber, 1967 [in CDW].

Film, London, Faber & Faber, 1967 [in CDW].

Breath, in *Gambit*, vol. 4, nr. 15, 1969 [in CDW].

Not I, London, Faber & Faber, 1973 [in CDW].

Esquisse radiophonique, in *Minuit*, nr. 5, 1973 [in PAS].

Fragment de théâtre I, in *Minuit*, nr. 8, 1974 [in PAS].

Pochade radiophonique, in *Minuit*, nr. 16, 1975 [in PAS].

Fragment de théâtre II, in Bishop-Federman 1976 [in PAS].

That Time, New York, Grove Press, 1976 [in CDW].

Footfalls, London, Faber & Faber, 1976 [in CDW].

Ghost Trio, in *Journal of Beckett Studies*, nr. 1, Winter 1976 [in CDW].

...but the clouds..., London, Faber & Faber, 1977 [in CDW].

A Piece of Monologue, in *The Keyton Review*, vol. I, nr. 3, Summer 1979 [in CDW].

Human Wishes, in Cohn 1980, pp. 295-305.

Rockaby, New York, Grove Press, 1981 [in CDW].

Ohio Impromptu, New York, Grove Press, 1981 [in CDW].

Catastrophe, Paris, Les Editions de Minuit, 1982 [in CAD].

What Where, New York, Grove Press, 1983 [in CDW].

Quad, London, Faber & Faber, 1984 [in CDW].

Nacht und Traüme, London, Faber & Faber, 1984 [in CDW].

Eleutheria, Paris, Les Editions de Minuit, 1995 [*Eleutheria* (Eng. Transl. Barbara Wright), London, Faber & Faber, 1996] posthumous.

Collections

[CDW] *The complete dramatic works*, London-Boston, Faber & Faber, 1986.

[COM] *Comédie et actes divers*, Paris, Les Editions de Minuit, 1972 [*Comédie, Va et vient, Cascando, Paroles et musique, Dis Joe, Acte sans paroles I, Acte sans paroles II, Film, Souffle*].

[PAS] *Pas suivi de quatre esquisses*, Paris, Les Editions de Minuit, 1978 [*Pas, Fragment de théâtre I, Fragment de théâtre II, Pochade radiophonique, Esquisse radiophonique*].

[CAD] *Catastrophe et autres dramaticules*, Paris, Les Editions de Minuit, 1986 [*Cette fois, Solo, Berceuse, Impromptu d'Ohio, Quoi où*].

Italian translations
Prose, essays, poetry

"Dante... Bruno. Vico.. Joyce", now in *Disiecta. Scritti sparsi ed un frammento drammatico* (It. Transl. Aldo Tagliaferri), Milano, Egea, 1991, pp. 19-42.

Proust (preface Sergio Moravia, It. Transl. Carlo Gallone), Milano, Sugarco, 1978.

Più pene che pane (It. Transl. Alessandro Roffeni), Milano, Sugarco, 1994.

Poesie in inglese (preface and It. Transl. Rodolfo J. Wilcock), Torino, Einaudi, 1964 [original version besides].

Murphy (It. Transl. Franco Quadri), Torino, Einaudi, 1962.

Trilogia. Molloy, Malone Muore, L'Innominabile (introduction and It. Transl. Aldo Tagliaferri), Torino, Einaudi, 1996.

Watt (It. Transl. and editing Gabriele Frasca), Torino, Einaudi, 1998.

Primo amore Novelle e testi per nulla (It. Transl. Franco Quadri and Carlo Cignetti), Torino, Einaudi, 1967.

Com'è (It. Transl. Franco Quadri), Torino, Einaudi, 1965.

Teste-morte (It. Transl. Valerio Frantiel and Guido Neri), Torino, Einaudi, 1969 [original version besides. Content: *from an abandoned work*, pp. 8-37; *assez*, pp. 40-63; *imagination morte imaginez*, pp. 66-75; *bing*, pp. 78-87].

Mercier e Camier (It. Transl. Luigi Buffarini), Milano, Sugarco, 1994.

L'immagine Senza Lo spopolatore (ed. Renato Oliva), Torino, Einaudi, 1972 e 1989 [original version besides].

Quello che è strano, via (It. Transl. Roberto Mussapi), Milano, SE, 1989 [original version besides].

Poesie. Poèmes suivi de Mirlitonnades (introduction and It. Transl. Giovanni Brogliolo), Torino, Einaudi, 1980 [original version besides].

Compagnia e Worstward ho (It. Transl. Roberto Mussapi), Milano, Jaca book, 1986.

Mal visto, mal detto (It. Transl. Renzo Guidieri), Torino, Einaudi, 1986.

Disiecta. Scritti sparsi ed un frammento drammatico (It. Transl. Aldo Tagliaferri), Milano, Egea, 1991.

Qual è la parola [What is the world. Comment dire] (It. Transl. Rosangela Barone), in *Poesia*, Milano, Crocetti, Febbraio 1991.

Racconti e teatro (It. Transl. Edda Meloni et alii), Torino, Einaudi, 1978.

Theatre and broadcasting (radio, tv, film)

[TC] *Teatro completo* (notes Paolo Bertinetti, It. Transl. Carlo Fruttero), Torino, Einaudi-Gallimard, 1994.

Desideri umani (It. Transl. Aldo Tagliaferri), in *Disiecta*, pp. 223-236.

BECKETT BIBLIOGRAPHY

AA.VV.
1971   *Samuel Beckett*, Paris, Lettres Modernes Minard.
1985   *A propos de Beckett*, Paris, Gallimard.
1991   *La Zattera di Babele. 1981-1991*, Palermo, La Zattera di Babele.
s.d.   *York Notes on Samuel Beckett's "Waiting for Godot"*, London, Longman.

ABBOTT, Porter H.
1973   *The Fiction of Samuel Beckett: Form and Effect*, Berkley, University of California Press.
1975   "King Laugh: Beckett's Early Fiction", in Cohn, Ruby (ed.), *Samuel Beckett: A Collection of Criticism*, New York, McGraw-Hill Book Company, pp. 51-62.
1983   "The Harpooned Notebook: *Malone Dies* and the Conventions of Intercalated Narrative", in Beja, Morris-Gontarski, Stan E.-Astier, Pierre (eds.), *Samuel Beckett. Humanistic Perspectives*, Ohio, Ohio State University Press, pp. 71-79.
1987   "Beckett and Autobiography", in Friedman, Alan Warren-Rossman, Charles-Sherzer, Dina (eds.), *Beckett Translating/Translating Beckett*, Pennsylvania State University Press, University Park, pp. 120-127.
1992   "Consorting with Spirits: The Arcane Craft of Beckett's Later Drama", in Brater, Enoch (ed.), *The Theatrical Gamut. Notes for a post-beckettian stage*, University of Michigan Press, pp. 91-106.
1993   "Late Modernism: Samuel Beckett and the Art of the Ouvre", in Brater, Enoch-Cohn, Ruby (eds.), *Around the Absurd. Essay on Modern and Postmodern Drama*, Michigan, University of Michigan Press, pp. 73-96.
1994   "Beginning again: the post-narrative art of *Texts for nothing* and *How it is*", in Pilling, John (ed.), *The Cambridge Companion to Beckett*, Cambridge, Cambridge University Press, pp. 106-123.
1996   *Beckett Writing Beckett. The Author in the Autograph*, Ithaca and London, Cornell University Press.

ABEL, Lionel
1963   *Metatheatre. A New View of Dramatic Form*, New York, Hill and Wang.

ACHESON, James
1992   "Beckett Re-Joycing: *Words and Music*", in Carey, Phyllis-Jewinski, Ed (eds.), *Re: Joyce 'n Beckett*, New York, Fordham University Press, pp. 50-60.
1993   "*Murphy*'s Metaphysics", in Gontarski, Stan E. (ed.), *The Beckett Studies Reader*, Florida, University Press of Florida, pp. 78-93.

1997 *Samuel Beckett's Artistic Theory and Practice*, London, Macmillan.

ACHESON, James - ARTHUR, Katheryna

1986 (eds.), *Beckett's Later Fiction and Drama: Text for "Company"*, London, Macmillan.

ADAMOV, Arthur

1968 "Adamov, Beckett, Ionesco", in *L'homme et l'enfant, Souvenirs, Journal*, Paris, Gallimard, pp. 111-116.

ADAMSON, Eve

1994 "Beckett in Repertory", in Oppenheimer, Lois, *Directing Beckett*, Michigan, The University of Michigan Press, pp. 268-276.

ADMUSSEN, Richard L.

1979 *The Samuel Beckett Manuscripts. A study*, Boston, G. K. Hall & Co.

ADORNO, Theodor

1961 "Versuch Endspiel zu verstehen", in *Noten zur Literatur*, Frankfurt am Main, Suhrkamp, vol. II, It. Transl.. G. Manzoni, "Tentativo di capire *Finale di partita*", in *Note per la letteratura 1943-1961*, Torino, Einaudi, 1979, pp. 267-308, now in Samuel Beckett, *Teatro completo*, Torino-Parigi, Einaudi Gallimard, 1994, pp. 658-694.

AKLAITIS, JoAnne

1990 "In Memory: Meeting Beckett", in *The Drama Review*, vol. 34, nr. 3, Fall 1990, pp. 11-12.

ALBEIRA, Philippe

1998 "Beckett and Hollinger", in Bryden, Mary (ed.), *Samuel Beckett and Music*, Oxford, Clarendon Press, pp. 87-97.

ALBRIGHT, Daniel

1981 *Representation and Imagination: Beckett, Nabokov, Kafka and Schoenberg*, Chicago, University of Chicago Press.

ALFANO, Giancarlo - CORTELLESSA, Andrea

2006 (eds.), *Beckett in Italia*, Roma, Edisup.

ALLEGRI, Luigi

1993 *La drammaturgia da Diderot a Beckett*, Roma, Laterza.

ALLUIN, Bernard

1987 *Les fleurs bleues de Raymond Queneau*, Lille, Societe Roman 20-50.

ALTER, Jean

1979 "Verso il matematesto a teatro: codificando Godot", in AA.VV., *Semiologia della rappresentazione. Teatro/televisione/fumetto* (ed. A. Helbo), Napoli, Liguori, pp. 47-66.

ALVARAREZ, Al

1973 *Beckett*, London, Fontana/Collins.

AMIRAN, Eyal

1993   *Wandering and home. Beckett's Metaphysical Narrative*, Pennsylvania, The Pennsylvania State University Press.

ANDERS, Günther

1956   *Die antiquiertheit des menschen*, München, Verlag C. H. Beck.

1965   "Being without Time: On Beckett's Play *Waiting for Godot*", in Esslin, Martin (ed.), *Samuel Beckett: A Collection of Critical Essays*, Englewood Cliffs, N.J., Prentice Hall, pp. 140-151.

ANDERSON, Robert-ROSEN, Steven J.

1993   "Beckett's Hamm and Shakespeare's Richard III: A Couple of Canettian Autocrats", in Drew, Anne Marie (ed.), *Past Crimson, Past Woe. The Shakespeare-Beckett Connection*, New York & London, Garland, pp. 91-98.

ANDREASEN, John-HAGBERG, Sylvia

1990   (eds.), *Alle tiders teater!*, Århus, Husets Forlag.

ANGELI, Siro

1953   "Il teatro di prosa", in *L'Osservatore Romano*, pp. 608-611.

ANHOUIL, Jean

1978   *Beckett*, Paris, s. e.

ANZIEU, Didier

1990   "Le théâtre d'Echo dans le récits de Beckett", in *Revue d'Estetique*, numéro hors-série (I ed. 1986), pp. 39-43.

1992   *Beckett et le psychanalyste*, [Paris], Éditions Mentha

ARIKHA, Avigdor

1990   "Un point pour le grand souffle", in *Revue d'Estetique*, numéro hors-série (I ed. 1986), pp. 3-5.

ARMSTRONG, Gordon S.

1990   *Samuel Beckett, W. B. Yeats, and Jack Yeats. Images and Words*, London and Toronto, Associated University Presses.

ARMSTRONG, William A.

1963   (ed.), *Experimental Drama*, London, G. Bell.

ARRABAL, Fernando

1967   "In connection with Samuel Beckett", in Calder, John (ed.), *Beckett at 60*, London, Calder and Boyars, p. 88.

1990   "L'ultima lettera di Beckett", in *Leggere*, Milano, n. 22 (Giugno 1990), pp. 22-23.

ARTUK, Simone Luise

1990   *La conscience dans le néant à la lumière de la problematique d'identité: une étude sur "L'Innommable" de Samuel Beckett*, Bonn, Romanisticher Verlag.

ASLAN, Odette

1982 "En attendant Godot de Samuel Beckett", in *Les voies de la création théâtrale*, Paris, CNRS, vol. X, pp. 187-238.

1988 *Roger Blin and Twentieth-Century Playwrights*, trad. ing. di Ruby Cohn, Cambridge, Cambridge University Press.

ASMUS, Walter

1990 "Réduire... (les deux mises en scène de Godot)", in *Revue d'Estetique*, numéro hors-série (I ed. 1986), pp. 349-357.

As no Other

1986 *As no Other Dare Fail*, London, John Calder.

ASTRO, Alan

1990 *Understanding Samuel Beckett*, South Carolina, University of South Carolina Press.

ATHANASON, Arthur N.

1993 *Endgame. The Ashbin Play*, New York, Twaine Publishers.

ATIENZA, Edward

1993 "If in Doubt, Drop Your Drawers: An Actor's Point of View", in Drew, Anne Marie (ed.), *Past Crimson, Past Woe. The Shakespeare-Beckett Connection*, New York & London, Garland, pp. 157-166.

AUSTER, Paul

1990 *Selected Poems and Essays 1970-1979*, London-Boston, Faber & Faber.

AXELROD, M.R.

1992 *The Politics of Style in the Fiction of Balzac, Beckett and Cortazar*, New York, St. Martin's.

BADIOU, Alain

1995 *Beckett. L'increvable désir*, Paris, Hachette.

BAIR, Deidre

1976 "La Vision, enfin", In Bishop, Tom-Federman, Raymond (eds.), *Samuel Beckett*, "Cahier de l'Herne", nr. 31, pp. 114-119.

1990 *Samuel Beckett: una biografia*, Milano, Garzanti.

BAJINI, Sandro

1959 "Beckett o l'emblema totale", in *Il Verri*, vol. III, nr. 2, April 1959, pp. 70-104.

BAKER, Phil

1997 *Beckett and the Mythology of Psychoanalysis*, London, Macmillan.

BAKEWELL, Michael-EWENS, Eric

[1961-62] (eds.), *From the Fifties. BBC Sound Radio Drama Series*, London, British Broadcasting Corporation, s.d.

BALDWIN, Hélène L.

1981 *Samuel Beckett's real silence*, Pennsylvania, Pennsylvania State University Press.

BANSANG, Michael

1984 "*Watt*-logique, démence, aphasie", in Rabate, Jean-Michel (ed.), *Beckett avant Beckett: essais sur le jeune Beckett (1930-1945)*, Paris, P.E.N.S., pp. 153-172.

BARALE, Michèle Aina-RABINOVITZ, Rubin

1988 *A Kwic Concordance to Samuel Beckett's Trilogy: Molloy, Malone Dies, and the Unnamable*, New York and London, Garland Publishing, 2 voll.

1990 *A Kwic Concordance to Samuel Beckett's Murphy*, New York and London, Garland Publishing.

BARCHICCHI, Alessandra

1997 *Samuel Beckett. I percorsi narrativi nei «Testi per nulla»*, Firenze, Libri Atheneum.

BARGE, Laura

1988 *God, the quest, the hero: thematic structures in Beckett's fiction*, Chappell Hill, University of North Carolina.

BARKER, Stephen

1990 "Conspicuous Absence: *Tracé* and Power in Beckett's Drama", in Butler, Lance St. John-Davis, Robin J. (eds.), *Rethinking Beckett. A Collection of Critical Essays*, London, Macmillan, pp. 181-205.

BARLOW, Clarence

1998 "Songs within Words: The Programme TXMS and the Performance of *Ping* on the Piano", in Bryden, Mary (ed.), *Samuel Beckett and Music*, Oxford, Clarendon Press, pp. 233-240.

BARNARD, Guy Christian

1970a *Samuel Beckett*, London, Dent.

1970b *Samuel Beckett New Approach: A Study of the Novels and Plays*, New York, Dodd, Mead and Company.

BARONE, Rosangela

1982 "*Play* di Samuel Beckett: l'Illusion Comique del XX secolo", in *Lingua e Stile*, a. XVII, nr. 3, Luglio-Settembre 1982.

BARRAULT, Jean-Louis

1990 "Artaud, Blin, Beckett ou le plus grand auteur des temps modernes", in *Revue d'Estetique*, numéro hors-série (I ed. 1986), pp. 175-178.

BARTOLUCCI, Giuseppe

1964 "Esistenzialismo e Metafisica in Samuel Beckett", in *Il calendario del popolo*, Gennaio-Febbraio 1964, pp. 6319-6320.

1989 "Quelli di Prima Porta agosto '65", in Bistolfi, Marina-Licata, Salvo (eds.), *Primo amore. Beckett-Quartucci*, Erice, La Zattera di Babele, p. 33.

BATAILLE, Georges

1971 "La Vérité dont nous sommes malades", in Nores, Dominique (ed.), *Les critiques de notre temps et Beckett*, Paris, Garnier, pp. 42-51.

1988 "Molloy's Silence", in Bloom, Harold (ed.), *Samuel Beckett's Molloy, Malone Dies, The Unnamable*, New York-New Haven Philadelphia, Chelsea House Publishers, pp. 13-21.

BAXTER, K.M.

1964 *Speak What We Feel. A Christian Looks at the Contemporary Theatre*, Liverpool and London, SCM Press.

BECKERMANN, Bernard

1986 "Beckett and the Act of Listening, in Brater, Enoch (ed.), *Beckett at 80/Beckett in Context*, New York, Oxford University Press, pp. 149-167.

Beckett

1971 "Beckett Symposium", in *New Theatre Magazine. Samuel Beckett Issue*, Reading, vol. XI, nr. 3, pp. 8-19.

1988 *Beckett und die Literatur der Gegenwart*, Heidelberg, Carl Winter Universitätsverlag.

BECKETT, Walter

1998 "Music in the Works of Samuel Beckett", in Bryden, Mary (ed.), *Samuel Beckett and Music*, Oxford, Clarendon Press, pp. 181-182.

Beckettiana

1992-1995 *Beckettiana. Cuadernos del Seminario Beckett*, Buenos Aires, Facultad de Filosofia y Letras, a. I-a. III, nr. 1-nr. 4.

BEER, Ann

1994 "Beckett's bilingualism", in Pilling, John (ed.), *The Cambridge Companion to Beckett*, Cambridge, Cambridge University Press, pp. 209-221.

BEGAM, Richard

1996 *Samuel Beckett and the end of modernity*, Stanford, Stanford University Press.

BEITCHMAN, Philip

1988 "A Question of Culture/Culture in Question: Samuel Beckett", in *I Am a Process with No Subject*, Gainesville, University of Florida Press, pp. 53-69.

BEJA, Morris-GONTARSKI, Stan E.-ASTIER, Pierre

1983 (eds.), *Samuel Beckett. Humanistic Perspectives*, Ohio, Ohio State University Press.

BELLINGHAM, Susan

1973 *The Samuel Beckett collection in McMaster University Library*, Hamilton, McMaster University.

BEN-ZVI, Linda

1986 *Samuel Beckett*, Boston, Twayne Publishers.

1987 "Phonetic Structure in Beckett: Frog Mag to Gaw", in Friedman, Alan Warren-Rossman, Charles-Sherzer, Dina (eds.), *Beckett Translating/Translating Beckett*, Pennsylvania State University Press, University Park, pp. 155-164.

1990 (ed.), *Women in Beckett. Performance and Critical Perspectives*, Urbana and Chicago, University of Illinois Press.

BENTLEY, Eric

1954 *The Dramatic Event*, Boston, Beacon Press.

1967 "The Talent of Samuel Beckett", in Cohn, Ruby (ed.), *Casebook on Waiting for Godot*, New York, Grove Press, pp. 59-67.

BERIO, Luciano

1998 "Interview", in Bryden, Mary (ed.), *Samuel Beckett and Music*, Oxford, Clarendon Press, pp. 189-190.

BERLIN, Normand

1986 "The Tragic Pleasure of 'Waiting for Godot'", in Brater, Enoch (ed.), *Beckett at 80/Beckett in Context*, New York, Oxford University Press, pp. 46-63.

BERNABEI, Alfio

1973 "Il teatro a Londra", in *Ridotto*, a. XXIII, nr. 3 (Marzo 1973), pp. 19-20.

BERNAL, Olga

1969 *Langage et fiction dans le roman de Beckett*, Paris, Gallimard.

1971a "La tentation des mots", in Nores, Dominique (ed.), *Les critiques de notre temps et Beckett*, Paris, Garnier, pp. 174-179.

1971b "Rien au-dehors, pénurie en dedans", in Nores, Dominique (ed.), *Les critiques de notre temps et Beckett*, Paris, Garnier, pp. 85-87.

1976 "Le Glissement hors du langage", in Bishop, Tom-Federman, Raymond (eds.), *Samuel Beckett*, "L'Herne", nr. 31, pp. 219-225.

BERNARD, Michel

1995 *Samuel Beckett et son sujet. Une apparition évanouissante*, Paris, Editions L'Harmattan.

BERNOLD, André

1992 *L'amitié de Beckett 1979-1989*, Paris, Hermann.

BERRETTINI, Célia

1977 *A linguagem de Beckett*, São Paulo, Editora Perspectiva.

BERSANI, Leo

1970 "Beckett and the End of Literature (The Trilogy: 'Molloy', 'Malone meurt', 'L'Innommable')", in *Balzac to Beckett. Center and Circumference in French fiction*, New York, Oxford University Press, pp. 300-328.

BERSANI, Leo-DUTOIT, Ulysse

1993 *The Art of Impoverishment. Beckett, Rothko, Resnais*, Cambridge-London, Harvard University Press.

BERTINETTI, Paolo

1984 *Invito alla lettura di Beckett*, Milano, Mursia.

BIMONTE, Ada

1976 *Nel labirinto di Samuel Beckett*, Roma, Bulzoni.

BIRKETT, Jennifer

1987 *Waiting for Godot by Samuel Beckett*, Basingstoke, Macmillan Educational.

BIRKENHAUER, Klaus

1971 *Beckett*, Hamburg, Rowol.

BISHOP, Lloyd

1989 *Romantic Irony in French Literature From Diderot to Beckett*, Nashville, Vanderbilt University Press.

BISHOP, Tom

1976 "Le Pénultième Monologue", in Bishop, Tom-Federman, Raymond (eds.), *Samuel Beckett*, "L'Herne", nr. 31, pp. 242-245.

1986 "La terza età di Beckett", in *Il Patalogo*, Milano, Ubulibri/Electa, nr. 9, pp. 228-229 [previously in *Le Monde*, 4-5 May 1986].

1987 "Beckett Transposing, Beckett Transposed: Plays on Television", in Friedman, Alan Warren-Rossman, Charles-Sherzer, Dina (eds.), *Beckett Translating/Translating Beckett*, Pennsylvania State University Press, University Park, pp. 167-173.

1990 "Transpositions pour la télévision: transmutations des œuvres de Beckett", in *Revue d'Estetique*, numéro hors-série (I ed. 1986), pp. 385-388.

BISHOP, Tom-FEDERMAN, Raymond

1976 (eds.), *Samuel Beckett*, "Cahier de l'Herne", nr. 31.

BISICCHIA, Andrea

1990 "Beckett en Italie", in *Revue d'Estetique*, numéro hors-série (I ed. 1986), pp. 454-458.

BISTOLFI, Marina-LICATA, Salvo

1989 (eds.), *Primo amore. Beckett-Quartucci*, Erice, La Zattera di Babele.

BLANCHOT, Maurice

1971   "Le vide et l'appel de l'œuvre", in Nores, Dominique (ed.), *Les critiques de notre temps et Beckett*, Paris, Garnier, pp. 118-126.

1988   "Where Now? Who Now?" in BLOOM, Harold (ed.), *Samuel Beckett's Molloy, Malone Dies, The Unnamable*, New York-New Haven Philadelphia, Chelsea House Publishers, pp. 23-29.

BLAU, Herbert

1965   *The Impossible Theatre. A Manifesto*, New York-London, Collier-Macmillan.

1967   "Notes from the Underground", in Cohn, Ruby (ed.), *Casebook on Waiting for Godot*, New York, Grove Press, pp. 113-121.

1987   *The Eye of Prey. Subversions of the Postmodern*, Bloomington and Indianapolis, Indiana University Press.

BLIN, Roger

1990   "Conversation avec Lynda Peskine", in *Revue d'Estetique*, numéro hors-série (I ed. 1986), pp. 159-169.

BLIN, Roger-BISHOP, Tom

1976   "Dialogue", in Bishop, Tom-Federman, Raymond (eds.), *Samuel Beckett*, "L'Herne", nr. 31, pp. 141-146.

BLOCKER, H. Gene

1979   *The Metaphysics of Absurdity*, Washington, University Press of America.

BLOOM, Harold

1987   (ed.), *Samuel Beckett's Waiting for Godot*, New York-New Haven Philadelphia, Chelsea House Publishers.

1988a (ed.), *Samuel Beckett's Endgame*, New York-New Haven Philadelphia, Chelsea House Publishers.

1988b (ed.), *Samuel Beckett's Molloy, Malone Dies, The Unnamable*, New York-New Haven Philadelphia, Chelsea House Publishers.

BLYHER von, Karl Alfred

1982   *Modernes französisches Theater: Adamov, Beckett, Ionesco*, Darmstadt, Wissenschaftliche Buchgesellschaft.

BOEHLER, Anne-BRAK, Dorothée-KNOWLSON, James

1990   "Essai de chronologie audio-visuelle", in *Revue d'Estetique*, numéro hors-série (I ed. 1986), pp. 467-472.

BONNEFOI, Geneviève

1971   "Le tombeau-refuge", in Nores, Dominique (ed.), *Les critiques de notre temps et Beckett*, Paris, Garnier, pp. 132-136.

BOOTH, W.C.

1974 *A Rethoric of Irony*, Chicago, University of Chicago Press.

BORIE, Monique

1981 *Mythe et théâtre aujourd'hui: une quête impossible?*, Paris, Librairie A.-G. Nizet.

BORRELI, Guy

1967 "Samuel Beckett et le sentiment de la dérélicion", in *Le théâtre moderne. II. Depuis la deuxième guerre mondiale*, Paris, pp. 45-55.

BORRIELLO, Antonio

1992 *Samuel Beckett Krapp's Last Tape. Dalla pagina alla messinscena*, Napoli, ESI.

BOSQUET, Alain

1976 "Poème pour Beckett", in Bishop, Tom-Federman, Raymond (eds.), *Samuel Beckett*, "L'Herne", nr. 31, pp. 152-154.

BOSSEUR, Jean-Yves

1990 "Between Word and Silence: *Bing*", in *Revue d'Estetique*, numéro hors-série (I ed. 1986), pp. 261-264 [now in Bryden, Mary (ed.), *Samuel Beckett and Music*, Oxford, Clarendon Press, 1998, pp. 241-247].

BOURDET, Gildas

1994 "Fizzle", in Oppenheimer, Lois, *Directing Beckett*, Michigan, The University of Michigan Press, pp. 155-160.

BOYLE, Kay

1975 "All Mankind is Us", in Cohn, Ruby (ed.), *Samuel Beckett: A Collection of Criticism*, New York, McGraw-Hill Book Company, pp. 15-19.

1991 *Collected Poems*, Port Towsend, Copper Canyon Press (I ed. 1938).

BRADBY, David

1984 *Modern French Drama 1940-1980*, Cambridge, Cambridge University Press.

BRADBURY, M.

1979 (ed.), *The Contemporary English Novel*, London, Arnold.

BRAK, Dorothée

1990a "Krapp à la luer manichéenne (des extraits du cahier de mise en scène de Samuel Beckett de *La Derniére Bande*", in *Revue d'Estetique*, numéro hors-série (I ed. 1986), pp. 319-330.

1990b "Quelques indications sur les éditions à tirage limité des œuvres de Samuel Beckett", in *Revue d'Estetique*, numéro hors-série (I ed. 1986), p. 424.

BRATER, Enoch

1983 "The *Company* Beckett Keeps: The Shape of Memory and One Fablist's Decay of Lying", in Beja, Morris-Gontarski, Stan E.-Astier, Pierre (eds.), *Samuel Beckett. Humanistic Perspectives*, Ohio, Ohio State University Press, pp. 157-171.

1986 "Introduction: The Origins of a Dramatic Style", in Brater, Enoch (ed.), *Beckett at 80/Beckett in Context*, New York, Oxford University Press, pp. 3-10.

1987 *Beyond Minimalism. Beckett's late style in the theatre*, Oxford-New York, New York University Press.

1989 *Why Beckett*, London, Thames and Hudson.

1992 (ed.), *The Theatrical Gamut. Notes for a post-beckettian stage*, University of Michigan Press.

1994 *The drama in the text: Beckett's late fiction*, New York-Oxford, Oxford University Press.

BRATER, Enoch-COHN, Ruby

1993 (eds.), *Around the Absurd. Essay on Modern and Postmodern Drama*, Michigan, University of Michigan Press.

BREE, Germaine

1976 "Les Abstracteurs de quintessence de Beckett", in Bishop, Tom-Federman, Raymond (eds.), *Samuel Beckett*, "L'Herne", nr. 31, pp. 318-325.

BREUER, Horst

1972 *Samuel Beckett*, München, Willelm Fink Verlag.

BREUER, Lee

1990 "Le théâtre narratif", in *Revue d'Estetique*, numéro hors-série (I ed. 1986), pp. 95-98.

BREUER, Rolf

1976 *Die Kunst der Paradoxie. Sinnsuche und Scheitern bei Samuel Beckett*, München, Willelm Fink Verlag.

1988 *Tragische Handlungsstrukturen. Eine Theorie der Tragödie*, München, Willelm Fink Verlag.

1993 "Paradox in Beckett", in *The Modern Language Review*, vol. 88, nr. 3 (July 1993), pp. 559-580.

BREUER, Rolf-GUNDEL, Harald-HUBER, Werner

1986 *Beckett Criticism in German. A Bibiography*, München, Willelm Fink Verlag.

BRIENZA, Susan D.

1987a "Perilous Journeys on Beckett's Stages: Traveling through Worlds", in Burkman, Katherine H. (ed.), *Myth and Ritual in the Plays of Samuel Beckett*, London and Toronto, Associated University Presses, pp. 28-49.

1987b "Sam No.2: Shepard Plays Beckett with an American Accent", in Friedman, Alan Warren-Rossman, Charles-Sherzer, Dina (eds.), *Beckett Translating/Translating Beckett*, Pennsylvania State University Press, University Park, pp. 181-195.

1987c *Samuel Beckett's New Worlds. Style in Metafiction*, Norman and London, University of Oklahoma Press.

1992 "Krapping Out: Images of Flow and Elimination as Creation in Joyce and Beckett", in Carey, Phyllis-Jewinski, Ed (eds.), *Re: Joyce 'n Beckett*, New York, Fordham University Press, pp. 117-146.

BROER, Lawrence

1987 "Beckett's Heroic Vision: Sounds of Hope, Exclamations of Grief in *Waiting for Godot*", in Hartigan Karelisa V. (ed.), *From the Bard to Broadway*, Lanham-London, University Press of America, pp. 11-19.

BROOK, Peter

1976 "Dire oui à la boue", in Bishop, Tom-Federman, Raymond (eds.), *Samuel Beckett*, "L'Herne", nr. 31, pp. 232-235 (It. Transl. in *Leggere*, Milano, nr. 22, Giugno 1990, pp. 18-20).

BROWN, J. R.

1968 *Modern British Dramatists*, Englewood Cliffs, Prentice Hall.

BRUN, Bernard

1984 "Sur le *Proust* de Beckett", in Rabate, Jean-Michel (ed.), *Beckett avant Beckett: essais sur le jeune Beckett (1930-1945)*, Paris, P.E.N.S., pp. 79-91.

BRUNEL, Pierre

1970 "Auteurs de Samuel Beckett- devanciers, épigones, et hérétiques", in *La Mort de Godot*, Paris, s. e.

BRUNKHORST, Martin-ROHMANN, Gerd-SCHOELL, Konrad

1988 *Beckett und die Literatur der Gegenwart*, Heidelberg, Carl Winter.

BRUZZO, Francois

1991 *Samuel Beckett*, Paris, Henri Veyrier.

BRYDEN, Mary

1991 "A Place Where None", in Fallaize, Elizabeth-Hallmark, Ron-Pickup, Ian (eds.), *Representations of belief. Essays in memory of G. V. Banks*, Birmingham, University of Birmingham, pp. 183-202.

1992a "Figures of Golgotha: Beckett's pinioned people", in Pilling, John-Bryden, Mary (eds.), *The Ideal Core of the Onion*, Reading, The Longdunn Press, pp. 99-135.

1992b "Samuel Beckett and the feminine-in-writing", in AA.VV., *Voices in the Air. French dramatists and the resources of language*, Glasgow, University of Glasgow, pp. 156-170.

1993 *Women in Samuel Beckett's Prose and Drama*, Boston, Barnes & Noble Books.

1995 "Beckett and The Three Dantean Smiles", in *Journal of Beckett Studies*, Florida, vol. 4, nr. 2, pp. 29-33.

1997 "Sounds and Silence: Beckett's Music", in *Samuel Beckett today/aujourd'hui*, Amsterdam, Atlanta, GA, nr. 6, pp. 279-288.

1998 "Beckett and the Sound of Silence", in Bryden, Mary (ed.), *Samuel Beckett and Music*, Oxford, Clarendon Press, pp. 21-46.

BULL, Peter

1967 "An Actor's Recollections", in Cohn, Ruby (ed.), *Casebook on Waiting for Godot*, New York, Grove Press, pp. 39-45.

BURKMAN, Katherine H.

1986 *The Arrival of Godot: Ritual Patterns in Modern Drama*, London and Rutherford, Associated University Presses.

1987 "Myth and Ritual in the Plays of Samuel Beckett: An Introduction", in Burkman, Katherine H. (ed.), *Myth and Ritual in the Plays of Samuel Beckett*, London and Toronto, Associated University Presses, pp. 13-18.

BUSI, Frederick

1980 *The Transformations of Godot. With a foreword by Willie Sypher*, Lexington, Kentucky, The University Press of Kentuky.

BUTLER, Christopher

1980 *After the Wake. An Essay on the Contemporary Avant-Garde*, Oxford, Clarendon Press.

BUTLER, Lance St. John

1984 *Samuel Beckett and the meaning of being: a study in ontological parable*, London, Macmillan.

1993 (ed.), *Critical Thoughts Series: 4. Critical Essays on Samuel Beckett*, England, Scholar Press.

BUTLER, Lance St.John-DAVIS, Robin J.

1988 (eds.) *'Make Sense Who May'. Essays on Samuel Beckett's Later Works*, London, Gerald Smythe.

1990 (eds.), *Rethinking Beckett. A Collection of Critical Essays*, London, Macmillan.

BÜTTNER, Gottfried

1984 *Samuel Beckett's Novel Watt* (Eng. Transl. Joseph Dolan), Philadelphia, Univerity of Pennsylvania Press.

1990 "A New Approach to *Watt*", in Butler, Lance St. John-Davis, Robin J. (eds.), *Rethinking Beckett. A Collection of Critical Essays*, London, Macmillan, pp. 169-180.

CADY, Andrea

1991 (ed.), *Women Teaching French: five papers on language and theory*, Loughborough, European Research Centre.

Cahiers

1963 *Cahiers de la Compagnie Renaud-Barrault. Samuel Beckett*, Paris, Julliard, nr. 44.

1966 *Cahiers de la Compagnie Renaud-Barrault. Ionesco, Beckett, Pinget*, Paris, Gallimard, nr. 53.

1983 *Cahiers de la Compagnie Renaud-Barrault. Duras, Beckett*, Paris, Gallimard, nr. 106.

CALDER, John

1967 (ed.), *Beckett at 60*, London, Calder and Boyars.

1976 "La Concentration de Samuel Beckett", in Bishop, Tom-Federman, Raymond (eds.), *Samuel Beckett*, "L'Herne", nr. 31, pp. 162-165.

1983 *A Samuel Beckett reader*, London, Picador.

CAMBRIA, Mariavita

1997 *Not I: Bodily Dissociation Between 'Insides' and 'Outsides'*, Dublin, Trinity College Dept. of "Theatre and Ireland", 14 April 1997.

CAMPBELL, James

1994 *Paris interzone: Richard Wright, Lolita, Boris Vian and others on the Left Bank, 1946-60*, London, Secker & Warburg.

1995 *Exiled in Paris : Richard Wright, James Baldwin, Samuel beckett, and others on the Left Bank*, New York, Scribner.

CAMPBELL, Julie

1997 "The semantic Krapp in *Krapp's Last Tape*", in *Samuel Beckett today/aujourd'hui*, Amsterdam, Atlanta, GA, nr. 6, pp. 63-71.

CAPONE, Giovanna

1967 *Drammi per voci. Dylan Thomas, Samuel Beckett, Harold Pinter*, Bologna, Patron.

CAPRIOLO, Ettore

1980 "Beckett di stagione", in *Il Patalogo*, Milano, Ubulibri/Electa, nr. 2, pp. 69-71.

CAREY, Phyllis

1987 "The Ritual of Human Techné in *Happy Days*", in Burkman, Katherine H. (ed.), *Myth and Ritual in the Plays of Samuel Beckett*, London and Toronto, Associated University Presses, pp. 144-150.

1992 "Stephen Dedalus, Belacqua Shuah, and Dante's *Pietà*", in Carey, Phyllis-Jewinski, Ed (eds.), *Re: Joyce 'n Beckett*, New York, Fordham University Press, pp. 104-116.

CAREY, Phyllis-JEWINSKI, Ed

1992 (eds.), *Re: Joyce 'n Beckett*, New York, Fordham University Press.

CARLSON, Marvin

1988 *Teorie del teatro. Panorama storico e critico*, Bologna, Il Mulino.

CARTERS, James & Son

s.d. "Catalogue No. 30: Samuel Beckett", London, James Carters & Son Ldt.

CASANOVA, Pascale

1997 *Beckett l'abstracteur. Anatomie d'une révolution littéraire*, Paris, Seuil.

CASCETTA, Annamaria

2000 Il Tragico e L'umorismo. Studio Sulla Drammaturgia Di Samuel Beckett, Le Lettere, Firenze.

CASCINI, Etta

1978 "Gli onori a Brecht e Beckett", in *Sipario*, a. XXXIII, nr. 389, Ottobre 1978, p. 18.

CASE, Sue-Ellen

1967 "Image and Godot", in Cohn, Ruby (ed.), *Casebook on Waiting for Godot*, New York, Grove Press, pp. 155-159.

CASTELLANO, Alberto

1988 "Un silenzio visivo", in *Filmcritica*, Roma, a. XXXIX, nr. 383 (Marzo 1988), pp. 150-158.

CASTELLI, Ferdinando

1977 *I cavalieri del nulla*, Milano, Massimo, pp. 222-252.

CATTANEI, Giovanni

1967a *Beckett*, Firenze, Il Castoro.

1967b "Beckett da Godot a Fin de Partie", in *Teatro e cinema*, Genova, a. I, nr. 1 (Gennaio-Marzo 1967), p. 45.

CAVELL, Stanley

1988 "Ending the Waiting Game: A Reading of Beckett's *Endgame*", in Bloom, Harold (ed.), *Samuel Beckett's Endgame*, New York-New Haven Philadelphia, Chelsea House Publishers, pp. 59-77.

CELATI, Gianni

1986 *Finzioni occidentali*, Torino, Einaudi.

CHABERT, Pierre

1983 "Samuel Beckett: lieu physique, théâtre du corps", in *Cahiers de la Compagnie Renaud-Barrault. Samuel Beckett*, Paris, Julliard, nr. 106, pp. 80-98.

1990a "Présentation", in *Revue d'Estetique*, numéro hors-série (I ed. 1986), pp. 9-21.

1990b "Textes non dramatiques montés au théâtre", in *Revue d'Estetique*, numéro hors-série (I ed. 1986), pp. 463-465.

CHABERT, Pierre-KRALIK, Erika

1990 "Chronologie des principales mises en scène en France", in *Revue d'Estetique*, numéro hors-série (I ed. 1986), p. 448.

CHAIKIN, Joseph

1991 *The Presence of the Actor*, New York, Theatre Communication Group (I ed. 1972).

CHALKER, John

1975 "The satiric shape of *Watt*", in Worth, Katharine (ed.), *Beckett the Shape Changer. A Symposium*, London&Boston, Routledge and Kegan Paul, pp. 19-37.

CHAMBERLAIN, Lori

1987 "'The Same Old Stories': Beckett's Poetics of Translation", in Friedman, Alan Warren-Rossman, Charles-Sherzer, Dina (eds.), *Beckett Translating/Translating Beckett*, Pennsylvania State University Press, University Park, pp. 17-24.

CHAMBERS, Ross

1963 "Beckett, homme des situations-limites", in *Cahiers de la Compagnie Renaud-Barrault. Samuel Beckett*, Paris, Julliard, nr. 44, pp. 37-62.

1965 "Beckett's Brinkmanship", in Esslin, Martin (ed.), *Samuel Beckett: A Collection of Critical Essays*, Englewood Cliffs, N.J., Prentice Hall, pp. 152-168.

1969 "An Approach to *Endgame*", in Chevigny, Bell Gale, *Twentieth Century Interpretations of "Endgame"*, Englewood Cliffs, N.J., Prentice-Hall.

1971 "Destruction des catégories du temps", in Nores, Dominique (ed.), *Les critiques de notre temps et Beckett*, Paris, Garnier, pp. 91-106.

CHAMPIGNY, Robert

1967 "*Waiting for Godot*: Myth, Words, Wait", in Cohn, Ruby (ed.), *Casebook on Waiting for Godot*, New York, Grove Press, pp. 137-144.

CHEMI, Tatiana

1996-1997 "Il Godot dimezzato. La percezione della realtà nei personaggi beckettiani", in *Porta di Massa. Laboratorio Autogestito di Filosofia. PERCEZIONE*, nr. 3, Autunno 1996-Inverno 1997, pp. 60-66.

2006 "Beckett, Pirandello e il metateatro", in Alfano, Giancarlo - Cortellessa, Andrea (eds.), *Beckett in Italia*, Roma, Edisup, pp. 121-138.

CHEVIGNY, Bell Gale

1969 (ed.), *Twentieth Century Interpretations of "Endgame"*, Englewood Cliffs, Prentice-Hall.

CHEVILLOT, Frédérique

1993 *La reouverture du texte. Balzac, Beckett, Robbe-Grillet, Roussel, Aragon, Calvino, Bénabou, Hébert*, Stanford, ANMA.

CHIARI, J.

1965 *Landmarks of Contemporary Drama*, London, Herbert Jenkins.

CHIAROMONTE, Nicola

1976 "Giorni Felici", "Aggiunte e chiose", "La predica di Beckett", in *Scritti sul teatro*, Torino, Einaudi, pp. 177-180.

CHRISTENSEN, Inger

1981 *The meaning of metafiction: a critical study of selected novels by Sterne, Nabokov, Barth and Beckett*, Bergen, Universitetsforlaget.

CHRISTIANSEN, Henning

1989 "Contrappunto a Beckett", in Bistolfi, Marina-Licata, Salvo (eds.), *Primo amore. Beckett-Quartucci*, Erice, La Zattera di Babele, p. 27.

CIORAN, E. M.

1976 "Quelques rencontres", in Bishop, Tom-Federman, Raymond (eds.), *Samuel Beckett*, "Cahier de l'Herne", nr. 31, pp. 101-105.

CITTI, Franco

1989 "Rappresentazione del vagabondo", in Bistolfi, Marina-Licata, Salvo (eds.), *Primo amore. Beckett-Quartucci*, Erice, La Zattera di Babele, p. 21.

CIXOUS, Hélène

1976 "Une passion: l'un peu moins que rien", in Bishop, Tom-Federman, Raymond (eds.), *Samuel Beckett*, "L'Herne", nr. 31, pp. 326-335.

CLAUSIUS, Claudia

1987 "Bad Habits While Waiting for Godot: The Demythification of Ritual", in Burkman, Katherine H. (ed.), *Myth and Ritual in the Plays of Samuel Beckett*, London and Toronto, Associated University Presses, pp. 124-143.

1991 "*Waiting for Godot* and the Chaplinesque Comic Film Gag", in Sclueter, June-Brater, Enoch (eds.), *Approaches to Teaching Beckett's Waiting for Godot*, New York, The Modern Language Association of America, pp. 71-78.

CLAUSSEN, Morten

1995 *Finn en mening den som kan: essays om humaniora, Sterne, Wilde, Kafka og Beckett*, Oslo, Bokvennen.

CLÉMENT, Bruno

1994 *L' Œuvre sans qualités. Rhétorique de Samuel Beckett*, Paris, Éditions du Seuil.

CLEMENTS, Roy

1992 *The Alternative Wisden on Samuel Barclay Beckett (1906-1989)*, s.l., Daripress.

CLURMAN, Harold

[1966] *The naked image. Observations on the modern theatre*, New York-London, Macmillan, s.d.

COCHRAN, Robert

1991 *Samuel Beckett. A Study of the Short Fiction*, New York, Twayne Publishers.

COCKERHAM, Harry

1975 "Bilingual playwright", in Worth, Katharine (ed.), *Beckett the Shape Changer. A Symposium*, London&Boston, Routledge and Kegan Paul, pp. 139-159.

COCO DAVANI, Maria Carmela

1977 *Godot. Il crack del codice*, Palermo, S. F. Flaccovio.

CODIGNOLA, Luciano

1969 *Il teatro della guerra fredda e altre cose*, Urbino, Argalia.

COE, Richard N.

1963 "Le Dieu de Samuel Beckett", in *Cahiers de la Compagnie Renaud-Barrault. Samuel Beckett*, Paris, Julliard, nr. 44, pp. 6-36.

1964 *Beckett*, Edimburgh and London, Oliver and Boyd.

1970 *Che cosa ha veramente detto Beckett*, Roma, Astrolabio.

1971 "L'approche du vide-plénitude", in Nores, Dominique (ed.), *Les critiques de notre temps et Beckett*, Paris, Garnier, pp. 106-117.

1983 "Beckett's English", in Beja, Morris-Gontarski, Stan E.-Astier, Pierre (eds.), *Samuel Beckett. Humanistic Perspectives*, Ohio, Ohio State University Press, pp. 36-57.

COHEN, David

1992 "'For This Relief Much Thanks': Leopold Bloom and Beckett's Use of Allusions", in Carey, Phyllis-Jewinski, Ed (eds.), *Re: Joyce 'n Beckett*, New York, Fordham University Press, pp. 43-49.

COHN, Ruby

1962 *Samuel Beckett: the Comic Gamut*, New Brunswick, Rutger University Press.

1965 "Philosophical Fragments in the Works of Samuel Beckett", in Esslin, Martin (ed.), *Samuel Beckett: A Collection of Critical Essays*, Englewood Cliffs, N.J., Prentice Hall, pp. 169-177.

1967 (ed.), *Casebook on Waiting for Godot*, New York, Grove Press.

1969 "Endgame", in Chevigny, Bell Gale, *Twentieth Century Interpretations of "Endgame"*, Englewood Cliffs, Prentice-Hall, pp. 40-52.

1973 *Back to Beckett*, Princeton, P.U.P.

1975 (ed.), *Samuel Beckett: A Collection of Criticism*, New York, McGraw-Hill Book Company.

1976 "«Watt» à la lumière du «Château»", in Bishop, Tom-Federman, Raymond (eds.), *Samuel Beckett*, "Cahier de l'Herne", nr. 31, pp. 306-317.

1980 *Just Play: Beckett's Theatre*, Princeton, P.U.P.

1982 *Contemporary dramatists*, New York, St. Martin's.

1983 "Beckett's Theater Resonance", in Beja, Morris-Gontarski, Stan E.-Astier, Pierre (eds.), *Samuel Beckett. Humanistic Perspectives*, Ohio, Ohio State University Press, pp. 3-15.

1986 "Growing (Up?) with Godot", in Brater, Enoch (ed.), *Beckett at 80/Beckett in Context*, New York, Oxford University Press, pp. 13-24.

1987a "Inexhaustibile Alan", in Friedman, Alan Warren-Rossman, Charles-Sherzer, Dina (eds.), *Beckett Translating/Translating Beckett*, Pennsylvania State University Press, University Park, pp. 227-232.

1987b "Mabou Mines Translation of Beckett", in Friedman, Alan Warren-Rossman, Charles-Sherzer, Dina (eds.), *Beckett Translating/Translating Beckett*, Pennsylvania State University Press, University Park, pp. 174-180.

1987c *Samuel Beckett's "Waiting for Godot" a casebook*, London, Macmillan.

1987d "Waiting", in Bloom, Harold (ed.), *Samuel Beckett's Waiting for Godot*, New York-New Haven Philadelphia, Chelsea House Publishers, pp. 41-51.

1990a "Animateurs de Beckett: Blin et Schneider", in *Revue d'Estetique*, numéro hors-série (I ed. 1986), pp. 189-194.

1990b "Mises en scène de Samuel Beckett", in *Revue d'Estetique*, numéro hors-série (I ed. 1986), pp. 443-444.

COLLERAN, Jeanne-MORONEY, Mayclaire

1993 "No Safe Spaces: Private and Public Violability in Shakespeare's *Measure for Measure* and Beckett's *Happy Days*", in Drew, Anne Marie (ed.), *Past Crimson, Past Woe. The Shakespeare-Beckett Connection*, New York & London, Garland, pp. 41-66.

COLOMBA, Sergio

1987 "Cartoline dal Purgatorio", in *Teatro festival*, nr. 8, Luglio-Agosto 1987, pp. 42-45.

1997 (ed.), *Le ceneri della commedia. Il teatro di Samuel Beckett*, Roma, Bulzoni.

CONLEY, Tom

1985 *Samuel Beckett: color, letter and line*, Cleveland, Visible Language.

CONNOR, Steven

1988 *Samuel Beckett: Repetition, Theory and Text*, New York and Oxford, Basil Blackwell.

1990 "'What? Where?' Presence and Repetition in Beckett's Theatre", in Butler, Lance St. John-Davis, Robin J. (eds.), *Rethinking Beckett. A Collection of Critical Essays*, London, Macmillan, pp. 1-19.

1992a "Authorship, Authority, and Self Reference in Joyce and Beckett", in Carey, Phyllis-Jewinski, Ed (eds.), *Re: Joyce 'n Beckett*, New York, Fordham University Press, pp. 147-159.

1992b "Between theatre and theory: *Long observation of the Ray*", in Pilling, John-Bryden, Mary (eds.), *The Ideal Core of the Onion*, Reading, The Longdunn Press, pp. 99-135.

1992c (ed.), *"Waiting for Godot" and "Endgame". New Casebooks*, London, Macmillan.

COOKE, Virginia

1985 (ed.), *Beckett on File*, London, Methuen.

COPELAND, Hannah C.

1975 *Art and the artist in the works of Samuel Beckett*, Netherlands, The Hague.

CORMIER, Ramona-PALLISTER, Janis L.

1979 *Waiting for Death. The Philosophical Significance of Beckett's En attendant Godot*, Alabama, The University of Alabama Press.

CORSARO, Antonio

1972 *Su Beckett*, Palermo, Libreria Gino.

CORTELLESSA, Andrea

1998 "Non mi basti più, Joyce", in *Alias*, nr. 21, 14 Novembre 1998, p. 22.

CORVIN, Michel

1969 *Le Théâtre Nouveau en France*, Paris, Presses Universitaires de France.

COSTA, Mario

1991 "Dalla scena al broadcasting: il caso di Samuel Beckett", in AA.VV., *Prima e dopo il teatro. Atti del convegno* (Fisciano, 27-28-29 Marzo 1990), ed. Rosa Meccia, s.l., Edizioni L'obliquo, pp. 111-118.

COSTAZ, Gilles

1990 "*Emmanuel Lê Quang Huy*, Beckett par Timar", in *Revue d'Estetique*, numéro hors-série (I ed. 1986), pp. 209-210.

COUISENEAU, Thomas

1990 *Waiting for Godot. Form in Movement*, Boston, Twayne.

1993 "*Watt*: Language as Interdicion and Consolation", in Gontarski, Stan E. (ed.), *The Beckett Studies Reader*, Florida, University Press of Florida, pp. 64-77.

COWELL, R.

1967 *Twelve Modern Dramatists*, Oxford, Perganon Press.

CRONIN, Anthony

1997 *Samuel Beckett: the last modernist*, London, HarperCollins (I ed. 1996).

CROUSSY, Guy

1971 *Beckett*, Paris, Hachette.

CRUICKSHANK, John

1962 (ed.), *The Novelist as Philosopher: Studies in French Fiction. 1935-1960*, London, Oxford University Press.

CULOTTA ANDONIANS, Cathleen

1989 *Samuel Beckett a reference guide*, Boston, G. K. Hall & Co.

CUNARD, Nancy

1969 *These Were the Hours: Memories of my Hours Press, Reanville and Paris, 1928-1931*, Carbondale, Southern Illinois Press.

CURRIE, W.T.

1978 *Brodie's Notes on Samuel Beckett's "Waiting for Godot"*, London, Pan Book's.

DAIKEN, Melanie

1998 "Working with Beckett Texts", in Bryden, Mary (ed.), *Samuel Beckett and Music*, Oxford, Clarendon Press, pp. 249-256.

D'ARCY, Margaretta

1980 "Irlanda", in Attisani, Antonio (ed.), *Enciclopedia del teatro del '900*, Milano, Feltrinelli, pp. 63-66.

DARZACQ, Dominique

1985 *Du théâtre comme il n'etait pas à prevoir mais comme il est à esperer*, Paris, Solin.

DAUVIGNAUD, Jean-LAGOUTTE, Jean

1974 "Beckett: ça est là...", in *Le Théâtre Contemporain. Culture et contre-culture*, Paris, Larousse, pp. 59-65.

DAVIES, Paul

1992 "*Stirring Still*: the disembodiment of Western tradition", in Pilling, John-Bryden, Mary (eds.), *The Ideal Core of the Onion*, Reading, The Longdunn Press, pp. 99-135.

1994a *The Ideal Real. Beckett's Fiction and Imagination*, London and Toronto, Associated University Presses.

1994b "Three novels and four *nouvelles*: giving up the ghost be born at last", in Pilling, John (ed.), *The Cambridge Companion to Beckett*, Cambridge, Cambridge University Press, pp. 43-66.

DAVIS, Anthony

1984 *No Symbols Where None Intended: Samuel Beckett Novels*, Horfield, Belston Night Works.

DAVIS, Reid

1994 "Fear and Laughing", in *Theater Week*, July 25-31, pp. 22-24.

DAVIS, Robin John

1979 *Samuel Beckett: checklist and index of his published works, 1967-1976*, Stirling, The Compiler.

DEARLOVE, Judith E.

1982 *Accomodating the Chaos: Samuel Beckett's Nonrelational Art*, Durhamm, Duke University Press.

1983 "'Syntax Upended in Opposite Corners': Alterations in Beckett's Linguistic Theories", in Beja, Morris-Gontarski, Stan E.-Astier, Pierre (eds.), *Samuel Beckett. Humanistic Perspectives*, Ohio, Ohio State University Press, pp. 122-128.

DE BOISDEFFRE, Pierre

1962 *Où va le roman?*, Paris, del DUCA.

de GAUDEMAR, Antoine

1989 "L'écrivain le plus bilingue du siècle", in *Liberation*, Paris, mercredi 27 Decembre 1989.

DELCAMPE, Armand

1990 "En attendant Godot... qu'on nous donne des poètes et tout sera sauvé", in *Revue d'Estetique*, numéro hors-série (I ed. 1986), pp. 217-219.

DELEUZE, Gilles

1983 *L'immagine-movimento*, Milano, Ubulibri.

1990 "Le plus grand film irlandais", in *Revue d'Estetique*, numéro hors-série (I ed. 1986), pp. 381-382.

DELORME-LOUISE, Marie-Nöelle

1990 "Comment dire, comment voir *Mal vu, mal dit*", in *Revue d'Estetique*, numéro hors-série (I ed. 1986), pp. 89-92.

DELYE, Huguette

1960 *Samuel Beckett ou la Philosophie de l'absurde*, Aix-en-Provence, Annales de la Faculté des Lettres.

DE MAGNY, Olivier

1963 "Samuel Beckett et la farce métaphisique", in *Cahiers Renaud-Barrault*, Paris, Julliard, Octobre 1963, pp. 67-72.

1971 "Nulle part- Personne", in Nores, Dominique (ed.), *Les critiques de notre temps et Beckett*, Paris, Garnier, pp. 87-91.

DETTMAR, Kevin J. H.

1990 "The Figure in Beckett's Carpet: *Molloy* and the Assault on Metaphor", in Butler, Lance St. John-Davis, Robin J. (eds.), *Rethinking Beckett. A Collection of Critical Essays*, London, Macmillan, pp. 68-88.

DEVINE, George

1967 "Last Tribute", in Calder, John (ed.), *Beckett at 60*, London, Calder and Boyars, p. 99.

D'HAEN, Theo-BERTENS, Hans

1993 (eds.), *British postmodern fiction*, Amsterdam, Rodopi.

DIAMOND, Elin

1975 "'what?... who?... no!... she!'. The Fictionalizers in Beckett's Plays", in Cohn, Ruby (ed.), *Samuel Beckett: A Collection of Criticism*, New York, McGraw-Hill Book Company, pp. 111-119.

DIBATTISTA, Maria

1991 *First Love. The Affections of Modern Fiction*, Chicago and London, The University of Chicago Press.

DIDIER-WEILL, Alain

1990 "Beckett; la deuxième mort", in *Revue d'Estetique*, numéro hors-série (I ed. 1986), pp. 147-148.

DI PIERRO, John C.

1981 *Structures in Beckett's Watt*, York, French Literature Publications Company.

DOBREZ, L. A. C.

1986 *The Existential and its Exist: Literary and Philosophical Perspectives on the Work of Beckett, Ionesco, Genet and Pinter*, London, Athlone.

DODSWORTH, Martin

1975 "*Film* and the religion of art", in Worth, Katharine (ed.), *Beckett the Shape Changer. A Symposium*, London&Boston, Routledge and Kegan Paul, pp. 161-182.

DOHERTY, Francis

1971 *Samuel Beckett*, London, Hutchinson University Library.

DOLL, Mary A.

1987 "Rites of Story: The Old Man ay Play", in Burkman, Katherine H. (ed.), *Myth and Ritual in the Plays of Samuel Beckett*, London and Toronto, Associated University Presses, pp. 73-85.

1988 *Beckett and Myth. An Archetypal Approach*, Syracuse, Syracuse University Press.

DOMENACH, Jean-Marie

1971 "L'Infra-Tragedie", in Nores, Dominique (ed.), *Les critiques de notre temps et Beckett*, Paris, Garnier, pp. 59-73.

DORT, Bernard

1967 *Teatro pubblico 1953-1966*, Padova, Marsilio.

1971 "La recharge en significations symboliques", in Nores, Dominique (ed.), *Les critiques de notre temps et Beckett*, Paris, Garnier, pp. 140-142.

1990 "L'acteur de Beckett: davantage de jeu", in *Reuve d'Estétique*, numero hors-série, pp. 227-234, now in Samuel Beckett, *Teatro completo*, Torino-Parigi, Einaudi Gallimard, 1994, pp. 759-771.

DOUGLAS, Stan

(ed.), *Samuel Beckett: teleplays*, Vancouver, The Gallery.

DRAKAKIS, John

1981 (ed.), *British Radio Drama*, Cambridge, Cambridge University Press.

DRECHSLER, Ute

1988 *Die "absurde farce" bei Beckett, Pinter und Ionesco*, Tübingen, Gunter Narr Verlag.

DREW, Anne Marie

1993 "No Deposit, No Return: The Cap and Bells in *Hamlet* and *Endgame*", in Drew, Anne Marie (ed.), *Past Crimson, Past Woe. The Shakespeare-Beckett Connection*, New York & London, Garland, pp. 79-90.

DREYESSE, Ursula

1973 (ed.), *Materialien zu Samuel Becketts 'Warten auf Godot'*, Frankfurt am Main, Suhrkamp Verlag.

DREYFUS, Dina

1971 "Les renouncements du roman", in Nores, Dominique (ed.), *Les critiques de notre temps et Beckett*, Paris, Garnier, pp. 73-79.

DUCKWORTH, Colin

1967 "The Making of *Godot*", in Cohn, Ruby (ed.), *Casebook on Waiting for Godot*, New York, Grove Press, pp. 89-101.

1972 *Angels of Darkness. Dramatic Effect in Beckett and Ionesco*, London, George Allen & Unwin.

1994 "Directing Beckett 'Down Under'", in Oppenheimer, Lois, *Directing Beckett*, Michigan, The University of Michigan Press, pp. 220-238.

DUKORE, Bernard F.

1973 "'Krapp's Last Tape' as Tragicomedy", in *Modern Drama*, vol. XV, March 1973, pp. 352-354.

DUMUR, Guy

1990 "La première fois que j'ai attendu Godot", in *Revue d'Estetique*, numéro hors-série (I ed. 1986), pp. 197-199.

DURBAND, Alan

1962 *Contemporary English*, London, Hutchinson Educational.

DUROZOI, Gérard

1972 *Samuel Beckett*, Paris, Bordas.

DUTHUIT, Georges

1965 (and Samuel Beckett), "Three Dialogues", in Esslin, Martin (ed.), *Samuel Beckett: A Collection of Critical Essays*, Englewood Cliffs, N.J., Prentice Hall, pp. 16-22.

DUTTON, Richard

1986 *Modern British Tragicomedy: Beckett, Pinter, Stoppard, Albee and Storey*, Brighton, Harvester.

DUX, Pierre

1990 "De la musique avant toute chose", in *Revue d'Estetique*, numéro hors-série (I ed. 1986), pp. 271-273.

EASTHOPE, Anthony

1968 "Hamm, Clov and dramatic method in 'Endgame'", in *Modern Drama*, vol. X, nr. 4 (February 1968), pp. 424-433, now in Chevigny, Bell Gale, *Twentieth Century Interpretations of "Endgame"*, Englewood Cliffs, Prentice-Hall, 1969, pp. 61-70.

EBERT, Harald

1974 *Samuel Becketts Dramaturgie der Ungewissheit*, Wien, Wihlelm Braumiller.

EDWARDS, Michael

1996 *Éloge de l'attente. T. S. Eliot et Samuel Beckett*, Paris, Belin.

EGEBAK, Niels

1973 *L'écriture de Samuel Beckett. Contribution à l'analyse sémiotique de textes littéraires contemporains*, København, Akademisk Forlag.

EHRARD, Peter

1976 *Anatomie de Samuel Beckett*, Bâle et Stuttgard, Birkhäuser Verlag.

ELAM, Keir

1986 "'Not I': Beckett's mouth and ars(e) rethorica", in Brater, Enoch (ed.), *Beckett at 80/Beckett in Context*, New York, Oxford University Press.

1994 "Dead heads: damnation-narration in the 'dramaticules'", in Pilling, John (ed.), *The Cambridge Companion to Beckett*, Cambridge, Cambridge University Press, pp. 145-166.

ELBORN, Geoffrey

1977 (ed.), *Hand and Eye. An Anthology for Sachewell Sitwell*, Edimburgh, The Tragara Press.

ELIOPULOS, James

1975 *Samuel Beckett's Dramatic Language*, Paris, The Hague.

ELLMAN, Richard

1986 *Samuel Beckett. Nayman of Noland*, Washington, Library of Congress.

1989 *Quattro dublinesi (Oscar Wilde, William Butler Yeats, James Joyce, Samuel Beckett)*, Milano, Leonardo (I ed. 1982).

ELOVAARA, Raili

1976 *The problem of identity in Samuel Beckett's prose. An approach from philosophies of existence*, Helsinki, Suomalainen Tiedeakatemia.

ENGEL, David

1985 (et alii), *The McGraw-Hill guide to world literature*, vol. II (Moliere to Beckett), New York, McGraw-Hill, 2 voll.

ENGERHARDT, Hartmut-METTLER, Dieter

1976 *Materialien zu Samuel Becketts Romanen 'Molloy', 'Malone stirbt', 'Der Namenlose'*, Frankfurt am Main, Suhrkamp Verlag.

ESSLIN, Martin

1961 *The Theatre of the Absurd*, New York, Anchor Books.

1962 "Samuel Beckett", in Cruickshank, John (ed.), *The Novelist as Philosopher: Studies in French Fiction. 1935-1960*, London, Oxford University Press, pp. 128-149.

1963 "Godot and His Children: The Theatre of Samuel Beckett and Harold Pinter", in Armstrong, William A. (ed.), *Experimental Drama*, London G. Bell, pp. 128-146.

1965 (ed.), *Samuel Beckett: A Collection of Critical Essays*, Englewood Cliffs, N.J., Prentice Hall.

1967a "Godot at San Quentin", in Cohn, Ruby (ed.), *Casebook on Waiting for Godot*, New York, Grove Press, pp. 83-89.

1967b "Samuel Beckett´s poems", in Calder, John (ed.), *Beckett at 60*, London, Calder and Boyars, pp. 55-60.

1969 "Samuel Beckett: The Search for the Self", in Chevigny, Bell Gale (ed.), *Twentieth Century Interpretations of "Endgame"*, Englewood Cliffs, Prentice-Hall, pp. 22-32.

1971   "Le bilinguisme", in Nores, Dominique (ed.), *Les critiques de notre temps et Beckett*, Paris, Garnier, pp. 151-152.

1975   *Il teatro dell'assurdo* (It. Transl. R. De Baggis e M. Trasatti), Roma, Abete (I ed. 1961).

1980   *Mediations: Essays on Brecht, Beckett, and the Media*, Baton Rouge, Louisiana State University Press.

1986a "Dionysos' Dianoetic Laugh", in Calder, John (ed.), *As No Other Dare Fail*, London, Calder, pp. 15-23, now in Samuel Beckett, *Teatro completo*, Torino-Parigi, Einaudi Gallimard, 1994, pp. 736-743.

1986b "Samuel Beckett-Infinity, Eternity", in Brater, Enoch (ed.*)*, *Beckett at 80/Beckett in Context*, New York, Oxford University Press, pp. 110-123.

1987a "A Poertry of Moving Images", in Friedman, Alan Warren-Rossman, Charles-Sherzer, Dina (eds.), *Beckett Translating/Translating Beckett*, Pennsylvania State University Press, University Park, pp. 65-76.

1987b "The Search of the Self", in Bloom, Harold (ed.), *Samuel Beckett's Waiting for Godot*, New York-New Haven Philadelphia, Chelsea House Publishers, pp. 23-40.

1990   "Une poésie d'images mouvantes", in *Revue d'Estetique*, numéro hors-série (I ed. 1986), pp. 391-403.

1992   "Beckett's German Context", in Brater, Enoch (ed.), *The Theatrical Gamut. Notes for a post-beckettian stage*, University of Michigan Press, pp. 41-50.

FARROW, Anthony

1991   *Early Beckett: Art and Allusion in More Pricks Than Kicks and Murphy*, New York, The Whitston Publishing Company Troy.

FASANO, Giancarlo

1962   "Samuel Beckett", in *Belfagor*, 31 Luglio 1962, p. 432.

1982   "Il caso Samuel Beckett", in *Studi di letteratura francese*, Firenze, Olschki, pp. 45-61

1983   "La scrittura come diversione", in AA.VV., *Scritti in onore di Giovanni Macchia*, Milano, Mondadori, pp. 320-335.

FEDERMAN, Raymond

1965   *Journey to Chaos: Samuel Beckett's Early Fiction*, Berkeley and Los Angeles, University of California Press.

1976a "L'Autre Pays", in Bishop, Tom-Federman, Raymond (eds.), *Samuel Beckett*, "L'Herne", nr. 31, pp. 155-156.

1976b "Le Paradoxe du menteur", in Bishop, Tom-Federman, Raymond (eds.), *Samuel Beckett*, "L'Herne", nr. 31, pp. 183-192.

1987 "The Writer as Self-Translator", in Friedman, Alan Warren-Rossman, Charles-Sherzer, Dina (eds.), *Beckett Translating/Translating Beckett*, Pennsylvania State University Press, University Park, pp. 7-16.

FEDERMAN, Raymond-FLETCHER, John

1970 *Samuel Beckett: His Works and His Critics (An Essay in Bibliography, 1929-1967)*, Berkeley and Los Angeles, University of California Press.

FEDERMAN, Raymond-GRAVER, Lawrence

1979 (eds.), *Samuel Beckett. The Critical Heritage*, London, Routledge & Kegan.

FEHSENFELD, Martha

1987 "From the Perspective of an Actress/Critic: Ritual Patterns in Beckett's *Happy Days*", in Burkman, Katherine H. (ed.), *Myth and Ritual in the Plays of Samuel Beckett*, London and Toronto, Associated University Presses, pp. 50-55.

1990a "Beckett aux U.S.A.: chronologie des mises en scène d'Alan Schneider (1956-1984)", in *Revue d'Estetique*, numéro hors-série (I ed. 1986), pp. 451-453.

1990b "De la boîte herménetique au regard implacable", in *Revue d'Estetique*, numéro hors-série (I ed. 1986), pp. 363-370.

FERRANTE, Luigi

1972 *Beckett, la vita il pensiero i testi esemplari*, Milano, Edizioni Accademia.

FINK, Guido

1979 "Ipotesi per *Not I*", in *Paragone*, Febbraio 1979, pp. 21-33.

FINNEY, Brian H.

1972 *'Since how it is'. A study of Samuel Beckett's later fiction*, London, Covent Garden Press.

1975 "*Assumption* to *Lessness*: Beckett's shorter fiction", in Worth, Katharine (ed.), *Beckett the Shape Changer. A Symposium*, London & Boston, Routledge and Kegan Paul, pp. 61-83.

FIORE, Enrico

1996 "Beckett, una risata d'infelicità sul palcoscenico dell'impotenza", in *Il Mattino*, 11 Gennaio 1996.

FISCHER-SEIDEL, Therese

1986 *Mythenparodie im modernen englischen und amerikanischen Drama: Tradition und Kommunikation bei Tennessee Williams, Edward Albee, Samuel Beckett und Harold Pinter*, Heidelberg, Carl Winter.

FITCH, Brian T.

1977 *Dimensions, structures et textualité dans la trilogie romanesque de Beckett*, Paris, Lettres Modernes Minard.

1987 "The Relationship Between *Compagnie* and *Company*: One Work, Two Texts, Two Fictive Universes", in Friedman, Alan Warren-Rossman, Charles-Sherzer, Dina (eds.), *Beckett Translating/ Translating Beckett*, Pennsylvania State University Press, University Park, pp. 25-35.

1988 *Beckett and Babel: An Investigation into the Status of the Bilingual Work*, Toronto, University of Toronto Press.

1991 *Reflections in the mind's eye: reference and its problematization in twentieth-century French fiction*, Toronto, University of Toronto Press.

FITZ-SIMON, Christopher

"Conservatives and shape-changers", in *The Irish Theatre*, London, Thames and Hudson, pp. 184-201.

FLETCHER, Beryl S.

1978 (et al.), *A Student's Guide to the Plays of Samuel Beckett*, London-Boston, Faber & Faber.

FLETCHER, John

1967 "In search of Beckett", in Calder, John (ed.), *Beckett at 60*, London, Calder and Boyars, pp. 29-33.

1962 "Samuel Beckett et Jonathan Swift: vers une étude comparée", in *Annales publiées par la Faculté des Lettres de Toulouse*, vol. 1, pp. 81-117.

1964 *The Novels of Samuel Beckett*, London, Chatto and Windus.

1965 "The Private Pain and the Whey of Words: a Survey of Beckett's Verse", in Esslin, Martin (ed.), *Samuel Beckett: A Collection of Critical Essays*, Englewood Cliffs, N.J., Prentice Hall, pp. 23-32.

1967a *Samuel Beckett's Art*, London, Chatto and Windus.

1967b "The First Director: Roger Blin", in Cohn, Ruby (ed.), *Casebook on Waiting for Godot*, New York, Grove Press, pp. 21-27.

1971 (ed.), *Waiting for Godot*, London, Faber & Faber.

1975 "Beckett as a Poet", in Cohn, Ruby (ed.), *Samuel Beckett: A Collection of Criticism*, New York, McGraw-Hill Book Company, pp. 41-50.

1976 "Ecrivain bilingue", in Bishop, Tom-Federman, Raymond (eds.), *Samuel Beckett*, "L'Herne", nr. 31, pp. 212-218.

1987 "Bailing Out of Silence", in Bloom, Harold (ed.), *Samuel Beckett's Waiting for Godot*, New York-New Haven Philadelphia, Chelsea House Publishers, pp. 11-22.

1992 "Joyce, Beckett, and the Short Story in Ireland", in Carey, Phyllis-Jewinski, Ed (eds.), *Re: Joyce 'n Beckett*, New York, Fordham University Press, pp. 20-30.

FLETCHER, John-SPURLING, John

1972a   *Beckett the Playwright*, New York, Hill and Wang.

1972b   *Samuel Beckett: A Study of his Plays*, London, Mehien.

FOSTER, Dennis A.

1987   *Confessions and Complicity in Narrative*, Cambridge, Cambridge University Press.

FOSTER, Paul

1980   *The beckettian impasse: a zen study of ontological dilemma in the novels of Samuel Beckett*, Erlangung der Doktorwürde der Neuphilologischen Fakultät, Universität Heidelberg.

1989   *Beckett and Zen: A Study of Dilemma in the Novels of Samuel Beckett*, London, Wisdom Publications.

FOSTER, Verna A.

1993   "'A sad tale's best for winter': Storytelling and Tragicomedy in the Late Plays of Shakespeare and Beckett", in Drew, Anne Marie (ed.), *Past Crimson, Past Woe. The Shakespeare-Beckett Connection*, New York & London, Garland, pp. 15-29.

FOUCRE, Michèle

1970   *Le geste et la parole dans le théâtre de Samuel Beckett*, Paris, Nizet.

FOURNIER, Edith

1971   "Pour que le verbe crée le monde", in Nores, Dominique (ed.), *Les critiques de notre temps et Beckett*, Paris, Garnier, pp. 170-174.

1990a   "L'art de l'évidence", in *Revue d'Estetique*, numéro hors-série (I ed. 1986), pp. 23-24.

1990b   "Liste chronologique des œuvres", in *Revue d'Estetique*, numéro hors-série (I ed. 1986), pp. 416-423.

1990c   "Marcel Mihalovici and Samuel Beckett: Musicians of Return'", in *Revue d'Estetique*, numéro hors-série (I ed. 1986), pp. 243-249 [now in Bryden, Mary (ed.), *Samuel Beckett and Music*, Oxford, Clarendon Press, 1998, pp. 131-139].

FOWLIE, Wallace

1961   *Dionysus in Paris. A Guide to Contemporary French Theatre*, London, Victor Gollancz.

FRANKEL, Margherita S.

1976   "Beckett e Proust: le triomphe de la parole", in Bishop, Tom-Federman, Raymond (eds.), *Samuel Beckett*, "L'Herne", nr. 31, pp. 281-294.

FRANZERO, C. M.

1964   "Il messaggio del pessimismo e della disperazione", in *Il dramma*, Roma, a. 40, nr. 330-331 (Marzo-Aprile 1964), pp. 91-93.

FRASCA, Gabriele

1985   "Dante in Beckett", in *Esperienze Letterarie*, a. X, nr. 4, pp. 37-55.

1988   *Cascando. Tre studi su Samuel Beckett*, Napoli, Liguori.

1989-1990   "La tegola dal cielo", in *Il piccolo Hans*, a. XVII, nr. 64, inverno 1989-1990, pp. 206-220.

1990-1991   "Le voci della radio", in *Il piccolo Hans*, a. XVIII, nr. 68, inverno 1990-1991, pp. 105-136.

1998   "Introduzione", in Samuel Beckett, *Watt* (It. Transl. and ed. Gabriele Frasca), Torino, Einaudi, pp. VII-LIV.

FRASER, G. S.

1967   "*Waiting for Godot*", in Cohn, Ruby (ed.), *Casebook on Waiting for Godot*, New York, Grove Press, pp. 133-137.

FRIEDMAN, Alan Warren-ROSSMAN, Charles-SHERZER, Dina

1987   (eds.), *Beckett Translating/Translating Beckett*, Pennsylvania State University Press, University Park.

FRIEDMAN, Melvin J.

1964a   (ed.), "Configuration critique de Samuel Beckett", in *Revue des Lettres Modernes*, nr. 100.

1964b   "Les Romans de Samuel Beckett et la Tradition du Grotesque", in *Revue des Lettres Modernes*, vol. I, nr. 94-99, pp. 31-50.

1970   (ed.), *Samuel Beckett Now*, Chicago, The University of Chicago Press.

1992   "Richard Ellman's *James Joyce* and Deidre Bair's *Samuel Beckett: A Biography*: The Triumphs and Trials of Literary Biography", in Carey, Phyllis-Jewinski, Ed (eds.), *Re: Joyce 'n Beckett*, New York, Fordham University Press, pp. 1-12.

FROST, Everett C.

1994   "A 'Fresh Go' for the Skull: Directing *All That Fall*, Smuel Beckett's Play for Radio", in Oppenheimer, Lois, *Directing Beckett*, Michigan, The University of Michigan Press, pp. 186-219.

1998   "The Note Man on the Word Man: Morton Feldman on Composing the Music for Samuel Beckett's *Words and Music* in *The Beckett Festival of Radio Plays*", in Bryden, Mary (ed.), *Samuel Beckett and Music*, Oxford, Clarendon Press, pp. 47-55.

FUSELLA, Patrizia

1995   *L'impossibilità di non essere. La negazione della mimesi e del soggetto in Not I di S. Beckett*, Napoli, Istituto Universitario Orientale.

FUSINI, Nadia

1990   "La macchia nel silenzio", in *Leggere*, Milano, nr. 22 (Giugno 1990), pp. 3-15.

1994   *B e B. Beckett e Bacon*, Milano, Garzanti.

GAGLIARDO, Francesca

1990   "*Happy Days*: Figure Matematiche nella Ripetizione", in *Il confronto letterario*, a. VII, nr. 14, Novembre 1990, pp. 329-334.

1992 "Processo catastrofico: la ribellione di Clov in *Endgame* di Samuel Beckett nella ricezione pragmatica del testo teatrale", in *Il confronto letterario*, a. IX, nr. 17, Maggio 1992, pp. 223-236.

GANS, Eric

1987 "Beckett and the Problem of Modern Culture", in Bloom, Harold (ed.), *Samuel Beckett's Waiting for Godot*, New York-New Haven Philadelphia, Chelsea House Publishers, pp. 95-110.

GARCIA LANDA, José Angel

1992 *Samuel Beckett y la narración reflexiva*, Zaragoza, Universidad de Zaragoza.

GARFORTH, Julian A.

1994 "George Tabori's Bair Essentials. A Perspective on Beckett Staging in Germany", in *Forum Modernes Theater*, Tübingen, Gunter Narr Verlag, vol. 9/1, pp. 59-75.

GARNER, Stanton B. jr.

1989 *The Absent Voice. Narrative Comprehension in the Theater*, Urbana and Chicago, University of Illinois Press.

GARSDAL, Lise

1998 "Og så til noget helt andet", in *Politiken*, København, 11 April 1998, p. 1.

GASCOIGNE, Bamber

1962 *Twentieth-Century Drama*, London, Hutchinson University Library.

GASKELL, Ronald

1972 "Beckett 'Endgame'", in *Drama and reality: the European theatre since Ibsen*, London, Routledge & Kegan Paul, pp. 147-154.

GASSMAN, Vittorio

1986 "Il mio Beckett", in *L'Espresso*, 13 Aprile 1986, p. 116.

GATTI, Guido

1992 *Il dramma come discorso etico: una lettura etica dei drammi di Ibsen, Ionesco, Miller, Camus, Betti, Durrenmat, Cechov, O'Neill, Beckett*, s. l., Leumann.

GENET, Jacqueline

1984 "Beckett et l'écriture des astres (*Murphy*)", in Rabate, Jean-Michel (ed.), *Beckett avant Beckett: essais sur le jeune Beckett (1930-1945)*, Paris, P.E.N.S., pp. 121-133.

GENETTI, Stefano

1992 *Les figures du temps dans l'oeuvre de Samuel Beckett*, s. l., Schena.

GESSANI, Alberto

1985 "L'ombra di Descartes", in *Il Pensiero*, vol. XXVI, Luglio-Dicembre 1985, pp. 119-135.

GESSNER, Niklaus

1957   *Die Unzulänglichkeit der Sprache*, Zürich, Juris Verlag.

GIBSON, Andrew

1990   *Reading narrative discourse: studies in the novel from Cervantes to Beckett*, London, Macmillan.

GIDAL, Peter

1986   *Understanding Beckett: A Study of Monologue and Gesture in the Works of Samuel Beckett*, New York, St. Martin's Press.

GILLESPIE, Michael Patrick

1992   "Textually Unhinibited: the Playfulness of Joyce and Beckett", in Carey, Phillys-Jewinski, Ed (eds.), *Re:Joyce'n Beckett*, New York, Fordham University Press, pp. 83-103.

GILLIAT, Penelope

1990   *To Wit, Skin and Bones of Comedy*, New York, Charles Scribner's Son.

GILMAN, Richard

1987a *The making of modern drama: a study of Bychner, Ibsen, Strindberg, Chekhov, Pirandello, Brecht, Beckett*, New York, Da Capo Press.

1987b "The Waiting Since", in Bloom, Harold (ed.), *Samuel Beckett's Waiting for Godot*, New York-New Haven Philadelphia, Chelsea House Publishers, pp. 67-78.

1988   "Beckett/79", in Bloom, Harold (ed.), *Samuel Beckett's Endgame*, New York-New Haven Philadelphia, Chelsea House Publishers, pp. 79-86.

GLASS, Philip

1987   *Music by Philip Glass*, New York, Harper and Row Publishers.

1990   "L'impossible identification", in *Revue d'Estetique*, numéro hors-série (I ed. 1986), pp. 265-266.

1998   "Interview", in Bryden, Mary (ed.), *Samuel Beckett and Music*, Oxford, Clarendon Press, pp. 191-194.

GLENAVY, Beatrice

1964   *Today we will only gossip*, London, Constable.

GLUCK REICH, Barbara

1979   *Beckett and Joyce. Friendship and Fiction*, Lewisburg-London, Associated University Presses.

GODIN, Georges-LA CHANCE, Michaël

1994   *Beckett. Entre le refus de l'art et le parcours mystique*, s. l., Le Castor Astral.

Godot

1992   "Godot, Beckett, Brassarel et les autres", in *Jeu. Cahiers de Théâtre*, Montréal.

GOLD, Alison Leslie

1991   *The Clarvoyant. A Novel of the Imaginated Life of Lucia Joyce*, Edimburgh, Mainstream.

GOLD, Hebert

1990 *Travels in San Francisco*, New York, Arcade.

GOLDMAN, Michael

1986 "Vitality and Dearness in Beckett's Plays", in Brater, Enoch (ed.), *Beckett at 80/Beckett in Context*, New York, Oxford University Press, pp. 67-83.

GOLDMAN, Richard M.

1969 "*Endgame* and its Scorekeepers", in Chevigny, Bell Gale (ed.), *Twentieth Century Interpretations of "Endgame"*, Englewood Cliffs, Prentice-Hall, pp. 33-39.

GONTARSKI, Stan E.

1977 *Beckett's Happy Days: a Manuscript Study*, Columbus, Ohio State University.

1983 "*Film* and Formal Integrity", in Beja, Morris-Gontarski, Stan E.-Astier, Pierre (eds.), *Samuel Beckett. Humanistic Perspectives*, Ohio, Ohio State University Press, pp. 129-136.

1985 *The intent of Undoing in Samuel Beckett's Dramatic Text*, Bloomington, Indiana University Press.

1986 (ed.), *On Beckett: Essays and Criticism*, New York, Grove Press.

1990 "«Ressasser tout ça» avec *Pas*", in *Revue d'Estetique*, numéro hors-série (I ed. 1986), pp. 151-156.

1992 (ed.), *The Theatrical Notebooks by Samuel Beckett. Endgame*, London, Faber & Faber, vol. II.

1993a "'Birth Astride of a Grave': Samuel Beckett's *Act Without Words I*", in Gontarski, Stan E. (ed.), *The Beckett Studies Reader*, Florida, University Press of Florida, pp. 29-34.

1993b "The *Journal of Beckett Studies*, The First Fifteen Years: An Introduction", in Gontarski, Stan E. (ed.), *The Beckett Studies Reader*, Florida, University Press of Florida, pp. 1-8.

GORDON, Lois

1996 *The world of Samuel Beckett 1906-1946*, New Haven-London, Yale University Press.

GRANT, Steve

1991 "Bum's the word", in *Time Out*, London, September 18-25, nr. 1100, pp. 16-18.

GRAVER, Lawrence

1989 *Beckett. Waiting for Godot*, Cambridge, Cambridge University Press.

GRAY, Katherine M.

1995-1996 "Troubling the Body: Toward a Theory of Beckett's Use of the Human Body Onstage", in *Journal of Beckett Studies*, vol. 5, nr. 1-2, Atumn 1995-Spring 1996, pp. 1-17.

GRAZIANI, Luisa Laura

1989 *Ancora una "stain upon the silence": Quad di Samuel Beckett*, Genova, Schena Editore.

GREENBERG, Rocky

1990 "Léclairage-partition", in *Revue d'Estetique*, numéro hors-série (I ed. 1986), pp. 239-240.

GREGORY, Horace

1961 "The Dying Gladiators of Samuel Beckett", in *The Dying Gladiators and Other Essays*, New York, Grove Press, pp. 165-176.

GRESSET, Michel

1971 "Le moment nu du bilan", in Nores, Dominique (ed.), *Les critiques de notre temps et Beckett*, Paris, Garnier, pp. 165-170.

GRINDEA, Miron

1998 "Beckett's involvement with Music", in Bryden, Mary (ed.), *Samuel Beckett and Music*, Oxford, Clarendon Press, pp. 183-185.

GROSSVOGEL, David I.

1958 *20th Century French Drama*, New York, Columbia University Press.

1962 *Four Playwrights and a Postscript. Brecht. Ionesco. Beckett. Genet*, Ithaca, Cornell Univerity Press.

GUICHARNAUD, Jaques and June

1967 "Existence Onstage: Samuel Beckett", in *Modern French Theatre from Girardoux to Genet*, New Haven, Yale University Press, pp. 230-258.

GUINOISEAU, Stephane

1995 *En Attendant Godot de Beckett: etude de l'oeuvre*, Paris, Hachette.

GUSSOW, Mel

1996 *Conversations with (and about) Beckett*, London, Nick Hern.

HAEFNER, Gerhard

1990 *Klassiker des englischen Romans im 20. Jahrhunderts: Joseph Conrad, D. H. Lawrence, James Joyce, Virginia Woolf, Samuel Beckett: Begryndung der Moderne und Abrechnung mit der Moderne*, Heidelberg, Carl Winter.

HAERDTER, Michaël

1990 "Samuel Beckett répète *Fin de partie*", in *Revue d'Estetique*, numéro hors-série (I ed. 1986), pp. 303-316.

HAGBERG, Per O.

1972 *The dramatic works of Samuel Beckett and Harold Pinter. A comparative analysis of main themes and dramatic tecnique*, London, s. e.

HALE, Jane Alison

1987 *The Broken Window. Beckett's Dramatic Perspective*, West Lafayette, Purdue University Press.

HALL, Ann C.

1993 "'Though women all above... Beneath is all the fiend's': Female Trouble in William Shakespeare's *King Lear* and Samuel Beckett's *Happy Days*", in Drew, Anne Marie (ed.), *Past Crimson, Past Woe. The Shakespeare-Beckett Connection*, New York & London, Garland, pp. 31-40.

HAMILTON, Alice

1976 *Condemned to life: the world of Samuel Beckett*, Grand Rapids, Eerdmans

HANDWERK, Gary J.

1985 *Irony and ethics in narrative: from Schlegel to Lacan*, New Haven-London, Yale University Press.

HANSFORD, Henry James

1983 *Skullscapes: imaginative strategies in the later prose of Samuel Beckett*, Reading, PhD Thesis.

1993a "'Imagination Dead Imagine': The Imagination and Its Context", in Gontarski, Stan E. (ed.), *The Beckett Studies Reader*, Florida, University Press of Florida, pp. 146-166.

1993b "'Imaginative Transactions' in 'La Falaise'", in Gontarski, Stan E. (ed.), *The Beckett Studies Reader*, Florida, University Press of Florida, pp. 203-213.

HANSON, Clare

1985 *Short stories and short fiction 1880-1980*, London, Macmillan.

HARDY, Barbara

1975 "The dubious consolation in Beckett's fiction: art, love and nature", in Worth, Katharine (ed.), *Beckett the Shape Changer. A Symposium*, London&Boston, Routledge and Kegan Paul, pp. 105-138.

HARMON, Murice

1984 (ed.), *The Irish Writer and the City*, London, Colin Smythe.

HART, Clive

1986 *Language and Structure in Beckett's Plays*, Great Britain, Colin Smythe.

HARRINGTON, John P.

1991a *Modern Irish Drama*, New York, Norton & Company.

1991b *The Irish Beckett*, Syracuse, Syracuse University Press.

1992a "Beckett, Joyce, and Irish Writings: The Example of Beckett's 'Dubliners' Story", in Carey, Phyllis-Jewinski, Ed (eds.), *Re: Joyce 'n Beckett*, New York, Fordham University Press, pp. 31-42.

1992b "Joyce and Beckett: A Preliminary Checklist of Publications", in Carey, Phyllis-Jewinski, Ed (eds.), *Re: Joyce 'n Beckett*, New York, Fordham University Press, pp. 184-193.

HARRISON BEAN, Kellie

1993 " The End Is in the Beginning: Story Telling in Shakespeare, Beckett (and Stoppard)", in Drew, Anne Marie (ed.), *Past Crimson, Past Woe. The Shakespeare-Beckett Connection*, New York & London, Garland, pp. 117-128.

HARVEY, Lawrence E.

1967 "Art and the Existential in *Waiting for Godot*", in Cohn, Ruby (ed.), *Casebook on Waiting for Godot*, New York, Grove Press, pp. 144-155.

1970 *Samuel Beckett Poet and Critic*, Princeton, P.U.P.

HASSAN, Ihab

1967 *The Literature of Silence. Henry Miller & Samuel Beckett*, New York, Alfred A. Knopf.

1971 *The dismemberment of Orpheus. Toward a postmodern literature*, s. l., s. e.

HAUCK, Gerhard

1992 *Reductionism in Drama and the Theatre. The Case of Samuel Beckett*, Maryland, Scripta Humanistica.

HAYMAN, David

1964 "Molloy à la recherche de l'absurde", in Friedman, Melvin J. (ed.), "Configuration critique de Samuel Beckett", in *Revue des Lettres Modernes*, nr. 100.

1987 "Beckett: Impoverishing the Means-Empowering the Matter", in Friedman, Alan Warren-Rossman, Charles-Sherzer, Dina (eds.), *Beckett Translating/Translating Beckett*, Pennsylvania State University Press, University Park, pp. 109-119.

HAYMAN, Ronald

1962 "Quest for Meaninglessness: The boundless poverty of *Molloy*", in Sutherland, William O. S. jr. (ed.), *Six Contemporary Novels*, Austin, The University of Texas University Press, pp. 90-112.

1968 *Samuel Beckett*, London, Heinemann.

1979 *Theatre and Anti-Theatre. New Movements Since Beckett*, London, Secker and Warburg.

HEDBERG, Johannes

1972 "Samuel Beckett's *Whoroscope*. A Linguistig-Literary Interpretation", in *Moderna språk monographs*, Saltsjö-Duvnäs, Tidskriften Moderna språk, nr. 1.

HEED, Sven

1996 *Roger Blin. Metteur en scène de l'avant-garde (1949-1959)*, s. l., Circé.

HENNING DEBEVEC, Sylvie

1985 "The guffaw of the Abderite: 'Murphy' and the Democritean universe", in *Journal of Beckett Studies*, London, nr. 10, pp. 5-20.

1988   *Beckett's Critical Complicity. Carnival, contestation and tradition*, Kentucky, University Press of Kentucky.

HENSEL, Georg

1970   *Beckett*, Hannover, Friedrich Verlag.

HEPPENSTALL, Rayner

1961   *The Fourfold Tradition*, London, Barrie and Rockliff.

HERBERT, Jocelyn

1967   "A letter", in Calder, John (ed.), *Beckett at 60*, London, Calder and Boyars, p. 98.

1993   *Jocelyn Herbert: a theatre workbook*, London, Art Books International.

HERBIN, Jean

1990   "Machine", "Noir", in *Revue d'Estetique*, numéro hors-série (I ed. 1986), p. 225.

HESLA, David H.

1971   *The Shape of Chaos. An Interpretation of the Art of Samuel Beckett*, Minneapolis, The University of Minnesota Press.

HESSING, Kees

1992   *Beckett on Tape. Productions of Samuel Beckett's Work on Film, Video and Audio*, Leiden, Academic Press Leiden.

HEWES, Henry

1967   "Mankind and Merdecluse", in Cohn, Ruby (ed.), *Casebook on Waiting for Godot*, New York, Grove Press, pp. 67-69

HIGDON, David Lean

1977   *Time and English Fiction*, London, The Macmillan Press.

HIGGINS, Aidan

1967   "Tribute", in Calder, John (ed.), *Beckett at 60*, London, Calder and Boyars, pp. 91-92.

HILDERSHEIMER, Wolfgang

1969   "Il cerimoniale simbolico del teatro dell'assurdo", in *Il Dramma*, a. 45, nr. 7, Aprile 1969, pp. 56-60.

HILL, Leslie

1988   "Fiction, Myth, and Identity in Samuel Beckett's Novel Trilogy", in Bloom, Harold (ed.), *Samuel Beckett's Molloy, Malone Dies, The Unnamable*, New York-New Haven Philadelphia, Chelsea House Publishers, pp. 85-94.

1990   *Beckett's Fiction in Different Words*, Cambridge, Cambridge University Press.

HINCHCLIFFE, A.P.

1969   "The Absurd", in Jump, J. D. (ed.), *The Critical Idiom*, London, Methuen, vol. 5.

HOBSON, Harold

1967a "An English Review", in Cohn, Ruby (ed.), *Casebook on Waiting for Godot*, New York, Grove Press, pp. 27-30.

1967b "The first night of *Waiting for Godot*", in Calder, John (ed.), *Beckett at 60*, London, Calder and Boyars, pp. 25-28.

HOEFER, Jaqueline

1965 "Watt", in Esslin, Martin (ed.), *Samuel Beckett: A Collection of Critical Essays*, Englewood Cliffs, N.J., Prentice Hall, pp. 62-76.

HOFFMANN, Frederick J.

1962 *Samuel Beckett the language of self*, Carbondale, Southern Illinois University Press.

1964a "L'inaississable moi: les 'M' de Beckett", in Friedman, Melvin J. (ed.), "Configuration critique de Samuel Beckett", in *Revue des Lettres Modernes*, nr. 100.

1964b *Samuel Beckett*, New York, Dutton.

HOFSTADTER, Dan

1992 *Temperaments. Artists Facing Their Work*, New York, Alfred A. Knopf.

HOKENSON, Jan

1975 "Three Novels in Large Blank Pauses", in Cohn, Ruby (ed.), *Samuel Beckett: A Collection of Criticism*, New York, McGraw-Hill Book Company, pp. 73-84.

HOMAN, Sidney

1984 *Beckett's Theaters. Interpretations for Performance*, London and Toronto, Associated University Presses.

1988 "*Endgame*: the Playwright Completes Himself", in Bloom, Harold (ed.), *Samuel Beckett's Endgame*, New York-New Haven Philadelphia, Chelsea House Publishers, pp. 123-146.

1992 *Filming Beckett's Television Plays. A Director's Experience*, London and Toronto, Associated University Presses.

HOOKER, Ward

1960 "Irony and Absurdity in the Avant-Garde Theatre", in *The Keyton Review*, vol. XXII, nr. 3, Summer 1960, pp. 436-454.

HUBERT, Marie-Claude

1976 "Primaute du corps dans le théâtre de Samuel Beckett", in *Travaux de Linguistique et de litterature publies par le Centre de Philologie et de Litteratures Romances*, Strasbourg, Universite de Strasbourg.

1987 *Langage et Corps Fantasmé dans le Théâtre des années cinquante. Ionesco. Beckett. Adamov*, s. l., Librairie José Corti.

HUBERT, Renée Riese

1976 "A la trace de «Bing»", in Bishop, Tom-Federman, Raymond (eds.), *Samuel Beckett*, "L'Herne", nr. 31, pp. 253-258.

1987 "*From an Abandoned Work*: The Encounter of Samuel Beckett and Max Ernst", in Friedman, Alan Warren-Rossman, Charles-Sherzer, Dina (eds.), *Beckett Translating/Translating Beckett*, Pennsylvania State University Press, University Park, pp. 199-211.

HUTCHINGS, William

1993 "'As Strange a Maze As E'er Man Trod': Samuel Beckett Allusions to Shakespeare's Last Plays", in Drew, Anne Marie (ed.), *Past Crimson, Past Woe. The Shakespeare-Beckett Connection*, New York & London, Garland, pp. 3-14.

HUTCHINSON, Mary

1967 "All the livelong way", in Calder, John (ed.), *Beckett at 60*, London, Calder and Boyars, pp. 93-95.

HYERS, Conrad

1996 *The Spirituality of Comedy. Comic Heroism in a Tragic World*, New Brunswick and London, Transaction Publisher.

In the Prison

1988 *In the Prison of His Days. A Miscellany for Nelson Mandela on His 70th Birthday*, Gigginstown, Lilliput.

IONESCO, Eugène

1962 *Notes et contre-notes*, Paris, Gallimard.

1976 "À propos de Beckett", in Bishop, Tom-Federman, Raymond (eds.), *Samuel Beckett*, "L'Herne", nr. 31, pp. 149-151.

ISER, Wolfgang

1966 "Samuel Beckett's Dramatic Language", in *Modern Drama*, Dicember 1966, pp. 251-259, now in Samuel Beckett, *Teatro completo*, Torino-Parigi, Einaudi Gallimard, 1994, pp. 699-707.

1978 *The implied reader*, London, Hopskins.

1988 "Subjectivity as the Autogenous Cancellation of Its Own Manifestations", in Bloom, Harold (ed.), *Samuel Beckett's Molloy, Malone Dies, The Unnamable*, New York-New Haven Philadelphia, Chelsea House Publishers, pp. 71-83.

1989 *Prospecting. From Reader Response to Literary Anthropology*, Baltimore, The John Hopkins University Press.

1992 "Counter-sensical Comedy and Audience Response in Beckett's 'Waiting for Godot'", in Connor, Steven (ed.), *Waiting for Godot and Endgame*, London, Macmillan, pp. 55-70.

ISOU, Isidore

1982   *Les pompiers du nouveau roman (Sarraute, Robbe-Grillet, Butor, Simenon, Beckett, Ionesco, Barthes, C. Mauriac)*, Paris, Centre de Creative.

JACQUART, Emmanuel C.

1974   *Le Thé, tre de dérision. Beckett, Ionesco, Adamov*, Paris, Gallimard.

1990   "«L'Ancien et le Nouveau»", in *Revue d'Estetique*, numéro hors-série (I ed. 1986), pp. 135-145.

JACQUART, Emmanuel C.-CHABERT, Pierre

1990   "Beckett: bibliographie", in *Revue d'Estetique*, numéro hors-série (I ed. 1986), pp. 425-438.

JACOBSEN, Josephine-MUELLER, William R.

1964   *The Testament of Samuel Beckett*, New York, Hill and Wang.

JANVIER, Ludovic

1966a   *Pour Samuel Beckett*, Paris, Les Edition de Minuit.

1966b   "Réduire à la parole", in *Cahiers de la Compagnie Renaud-Barrault. Samuel Beckett*, Paris, Julliard, nr. 53, pp. 42-48.

1967   "Cyclical Dramaturgy", in Cohn, Ruby (ed.), *Casebook on Waiting for Godot*, New York, Grove Press, pp. 166-171.

1969   *Samuel Beckett par lui-même*, Paris, Editions Seuil.

1971a   "A l'écoute d'un vieux bonheur", in Nores, Dominique (ed.), *Les critiques de notre temps et Beckett*, Paris, Garnier, pp. 136-138.

1971b   "L'Humour et le Vertige comblé par la mathématique", in Nores, Dominique (ed.), *Les critiques de notre temps et Beckett*, Paris, Garnier, pp. 19-23.

1971c   "Le dépassement de la parole manquée", in Nores, Dominique (ed.), *Les critiques de notre temps et Beckett*, Paris, Garnier, pp. 180-182.

1975   "Place of Narration/Narration of Place", in Cohn, Ruby (ed.), *Samuel Beckett: A Collection of Criticism*, New York, McGraw-Hill Book Company, pp. 98-110.

1976a   "Au travail avec Beckett", in Bishop, Tom-Federman, Raymond (eds.), *Samuel Beckett*, "L'Herne", nr. 31, pp. 137-140.

1976b   "Lieu dire", in Bishop, Tom-Federman, Raymond (eds.), *Samuel Beckett*, "L'Herne", nr. 31, pp. 193-205.

1990   "Roman et théâtre", in *Revue d'Estetique*, numéro hors-série (I ed. 1986), pp. 45-54.

JANVIER, Ludovic-FEDERMAN, Raymond-FOURNIER, Edith

1990   "Chronologie", in *Revue d'Estetique*, numéro hors-série (I ed. 1986), pp. 405-415.

JANVIER, Ludovic-VAQUIN-JANVIER, Agnès

1990   "Traduire *Watt* avec Beckett", in *Revue d'Estetique*, numéro hors-série (I ed. 1986), pp. 57-64.

JEWINSKI, Ed

1990 "Beckett's *Company*, Post-structuralism, and *Mimetalogique*", in Butler, Lance St. John-Davis, Robin J. (eds.), *Rethinking Beckett. A Collection of Critical Essays*, London, Macmillan, pp. 141-159.

1992 "James Joyce and Samuel Beckett: From Epiphany to Anti-Epiphany", in Carey, Phyllis-Jewinski, Ed (eds.), *Re: Joyce 'n Beckett*, New York, Fordham University Press, pp. 160-174.

JOHNS, Gregory-KAZAN, Jean

1993 *In the Dim Void: Samuel Beckett's Late Trilogy*, England, Crescent Moon.

JOHNSTON, Denis

1967 "An Irish Evaluation", in Cohn, Ruby (ed.), *Casebook on Waiting for Godot*, New York, Grove Press, pp. 31-39.

JOLAS, Maria

1967 "A Bloomlein for Sam", in Calder, John (ed.), *Beckett at 60*, London, Calder and Boyars, pp. 14-16.

JONES, Tony

1991 "Beckett's Stage People: more than merely Players", in Fallaize, Elizabeth-Hallmark, Ron-Pickup, Ian (eds.), *Representations of belief. Essays in memory of G. V. Banks*, Birmingham, University of Birmingham, pp. 203-211.

JORDAN, John

1962 "The Irish Theatre-Retrospect and Premonition", in AA.VV., *Contemporary Theatre*, London, Edward Arnold Publishers, pp. 165-184.

JOSIPOVICH, G.

1976 (ed.), *The Modern English Novel*, London, Open Books Publisher.

JULIET, Charles

1986 *Rencontre avec Samuel Beckett*, Fontfroide-le-Haut, Fata Morgana.

1995 *Conversations with Samuel Beckett and Bram van Velde*, Leiden, Academic Press Leiden.

JUNKER, Mary

1995 *Beckett. The Irish Dimension*, Dublin, Wolfhound Press.

KAELIN, Eugene Francis

1981 *The unhappy consciousness: the poetic plight of Samuel Beckett*, Dordrecht-Boston-London, Reidel Publishing Company.

KALB, Jonathan

1989 *Beckett in Performance*, New York, Cambridge University Press.

1993 *Free Admissions. Collected Theater Writings*, New York, Limelight.

1994 "The mediated Quixote: the radio and television plays, and *Film*", in Pilling, John (ed.), *The Cambridge Companion to Beckett*, Cambridge, Cambridge University Press, pp. 124-144.

KAMYABI MASK, Ahmad

1990 *Dernière rencontre avec Samuel Beckett*, [Paris], Caractères.

KARL, Frederik R.

1962a *A Reader's Guide To The Contemporary English Novel*, New York, Farrar, Straus and Cudahy.

1962b *The Contemporary English Novel*, New York, Farrar, Straus and Cudahy.

KAWIN, B.F.

1972 *Telling It Again and Again*, London, Cornell University Press.

1982 *The Mind of the Novel*, Princeton, P.U.P.

KEARNEY, Patrick J.

1987 *The Paris Olympia Press*, London, Black Spring Press.

KELLMAN, Steven G.

1980 *The Self-Begetting Novel*, London, The Macmillan Press.

KELLY, Katherine

1993 "The Orphic Mouth in *Not I*", in Gontarski, Stan E. (ed.), *The Beckett Studies Reader*, Florida, University Press of Florida, pp. 121-128.

KELLY, Lionel

1992 "Beckett's *Human Wishes*", in Pilling, John-Bryden, Mary (eds.), *The Ideal Core of the Onion*, Reading, The Longdunn Press, pp. 99-135.

KENNEDY, Andrew K.

1975 *Six dramatists in search of a language. Shaw. Eliot. Beckett. Pinter. Osborne. Arden*, Cambridge, Cambridge University Press.

1983 *Dramatic Dialogue. The Duologue of Personal Encounter*, Cambridge, Cambridge University Press.

1989 *Samuel Beckett*, Cambridge, Cambridge University Press.

KENNEDY, Sighle

1971 *Murphy's Bed. A Study of Real Sources and Sur-real Associations in Samuel Beckett's First Novel*, Lewisburg, Bucknell University Press.

KENNER, Hugh

1961 *Samuel Beckett: A Critical Study*, New York, Grove Press.

1962 *Samuel Beckett*, London, Calder.

1964 *Flaubert, Joyce and Beckett. The Stoic Comedians*, London, Allen.

1965 "The Cartesian Centaur", in Esslin, Martin (ed.), *Samuel Beckett: A Collection of Critical Essays*, Englewood Cliffs, N.J., Prentice Hall, pp. 52-61.

1967a	"Life in the Box", in Cohn, Ruby (ed.), *Casebook on Waiting for Godot*, New York, Grove Press, pp. 107-113.
1967b	"Progress report 1962-65", in Calder, John (ed.), *Beckett at 60*, London, Calder and Boyars, pp. 61-77.
1973	*A Reader's Guide to Samuel Beckett*, London, Thames & Hudson.
1975	"Shades of Syntax", in Cohn, Ruby (ed.), *Samuel Beckett: A Collection of Criticism*, New York, McGraw-Hill Book Company, pp. 21-31.
1983	*A Colder Eye. The Modern Irish Writers*, London, Allen Lane.
1987a	*The Mechanic Muse*, New York, Oxford University Press.
1987b	"*Waiting for Godot*", in Bloom, Harold (ed.), *Samuel Beckett's Waiting for Godot*, New York-New Haven Philadelphia, Chelsea House Publishers, pp. 53-66.
1988	"The Trilogy", in Bloom, Harold (ed.), *Samuel Beckett's Molloy, Malone Dies, The Unnamable*, New York-New Haven Philadelphia, Chelsea House Publishers, pp. 31-49.
1990	*Historical Fictions*, San Francisco, North Point Press.

KERMODE, Frank

1962a	*Continuities*, New York, Random House.
1962b	*Puzzles and Epiphanies. Essays and Reviews 1958-1961*, New York and London, Routledge & Kegan Paul.
1970	*Modern Essays*, London, Fontana-Collins.

KERN, Edith

1964	"Samuel Beckett et les poches de Lemuel Gulliver", in Friedman, Melvin J. (ed.), "Configuration critique de Samuel Beckett", in *Revue des Lettres Modernes*, nr. 100.
1966	"Beckett and the spirit of the Commedia dell'Arte", in *Modern Drama*, Columbia, Artcsaft Press, vol. 9, nr. 3 (December 1966), pp. 260-267.
1970	*Existential Thought and Fictional Tecnique: Kierkegaard, Sartre, Beckett*, New Haven, Yale University Press.
1977	"Beckett as Homo Ludens", in *Journal of Modern Literature*, Philadelphia, vol. 6, nr. 1 (February 1977), pp. 47-60.
1980	*The Absolute Comic*, New York, Columbia University Press.
1983	"Beckett's Modernity and Medieval Affinities", in Beja, Morris-Gontarski, Stan E.-Astier, Pierre (eds.), *Samuel Beckett. Humanistic Perspectives*, Ohio, Ohio State University Press, pp. 26-35.

KIM, Earl

1998	"A Note: *Dead Calm*", in Bryden, Mary (ed.), *Samuel Beckett and Music*, Oxford, Clarendon Press, p. 257.

KITCHIN, L.

1962   *Mid-Century Drama*, London, Faber & Faber.

KNOWLSON, James

1971   *Samuel Beckett: an exhibition*, London, Turret.

1972   *Light and Darkness in the Theatre of Samuel Beckett*, London, Turret.

1980   (ed.), *Samuel Beckett:Krapp's Last Tape*, London, Brutus Book Limited.

1983   "Beckett's 'Bits of Pipe'", in Beja, Morris-Gontarski, Stan E.-Astier, Pierre (eds.), *Samuel Beckett. Humanistic Perspectives*, Ohio, Ohio State University Press, pp. 16-25.

1985   (ed.), *Happy Days: Samuel Beckett's Production Notebook*, London-Boston, Faber & Faber.

1986a   (ed.), *Beckett at Eighty a celebration*, Reading, The Beckett Archive.

1986b   "Ghost Trio/Geister Trio", in Brater, Enoch (ed.), *Beckett at 80/Beckett in Context*, New York, Oxford University Press, pp. 193-207.

1990   "Samuel Beckett metteur en scène: ses cahiers de mise en scène et leur interprétation critique", in *Revue d'Estetique*, numéro hors-série (I ed. 1986), pp. 277-289.

1992   *The Theatrical Notebooks by Samuel Beckett. Krapp's Last Tape*, London, Faber & Faber.

1996   *Damned to Fame*, London, Bloomsbury.

KNOWLSON, James-PILLING, John

1979   *Frescoes of the Skull: The Later Prose and Drama of Samuel Beckett*, London, John Calder.

KOSTELANETZ, Richard

1964   (ed.), *On Contemporary Literature*, New York, Avon.

KOTT, Jan

1966   "A note on Beckett's Realism", in *Tulane Drama Rview*, vol. X, nr. 3, pp. 156-159, now in Samuel Beckett, *Teatro completo*, Torino-Parigi, Einaudi Gallimard, 1994, pp. 695-699.

1968   *Theatre notebook*, London, Methuen.

1971a   "Ce monde tragique et grotesque", in Nores, Dominique (ed.), *Les critiques de notre temps et Beckett*, Paris, Garnier, pp. 25-35.

1971b   "L'Icona e l'Assurdo", in *Biblioteca teatrale*, Roma, Bulzoni, nr. 1, Primavera 1971, pp. 3-14 (I ed. 1969).

KRALIK, Erika

1990   "Mises en scène par la Compagnie Renaud-Barrault", in *Revue d'Estetique*, numéro hors-série (I ed. 1986), pp. 449-450.

KRANCE, Charles

1975   "L'ouvre-boît et la conscience narrative dans 'Comment c'est'", in AA.VV., *Saggi e ricerche di letteratura francese*, Roma, Bulzoni.

1990 "*Worstward Ho* and *On*-words: Writing to(wards) the Point", in Butler, Lance St. John-Davis, Robin J. (eds.), *Rethinking Beckett. A Collection of Critical Essays*, London, Macmillan, pp. 124-140.

1993 *Samuel Beckett's Company/Compagnie and A Piece of Monologue/Solo. A Bilingual Variorum Edition*, New York and London, Garland.

1996 *Samuel Beckett's Mal vu mal dit/Ill seen Ill said. A Bilingual, Evolutionary and Synoptic Variorum Edition*, New York and London, Garland.

KRISTEVA, Julia

1976 "Le Père, l'amour, l'exil", in Bishop, Tom-Federman, Raymond (eds.), *Samuel Beckett*, "Cahier de l'Herne", nr. 31, pp. 246-252.

KRISTIANSEN, Mikael Ørting

2002 "Den Bogstavelige Humor Eller Bogstavelighedens Komiske Effekt", in *Le philosophoire. Laboratoire de philosophie - Le Rire*, nr. 17, 2002/2, pp. 103-109.

KROLL, Jeri L.

1993 "Belacqua as Artist and Lover: 'What a Misfortune'", in Gontarski, Stan E. (ed.), *The Beckett Studies Reader*, Florida, University Press of Florida, pp. 35-63.

LAAS, Henner

1978 *Samuel Beckett. Dramatische Form als Medium der Reflexion*, Bonn, Bouvier Verlag Hebert Grundmann.

LAHR, John

1970 *Notes on a Cowardly Lion*, London, Allen Lane The Penguin Press (I ed. 1969).

LAKE, Carlton

1984 (ed.), *No symbols where none intended*, Austin, Humanities Research Center.

LALANDE, Bernard

1977 En attendant Godot: Beckett: analyse critique, Paris, Hatier.

LAMONT, Rosette C.

1964 "La Farce metaphysique de Samuel Beckett", in Friedman, Melvin J. (ed.), "Configuration critique de Samuel Beckett", in *Revue des Lettres Modernes*, Paris, nr. 100, pp. 99-116

1965 "Death and Tragi-Comedy: Three Plays of the New Theatre", in *The Massachussetts Review*, vol. 6, nr. 2 (Winter-Spring 1965), pp. 381-402.

1976 "Krapp, un anti-Proust", in Bishop, Tom-Federman, Raymond (eds.), *Samuel Beckett*, "Cahier de l'Herne", nr. 31, pp. 295-305.

1987a "Crossing the Iron Curtain: Political Parables", in Friedman, Alan Warren-Rossman, Charles-Sherzer, Dina (eds.), *Beckett Translating/Translating Beckett*, Pennsylvania State University Press, University Park, pp. 77-84.

1987b "To Speak the Words of 'The Tribe'. The Wordlessness of Samuel Beckett's Metaphisical Clowns", in Burkman, Katerine (ed.), *Myth and Ritual in the Plays of Samuel Beckett*, London and Toronto, Associated University Presses, pp. 56-70.

LANE, John Francis

1973 "Beckett più Finney", in *Sipario*, Roma, nr. 232 (Aprile 1973), pp. 28-30.

LAWLEY, Paul

1988 "Symbolic Stucture and Creative Obligation in *Endgame*", in Bloom, Harold (ed.), *Samuel Beckett's Endgame*, New York-New Haven Philadelphia, Chelsea House Publishers, pp. 87-110.

1993 "*Embers*: An Interpretation", in Gontarski, Stan E. (ed.), *The Beckett Studies Reader*, Florida, University Press of Florida, pp. 94-120.

1994 "Stages of identity: from *Krapp's Last Tape* to *Play*", in Pilling, John (ed.), *The Cambridge Companion to Beckett*, Cambridge, Cambridge University Press, pp. 88-105.

LAWS, Catherine

1998 "Morton Feldman's *Neither*: A Musival Translation of Beckett's Text", in Bryden, Mary (ed.), *Samuel Beckett and Music*, Oxford, Clarendon Press, pp. 57-85.

LECERCLE, Ann

1984 "*Echo's Bones*-La redontable symétrie de l'œuf-pourri ou Une poétique de la suture", in Rabate, Jean-Michel (ed.), *Beckett avant Beckett: essais sur le jeune Beckett (1930-1945)*, Paris, P.E.N.S., pp. 47-78.

LEE, Richard

1976 "The fictional topography of Samuel Beckett", in Josipovich, G. (ed.), *The Modern English Novel*, London, Open Books Publisher.

LEES, Heath

1993 "*Watt*: Music, Tuning, and Tonality", in Gontarski, Stan E. (ed.), *The Beckett Studies Reader*, Florida, University Press of Florida, pp. 167-185.

LENNON, Peter

1994 *Foreign correspondent: Paris in the sixties*, London, Picador.

LE SAGE, Laurent

1962 *The French New Novel. An Introduction and a Sampler*, University Park, The Pennsylvania State University Press.

LEVENTHAL, Abraham Jacob

1965 "The Beckett Hero", in Esslin, Martin (ed.), *Samuel Beckett: A Collection of Critical Essays*, Englewood Cliffs, N.J., Prentice Hall, pp. 37-51.

1967 "The Thirties", in Calder, John (ed.), *Beckett at 60*, London, Calder and Boyars, pp. 7-13

1976 "Les Anée Trente", in Bishop, Tom-Federman, Raymond (eds.), *Samuel Beckett*, "L'Herne", nr. 31, pp. 109-113.

LEVY, Alan

1967 "The Long Wait for Godot", in Cohn, Ruby (ed.), *Casebook on Waiting for Godot*, New York, Grove Press, pp. 74-79.

LEVY, Eric P.

1980 *Beckett and the Voice of Species. A Study of the Prose Fiction*, Totowa, Gill and Macmillan.

LEVY, Shimon

1990 *Samuel Beckett's Self-Referential Drama The Three I's*, London, Macmillan.

LEWIS, Jim

1990a "Beckett et la caméra", in *Revue d'Estetique*, numéro hors-série (lla I ed. 1986), pp. 371-379.

1990b "Mises en scène des pièces de télévision par Samuel Beckett à Stuttgart pour la S.D.R.", in *Revue d'Estetique*, numéro hors-série (I ed. 1986), p. 466.

LIBERA, Antoni

1983 "*The Lost Ones*: A Myth of Human History and Destiny", in Beja, Morris-Gontarski, Stan E.-Astier, Pierre (eds.), *Samuel Beckett. Humanistic Perspectives*, Ohio, Ohio State University Press, pp. 145-156.

LIBERTINI, Angelo-SINISCALCHI, Claudio

1992 *Il nulla e l'infinito: una lettura spirituale dell'opera di Samuel Beckett*, Roma, Ente dello Spettacolo.

LICATA, Salvo

1989a "Forse", in Bistolfi, Marina-Licata, Salvo (eds.), *Primo amore. Beckett-Quartucci*, Erice, La Zattera di Babele, pp. 3-6.

1989b "La non-cravatta. Conservazione con Sandro Lombardi", in Bistolfi, Marina-Licata, Salvo (eds.), *Primo amore. Beckett-Quartucci*, Erice, La Zattera di Babele, pp. 23-24.

LINDON, Jérôme

1967 "First meeting with Samuel Beckett", in Calder, John (ed.), *Beckett at 60*, London, Calder and Boyars, pp. 17-19.

LITTLE, Janet Patricia

1981 *Beckett: "En Attendant Godot" and "Fin de Partie". Critical Giudes to French Texts*, London, Grant & Cutler.

LITTLE, Roger

1994 "Beckett's poems and verse translations or: Beckett and the limits of poetry", in Pilling, John (ed.), *The Cambridge Companion to Beckett*, Cambridge, Cambridge University Press, pp. 184-195.

LOCATELLI, Carla

1984   *La disdetta della parola. L'ermeneutica del silenzio nella prosa inglese di Samuel Beckett*, Bologna, Pàtron.

1990a   "Comic strategies in Samuel Beckett's narratives", in *Le forme del comico: Atti dell'VIII Convegno dell'Associazione Italiana di Anglistica* (Torino, ottobre 1985), eds. Carla Marengo Vaglio, P. Bertinetti, G. Cortese, Alessandria, Ed. dell'Orso.

1990b   *Unwording the World. Samuel Beckett's Prose Works After the Nobel Prize*, Pennsylvania, University of Pennsylvania Press.

1992   "Delogocentrating Silence: Beckett's Ultimate Unwording", in Brater, Enoch (ed.), *The Theatrical Gamut. Notes for a post-beckettian stage*, University of Michigan Press, pp. 67-89.

LODGE, David

1979   *The Modes of Modern Writing*, London, Edward Arnolds.

LONSDALE, Michael

1990   "Un précurseur du théâtre musical", in *Revue d'Estetique*, numéro hors-série (I ed. 1986), pp. 255-259.

LOUZOUN, Myriam

1982   "'Fin de Partie' de Samuel Beckett. Effacement et dynamisme formel", in *Les voies de la création théâtrale*, Paris, CNRS, vol. V, pp. 377-445.

LOXERTMAN, Alan S.

1992   "'The More Joyce He Knew the More He Could' and 'More Than I Could': Theology and Fictional Tecnique in Joyce and Beckett", in Carey, Phyllis-Jewinski, Ed (eds.), *Re: Joyce 'n Beckett*, New York, Fordham University Press, pp. 61-82.

LOWE, N. F.

1995   "The dirty jokes in *Waiting for Godot*", in *The Modern Language Review*, vol. 10, nr. 1 (January 1995), pp. 14-17.

LUDVIGSEN, Christian

1967   "Dramatikeren som iscenesætter i sin egen tekst", in *Teatrets Teori og Teknikk*, Oslo, nr. 5, pp. 4-10.

1997   *Det begyndte med Beckett – min egen teaterhistorie*, Århus, Institut for Dramaturgi.

LUKACS, Georges

1971   "Dissolution de l'homme et du monde", in Nores, Dominique (ed.), *Les critiques de notre temps et Beckett*, Paris, Garnier, pp. 80-85.

LYMAN, S.

1976   (ed.), *Perspectives on Plays*, London, Rotledge.

LYONS, Charles R.

1983   *Samuel Beckett*, New York, Grove Press.

1986 "'Happy Days' and Dramatic Convention", in Brater, Enoch (ed.), *Beckett at 80/Beckett in Context*, New York, Oxford University Press, pp. 84-101.

LYONS, W. H.

1980 "Backtracking Beckett", in Burns, C. A. (ed.), *Literature and Society. Studies in nineteenth and twentieth century French literature*, Birmingham, University of Birmingham, pp. 214-220.

MacGOWRAN, Jack

1967 "Working with Samuel Beckett", in Calder, John (ed.), *Beckett at 60*, London, Calder and Boyars, pp. 23-24.

MACIEL, L. C.

1959 *Samuel Beckett e a solidão humana*, Porto Alegre, Instituto Estadual do Luero.

MACNEICE, Louis

1965 *Varieties of Parable*, Cambridge, The University Press.

MAGNAN, Jean-Marie

1976 "Les Chaines et Relais du néant", in Bishop, Tom-Federman, Raymond (eds.), *Samuel Beckett*, "L'Herne", nr. 31, pp. 259-265.

MAILER, Norman

1961 *Advertisement for Myself*, London, Andre Deuttch.

1967 "A Public Notice", in Cohn, Ruby (ed.), *Casebook on Waiting for Godot*, New York, Grove Press, pp. 69-74.

MAIOCCHI FATTORI, Annamaria

(ed.), *Beckett e il teatro dell'assurdo. Crisi di una civiltà*, Milano, Università Bocconi.

MANDELL, Alan

1990 "La représentation de Godot au Pénitencier de San Quentin (U.S.A.) et la création de la Compagnie théâtrale del San Quentin", in *Revue d'Estetique*, numéro hors-série (I ed. 1986), pp. 201-202.

MANNERS, Marya

1967 "An American Reaction", in Cohn, Ruby (ed.), *Casebook on Waiting for Godot*, New York, Grove Press, pp. 30-31.

MANZONI, Giacomo

1998 "Towards *Parole da Beckett*", in Bryden, Mary (ed.), *Samuel Beckett and Music*, Oxford, Clarendon Press, pp. 213-232.

MARCOULESCO, Ileana

1993 "Beckett and the Temptation of Solipsism", in Gontarski, Stan E. (ed.), *The Beckett Studies Reader*, Florida, University Press of Florida, pp. 214-225.

MARECHAL, Marcel

1990   "Une partition fantastique", in *Revue d'Estetique*, numéro hors-série (I ed. 1986), pp. 205-206.

MARIN, Maguy

1990   "May B...", in *Revue d'Estetique*, numéro hors-série (I ed. 1986), p. 359.

MARISSEL, André

1963   *Samuel Beckett*, Paris, Editions Universitaires.

MAROWITZ, Charles

1962   "Paris Log", in *Encore*, March-April 1962, vol. 9, nr. 36, pp. 37-46.

MARVEL, Laura

1993   "The Failure of *Telos* in *King Lear* and *Endgame*", in Drew, Anne Marie (ed.), *Past Crimson, Past Woe. The Shakespeare-Beckett Connection*, New York & London, Garland, pp. 99-116.

MASIH, I. K.

1981   *Plays of Samuel Beckett*, New Delhi, Arnold-Heinemann.

MASK KAMYABI, Ahmad

1990   *Dernière rencontre avec Samuel Beckett*, Paris, Editions Caractères.

MASON, Amanda

1988   *An Examination of Proxemic and the Visual Semiotic in a Production of Samuel Beckett's Waiting for Godot*, Polytecnic of North London, M. A. in Modern Drama Studies.

Materialien

1968   *Materialien zu Becketts 'Endspiel'*, Frankfurt am Main, Surkamp Verlag.

MATTEWS, Herbert

1967   *The Primal Curse. The Myth of Chain and Abel in the Theatre*, London, Chatto and Windus.

MAUGHLIN, Susan

1987   "Liminality: An Approach to Artistic Process in *Endgame*", in Burkman, Katherine H. (ed.), *Myth and Ritual in the Plays of Samuel Beckett*, London and Toronto, Associated University Presses, pp. 86-99.

MAURIAC, Claude

1958   *L'allittérature contemporaine*, Paris, Albil Michel.

MAYBERRY, Bob

1989   *Theatre of Discord. Dissonance in Beckett, Albee, and Pinter*, London and Toronto, Associated University Presses.

MAYOUX, Jean-Jacques

1960   *Vivant Piliers. Le roman anglo-saxon et les symboles*, Paris, Julliard.

1965   "Samuel Beckett and Universal Parody", in Esslin, Martin (ed.), *Samuel Beckett: A Collection of Critical Essays*, Englewood Cliffs, N.J., Prentice Hall, pp. 77-91.

1966 "Beckett et l'humour", in *Cahier Renaud-Barrault*, Paris, Gallimard, Février 1966, pp. 33-41.

1969 *Über Beckett*, Frankfurt am Main, Surkamp Verlag.

1971 "Solitude de l'homme", in Nores, Dominique (ed.), *Les critiques de notre temps et Beckett*, Paris, Garnier, pp. 56-59.

1974 *Beckett*, London, Longman.

MAYS, J. C. C.

1984 "Les racines irlandaises du jeune Beckett", in Rabate, Jean-Michel (ed.), *Beckett avant Beckett: essais sur le jeune Beckett (1930-1945)*, Paris, P.E.N.S., pp. 11-26.

McCARTHY, Gerry

1992 "«Codes from a Mixed-up Machine»: The Disintegrating Actor in Beckett, Shepard, and, Surprisingly, Shakespeare", in Brater, Enoch (ed.), *The Theatrical Gamut. Notes for a post-beckettian stage*, University of Michigan Press, pp. 171-187.

1994 "Emptying the Theater: On Directing the Plays of Samuel Beckett", in Oppenheimer, Lois, *Directing Beckett*, Michigan, The University of Michigan Press, pp. 250-267.

McCORMACK, W. J.

s. d. *From Burke to Beckett: Ascendancy, Tradition and Betrayal in Literary History*, Cork, Cork University Press.

McGRORY, Katleen-UNTERECKER, John

1976 (eds.), *Yeats, Joyce and Beckett: new fight on three modern Irish writers*, Lewisburg, Bucknell University Press.

McMILLAN, Dougald

1975a "Samuel Beckett and the Visual Arts: the Embarrassement of Allegory", in Cohn, Ruby (ed.), *Samuel Beckett: A Collection of Criticism*, New York, McGraw-Hill Book Company, pp. 121-135.

1975b *Transition: History of a Literary Era. 1927-1938*, London, Calder and Boyars.

1990 "*Eleutheria*: le discours de la méthode inédit de Samuel Beckett", in *Revue d'Estetique*, numéro hors-série (I ed. 1986), pp. 101-109.

McMILLAN, Dougald-FEHSENFELD, Martha

1988 *Beckett in the Theatre. The Author as practical Playwright and Director*, London, John Calder.

McMULLAN, Anna

1989 *Between spaces: the dynamic principle in Samuel Beckett's later drama*, Reading, PhD Thesis.

1993 *Theatre on Trial. Samuel Beckett's later drama*, New York and London, Routledge.

1994 "Beckett as director: the art of mastering failure", in Pilling, John (ed.), *The Cambridge Companion to Beckett*, Cambridge, Cambridge University Press, pp. 196-208.

McMULLAN, Audrey

1990a "Chronologie des principales mises en scène des pièces de Samuel Beckett en Angleterre", in *Revue d'Estetique*, numéro hors-série (I ed. 1986), pp. 445-446.

1990b "La forme en movement", in *Revue d'Estetique*, numéro hors-série (I ed. 1986), pp. 337-341

McNAMARA, Robert

1994 "On Directing Beckett: In and Out of Ireland", in Oppenheimer, Lois, *Directing Beckett*, Michigan, The University of Michigan Press, pp. 277-291.

MEGGED, Matti

1985 *Dialogue in the Void: Beckett and Giacometti*, New York, Lumen Books.

MELDOLESI, Claudio

1997 "Dal no *Taniko* a *Il Consenziente* e *Il Dissenziente*, Chiarimenti della dramaturgie d'autore, anche sui confini dell'*Opera da tre soldi* e di *Godot*", in *Teatro e Storia*, a. XII, nr. 19, pp. 185-200.

MELESE, Pierre

1966-1969 *Samuel Beckett*, Paris, Seghers.

MEMOLA, Massimo

1982 "Crisi e frantumazione del soggetto nell'opera di Samuel Beckett", in *Quaderni di teatro*, Firenze, Vallecchi, nr. 17, a. V (agosto 1982), pp. 151-178.

1983 "Per un'interpretazione materialistica dell'opera di Samuel Beckett", in *Quaderni di Teatro*, Firenze, Vallecchi, a. V, nr. 20, Maggio 1983, pp. 39-73.

MERCIER, Vivian

1977 *Beckett/Beckett*, New York, Oxford University Press.

METHA, Xerxes

1994 "Ghosts", in Oppenheimer, Lois, *Directing Beckett*, Michigan, The University of Michigan Press, pp. 170-185.

METMAN, Eva

1965 "Reflections on Samuel Beckett's Plays", in Esslin, Martin (ed.), *Samuel Beckett: A Collection of Critical Essays*, Englewood Cliffs, N.J., Prentice Hall, pp. 117-139.

MEYER, Hans

1972 "Brecht Beckett e un come", in *Sipario*, n. 319, Dicembre 1972, pp. 13-16.

MIGNON, Paul-Louis

1969 "Beckett", in *Le théâtre contemporain*, Paris, Hachette, pp. 87-89.

MIHALOVICI, Marcel

1967 "My collaboration with Samuel Beckett", in Calder, John (ed.), *Beckett at 60*, London, Calder and Boyars, pp. 20-22.

MILLER, Lawrence

1992 *Samuel Beckett. The Epressive Dilemma*, New York, St. Martin's Press.

MINIHAN, John

1995 *Samuel Beckett: photographs* (with an introduction by Aidan Higgins), London, Secker & Warburg.

MITCHELL, Breon

1983 *A Beckett Bibliography: new works 1972-1982*, West Lafayette, Dept. of English, Purdue University.

1987 "Seeing the Unsayable: Beckett and H. M. Ehrardt", in Friedman, Alan Warren-Rossman, Charles-Sherzer, Dina (eds.), *Beckett Translating/Translating Beckett*, Pennsylvania State University Press, University Park, pp. 212-233.

MOLLOY, Frank

1985 "Parody in Modern Irish Fiction: Samuel Beckett and Flann O'Brien", in Petr, Pavel-Roberts, David-Thompson, Philip (eds.), *Comic Relations. Studies in the Comic Satire and Parody*, Frankfurt am Main, Verlag Peter Lang, pp. 239-246.

MONNIER, Adrienne

1961 *Dernières Gazettes et Écrits divers*, Paris, Mercure de France.

MONTEITH, Charles

1967 "Personal Note", in Calder, John (ed.), *Beckett at 60*, London, Calder and Boyars, p. 87.

MONTESSORI, Chiara

1991 "Percorsi paralleli e destabilizzazione narrativa nel *Murphy* di Samuel Beckett", in *Il confronto letterario*, a. VIII, nr. 16, Novembre 1991, pp. 439-448.

MOONEY, Michael E.

1990 "*Watt*: Samuel Beckett's Sceptical Fiction", in Butler, Lance St. John-Davis, Robin J. (eds.), *Rethinking Beckett. A Collection of Critical Essays*, London, Macmillan, pp. 160-168.

MOORJANI, Angela B.

1982 *Abysmal Games in the Novels of Samuel Beckett*, Chapel Hill, University of North Carolina Press.

1987 "The *Magna Mater* Myth in Beckett's Fiction: Subtext and Subvertion", in Friedman, Alan Warren-Rossman, Charles-Sherzer, Dina (eds.), *Beckett Translating/Translating Beckett*, Pennsylvania State University Press, University Park, pp. 149-154.

1990 "Beckett's Devious Deictics", in Butler, Lance St. John-Davis, Robin J. (eds.), *Rethinking Beckett. A Collection of Critical Essays*, London, Macmillan, pp. 20-30.

1992 *The Aesthetics of Loss and Lessness*, London, Macmillan.

MORICONI, Valentina

1990 *Beckett e altro "Assurdo"*, Napoli, Guida.

MORISETTE, Bruce

1964 "Les Idées de Robbe-Grillet sur Beckett", in Friedman, Melvin J. (ed.), "Configuration critique de Samuel Beckett", in *Revue des Lettres Modernes*, nr. 100.

MOROT-SIR, Edouard

1976 *Samuel Beckett and Cartesian Emblems*, s. l., s. e.

1988 "Gramatical Insincerity in *The Unnamable*", in Bloom, Harold (ed.), *Samuel Beckett's Molloy, Malone Dies, The Unnamable*, New York-New Haven Philadelphia, Chelsea House Publishers, pp. 131-144

MORRISON, Kristin

1983a *Canters and Chronicles: The Use of Narrative in the Plays of Samuel Beckett and Harold Pinter*, Chicago, University of Chicago Press.

1983b "Neglected Biblical Allusions in Beckett's Plays: 'Mother Pegg' Once More", in Beja, Morris-Gontarski, Stan E.-Astier, Pierre (eds.), *Samuel Beckett. Humanistic Perspectives*, Ohio, Ohio State University Press, pp. 91-98.

MORTEO, Gian Renzo

1965 "Incontro con Roger Blin", in *I Quaderni del Teatro Stabile di Torino*, Torino, Ed. del Teatro Stabile, nr. 3 (26 Marzo 1965), pp. 95-105.

MOYNAHAM, Julian

1995 *Anglo-Irish. The Literary Imagination in a Hyphenated Culture*, Princeton, Princeton University Press.

MURCH, Anne C.

1993 "Quoting from *Godot*: Trends in Contemporary French Theater", in Gontarski, Stan E. (ed.), *The Beckett Studies Reader*, Florida, University Press of Florida, pp. 186-202.

MURPHY, P.(eter) J.(ohn)

1990 *Reconstructing Beckett. Language for Being in Samuel Beckett's Fiction*, Toronto, University of Toronto Press.

1992 "On first looking into Beckett's *The Voice*", In PILLING, John-BRYDEN, Mary (eds.), *The Ideal Core of the Onion*, Reading, The Longdunn Press, pp. 99-135.

1994 "Beckett and the philosophers", in Pilling, John (ed.), *The Cambridge Companion to Beckett*, Cambridge, Cambridge University Press, pp. 222-240.

MURPHY, P. J.-HUBER, Werner-BREUER, Rolf-SCHOELL, Konrad

1994 *Critique of Beckett Criticism: A Guide to Research in English, French, and German*, Columbia, Camden House.

MURRAY, Patrick

1970　*The tragic comedian. A study of Samuel Beckett*, Cork, The Mercier Press.

NADEAU, Maurice

1963　"Le chemin de la parole au silence", in *Cahiers de la Compagnie Renaud-Barrault. Samuel Beckett*, Paris, Julliard, nr. 44, pp. 63-66.

1965　"Samuel Beckett: Humor and the Void", in Esslin, Martin (ed.), *Samuel Beckett: A Collection of Critical Essays*, Englewood Cliffs, N.J., Prentice Hall, pp. 33-36.

1971a　"De la parole au silence", in Nores, Dominique (ed.), *Les critiques de notre temps et Beckett*, Paris, Garnier, pp. 152-161.

1971b　"Occupée à mourir", in Nores, Dominique (ed.), *Les critiques de notre temps et Beckett*, Paris, Garnier, pp. 38-42.

NEIZVESTNY, Ernst

1990　*Space, Time, and Syntesis in Art. Essays on Art, Literature, and Philosophy*, Oakville, Mosaic Press.

NORES, Dominique

1971　(ed.), *Les critiques de notre temps et Beckett*, Paris, Garnier.

NØJGAARD, Morten

1978　"Tempo drammatico e tempo narrativo. Saggio sui livelli temporali ne «La dernière bande» di Beckett", in *Biblioteca teatrale*, nr. 20, pp. 65-73.

O'BRIEN, Eoin-KNOWLSON, James

1986　*The Beckett Country. An Exhibition for Samuel Beckett's Eightieth Birthday*, Dublin, The Black Cat Press.

O'BRIEN JOHNSON, Toni

1984　"*The Well of the Saints* and *Waiting for Godot*: two Ways of Avoiding Urbanity", in Harmon, Maurice (ed.), *The Irish Writer and the City*, London, Colin Smythe, pp. 90-102.

O'HARA, James D.

1970　(ed.), *Twentieth Century interpretations of Molloy, Malone Dies, The unnamable*, Englewood Cliffs, Prentice Hall.

1993　"Jung and the 'Molloy' Narrative", in Gontarski, Stan E. (ed.), *The Beckett Studies Reader*, Florida, University Press of Florida, pp. 129-145.

OLIVA, Renato

1965　"Il teatro di Samuel Beckett", in *Quaderni del Teatro Stabile della città di Torino*, Torino, Ed. del Teatro Stabile, nr. 3 (26 Marzo 1965), pp. 71-91.

1967　*Samuel Beckett. Prima del silenzio*, Milano, Mursia.

1972　"Appunti per una lettura dell'ultimo Beckett", in Samuel Beckett, *L'immagine, Senza Lo spopolatore*, Torino, Einaudi, pp. 95-121.

OMESCO, I.

1978   *La metamorphose de la tragédie*, Vendôme, Presse Universitaire de France.

O'NAN, Martha B.

1962   *The role of mind in Hugo, Faulkner, Beckett and Gass*, s. l., s. e.

ONIMUS, Jean

1968   *Beckett. Les écrivains devant Dieu*, Bruges, Desclée de Brouwer.

1970   *Samuel Beckett, ultimo traguardo*, Bologna, Dehoniane.

1971a   "Faire parler l'existence", in Nores, Dominique (ed.), *Les critiques de notre temps et Beckett*, Paris, Garnier, pp. 52-55.

1971b   "Les rêves de lévasion et du repos", in Nores, Dominique (ed.), *Les critiques de notre temps et Beckett*, Paris, Garnier, pp. 126-131.

OPPENHEIMER, Lois

1994   *Directing Beckett*, Michigan, The University of Michigan Press.

OPPENHEIMER, Lois-BUNING, Marius

1996   (eds.) *Beckett on and on...*, London, Associated University Presses.

ORR, John

1981   *Tragic Drama & Modern Society*, London, Macmillan.

1991   *Tragicomedy and Contemporary Culture: Play and Performance from Beckett to Shepard*, London, Macmillan.

OSTROVSKY, Erika

1969   "Jules Laforgue and Samuel Beckett: a rapprochement", in *Jules Laforgue*, Carbondale-Edwardsville-London-Amsterdam, s. e., pp. 130-145.

1976   "Le silence de Babel", in Bishop, Tom-Federman, Raymond (eds.), *Samuel Beckett*, "L'Herne", nr. 31, pp. 206-211.

Ottant'anni

1986   *Ottant'anni. Il compleanno di Samuel Beckett*", in *Il Patalogo*, Milano, Ubulibri/Electa, nr. 9, p. 227.

OVERBECK, Lois More

1987   "«Getting On»: Ritual as Façon in Beckett's Plays", in Burkman, Katherine H. (ed.), *Myth and Ritual in the Plays of Samuel Beckett*, London and Toronto, Associated University Presses, pp. 21-27.

PAINE, Sylvia

1981   *Beckett, Nabokov, Nin. Motives and Modernism*, Port Washington, Kenniktat.

PAOLINI, Giulio

1989   "L'«ascolto» di un'immagine", in Bistolfi, Marina-Licata, Salvo (eds.), *Primo amore. Beckett-Quartucci*, Erice, La Zattera di Babele, p. 26.

PASQUIER, Marie-Claire

1983 "Blanc, gris, noir, gris, blanc", in *Cahiers de la Compagnie Renaud-Barrault. Samuel Beckett*, Paris, Julliard, nr. 106, pp. 61-79.

1984 "La rose et le homard-Vie et mort de Belacqua Shuah", in Rabate, Jean-Michel (ed.), *Beckett avant Beckett: essais sur le jeune Beckett (1930-1945)*, Paris, P.E.N.S., pp. 27-45.

PASSERI PIGNONI, Vera

1967 "L'attesa di Beckett", in *Teatro contemporaneo*, Firenze, Città di Vita, pp. 44-48.

PASTORELLO, Félie

1982 "La réception par la presse", in *Les voies de la création thé, trale*, Paris, CNRS, vol. X, pp. 241-250.

PAZ, Octavio

1990 "Samuel Beckett e la poesia messicana", in *Leggere*, Milano, nr. 22 (Giugno 1990), p. 21.

PEACHE, Charles

1975 "The labours of poetical excavation", in Worth, Katharine (ed.), *Beckett the Shape Changer. A Symposium*, London&Boston, Routledge and Kegan Paul, pp. 39-59.

PEARCE, Richard

1970 *Stages of the Clown. Perspectives on Modern Fiction from Dostoyevsky [sic] to Beckett*, Southern Illinois, Southern Illinois University Press.

PERCHE, Louis

1969 *Beckett. L'enfer à notre portée*, Paris, Le Centurion.

PERLOFF, Carey

1994 "Three Women and a Mound: Directing *Happy Days*", in Oppenheimer, Lois, *Directing Beckett*, Michigan, The University of Michigan Press, pp. 161-169.

PERLOFF, Majorie

1987a *The Dance of Intellect: Studies in the Poetry of the Pound Tradition*, Cambridge, Cambridge University Press.

1987b "Une voix pas la mienne: French/English Reader", in Friedman, Alan Warren-Rossman, Charles-Sherzer, Dina (eds.), *Beckett Translating/Translating Beckett*, Pennsylvania State University Press, University Park, pp. 36-48.

PERNIOLA, Mario

1961 "Beckett e la scrittura esistenziale", in *Tempo presente*, nr. 9-10, Settembre-Ottobre 1961, pp. 727-733.

PETER, John

1987 *Vladimir's Carrot. Modern Drama and the Modern Imagination*, London, André Deutsch.

PIETTE, Adam

1996 *Remembering and the Sound of Words: Mallarme, Proust, Joyce, Beckett*, Oxford, Clarendon Press.

PILLING, John

1976 *Samuel Beckett*, London, Routledge and Kegan Paul.

1992 "From a (W)horoscope to *Murphy*", in Pilling, John-Bryden, Mary (eds.), *The Ideal Core of the Onion*, Reading, The Longdunn Press, pp. 99-135.

1994a "Beckett's English fiction", in Pilling, John (ed.), *The Cambridge Companion to Beckett*, Cambridge, Cambridge University Press, pp. 17-42.

1994b (ed.), *The Cambridge Companion to Beckett*, Cambridge, University Press.

1998a *Beckett before Godot*, Cambridge, Cambridge University Press.

1998b "*Proust* and Shopenhauer: Music and Shadows", in Bryden, Mary (ed.), *Samuel Beckett and Music*, Oxford, Clarendon Press, pp. 173-178.

PILLING, John-BRYDEN, Mary

1992 (eds.), *The Ideal Core of the Onion*, Reading, Beckett International Foundation.

PILLING, John-KNOWLSON, James

1979 *Frescoes of the Skull: The Later Prose and Drama of Samuel Beckett*, London, John Calder.

PINGET, Robert

1967 "My dear Sam", in Calder, John (ed.), *Beckett at 60*, London, Calder and Boyars, pp. 84-85.

1976 "Lettre", in Bishop, Tom-Federman, Raymond (eds.), *Samuel Beckett*, "Cahier de l'Herne", nr. 31, pp. 160-161.

1990 "Notre ami", in *Revue d'Estetique*, numéro hors-série (I ed. 1986), pp. VII-1.

1993 *Robert Pinget a la lettre: entretiens avec Madeleine Renouard*, Paris, Belfond.

PINGAUD, Bernard

1971a "Importance de Beckett à sa date", in Nores, Dominique (ed.), *Les critiques de notre temps et Beckett*, Paris, Garnier, pp. 35-38.

1971b "Le langage irréel", in Nores, Dominique (ed.), *Les critiques de notre temps et Beckett*, Paris, Garnier, pp. 161-164.

PINTER, Harold

1967 "Beckett", in Calder, John (ed.), *Beckett at 60*, London, Calder and Boyars, p. 86.

PISANTI, Tommaso

1978 *Anger and silence. Il nuovo Teatro inglese*, Napoli, Loffredo.

PONCE, Fernando

1970 *Samuel Beckett*, Madrid, E.P.S.E.A.

POUNTNEY, Rosemary

1981 *Waiting for Godot: notes*, Harlow, Longman.

1988 *Theatre of Shadows. Samuel Beckett's Drama 1956-1976*, London, Colin Smythe.

PRINGET, Christian

1993 "A Descent From Clowns", in *Journal of Beckett Studies*, Florida, nr. 1, vol. 3 (1993), pp. 1-19.

PRINZ, Jessica

1987 "The Fine Art of Inexpression: Beckett and Duchamp", in Friedman, Alan Warren-Rossman, Charles-Sherzer, Dina (eds.), *Beckett Translating/Translating Beckett*, Pennsylvania State University Press, University Park, pp. 95-106.

PRONKO, Leonard Cabell

1962 "Samuel Beckett", in *Avant-Garde: The Experimental Theatre in France*, Berkeley and Los Angeles, University of California Press, pp. 22-58.

QUADRI, Franco

1976 *L'avanguardia teatrale in Italia. 1960-1976*, Torino, Einaudi, 2 voll.

1987 (ed.), *Per Beckett*, Milano, UBULIBRI.

1989 "Il tempo dell'altro Beckett", in *Il Patalogo*, Milano, Ubulibri/Electa, nr. 13, pp. 180-181.

1995 "Sul viso di Winnie c'è una vita intera", in *La Repubblica*, 10 Dicembre 1995, p. 36.

QUARTUCCI, Carlo

1989a "In fondo alla lunga notte", in Bistolfi, Marina-Licata, Salvo (eds.), *Primo amore. Beckett-Quartucci*, Erice, La Zattera di Babele, pp. 9-11.

1989b "Scena in colloquio. Giulio Paolini", in Bistolfi, Marina-Licata, Salvo (eds.), *Primo amore. Beckett-Quartucci*, Erice, La Zattera di Babele, p. 25.

1997 "Conversazione con gli studenti", c/o Galleria Toledo, Napoli, 14.2.1997.

RABATE, Etienne

1984 "Watt à l'ombre de Plume-L'écriture du désœuvrement", in Rabate, Jean-Michel (ed.), *Beckett avant Beckett: essais sur le jeune Beckett (1930-1945)*, Paris, P.E.N.S., pp. 173-185.

RABATE, Jean-Michel

1984 "Quelques figures de la première (et la dernière) antropomorphie de Beckett", in Rabate, Jean-Michel (ed.), *Beckett avant Beckett: essais sur le jeune Beckett (1930-1945)*, Paris, P.E.N.S., pp. 135-151.

1996 *The Ghosts of Modernity*, Gainesville, University Press of Florida.

RABINOVITZ, Rubin

1983 "Unreliable Narrative in *Murphy*", in Beja, Morris-Gontarski, Stan E.-Astier, Pierre (eds.), *Samuel Beckett. Humanistic Perspectives*, Ohio, Ohio State University Press, pp. 58-70.

1984 *The Development of Samuel Beckett's Fiction*, Urbana and Chicago, University of Illinois Press.

1987 "Beckett, Dante, and the Metaphorical Representation of Intangible Reality", in Friedman, Alan Warren-Rossman, Charles-Sherzer, Dina (eds.), *Beckett Translating/Translating Beckett*, Pennsylvania State University Press, University Park, pp. 57-64.

1990 "Repetition and Underlying Meanings in Samuel Beckett's Trilogy", in Butler, Lance St. John-Davis, Robin J. (eds.), *Rethinking Beckett. A Collection of Critical Essays*, London, Macmillan, pp. 31-67.

1992 *Innovation in Samuel Beckett's Fiction*, Urbana and Chicago, University of Illinois Press.

RAETHER, Martin

1980 *Der Acte gratuit: Revolte und Literatur: Hegel, Dostojewskij, Nietzsche, Gide, Sartre, Camus, Beckett*, Heidelberg, Carl Winter.

RAMAKRISHNA, Lalita

1997 *Samuel Beckett: Time and Self in His Plays*, New Delhi, Harman Publishing House.

RATHIEN, Friedhelm

1990 *Reziproke Radien. Arno Schmidt und Samuel Beckett*, München, edition text+kritik.

REAVEY, Georges

1976 "Première vision de 'Oh les beaux jours', 1962", in Bishop, Tom-Federman, Raymond (eds.), *Samuel Beckett*, "L'Herne", nr. 31, pp. 157-159.

REBER, Trudis

1971 *Samuel Beckett*, s. l., s. e.

REDFERN, Walter

1998 "A Funny-bone to Pick with Beckett", in *Journal of Beckett Studies*, vol. 8, nr. 1, pp. 101-118.

1999 "Bad Jokes and Beckett", in Parkin, John (ed.), *French humour: papers based on a colloquium held in the French Department of the University of Bristol, November 30th 1996*, Amsterdam, Rodopi.

REGAN, Denis

1992 "Beckett and Joyce et Beckett-esque: A One-Act Play", in Carey, Phyllis-Jewinski, Ed (eds.), *Re: Joyce 'n Beckett*, New York, Fordham University Press, pp. 175-184.

REID, Alec

1964 "Krapp's Last Tape Samuel Beckett", in Harward, T.B. (ed.), *European Patterns*, Dublin, The Dolmen Press, pp. 38-43.

1969 *All I can manage, more than I could*, Dublin, Dolmen Press (I ed. 1968).

1975 "From Beginning to Date: Some Thoughts on the Plays of Samuel Beckett", in Cohn, Ruby (ed.), *Samuel Beckett: A Collection of Criticism*, New York, McGraw-Hill Book Company, pp. 63-72.

RENAUD, Madelaine

1967 "Beckett the magnificant", in Calder, John (ed.), *Beckett at 60*, London, Calder and Boyars, pp. 81-83.

1990 "Laisser parler Beckett, ou le sac de Winnie", in *Revue d'Estetique*, numéro hors-série (I ed. 1986), pp. 171-172.

RENNER, Charlotte

1988 "The Self-Multiplying Narrators of *Molloy*, *Malone Dies* and *The Unnamable*", in Bloom, Harold (ed.), *Samuel Beckett's Molloy, Malone Dies, The Unnamable*, New York-New Haven Philadelphia, Chelsea House Publishers, pp. 95-114.

RENTON, Andrew

1990 *"He all but said...": evasion and referral in the later prose and drama of Samuel Beckett*, Reading, PhD Thesis.

1992 "*Wostward Ho* and the end(s) of representation", in Pilling, John-Bryden, Mary (eds.), *The Ideal Core of the Onion*, Reading, The Longdunn Press, pp. 99-135.

1994 "Disabled figures: from the *Residua* to *Stirring still*", in Pilling, John (ed.), *The Cambridge Companion to Beckett*, Cambridge, Cambridge University Press, pp. 167-183.

RESTIVO, Giuseppina

1990 "Il regime delle emozioni in 'Endgame' di Samuel Beckett", in *Le forme del comico: Atti dell'VIII Convegno dell'Associazione Italiana di Anglistica* (Torino, Ottobre 1985), eds. Carla Marengo Vaglio, P. Bertinetti, G. Cortese, Alessandria, Ed. dell'Orso, pp. 489-511.

1991 *Le soglie del postmoderno: 'Finale di partita'*, Bologna, Il Mulino.

REYNOLDS, Roger

1998 "The Indifference of the Broiler to the Broiled", in Bryden, Mary (ed.), *Samuel Beckett and Music*, Oxford, Clarendon Press, pp. 195-211.

RICKS, Christopher

1993 *Beckett's Dying Words. The Clarendon Lectures*, Oxford, Clarendon.

RIFBJERG, Klaus

1983 *Patience: en Beckett-idyl*, København, Gyldendal.

1997 "Den sidste modernist", in *Politiken*, København, 2 Juli 1997, p. 1.

RIPELLINO, Angelo Maria

1965 *Il trucco e l'anima*, Torino, Einaudi.

ROBBE GRILLET, Alain

1965 "Samuel Beckett, or 'Presence' in the Theatre", in Esslin, Martin (ed.), *Samuel Beckett: A Collection of Critical Essays*, Englewood Cliffs, N.J., Prentice Hall, pp. 108-115.

1971 "Retour à la signification", in Nores, Dominique (ed.), *Les critiques de notre temps et Beckett*, Paris, Garnier, pp. 142-151.

ROBINSON, Fred Miller

1991 "Tray Bong! *Godot* and Music Hall", in Sclueter, June-Brater, Enoch (eds.), *Approaches to Teaching Beckett's Waiting for Godot*, New York, The Modern Language Association of America, pp. 64-70.

1992 "Didi's and Gogo's Time Routine", in *Comic Moments*, Athens & London, The University of Georgia Press, pp. 54-62.

ROBINSON, Jeremy

1992 *Samuel Beckett Goes into the Silence*, Kidderminster, Crescent Moon.

ROBINSON, Michael

1969 *The long sonata of the dead*, London, R. Hart-Davis.

ROCHE, Anthony

s. d. *Contemporary Irish Drama: From Beckett to McGuinness. Gill's Studies in Irish Literature*, London, Gill & Macmillan.

RODOTA', Maria Laura

1992 "E Beckett salta fuori dal cassetto", in *L'Espresso*, 6 Dicembre 1992, p. 123.

RODRIGUEZ-GAGO, Antonia

1990 "Beckett sur la scène espagnole", in *Revue d'Estetique*, numéro hors-série (I ed. 1986), pp. 459-462.

1992 "Molloy's «Happy Nights» and Winnie's «Happy Days»", in Brater, Enoch (ed.), *The Theatrical Gamut. Notes for a post-beckettian stage*, University of Michigan Press, pp. 29-40.

ROJTMAN, Betty

1987 *Forme et signification dans le Théâtre de Beckett*, Paris, Nizet (II ed.).

ROMANO, Augusto-TREVI, Mario

1975 *Studi sull'ombra*, Venezia-Padova, Marsilio.

ROMANO, Vincenzo

1975 *La fine di un inizio. (Interpretazione dell'"Endgame' di Samuel Beckett)*, Bari, Grandolfo.

1977 *Paralisi e cosmicità*, Bari, Damiani.

RONEN, Ilan

1994 "*Waiting for Godot* as Political Theater", in Oppenheimer, Lois, *Directing Beckett*, Michigan, The University of Michigan Press, pp. 239-249.

RONFANI, Ugo

1976 "Morire giovani", in *Il Dramma*, a. LII, nr. 1-2, Giugno-Luglio 1976, pp. 89-96.

ROOF, Judith A.

1987 "A Blink in the Mirror: From Oedipus to Narcissus and Back in the Drama of Samuell Beckett", in Burkman, Katherine H. (ed.), *Myth and Ritual in the Plays of Samuel Beckett*, London and Toronto, Associated University Presses, pp. 151-163.

1993 "Critical Figures: Shakespeare, Beckett and the Survival of Theatre", in Drew, Anne Marie (ed.), *Past Crimson, Past Woe. The Shakespeare-Beckett Connection*, New York & London, Garland, pp. 129-146.

ROSATI, Carlo

1974 "Giorni felici di Samuel Beckett", in *Sipario*, nr. 343 (Dicembre 1974).

ROSE, Margaret

1989 *The symbolist theatre tradition from Maeterlinck and Yeats to Beckett and Pinter*, Milano, Unicopoli.

ROSEN, Carol

1983 *Plays of impasse. Contemporary drama set in confying institutions*, Princeton, P.U.P.

ROSEN, Steven J.

1976 *Samuel Beckett and the Pessimistic Tradition*, New Brunswick, Rutgers University Presses.

ROSSET, Clément

1990 "La force comique", in *Critique. Revue générale des publications française et étrangère*, Paris, CNL, tome LXVI, nr. 512-520, Août-Septembre, pp. 708-712.

ROUSSEAU, Josanne

1990 "Le corps du fantasme", in *Revue d'Estetique*, numéro hors-série (I ed. 1986), pp. 221-222.

ROUSSENAUX, André

1955 "L'homme désintégré de Samuel Beckett", in *Littérature du Vingtième Siècle*, vol. V, Paris, Éditions Albin Michel, 7 voll., pp. 105-113.

ROVATTI, Pieraldo

1964 "Note sul teatro di Beckett", in *Aut Aut*, nr. 81, Maggio 1964, pp. 74-88.

RUSSEL BROWN, John-HARRIS, Bernard

1962 *Contemporary Theatre*, London, Edward Arnold Ldt.

RYNGAERT, Jean-Pierre

1993 *Lire En Attendant Godot de Beckett*, Paris, Dunod.

SAGE, Victor

1975 "Innovation and continuity in *How it is*", in Worth, Katharine (ed.), *Beckett the Shape Changer. A Symposium*, London & Boston, Routledge and Kegan Paul, pp. 85-103.

SAINT-MARTIN, Fernande

1976 *Samuel Beckett et l'Univers de la Fiction*, Montréal, Les Presses de l'Université de Montréal.

SAISON, Maryvonne

1990 "Mettre en scène l'irreprésentable", in *Revue d'Estetique*, numéro hors-série (I ed. 1986), pp. 85-87.

Samuel Beckett

1971 *Samuel Beckett. Calepins de bibliographie*, Paris, Lettres Modernes Minard.

1976a   *Samuel Beckett inszeniert "Glyckliche Tage": Probenprotokoll der Inszenierung von Samuel Beckett in der "Werkstatt" des Berliner Schiller-Theaters*, aufgezeichnet von Alfred Hybner, Frankfurt am Main, Suhrkamp Taschenbycher.

1976b   *Samuel Beckett: the art of rethoric*, Chapel Hill, University of North Carolina.

1990   *Samuel Beckett*, in *Revue d'Esthétique*, numéro hors série (I ed. 1986).

1992-1997   *Samuel Beckett Today/Aujourd'hui*, Amsterdam, Editions Rodopi.

SANDULESCU, George G.

1986   *A Beckett Synopsis*, Great Britain, Colin Smythe.

SANTINI, Orazio

1976   *Il teatro drammatico contemporaneo. (Pirandello, Betti, Sartre, Camus, Beckett, Jonesco* [sic]*, Brecht, Eliot, Fabbri)*, Mantova, Grassi.

SARRAZAC, Jean-Pierre

1980a   "Samuel Beckett", in Attisani, Antonio (ed.), *Enciclopedia del teatro del '900*, Milano, Feltrinelli, pp. 173-174.

1980b   "Teatro dell'Assurdo", in Attisani, Antonio (ed.), *Enciclopedia del teatro del '900*, Milano, Feltrinelli, pp. 517-518.

SARRIS, Andrew

1969   "Buster Keaton and Samuel Beckett", in *Columbia Forum*, vol. 12, nr. 4, Winter 1969, pp. 42-43.

SASTRE, Alfonso

1967   "Seven Notes on *Waiting for Godot*", in Cohn, Ruby (ed.), *Casebook on Waiting for Godot*, New York, Grove Press, pp. 101-107.

1976   "Avant-gard et Réalité, in Bishop, Tom-Federman, Raymond (eds.), *Samuel Beckett*, "L'Herne", nr. 31, pp. 236-241.

SAUNDERS, Jeffrey

1993   *The mortal microcosm: creativity and the body in the fiction of Samuel Beckett 1932-1961*, manuscript PhD Thesis, Reading.

SAVIGNEAU, Josyane

1986   "Aspettando Samuel", in *Il Patalogo*, Milano, Ubulibri/Electa, nr. 9, pp. 227-228.

SCANLAN, Robert

1989   "Beckett fuori di scena", in *Teatro festival*, nr. 12, Gennaio-Febbraio 1989, pp. 52-58.

1994   "Performing Voices: Notes from Stagings of Beckett's Work", in Oppenheimer, Lois, *Directing Beckett*, Michigan, The University of Michigan Press, pp. 145-154.

SCARLINI, Luca

1996   (ed.), *Un altro giorno felice. La fortuna dell'opera teatrale di Samuel Beckett in Italia 1953-1996*, Firenze, Maschietto & Musolino.

SCHECHNER, Richard

1967 "There's Lots of Time in *Godot*", in Cohn, Ruby (ed.), *Casebook on Waiting for Godot*, New York, Grove Press, pp. 175-188.

SCHNEIDER, Alan

1958 "Waiting for Beckett. A personal chronicle", in *Chelsea Review*, nr. 2 (Autumn 1958), pp. 3-20, now in Samuel Beckett, *Teatro completo*, Torino-Parigi, Einaudi Gallimard, 1994, pp. 643-658.

1967 "The First American Director", in Cohn, Ruby (ed.), *Casebook on Waiting for Godot*, New York, Grove Press, pp. 51-59.

1976 "Comme il vous plaira", in Bishop, Tom-Federman, Raymond (eds.), *Samuel Beckett*, "L'Herne", nr. 31, pp. 123-136.

1987 *Entrances. An American Director's Journey*, s. l., Limelight (I ed. 1986).

1990 "A. Schneider et le théâtre de Beckett aux U.S.A.", in *Revue d'Estetique*, numéro hors-série (I ed. 1986), pp. 181-186.

1994 "On *Play* and Other Plays", in Oppenheimer, Lois, *Directing Beckett*, Michigan, The University of Michigan Press, pp. 315-318.

SCHOELL, Konrad

1967 *Das Theater Samuel Becketts*, Munchen, Wilhelm Fink.

SCHOU, Søren

"Becketts musik", in *Weekendavisen Bøger*, København, 31 Juli-6 August 1998, p. 15.

SCHULZ, Hans J.

1973 *This hell of stories. A Hegelian approach to the novels of Samuel Beckett*, The Hague, Mouton.

SCHURMAN, Susan

1987 *The Solipsistic Novels of Samuel Beckett*, Köln, Pahl-Rugenstein Verlag.

SCHWAB, Gabriele

1994 *Subjects without selves: transitional texts in modern fiction*, Cambridge, Harvard University Press.

SCOTT, Alan

2012 "A Desperate Comedy: Hope and alienation in Samuel Beckett's Waiting for Godot", in *Educational Philosophy and Theory*, pp. 1-13.

SCOTT, Nathan A.

1965a *Samuel Beckett*, London, Bowes.

1965b *Man in the Modern Theatre*, Richmond, John Knox Press.

SEAVER, Richard

1976a "Beckett vient à l'Olympia Press", in Bishop, Tom-Federman, Raymond (eds.), *Samuel Beckett*, "Cahier de l'Herne", nr. 31, pp. 97-100.

1976b (ed.), *I Can't Go On, I'll Go On. A Samuel Beckett Reader*, New York, Grove Weidenfeld.

SEGRE, Cesare

1973 *La fonction du langage dans l'Acte sans paroles de Samuel Beckett*, Urbino, Università di Urbino.

1974 *Le strutture del tempo*, Torino, Einaudi.

SEN, Supti

1970 *Samuel Beckett. His mind and art*, s. l., s. e.

SERREAU, Geneviève

1966 *Histoire du 'Nouveau Théâtre'*, Paris, Gallimard.

1967 "Beckett's Clowns", in Cohn, Ruby (ed.), *Casebook on Waiting for Godot*, New York, Grove Press, pp. 171-175.

1971 "Entrée des clowns", in Nores, Dominique (ed.), *Les critiques de notre temps et Beckett*, Paris, Garnier, pp. 14-19.

SEYRIG, Delphine

1990 "Haute précision", in *Revue d'Estetique*, numéro hors-série (I ed. 1986), pp. 343-346.

SHAINBERG, Lawrence

1996 *Beckett. Shainberg racconta Beckett*, Roma, Minimum Fax.

SHANK, Theodore J.

1963 (ed.), *A Digest of 500 Plays. Plot Outlines and Production Notes*, New York-London, Collier-Macmillan.

SHEEDY, John J.

1966 "The comic Apocalypse of King Hamm", in *Modern Drama*, Columbia, Artcraft Press, vol. 9, nr. 3 (December 1966), pp. 310-318.

1967 "The Net", in Cohn, Ruby (ed.), *Casebook on Waiting for Godot*, New York, Grove Press, pp. 159-166.

SHENKER, Israel

1997 "Samuel Beckett 'Ero l'opposto di Joyce'", in *La Repubblica*, 24 Giugno 1997, p. 43.

SHERINGHAM, Michael

1985 *Beckett: "Molloy". Critical Guides to French Texts*, London, Grant & Cutler.

SHERZER, Dina

1976 *Structure de la trilogie de Beckett: 'Molloy', 'Malone meurt', 'L'Innommable'*, Paris, Mouton.

1987 "Words About Words: Beckett and Language", in Friedman, Alan Warren-Rossman, Charles-Sherzer, Dina (eds.), *Beckett Translating/Translating Beckett*, Pennsylvania State University Press, University Park, pp. 49-54.

SHITH, H. A.

1962 "Dipsychus Among the Shadows", in Brown-Harris (eds.), *Contemporary Theatre*, London, Arnold.

Signature

1975 *Signature Anthology*, London, Calder & Boyars.

SIMON, Alfred

1983 *Samuel Beckett*, Paris, Pierre Belfond.

1990a "Chronologie des principales mises en scène en français et en anglais", in *Revue d'Estetique*, numéro hors-série (I ed. 1986), pp. 439-442.

1990b "Du théâtre de l'écriture à l'écriture de la scène", in *Revue d'Estetique*, numéro hors-série (I ed. 1986), pp. 71-83, now in Samuel Beckett, *Teatro completo*, Torino-Parigi, Einaudi Gallimard, 1994, pp. 744-759.

SIMON, Bennett

1988 *Tragic Drama and the Family: Psychoanalytic Studies from Aeschilus to Beckett*, Yale, Yale University Press.

SIMON, Richard Keller

1987 "Beckett, Comedy, and the Critics: A Study of Two Contexts, in Friedman, Alan Warren-Rossman, Charles-Sherzer, Dina (eds.), *Beckett Translating/Translating Beckett*, Pennsylvania, The Pennsylvania State University Press, pp. 85-94.

SIMPSON, Alan P.

1962 *Beckett and Behan and a Theatre in Dublin*, London, Routledge and Kegan Paul.

1967a "Samuel Beckett", in Calder, John (ed.), *Beckett at 60*, London, Calder and Boyars, pp. 96-97.

1967b "The First Irish Director", in Cohn, Ruby (ed.), *Casebook on Waiting for Godot*, New York, Grove Press, pp. 45-51.

SIMPSON, Ekundayo

1978 *Samuel Beckett: traducteur de lui-même. Aspects de bilinguisme littéraire*, Québec, Centre International de recherche sur le bilinguisme.

SMITH, Frederik N.

1983a "Beckett's verbal slapstick", in *Modern fiction studies*, West Lafayett, Purdue University, vol. 29, nr. 1 (Spring 1983), pp. 43-55.

1983b "Fiction as Composing Process: *How It Is*", in Beja, Morris-Gontarski, Stan E.-Astier, Pierre (eds.), *Samuel Beckett. Humanistic Perspectives*, Ohio, Ohio State University Press, pp. 107-121.

1987 "'A Land of sanctuary': Allusions to the Pastoral in Beckett's Fiction", in Friedman, Alan Warren-Rossman, Charles-Sherzer, Dina (eds.), *Beckett Translating/Translating Beckett*, Pennsylvania State University Press, University Park, pp. 128-139.

SMITH, Joseph H.

1991 (ed.), *World of Samuel Beckett*, Baltimore and London, John Hopkins University Press.

SMITH, Roc C.

1988 "Naming the M/inotaur: Beckett's Trilogy and the Failure of Narrative", in Bloom, Harold (ed.), *Samuel Beckett's Molloy, Malone Dies, The Unnamable*, New York-New Haven Philadelphia, Chelsea House Publishers, pp. 115-122.

SMUDA, Manfred

Becketts Prosa als Metasprache, Munchen, Wilhelm Fink.

SODDU, Ubaldo

1973 "Beckett '73", in *Sipario*, nr. 324 (Maggio 1973), p. 38.

SOLOV, Sandra

1990 "Les notes de mises en scène de *Fin de partie*", in *Revue d'Estetique*, numéro hors-série (I ed. 1986), pp. 291-301.

SPINALBELLI, Rosalba

1982 *'Endgame': gioco al massacro del linguaggio*, Bologna, Centro Stampa "Lo Scarabeo".

STAIB, Philippe

1967 "*A Propos* Samuel Beckett", in Calder, John (ed.), *Beckett at 60*, London, Calder and Boyars, pp. 89-90.

STANLEY, Thomas F.

1996 (ed.), *Shouting in the evening. British Theater 1956-1996*, Austin, Harry Ransom Humanities Research Center.

STATES, Bert O.

1978 *The Shape of Paradox: An Essay on 'Waiting for Godot'*, Berkeley and Los Angeles, University of California.

1985 *Great Reckonings in Little Rooms on the Phenomenology of Theatre*, Berkeley and Los Angeles, University of California.

1987 "The Language of Myth", in Bloom, Harold (ed.), *Samuel Beckett's Waiting for Godot*, New York-New Haven Philadelphia, Chelsea House Publishers, pp. 79-94.

STEPHANE, Nicole

1995 "Beckett a Sarajevo", in *Filmcritica*, a. XLVI, nr. 454, Aprile 1995, p. 224.

STRAUSS, Walter A.

1976 "Le Belacqua de Dante et les Clochards de Beckett", in Bishop, Tom-Federman, Raymond (eds.), *Samuel Beckett*, "Cahier de l'Herne", nr. 31, pp. 269-280.

STREHLER, Giorgio

1990 "Beckett ou le tromphe de la vie", in *Revue d'Estetique*, numéro hors-série (I ed. 1986), pp. 213-215.

STYAN, J. L.

1968 *The Dark Comedy*, Cambridge, Cambridge University Press.

SULLIVAN, Victoria

1993 "Clowns, Fools, and Blind Men: *King Lear* and *Waiting for Godot*", in Drew, Anne Marie (ed.), *Past Crimson, Past Woe. The Shakespeare-Beckett Connection*, New York & London, Garland, pp. 67-78.

SUTHERLAND, William O. S.

1962 (ed.), *Six Contemporary Novels: Six Introductory Essays in Modern Fiction*, Austin, University of Texas.

SUVIN, Darko

1967 "Preparing for *Godot*-or the Purgatory of Individualism", in Cohn, Ruby (ed.), *Casebook on Waiting for Godot*, New York, Grove Press, pp. 121-133.

SWERLING, Anthony

1971 *Strindberg's impact in France. 1920-1960*, Cambridge, Trinity Lane Press.

SZANTO, George H.

1972 *Narrative consciousness. Structure and perception in the fiction of Kafka, Beckett and Robbe-Grillet*, London, s. e.

SZENDY, Peter

1998 "End Games", in Bryden, Mary (ed.), *Samuel Beckett and Music*, Oxford, Clarendon Press, pp. 99-129.

SZONDI, Peter

1962 *Teoria del dramma moderno*, Torino, Einaudi.

TAGLIAFERRI, Aldo

1967 *Beckett e l'iperdeterminazione letteraria*, Milano, Feltrinelli.

1976 "Novelli e Beckett: Com'è", in *Novelli*, Milano, Feltrinelli, pp. 44-46.

1988 "Il sacro di Beckett", in *Alfabeta*, Milano, a. 10, nr. 107, Aprile 1988, pp. 32-33.

1991 "Primo tempo beckettiano", in *Modernismo/Modernismi*, Milano, Principato, pp. 515-530.

1993 "A propos de *Fin de partie*", in *Europe*, Giugno-Luglio 1993, pp. 132-142, now in' Samuel Beckett, *Teatro completo*, Torino-Parigi, Einaudi Gallimard, 1994, pp. 771-782.

1996 "Introduzione", in Samuel Beckett, *Trilogia* (It. Transl. and ed. A. Tagliaferri), Torino, Einaudi, pp. VII- LXIV.

TAKAHASHI, Yasunari

1975 "The Fools Progress", in Cohn, Ruby (ed.), *Samuel Beckett: A Collection of Criticism*, New York, McGraw-Hill Book Company, pp. 33-40.

1982 "The theatre of the Mind", in *Encounter*, aprile 1982, pp. 68-70, now in Samuel Beckett, *Teatro completo*, Torino-Parigi, Einaudi Gallimard, 1994, pp. 728-736.

1983 "Qu'est-ce qui arrive? Some Structural Comparisons of Beckett's Plays and Noh", in Beja, Morris-Gontarski, Stan E.-Astier, Pierre (eds.), *Samuel Beckett. Humanistic Perspectives*, Ohio, Ohio State University Press, pp. 99-106.

1992 "Memory Inscribed in the Body: *Krapp's Last Tape* and the Noh Play *Izutsu*", in Brater, Enoch (ed.), *The Theatrical Gamut. Notes for a post-beckettian stage*, University of Michigan Press, pp. 51-65.

TANNER, James T. F.-DON VANN, J.

1969 *Samuel Beckett. A Checklist of Criticism*, Kent, The Kent State University Press.

TATO', Carla

1989 "Il corpo spezzato", in Bistolfi, Marina-Licata, Salvo (eds.), *Primo amore. Beckett-Quartucci*, Erice, La Zattera di Babele, pp. 18-20.

TAYLOR WATSON, Simon

1968 *French Writing Today*, London, Penguins Books.

TEW, Philip

2003 "*Three Dialogues* As A Laughable Text? Beckett's Bergsonian Comedy", in *Samuel Beckett Today / Aujourd'hui*, Vol. 13, pp. 105-118.

The Samuel Beckett Collection

1978 *The Samuel Beckett Collection*, Reading, The Library University of Reading.

THIBAULT, Rémy

1991 *En attendant Godot/Fin de partie*, Paris, Editions Nathan.

THIHER, Allen

1983 "Wittgenstein, Heidegger, the Unnamable, and Some Thoughts on the Status of Voice in Fiction", in Beja, Morris-Gontarski, Stan E.-Astier, Pierre (eds.), *Samuel Beckett. Humanistic Perspectives*, Ohio, Ohio State University Press, pp. 80-90.

THOMSON, Duncan

1994 *Arikha*, London, Phaidon.

TINAZZI, Giorgio

1993 "Samuel Beckett e Buster Keaton", in *Belfagor*, a. XLV, 30 Settembre 1993, fasc. V, pp. 509-518.

TINDALL YORK, William

1960 *Beckett's Bums*, London, Privately Printed.

1964   *Samuel Beckett*, New York and London, Columbia University Press.

TODOROV, Tzvetan

1990   "L'espoir chez Beckett", in *Revue d'Estetique*, numéro hors-série (I ed. 1986), pp. 27-36.

TOPIA, André

1984   "*Murphy* ou Beckett baroque", in Rabate, Jean-Michel (ed.), *Beckett avant Beckett: essais sur le jeune Beckett (1930-1945)*, Paris, P.E.N.S., pp. 93-119.

TOPSFIELD, Valerie

1988   *The Humour of Samuel Beckett*, London, Macmillan.

TORRESANI, Giorgio

1966   "Samuel Beckett", in *Il Dramma*, a. 42, nr. 359/360 (Agosto-Settembre 1966), pp. 124-126.

TOUCHARD, Pierre-Aimé

1965   "Le Théâtre français de 1918 à nos jours", in AA.VV., *Encyclopédie de la Pléiade*, Paris, Gallimard, vol. XIX, pp. 1383-1404.

TREVICO, Rosa Giannetta

1982   "*Giorni felici*: un inferno piccolo borghese", in *Sipario*, nr. 412-413, Agosto-Settembre 1982, pp. 12-14.

TREZISE, Thomas

1990   *Into the Breach. Samuel Beckett and the Ends of Literature*, Princeton, Princeton University Press.

TRIELOFF, Barbara

1990   "'Babel of Silence': Beckett's Post-Trilogy Prose Articulated", in Butler, Lance St. John-Davis, Robin J. (eds.), *Rethinking Beckett. A Collection of Critical Essays*, London, Macmillan, pp. 89-104.

TSENG, Li-Ling

1987   *The 'syntax of weakness' in Samuel Beckett's later shorter prose (1963-1975)*, Reading, PhD Thesis.

TYNAN, Kathleen

1994   (ed.), *Kenneth Tynan Letters*, London, Weidenfeld and Nicholson.

TYNAN, Kenneth

1969   *Oh!Calcutta!*, New York, Grove Press.

UBERSFELD, Anne

1990   "Beckett dit: «Je raconte»", in *Revue d'Estetique*, numéro hors-série (I ed. 1986), pp. 67-69.

UPDIKE, John

1965   *Assorted Prose*, London, Andre Deutsch.

UWAH OKEBARAM, Godwin

1989   *Pirandellism and Samuel Beckett's Plays*, Potomac, Scripta Humanistica.

VAHANIAN, Gabriel

1967 *The Death of God. The Culture of Our Post-Christian Era*, New York, George Braziller (I ed. 1957).

VALENCY, M.

1980 *The End of the World*, New York, Oxford University Press.

VALENTINI, Valentina

1991 "L'autoriflessività della drammaturgia letteraria contemporanea (Bernhard, Müller, Beckett)", in AA.VV., *Prima e dopo il teatro. Atti del convegno* (Fisciano, 27-28-29 Marzo 1990), ed. Rosa Meccia, s. l., Edizioni L'obliquo, pp. 195-206.

VANNIER, Jean

1971 "Un nouveau contenu", in Nores, Dominique (ed.), *Les critiques de notre temps et Beckett*, Paris, Garnier, pp. 138-140.

VASQUEZ MONTALBAN, Manuel

1990 *Gli uccelli di Bankok*, Milano, Feltrinelli, pp. 32; 234.

VENTIMIGLIA, Dario

1973 *Il teatro di Samuel Beckett*, Padova, Liviana.

VESTNER, Heinz

1980 *Erzæhlstruktur und Erzæhlstrategie in Samuel Becketts Molloy, Malone dies und The unnamable*, s. l., s. e.

VIGORELLI, Giancarlo

1969 "Il Nobel a Beckett", in *Il Dramma*, nr. 14-15 (Novembre-Dicembre 1969), pp. 35-38.

VISCONTI, Laura

1990 *Archetipi beckettiani*, Pescara, Tracce.

Voies

1982 *Voies (Les) de la création théâtrale*, vol. X, Paris, CNRS.

VÖLKER, Klaus

1986 *Beckett in Berlin*, Berlin, Frölich & Kaufmann.

WARDLE, Irving

1978 *The Theatres of George Devine*, London, Wardle.

WARRILOW, David

1990 "La musique, pas le sens", in *Revue d'Estetique*, numéro hors-série (I ed. 1986), pp. 251-253.

WATSON, David

1991 *Paradox & Desire in Samuel Beckett's Fiction*, London, Macmillan.

WATSON, Dwight

1993 "'Rounded with a Sleep': Director's Notes for *Waiting for Godot* and *The Tempest*", in Drew, Anne Marie (ed.), *Past Crimson, Past Woe. The Shakespeare-Beckett Connection*, New York & London, Garland, pp. 147-156.

WATT, Stephen

1987 "Beckett by Way of Baudrillard: Toward a Political Reading of Samuel Beckett's Drama", in Burkman, Katherine H. (ed.), *Myth and Ritual in the Plays of Samuel Beckett*, London and Toronto, Associated University Presses, pp. 103-123.

WAUGU, Patricia

1984 *Metafiction. The Theory and Practice of Self-Conscious Fiction*, London and New York, Methuen.

WEBB, Eugene

Samuel Beckett: a study of his novels, London, Owen.

1972a *Samuel Beckett*, Seattle, University of Washington Press.

1972b *The Plays of Samuel Beckett*, London, Owen.

WEBER, Brigitta

1998 "*That Time*: Samuel Beckett and Wolfgang Fortner", in Bryden, Mary (ed.), *Samuel Beckett and Music*, Oxford, Clarendon Press, pp. 141-158.

WEBER-CAFLISH, Antoinette

1994 *Chacun son Dépeupleur. Sur Samuel Beckett*, Paris, Les Éditions de Minuit.

WELLERSHOFF, Dieter

1965 "Failure of Attempt at De-Mythologization: Samuel Beckett's Novels", in Esslin, Martin (ed.), *Samuel Beckett: A Collection of Critical Essays*, Englewood Cliffs, N.J., Prentice Hall, pp. 92-107.

1976 "Toujours moins, presque rien", in Bishop, Tom-Federman, Raymond (eds.), *Samuel Beckett*, "Cahier de l'Herne", nr. 31, pp. 169-182.

WETZESTEON, Ross

1994 (ed.), *The Best of Off-Broadway & Contemporary Obie-Winning Plays*, New York, Penguins.

WHITAKER, Thomas R.

1986 "'Wham, Bam, Thank you Sam': The Presence of Beckett", in Brater, Enoch (ed.), *Beckett at 80/Beckett in Context*, New York, Oxford University Press, pp. 208-229.

WHITE, Harry

1998 "'Something is Taking its Course': Dramatic Exactitude and the Paradigm of Serialism in Samuel Beckett", in Bryden, Mary (ed.), *Samuel Beckett and Music*, Oxford, Clarendon Press, pp. 159-171.

WHITELAW, Billie

1990 "Travailler avec Samuel Beckett", in *Revue d'Estetique*, numéro hors-série (I ed. 1986), pp. 333-335.

1995 *Billie Whitelaw... Who he? An Autobiography*, Great Britain, Hodder & Stoughton.

WILLIAMS, Raymond

1966 "Tragic Deadlok and Stalenmate: Checov, Pirandello, Ionesco, Beckett", in *Modern Tragedy*, Standford, Standford University Press.

WILMER, S. E.

1992 (ed.), *Beckett in Dublin*, Dublin, Lilliput.

WILSON, Colin

1962 *The Strenght to Dream. Literature and the Imagination*, London, Victor Gollancz.

WINKGENS, Meinhard

Das Zeitproblem in Samuel Becketts Dramen, Bern, Herbert Lang.

WOLF, Daniel-FANCHER, Edwin

1962 (ed.), *The Village Voice Reader*, New York, Doubleday & Company.

WOOD, Rupert

1994 "An endgame of aesthetics: Beckett as essayist", in Pilling, John (ed.), *The Cambridge Companion to Beckett*, Cambridge, Cambridge University Press, pp. 1-16.

WOODWARK, Kathleen-MURRAY, M.

1986 *Aging-Literature-Psychoanalysis*, Bloomington, Indiana University Press.

WORTH, Katharine

1975 "The space and the sound in Beckett's theatre", in Worth, Katharine (ed.), *Beckett the Shape Changer. A Symposium*, London & Boston, Routledge and Kegan Paul, pp. 183-218.

1978 *The Irish Drama of Europe from Yeats to Beckett*, London, The Athlone Press.

1981 "Beckett and the radio medium", in Drakakis, John (ed.), *British Radio Drama*, Cambridge, Cambridge University Press, pp. 191-217.

1986 "Beckett's Auditors: 'Not I' to 'Ohio Impromptu'", in Brater, Enoch (ed.), *Beckett at 80/ Beckett in Context*, New York, Oxford University Press, pp. 168-192.

1990a "Journal de *Cascando*", in *Revue d'Estetique*, numéro hors-série (I ed. 1986), pp. 267-268.

1990b *Waiting for Godot and Happy Days. Text and Performance*, London, Macmillan.

1998 "Words for Music Perhaps", in Bryden, Mary (ed.), *Samuel Beckett and Music*, Oxford, Clarendon Press, pp. 9-20.

WORTON, Michael

1994 "*Waiting for Godot* and *Endgame*: theatre as text", in Pilling, John (ed.), *The Cambridge Companion to Beckett*, Cambridge, Cambridge University Press, pp. 67-87.

YAMASAKI TOYAMA, Jean

1991   *Beckett's Game. Self and Language in the Trilogy*, New York, Peter Lang.

YOUNG, Jordan R.

1987   *The Beckett Actor. Jack MacGowran, Beginning to End*, Beverly Hills, Moonstone Press.

ZACCARIA, Paola

1990   "*Fizzles* by Samuel Beckett: The Failure of the Dream of a Nver-ending Verticality", in Butler, Lance St. John-Davis, Robin J. (eds.), *Rethinking Beckett. A Collection of Critical Essays*, London, Macmillan, pp. 105-123.

1992   *Forme della ripetizione. Le ipertrofie di Edgar Allan Poe. I deficit di Samuel Beckett*, Torino, Tirrenia Stampatori.

ZARD, Philippe

1991   *En attendant Godot*, Paris, Bordas.

ZEGEL, Sylvain

1967   "The First Review", in Cohn, Ruby (ed.), *Casebook on Waiting for Godot*, New York, Grove Press, p. 11.

ZEIFMAN, Hersh

1975   "Religious Imagery in the Plays of Samuel Beckett", in Cohn, Ruby (ed.), *Samuel Beckett: A Collection of Criticism*, New York, McGraw-Hill Book Company, pp. 85-97.

1983   "*Come and Go*: A Criticule", in Beja, Morris-Gontarski, Stan E.-Astier, Pierre (eds.), *Samuel Beckett. Humanistic Perspectives*, Ohio, Ohio State University Press, pp. 137-144.

1987   "'The Core of the Eddy': *Rockaby* and Dramatic Genre", in Friedman, Alan Warren-Rossman, Charles-Sherzer, Dina (eds.), *Beckett Translating/Translating Beckett*, Pennsylvania State University Press, University Park, pp. 140-148.

ZILLIACUS, Clas

1976   *Beckett and Broadcasting. A study of Works of Samuel Beckett for Radio and Television*, Abo, Abo Akademi.

1993   "*Act without words I* as cartoon and codicil", in *Samuel Beckett Today/Aujourd'hui*, Amsterdam-Atlanta, G. A., pp. 295-304.

ZIVELLI, Giuseppe

1970-71   *Il teatro di Samuel Beckett*, Napoli, Istituto Universitario Orientale.

ZURBRUGG, Nicholas

1983   "Beckett, Proust, and Burroughs, and the Perils of 'Image Warfare'", in Beja, Morris-Gontarski, Stan E.-Astier, Pierre (eds.), *Samuel Beckett. Humanistic Perspectives*, Ohio, Ohio State University Press, pp. 172-187.

1988   *Beckett and Proust*, London, Colin Smythe.

* GENERAL BIBLIOGRAPHY *

Silent movies

AA.VV.
1960   *Immagini del cinema muto americano*, Torino, Tipografia Manifesti.

ALVEY, Glenn H. jr.
1952   *Dizionario dei termini cinematografici. Italiano-Inglese. English-Italian*, Roma, Casa Editrice Mediterranea.

ASPLUND, Uno
1971   *Chaplin's films. A filmography*, Newton Abbott, David & Charles.

BARSON, Michael
1988   (ed.), *Flyweel, Shyster, and Flyweel. The Marx Brother's lost radio show*, New York, Pantheon Books.

BERNARDI, Alessandro
1975   "Il gioco e la ricerca nelle 'gags' dei Marx brothers", in *Cinema Nuovo*, Firenze, a. XXIV, nr. 235-236, Maggio-Agosto 1975, pp. 244-248.

BLESH, Rudi
1966   *Keaton*, London, Secker & Warburg.

BROWN, Pam
1991   *Charlie Chaplin, the star of silent films whose inspiration gave hope and laughter to the world*, Watford, Exley.

BROWNLSON, Kevin
1980   *Hollywood. L'era del muto*, Milano, Garzanti.

CAHN, William
1966   *Harold Lloyd's World of Comedy*, London, George Allen and Unwin Ldt.

CAUDA, Ernesto
1936-44 *Dizionario poliglotta della cinematografia (tedesco, inglese, francese, italiano)*, Città di Castello, Tip. Leonardo Da Vinci.

CELATI, Gianni
1976   "Il corpo comico nello spazio", in *Il Verri*, nr. 3, Novembre 1976, pp. 22-32.

CHERCHI USAI, Paolo
         (ed.), *Vitagraph Co. of America: il cinema prima di Hollywood*, Pordenone, Studio Tesi.
1991   *Una passione infiammabile: guida allo studio del cinema muto*, Torino, UTET.

CHAPLIN, Charles

1964a   *My Autobiography*, London, The Bodley Head.

1964b   *My Early Years*, London, Heinemann.

COURSODON, Jean Pierre

1973   *Buster Keaton*, Seghers, Cinema Club.

1965   *Laurel & Hardy*, Paris, Anthologie du Cinéma.

CREMONINI, Giorgio

1975   "Linguaggio e storia nel cinema del grande Charlot-Chaplin", in *Cinema Nuovo*, Firenze, a. XXIV, nr. 235-236, Maggio-Agosto 1975, pp. 234-241.

1976   "Per una definizione del gag cinematografico", in *Il Verri*, nr. 3, Novembre 1976, pp. 94-109.

1978   *Il comico e l'altro. Il comico nel cinema americano*, Bologna, Cappelli.

1995a   *Buster Keaton*, Milano, Il Castoro.

1995b   *Charlie Chaplin*, Milano, Il Castoro.

DARDIS, Tom

1979   *Keaton. The man who wouldn't lie down*, London, Penguin.

1983   *Harold Lloyd*, New York, the Viking Press.

DI GIAMMATTEO, Fernaldo

1985   *Dizionario universale del cinema*, Roma, Editori Riuniti, 2 voll.

FINK, Guido

1980   "Scusi il ritardo... Pantomima tradizionale e comici del muto", in De Marinis, Marco (ed.), *Mimo e mimi. Parole e immagini per un genere teatrale del Novecento*, Firenze, Usher, pp. 233-242.

FRANKLIN, Joe

1973   *Classics of the silent screen*, Secaucus, The Citadel Press.

GEHRING, Wes D.

1983   *Charlie Chaplin. A Bio-Bibliography*, Wesport-London, Greenwood Press.

GIUSTI, Marco

1995   *Laurel & Hardy*, Milano, Il Castoro.

GRIGNAFFINI, Giovanna

1986   *Sapere e teorie del cinema: il periodo del muto*, Bologna, CLUEB.

HAVEL, Václav

1980   "The Anatomy of the Gag", in *Modern Drama*, vol. XXIII, nr. 1, March 1980, pp. 13-24 (I ed. 1966).

HOYT, Edwin P.

1977   *Sir Charlie*, London, Robert Hale.

KEATON, Buster-SAMUELS, Charles

1995   *Memorie a rotta di collo*, Milano, Feltrinelli (I ed.1960 *My wonderful world of slapstick*).

LA POLLA, Franco

1976   "I baffi di Groucho", in *Il Verri*, nr. 3, Novembre 1976, pp .73-93.

LEBEL, J.-P.

1967   *Buster Keaton,* London-New York, Zwemmer.

LLOYD, Harold

1971   *An American Comedy*, New York, Dover Publications.

LYONS, Timothy J.

1979   *Charlie Chaplin: a guide to references and resources*, Boston, Hall & Co.

MALAND, Charles J.

1989   *Chaplin and American culture: the evolution of a star image*, Princeton, Princeton University Press.

MANVELL, Robert

1974   *Chaplin*, London, The Anchor Press.

MARTINI, Andrea

1995   *I fratelli Marx*, Milano, Il Castoro.

MARX, Groucho

1992   *Le lettere di Groucho Marx*, Milano, Adelphi (I ed. 1967).

MOEWS, Daniel

1977   *Keaton. The Silent Features Close Up*, Berkley and Los Angeles, University of California Press.

PAOLELLA, Roberto

1956   *Storia del cinema muto*, Napoli, Giannini.

PASOLINI, Pier Paolo

1971   "La «gag» in Chaplin come metafora dell'azione come linguaggio", in *Bianco e Nero*, nr. 3-4 (Marzo-Aprile 1971), p. 36.

ROBINSON, David

1969   *Buster Keaton*, London, Martin Secker & Warburg.

1985   *Chaplin. His Life and Art*, London, Collins.

VERDONE, Mario

1990a   "Funny faces. I clowns del cinema britannico primitivo", in Pretini, Giancarlo (ed.), *Thesaurus circensis*, 2 voll., Udine, Trapezio libri, vol. II, pp. 1155-1160.

1990b   "Genesi e sviluppo del 'comico' di Sennett", in Pretini, Giancarlo (ed.), *Thesaurus circensis*, 2 voll., Udine, Trapezio libri, vol. II, pp. 1185-1192.

WEAD, George-LELLIS, George

The Film Career of Buster Keaton, Boston, Hall & Co.

Circus

AA.VV.

1984   *Arte del clown*, Roma, Gremese.

ADRIAN-CERVELLATI, Alessandro

1954-1968   "Medrano", in D'Amico, Silvio (ed.), *Enciclopedia dello Spettacolo*, 12 voll., Roma, Le Maschere, vol. II, pp. 359-360.

BALSIMELLI, Rossano

1982   *Guida al mimo e al clown*, Milano, Rizzoli.

BOLTON, Reg

1987   *New Circus*, London, Calouste Gulbenkian Foundation.

BOUISSAC, Paul

1976   *Circus and Culture: A Semiotic Approach*, Bloomington, Indiana University Press.

CERVELLATI, Alessandro

        Storia del clown, Firenze, Marzocco.

1956   *Storia del circo*, Bologna, Il Resto del Carlino.

1961   *Questa sera grande spettacolo. Storia del circo italiano*, Milano, Edizioni Avanti!.

1962   *Il Circo e il Music-Hall*, Bologna, Tamari Editori.

CLARKE, John S.

1936   *Circus parade*, London, B. T. Batsford.

DISHER, Willson

1985   *Clowns & pantomimes*, Salem, Ayer.

GREENWOOD, Isaac J.

1970   *The Circus: its origins and growth prior to 1835*, New York, Burt Franklin (I ed.1898).

HUGILL, Beryl

1980   *Bring on the clowns*, Newton Abbot-London, David & Charles.

JONES, Louisa E.

1984   *Sad clowns and pale Pierrots: literature and the popular comic arts in 19th century France*, Lexington, French Forum.

LEVY, Pierre Robert

1977   "Les clowns", in Renevey, Monica J. (ed.), *Le grand livre du cirque*, 2 voll., Genève, Bibliothèque des arts, vol. II, pp. 81-136.

MANETTI, Giovanni

1980 "Entrate clownesche. Semantica del corpo comico", in De Marinis, Marco (ed.), *Mimo e mimi. Parole e immagini per un genere teatrale del Novecento*, Firenze, Usher, pp. 243-253.

MARIEL, Pierre

1923 *Les Fratellini. Histoire de trois clowns*, Paris, Soc. Anon. d'éditions.

MC VICAR, Wes

1987 *Clown act omnibus: everything you need to know about clowning plus over 200 clown stunts*, Colorado Springs, Meriwether Publisher.

MIDDLEMISS, J.L.

1987 *A zoo on wheels: Bostock and Wombwell menagerie*, Burton on Trent, Dalebrook.

PRETINI, Giancarlo

1987a *L'anima del circo*, Udine, Trapezio Libri.

1987b *La grande cavalcata*, Udine, Trapezio Libri.

1988 *Il circo di carta*, Udine, Trapezio Libri.

1990 (ed.), *Thesaurus circensis*, Udine, Trapezio libri, 2 voll.

RÉMY, Tristan

1974 *Arrivano i clowns*, Milano, Il Formichiere (I ed. *Entrée clownesques*, 1962).

RENEVEY, Monica J.

1977 (ed.), *Le grand livre du cirque*, Genève, Bibliothèque des arts, 2 voll.

1985 *Il circo e il suo mondo*, Roma-Bari, Laterza.

RICHET, Michèle

1965 "Le Cirque", in AA.VV., *Encyclopédie de la Pléiade*, Paris, Gallimard, vol. XIX, pp. 1520-1542.

STAROBINSKI, Jean

1984 *Ritratto dell'artista da saltimbanco*, Torino, Boringhieri.

TORSELLI, Giorgio

1971 *Il circo*, Roma, Fratelli Palombi.

TYRWHIT-DRAKE, Garrand (Sir)

1946 *The English Circus and Fair Ground*, London, Methuen & Co.

VERDONE, Mario

1954-1968 "Boswell", in D'Amico, Silvio (ed.), *Enciclopedia dello Spettacolo*, 12 voll., Roma, Le Maschere, vol. II, p. 885.

VIGANO', Antonio

1985 *Nasi rossi: il clown tra il circo e il teatro*, Montepulciano, Editori del Grifo.

VOLTA, Ornella

"Il mito del clown", in *Il Dramma*, nr. 3 (Marzo 1975), p. 5.

Commedia dell'Arte

CAMPORESI, Piero

1991   *Rustici e buffoni*, Torino, Einaudi.

FERRONE, Siro

1993   *Attori, mercanti, corsari: la Commedia dell'Arte in Europa tra Cinque e Seicento*, Torino, Einaudi.

GRECO, Franco Carmelo

1988   (ed.), *Quante storie per Pulcinella. Combien d'histoires pour Polichinelle*, Napoli, ESI.

1990   (ed.), *Pulcinella. Una maschera tra gli specchi*, Napoli, ESI.

MANGO, Achille-LOMBARDI, Maria Rosaria

1969-70   *Le origini della Commedia dell'Arte*, Salerno, Libreria Internazionale Editrice.

MAROTTI, Ferruccio

1991   *La Commedia dell'Arte: storia, testi, documenti*, Roma, Bulzoni.

MOLINARI, Cesare

1984   *La Commedia dell'Arte*, Milano, Mondadori.

TAVIANI, Ferdinando

1969   *La Commedia dell'Arte e la società barocca. La fascinazione del teatro*, Roma, Bulzoni.

TAVIANI, Ferdinando-SCHINO, Mirella

1986   *Il segreto della Commedia dell'Arte. La memoria delle compagnie italiane del XVI, XVII e XVIII secolo*, Firenze, La Casa Usher (I 1982).

TESSARI, Roberto

1984   *Commedia dell'Arte: la maschera e l'ombra*, Milano, Mursia.

Music-Hall, Vaudeville, Cabaret

AA.VV.

1931   *Les spectacles a travers les ages. Théâtre. Cirque. Music-Hall. Café-Concerts. Cabarets artistiques*, Paris, Editions du cygne.

1986   *Music Hall The Business of Pleasure* (P. Bailey ed.), Milton Keynes, Open University Press.

1989   *Cabaret performance 1890-1920*, New York, PAJ, vol. I.

1993   *Cabaret performance 1920-1940*, Baltimore-London, John Hopkins University Press, vol. II.

ALLEN, Robert C.

1980   *Vaudeville and film, 1895-1915: a study in media interaction*, New York, Arno Press.

BUSBY, Roy

1976   *British Music Hall*, London, Paul Elek.

CHESHIRE, David F.

1971   "A Chronology of Music Hall", in *Theatre quarterly*, vol. I, nr. 4 (October-December 1971), pp. 41-45.

COCCO, Maria Rosaria

1990   *Arlecchino, Shakespeare e il marinaio. Teatro popolare e melodramma in Inghilterra (1800-1850)*, Napoli, IUO.

CORIO, Ann-DI MONA, Joseph

This was the burlesque, New York, Grosset & Dunlap.

DAMASE, Jaques

1965   "Le Music-hall", in AA.VV., *Encyclopédie de la Pléiade*, Paris, Gallimard, vol. XIX, pp. 1543-1575.

EdS

1954-1968 D'Amico, Silvio (ed.), *Enciclopedia dello Spettacolo*, Roma, Le Maschere, 12 voll.

FAZIO, Mara

1980   "Introduzione" and "Cenni biografici su Karl Valentin", in Karl Valentin, *Tingeltangel* (ed. Mara Fazio), Milano, Adelphi, pp. 11-30.

FO, Dario

1982   "La violence de la marionnette et du masque", in AA.VV., *Totò l'acteur du varietà. Sketches théâtraux et filmiques présentés par Dario Fo et Federico Fellini*, Paris, Editions Dramaturgie, pp. 9-17.

GAULTIER, Gilles

1981   "Karl Valentin. La vision d'un monde étriqué", in *Cinema*, Paris, nr. 267 (Marzo 1981), pp. 6-14.

GILBERT, Douglas

1963   *American Vaudeville: its life and times*, New York, Dover.

HESSE, Hermann

1980   "Una serata ai Kammerspiele", in Karl Valentin, *Tingeltangel* (ed. Mara Fazio), Milano, Adelphi, pp. 207-208.

JHERING, Herbert

1954-1968 "Valentin", in D'Amico, Silvio (ed.), *Enciclopedia dello Spettacolo*, 12 voll., Roma, Le Maschere, vol. IX, pp. 1391-1392.

LEE, Ed

1982   *Folksong & Music hall*, London, Routledge & Kegan Paul.

MANDER, Raymond-MITCHENSON, Joe

1969   *Musical Comedy. A Story in Pictures*, London, Peter Davies.

1971   *Revue. A Story in Pictures*, London, Peter Davies.

MATTER SINISCALCHI, Adelheid

1990   *La satira politica nel cabaret tedesco del secondo dopoguerra*, Napoli, ESI.

McGraw-Hill

1972   *McGraw-Hill Encyclopedia of World Drama*, 4 voll., New York, McGraw-Hill.

Mc LEAN, Albert F.

1971   "U.S. vaudeville and the urban comics", in *Theatre quarterly*, vol. I, nr. 4 (October-December 1971), pp. 47-52.

MERLE, Pierre

1985   *Le café théâtre*, Paris, Presses Universitaires de France.

POLGAR, Alfred

1980   "Karl Valentin", in Karl Valentin, *Tingeltangel* (ed. Mara Fazio), Milano, Adelphi, pp. 209-211.

RÉMY, Tristan

1965   "Le Mime", in AA.VV., *Encyclopédie de la Pléiade*, Paris, Gallimard, vol. XIX, pp. 1593-1519.

SCHULTE, Michael

1971   "Un Chaplin della parola", in *Sipario*, nr. 305 (Ottobre 1971), pp. 11-15.

SEGEL, Harold B.

1987   *Turn of the century cabarets: Paris, Barcelona, Berlin, Munich, Vienna, Cracow, Moscow, St. Petersburg, Zurich*, New York, Columbia University Press.

SNYDER, Robert W.

1989   *The voice of the city: vaudeville and popular culture in New York*, New York-Oxford, Oxford University Press.

TUCHOLSKY, Kurt

1980   "Quello che pensa a rovescio", in Karl Valentin, *Tingeltangel* (ed. Mara Fazio), Milano, Adelphi, pp. 199-203.

VALENTIN, Karl

1980   *Tingeltangel* (ed. Mara Fazio), Milano, Adelphi.

WBE

1977   *(The) World Book Encyclopedia*, Chicago, Field Enterprises Educational Corporation, voll. 22 ["Joe Miller", vol. XIII, p. 468].

WEINMANN, Alexander-WARRACK, John

1980   "Diabelli, Anton", in Sadie, Stanley (ed.), *The New Grove Dictionary of Music and Musicians*, 20 voll., London, Macmillan, vol. V, pp. 414-415.

Who Was Who

1978   *Who Was Who in the Theatre: 1912-1976. A Biographical Dictionary of Actors, Actresses, Directors, Playwrights, and Producers of the English-Speaking Theatre*, 4 voll., London, Pitman.

WILMETH, Don B.-MILLER, Tice L.

1993   (eds.), "Bill Irwin", in *Cambridge Guide to American Theatre*, Cambridge, Cambridge University Press, pp. 250-251.

Irish theatre

FITZ-SIMON

1983   Christopher, *The Irish Theatre*, London, Thames & Hudson.

LUNARI, Gigi

1960   *Il movimento drammatico irlandese (1899-1922)*, Bologna, Cappelli.

MERCIER, Vivian

1962   *The Irish comic tradition*, Oxford, Claredon Press.

MICHAIL, E. H.

1988   *The Abbey Theatre*, London, Macmillan.

O'CASEY, Sean

1957   *Collected Plays*, London, Macmillan & Co., 5 voll.

O'CONNELL, Dan

1967   "Ireland", in Hartnoll, Phyllis (ed.), *The Oxford Companion to the Theatre*, London, Oxford University Press, pp. 472-477.

Ó hAodha, Micheál

1974   *Theatre in Ireland*, Oxford, Basil Blackwell.

POPE MACQUEEN, W.

1949   *Gaiety. Theatre of Enchantment*, London, W. H. Allen.

ROBINSON, Lennox

1951   *Ireland's Abbey Theatre. A History 1899-1951*, London, Sidgwick and Jackson Limited.

SYNGE, John Millington

1963   *The Plays and Poems*, London, Methuen & Co.

TRUNINGER, Annelise

1976 *Paddy and the Paycock. A Study of the Stage Irishman from Shakespeare to O'Casey*, Bern, Francke Verlag.

WATERS, Maureen

1984 *The comic Irishman*, Albany, State University of New York Press.

Radio

BEVILACQUA, Giuseppe

1949 "La radio e la parola", in *Repertorio. Rassegna quindicinale di radiocommedie*, a. I, nr. 7, 20 Luglio 1949, pp. 22-24.

BIZZARRI, Carla

1949 "La grande famiglia della BBC", in *Repertorio. Rassegna quindicinale di radiocommedie*, a. I, nr. 7, 20 Luglio 1949, pp. 27-29.

BURNS, Tom

1979 *La BBC tra pubblico e privato*, Torino, ERI.

CLERICI, Carlotta

1998 "La drammaturgia contemporanea è di scena su radio France", in *Hystrio*, a. XI, nr. 3, pp. 24-25.

DOGLIO, Daniele-RICHERI, Giuseppe

1980 *La radio*, Milano, Mondadori.

GIANNACHI, Gabriella

1998 "E l'Inghilterra scoprì il rumore del silenzio", in *Hystrio*, a. XI, nr. 3, pp. 28-29.

GUERRINI, Tito

1949 "Radioteatro e cinema sonoro", in *Repertorio. Rassegna quindicinale di radiocommedie*, a. I, nr. 7, 20 Luglio 1949, pp. 25-26.

MONTELEONE, Franco

1994 (ed.), *La radio che non c'è. Settant'anni di un grande futuro*, Roma, Donzelli.

PACI, Roberta

1998 "Da Weimar all'elettronica i mille volti dell'Hörspiele", in *Hystrio*, a. XI, nr. 3, pp. 26-27.

PICCIALUTI CAPRIOLI, Maura

1976 (ed.), *Radio Londra 1940/1945*, Roma, s.e., 2 voll.

PRADALIE, Roger

1951 *L'art radiophonique*, Paris, Presses Universitaires de France.

Contemporary Theatre Theories

AA.VV.

1986   *Testo e messa in scena in Pirandello*, Roma, La Nuova Scientifica.

ARTAUD, Antonin

1958   *The Theatre and its Double*, New York, Grove.

1968   *Il teatro e il suo doppio*, Torino, Einaudi.

BARBA, Eugenio

1981   *Il Brecht dell'Odin*, Milano, Ubulibri.

1985   *Il corpo dilatato*, Roma, La Goliardica.

1993   *La canoa di carta*, Bologna, Il Mulino.

1996   *Teatro. Solitudine, mestiere, rivolta*, Milano, Ubulibri.

1998   *La terra di cenere e diamanti. Il mio apprendistato in Polonia*, Bologna, Il Mulino.

BARBA, Eugenio-SAVARESE, Nicola

1990   *L'arte segreta dell'attore. Dizionario di antropologia teatrale*, Lecce, Argo.

BRECHT, Bertolt

1962 and 1975   *Scritti teatrali*, Torino, Einaudi, 3 voll.

1964   *Brecht on Theatre. The Development of an Aesthetic*. London, Methuen.

1969   *Theaterarbeit*, Milano, Mondadori.

1970   *Me-Ti. Libro delle svolte*, Torino, Einaudi.

1976   *Diario di lavoro*, Torino, Einaudi.

1980   "Karl Valentin", in Karl Valentin, *Tingeltangel* (ed. Mara Fazio), Milano, Adelphi, p. 205.

CRAIG, Edward Gordon

1971   *Il mio teatro*, Milano, Feltrinelli.

DE MARINIS, Marco

1993   *Mimo e teatro nel Novecento*, Firenze, La Casa Usher.

GROTOWSKI, Jerzy

1970   *Per un teatro povero*, Roma, Bulzoni.

JARRY, Alfred

1969   *Essere e vivere*, Milano, Adelphi, 3 voll.

von KLEIST, Heinrich

1986   *Sul teatro di marionette. Aneddoti. Saggi*, Parma, Guanda.

LE COQ, Jaques

1980   "L'espressione fisica dell'attore", in De Marinis, Marco (ed.), *Mimo e mimi. Parole e immagini per un genere teatrale del Novecento*, Firenze, Usher, pp. 201-205.

MELDOLESI, Claudio

1984   *Fondamenti del teatro italiano*, Firenze, Sansoni.

RICHARDS, Thomas

1997   *Al lavoro con Grotowski sulle azioni fisiche*, Milano, Ubulibri (I ed. 1993).

STANISLAVSKIJ, Konstantin

1963   *La mia vita nell'arte*, Torino, Einaudi.

1980   *L'attore creativo*, Firenze, La Casa Usher.

1988   *Il lavoro dell'attore sul personaggio*, Roma-Bari, Laterza.

1991   *Il lavoro dell'attore su se stesso*, Bari, Laterza.

TAVIANI, Ferdinando

1997   *Uomini di scena uomini di libro*, Bologna, Il Mulino.

VICENTINI, Claudio

1993   *Pirandello. Il disagio del teatro*, Padova, Marsilio.

Comedy, humour, laughter

AA.VV.

1983   *Ambiguità del comico*, Palermo, Sellerio.

ALMANSI, Guido

1976   "Come scrivere ad Alice", in *Il Verri*, nr. 3, Novembre 1976, pp. 33-52.

BAKHTIN, Michail

1968   *Rabelais and His World*, Bloomington, Indiana University Press.

1982   *L'opera di Rabelais e la cultura popolare. Riso, carnevale e festa nella tradizione medievale e rinascimentale*, Torino, Einaudi (I ed. 1965).

BARILLI, R.

1982   *Comicità di Kafka: un'interpretazione sulle tracce del pensiero freudiano*, Milano.

BAUDELAIRE, Charles

1976   "De l'essence du rire et généralement du comique dans les arts plastiques", now in *Oeuvres complètes*, 2 voll., Paris, Gallimard, vol. II, pp. 525-543 (I ed. 1855).

BERGSON, Henri

1987   *Il riso. Saggio sul significato del comico*, Roma-Bari, Laterza (I ed. 1916).

2002   *Laughter: An Essay on the Meaning of the Comic*, The Project Gutemberg EBook, nr. 4352. Retrieved from www.gutenberg.org/catalog/world/readfile?fk_files=1455542&pageno=1

BOOTH, Wayne C.

1975   *A Rethoric of Irony*, Chicago and London, The University of Chicago Press.

CRYSTAL, David

1987   *The Cambridge Encyclopedia of Language*, Cambridge, Cambridge University Press.

ELGOZY, Georges

1979   *De l'humour*, Paris, Editions Denoël.

FEINBERG, Leonard

1978   *The Secret of Humor*, Amsterdam, Editions Rodopi.

FERRONI, Giulio

1974   *Il comico nelle teori contemporanee*, Roma, Bulzoni.

FREUD, Sigmund

2002   *The Joke and Its Relation to the Unconscious*, London, Penguin Books.

GORI, Gino

1978   *Il grottesco e altri studi teatrali*, Roma, Bulzoni.

GUREWITCH, Morton

1975   *Comedy. The irrational vision*, Ithaca and London, Cornell University Press.

LALO, Charles

1954   *Estetica del ridere*, Milano, Viola.

LEVI, Eugenio

1957   *Il comico di carattere da Teofrasto a Pirandello*, Torino, Einaudi.

LEVI, Giulio Augusto

1913   *Il comico*, Genova, Formiggini.

MANETTI, Giovanni

1976   "Per una semiotica del comico", in *Il Verri*, nr. 3, Novembre 1976, pp. 130-152.

MUSACCHIO, Enrico-CORDESCHI, Sandro

1985   *Il riso nelle poetiche rinascimentali*, Bologna, Cappelli.

OLBRECHT-TYTECA, Lucie

1977   *Il comico del discorso*, Milano, Feltrinelli.

PERNIOLA, Mario

1976   "Il Witz come elusione del conflitto", in *Il Verri*, nr. 3, Novembre 1976, pp. 7-21.

PIRANDELLO, Luigi

1974   *On Humour*, Chapel Hill, The University of North Carolina Press.

1986   *L'umorismo*, Milano, Mondadori (I ed. 1908).

POOLE, Gordon

1976   "Il «nonsense» di Lewis Carroll", in *Il Verri*, nr. 3, Novembre 1976, pp. 53-72.

VIOLI, Patrizia

1976   "Comico e Ideologia", in *Il Verri*, nr. 3, Novembre 1976, pp. 110-130.

WAITH, E. M.

1952 *The Pattern of Tragicomedy in Beaumont and Fletcher*, New Haven, Yale University Press.

Jewish Humour

BERGER, Arthur Asa

1993 *Anatomy of Humor*, New Brunswick, Transaction Publishers.

BERGER, Peter L.

1997 *Redeeming Laughter. The Comic Dimension of Human Experience*, Berlin, Walter de Gruyter & Co.

GROTJAHN, Martin

1970 "Jewish jokes and Their Relationship to Masochism", in Mendel, Werner (ed.), *A celebration of laughter*, Los Angeles, Mara Books, pp. 135-144.

TELUSHKIN, Rabbi Joseph

1992 *Jewish Humor*, New York, William Morrow and Co.

Theatre Semiotics

AA.VV.

1979 *Semiologia della rappresentazione*, Napoli, Liguori.

BOGATYRËV, Pëtr

1982 *Semiotica della cultura popolare* (ed. M. Solimini), Verona, Bertani (I ed. 1975).

DE MARINIS, Marco

1982 *Semiotica del teatro. L'analisi testuale dello spettacolo*, Milano, Bompiani.

1988 *Capire il teatro. Lineamenti di una nuova teatrologia*, Firenze, La Casa Usher.

ECO, Umberto

1979 *Lector in fabula*, Milano, Bompiani.

ELAM, Keir

1988 *Semiotica del teatro*, Bologna, Il Mulino.

GREIMAS, A. J.-COURTES, J.

1986 *Semiotica. Dizionario ragionato della teoria del linguaggio*, Firenze, La Casa Usher (I ed. 1979).

KRISTEVA, Julia

1980 *Materia e senso. Pratiche significanti e teorie del linguaggio*, Torino, Einaudi (I ed. 1968-77).

LOTMAN, Yuri

1980   "La semiotica della scena", in *Teatro*, nr. 1, pp. 89-99.

MARCHESE, Angelo

1984   *Dizionario di retorica e di stilistica. Arte e artificio nell'uso delle parole retorica, stilistica, metrica, teoria della letteratura*, Milano, Mondadori (I ed. 1978).

MOLINARI, Cesare-OTTOLENGHI, Valeria

1979   *Leggere il teatro*, Firenze, Vallecchi.

SEGRE, Cesare

1984   *Teatro e romanzo*, Torino, Einaudi.

UBERSFELD, Anne

1984   *Theatricòn. Leggere il teatro*, Roma, La Goliardica.

Other

AA.VV.

1981   *Enciclopedia Garzanti di Filosofia*, Milano, Garzanti.

APPERSON, G. L.

1993   *The Wordsworth Dictionary of Proverbs*, Ware, Wordsworth Reference.

AUSTER, Paul

1988   *The New York Trilogy. City of Glass, Ghosts, The Locked Room*, London, Faber & Faber.

CROCE, Benedetto

1921   *La poesia di Dante*, Bari, Laterza.

DANTE

2005   (Eng. Trans. Rev.) *The Divine Comedy*, The Project Gutemberg EBook, nr. 8800.

FREEDMAN, Terry and David

1996   *The Wordsworth Dictionary of Cliché*, Ware, Wordsworth Reference.

GIACALONE, Giuseppe

1975   (ed.) *La Divina Commedia*, Roma, Signorelli.

GOLDEN, Leon

1976   "Aristotle and the Audience for Tragedy", in *Mnemosyne*, Fourth Series, Vol. 29, Fasc. 4, pp. 351-359.

GRAY, Thomas

1966   *On a distant prospect of Eton College*, in *The Complete Poems*, Oxford, Clarendon Press, pp. 7-10.

HORACE

2005 *The Art Of Poetry An Epistle To The Pisos*. Project Gutenberg, EBook nr. 9175. Retrieved from www.gutenberg.org/dirs/etext05/8artp10.txt.

1969 *Ars Poetica*, (It. Transl. and ed. Medardo Albanese), Napoli, Loffredo.

JOYCE, James

1986 *Ulysses*, London, Penguin (I ed. 1922).

MARCHESE, Giovanni-ROSSI, Salvatore

1982 *La Divina Commedia. Lettura de il Purgatorio*, Palermo, Palumbo.

SHAKESPEARE

1994 *The Complete Works*, Oxford, Clarendon Press.

VOLTAIRE

1968 *Candide ou l'optimisme*, Genève, Librairie Droz.